Sunil Manohar Gavaskar wa[...] in Bombay, where he attended S[...] Xavier's College. He inherited h[...] parents and uncle and justified t[...] at the age of twelve, he distinguished himself in inter-school tournaments. The College XI, the Irani Cup and the Ranji Trophy paved the way for his selection in Test cricket. In 1971, Gavaskar made his debut in the West Indies where he scored an astounding 774 runs in four Tests at an average of 154.8. So brilliant was his game that the West Indians composed a calypso in his honour whose refrain was "We couldn't out Gavaskar at all."

Gavaskar has played Test cricket for India all over the world, besides playing regularly for the Ranji Trophy, Irani cup and Duleep Trophy. He remains one of cricket's greatest gentlemen. Readers will remember how often, and how generously he praises other cricketers and how modest he is about his own achievements. With 30 Test centuries to his credit, Gavaskar has surpassed Sir Donald Bradman's 35 year-old record of 29 Test centuries. He has been a regular contributor to various newspapers and magazines, while also being a commentator on television.

The Sunil Gavaskar Omnibus

Sunil Gavaskar

Rupa • Co

First published 1999
First Rupa Paperback 1999
Second impression 2003

Copyright © Sunil Gavaskar 1999

Published by
Rupa . Co
7/16, Ansari Road, Daryaganj,
New Delhi 110 002

Sales Centres:

Allahabad Bangalore Chandigarh Chennai
Dehradun Hyderabad Jaipur Kathmandu
Kolkata Ludhiana Mumbai Pune

ISBN-81-7167-400-3

Typeset in Clearly Roman by
Nikita Overseas Pvt Ltd,
1410, Chiranjiv Tower,
43 Nehru Place,
New Delhi 110 019

Printed in India by
Gopsons Papers Ltd.
A-14 Sector 60
Noida 201 301

Contents

SUNNY DAYS

SUNNY DAYS

1

The First Step

I MAY NEVER HAVE BECOME A CRICKETER AND THIS BOOK WOULD certainly not have been written, if an eagle-eyed relation, Mr Narayan Masurekar, had not come into my life the day I was born (10 July 1949). It seems that Nan-kaka (as I call him), who had come to see me in hospital on my first day in this world, noticed a little hole near the top of my left ear lobe. The next day he came again and picked up the baby lying on the crib next to my mother. To his utter horror, he discovered that the baby did not have the hole on the left ear lobe. A frantic search of all the cribs in the hospital followed, and I was eventually located sleeping blissfully beside a fisherwoman, totally oblivious of the commotion I had caused! The mix-up, it appears, followed after the babies had been given their bath.

Providence had helped me retain my true identity, and in the process, charted the course of my life. I have often wondered what would have happened if nature had not marked me out, by giving me that small hole on my left ear lobe; and if Nankaka had not noticed this abnormality. Perhaps I would have grown up to be an obscure fisherman, toiling somewhere along the west coast. And what about the baby who, for a spell, took my place? I do not know if he is interested in cricket, or whether he will ever read this book. I can only hope that, if he does, he will start taking a little more interest in Sunil Gavaskar.

My most vivid recollection of my childhood cricket-playing days is the time I almost broke my mother's nose. She used to bowl to me in the small gallery of our house where we played our daily match with a tennis ball. Since the area was small she would kneel to bowl, or rather lob the ball to me. I hit one straight back and caught her bang on the nose, which started bleeding. Although it was a tennis ball, the distance between the two of us was very short, which accounts for the force with which the ball hit her. I was frightened but she shrugged it off, washed her face and, as the bleeding stopped, we continued the game. But, for the rest of the day it was only forward defence for me. I restrained myself and played no attacking shot.

Cricket, to use a cliché, is in my blood. My father was a good club cricketer in his days and a keen student of the game. Even now we have interesting discussions on various aspects of the game and I have found his advice invaluable in the development of my career. And, as mentioned earlier, I have had the privilege of having a cricketing mother, who helped me to take the first steps in the game I have come to love. My uncle, Madhav Mantri, who played for India in four official Tests, though not very successfully, was a force to reckon with in first-class games. Whenever I went to my uncle's house my favourite pastime used

4

to be to take out his pullovers and caress them with a sense of longing. I was so attracted by the India Test pullovers that once I even dared to ask him if I could take one, since he had so many. My uncle told me that one has to sweat and *earn* the India 'colours' and I too should work hard to earn the distinction. That is a lesson I have never forgotten. Looking back, I am glad that my uncle did not succumb to my childish fancy and, instead, taught me that there was no short cut to the top. I was also fascinated by the many souvenirs he had and the large number of trophies he had won. What I liked most was the stump bearing the autographs of the 1952 India and England teams, and I loved to linger over the autograph of every player.

Right from the start I wanted to become a batsman and I hated losing my wicket. This became such an obsession with me that, if the rest of the boys ever got me out, I would fight and eventually walk home with the bat and the ball. This would bring the game to an abrupt end since nobody else had a ball or bat. The boys cursed and called me names, but the tension did not last long and we generally got on very well. Among these early comrades with whom I played were the Ambaye brothers, the Mandrekar brothers and several others who made up our team. Whenever I batted they would decide beforehand that they would appeal at a particular ball and, whether I was out or not, I had to go by the majority verdict! We often played matches against teams made up of boys living in the neighbouring building and there was tremendous interest in the trophies, as we called them. These trophies were small white-metal cups for which we all contributed and bought for as little as Rs. 1.50.

In our neighbourhood were Sudhir Naik, Sharad Hajare and, of course, Milind Rege, who lived in the same building in which we had a flat. We often played against each other in those days. Years later, when all of us were in the Bombay Ranji Trophy team, it seemed as if Chickalwadi and Shivaji Park were representing Bombay!

I joined St. Xavier's High School, which had a fairly good cricket team at that time. While we were just juniors we would run during the lunch recess to watch the senior boys play. Feroze Patka was then the idol of almost every Xavierite and Vinay Chaudhari, the skipper, was equally popular. When St. Xavier's won the Harris Shield under Chaudhari's captaincy, every Xavierite went delirious with joy. We had interclass matches which were very important, because the school junior team was selected on the basis of performances in these encounters. Even on holidays we went to play the school matches, very often with just one leg-guard and no batting gloves. I used to bowl, also, at that time and managed to bag quite a few wickets.

One day, as I was leaving home to play a match, my father stopped me to introduce me to Mr Kamal Bhandarkar, the former Maharashtra player, who is always prepared to coach anybody who shows a keenness to learn. He had come to invite us for a wedding and, seeing that I was going for a game, he asked me to show him my forward defence. When I did so, Mr Bhandarkar pointed out that my bat was at an angle and there was the danger of the ball being deflected towards the slips. Then he showed me the proper grip and, even now, when I find myself in difficulties I remember those words and check if my grip is correct. Anyway, the ball still goes to the slips! Mr Bhandarkar is, I think, one of the best cricket coaches in India and he is prepared to sit up all night to discuss any cricketing problem one might have. Years later I was thrilled when he invited me, along with Dilip Sardesai, to his coaching camp at the P.Y.C. Gymkhana to talk to the young boys under his charge.

My first chance of playing in the Harris Shield came when

Milind Rege went down with chickenpox. I went in to bat at number ten, and remained unbeaten with 30 runs. Next morning I got up early to look at the newspaper, all excited in the expectation of reading my name in print for the first time. I was, however, disappointed because the name had been printed as 'G. Sunil 30 not out'. Thus began my career in school cricket. The next thing I had set my heart on was to earn the Bombay Schools 'cap'.

My first season for the Bombay Schools began disastrously. I fielded badly and was dropped from the side after I had scored only 8 runs. It was then that I realised that I had to improve my fielding. I worked hard to become a good fielder and soon my efforts bore fruit. I became a close-in fielder, specialising in the slips. Concentration, I feel, is my strongest point and this keeps me going in the slips even when the batsmen are batting well that there is no chance of their edging or snicking the ball in my direction.

My second year for the Bombay Schools was better and the third and final year (1965-66) was the best. In the quarterfinals of the Cooch-Behar Trophy I scored 246 not out and put on 421 runs for the first wicket with Anwar Qureshi, who also got a double hundred. In the semifinals I got 222 and in the final my score was 85. This led to my selection for the All-India Schools' Team against the London Schoolboys, who were touring India. I was also the proud recipient of the J.C. Mukherjee Trophy for the Best Schoolboy Cricketer of the Year – my first prize in a national competition.

In the first Test against the London Schools I scored 116. I did not wear a thigh-guard till then and, during the early part of the innings, I was hit by a ball on the thigh. It hurt me terribly, and the skipper of the team, realising my discomfiture, asked the bowlers 'to do it again'. This only made me more determined and I batted on without flinching. I have found that any physical pain now puts my back up and I invariably play better.

I played in the first four Tests and scored an aggregate of 309 runs. I had to stand down from the last Test because of my forthcoming annual examination. The Indian Schools, however, won the match and, with it, the series. This was my final year at school, but before going on to university, I attended a coaching camp organised by the Board of Control at Hyderabad. There were thirty schoolboy cricketers in the camp, and Mr T.S. Worthington, the former England player, was our coach. Mr Worthington changed my Indian technique to the English one and gave me many invaluable tips. The month I spent in Hyderabad meant that I missed the first ten days of my college life.

2

Lotuses in the Slush

ST. XAVIER'S COLLEGE AT THAT TIME BOASTED OF A CRICKET TEAM that had several first-class players. Ashok Mankad was the captain and Kailash Gattani led the side later on. We, however, invariably lost to Siddharth College, except in my final year when we beat our traditional rivals by a convincing margin.

My parents gave me every encouragement and, as an inducement, promised me ten rupees for every hundred I scored. Even in those days the value of money was not lost on me, and I remember one year when I almost put the household budget in disarray with my centuries. My father, however, was delighted and paid up cheerfully. Often, when he returned home in the evening, he would take out his wallet and ask me if I had scored a century and would be most disappointed if I said no.

While I was encouraged to develop my talents as a cricketer, my parents never failed to emphasise the importance of doing equally well academically. In fact, cricket was never allowed to interfere with my studies. Once, when I got a really bad report from school, my father was so upset that he refused to let me play in the interschool tournament. My principal, the late Reverend L. Serkis, however, met my father and assured him that he would personally look after my studies. It was then that my father relented and I was allowed to play in the tournament.

I'll never forget my first match against Siddharth College. We scored about 311 runs, of which Ashok Mankad alone contributed 140-odd. When Ashok reached his century, some Xavierites drove a car, almost up to the wicket, and garlanded their hero. When Siddharth College batted, Kiran Adhikari scored a century and when he completed his ton, some of the Siddharth boys came up on a motorbike and garlanded him. This must have upset Adhikari's concentration because he was soon out leg-before wicket, leaving Siddharth's last pair to score 20 runs for victory. They did so but even now I feel they should never have won. I was keeping wickets then and the first ball that the number eleven batsman faced caught him on the backfoot plumb in front of the stumps. It was a plain straight delivery, and it could not possibly have missed the middle stump. However, the more aggressive among the Siddharth College boys, wielding knives and sticks, looked very menacing and the umpire dared not give the batsman out. Frankly, I don't blame the umpire at all for adhering to the old adage, discretion is the better part of valour.

Immediately after this incident, there was the tea interval. Our cricket secretary, however, told us not to bother to come to the pavilion, but run straight to the cars they had lined up and make a quick getaway. Being the wicketkeeper I was stranded, and soon found myself encircled by the mob. Luckily one of the dadas (senior boys) of Siddharth College escorted me, all the time assuring me that there was no cause for worry, I was safe, but I wondered what would have happened if St. Xavier's had won. My team-mates, who were able to reach the cars and were rushing away from the ground, were, however, unlucky. The waiting crowd smashed the windscreen and caused considerable damage to the cars.

Soon afterwards I was selected to play for the Bombay University team. The West Zone tournament that year was held in Poona and in the first two fixtures I hit centuries. The second century was a better effort as we played against bowlers like Uday, Ashok Joshi and Pankaj Zaveri, all established Ranji Trophy players from Gujarat. I used to bat one wicket down at that time, because Sudhir Naik and Ramesh Nagdev were the regular openers.

We lost in the final to Osmania University, who won the Rohinton-Baria Trophy for the first time. Osmania, with their balanced attack, used to bundle the other sides out on the matting track. Their left-arm spinner Mumtaz Hussain, the hero of the tournament, proved deadly with his disguised chinaman and regular orthodox spin. In the second innings Ramesh Nagdev and I were going strong after Naik's cheap dismissal. But Nagdev was not able to fathom Mumtaz Hussain's spin when he bowled the chinaman. I thought I knew, so in a purely psychological move I called out loud to Nagdev at the non-striker's end: 'Don't worry, Ramesh, I know when he bowls that one.' When Mumtaz heard this, he smiled mysteriously and tossed the ball up to me for the next few deliveries. I came down the wicket, but managed to hit only one four while the others went straight to the fielders. Mumtaz tossed up the last ball of the over slightly outside the off-stump. Too late I realised that

11

he had bowled a googly and was stranded yards down the track, to be easily stumped. We had learnt our lesson and when South Zone met West Zone for the first-ever Vizzy Trophy Inter-Zone final, Mumtaz got only three wickets in two innings. Unfortunately, the next time I saw him bowl at Hyderabad he seemed to have changed his style, and from a lovely high action he seemed to be bowling almost halfway down. He still does a good job for Hyderabad, but the magic seems to have disappeared.

Conard Hunte, the West Indies stalwart, who was the chief guest at the Vizzy Trophy final, came in the afternoon when I was batting. He seemed quite impressed with my performance and was kind enough to make a reference to me in his speech. Jayantilal also came in for some praise from Hunte.

Earlier in the season Hunte's batting technique had been evident during his century against India in the Bombay Test. His backlift, so straight and high, was the thing I had my eyes glued on, and also the way his front-foot was always where the ball was pitched. It was an unforgettable and rewarding experience. I must confess that I have tried to model my batting on Hunte's style.

While returning from the interuniversity tournament, we read that four university players were in the Bombay Ranji Trophy team, announced the previous day. Rege and I were the two newcomers, while Naik and Varde had already played in the Ranji Trophy. Both of us, of course, never made the eleven, but I was made the twelfth man. It was here that I really got to know Ajit Wadekar. I had met him earlier, but it was as Madhav Mantri's nephew. Now I was in the same team, we shared a lunch table and I could talk to him freely. Ajit completed a magnificent century and then his bat broke. I rushed out with some bats after searching his kitbag, in vain, for a spare bat. I carried my own bat also and I don't know why, but somehow of all those bats, Ajit chose mine. He banged the next three balls for boundaries, and going for a fourth, was caught behind.

As he sat in his corner in the dressing room, he handed back the bat to me with a thanks. I ventured to say, 'It brought you bad luck'. To which Ajit replied, 'May be, but those three shots were the best of the innings.' Ajit Wadekar always had a word for me then and though he and Ramakant Desai often pulled my leg it was in good spirit and I liked it. Baloo Gupte was another player who helped me along and made me feel at ease in the company of the other stalwarts I had only read about, but had never come in contact with. Somehow Baloo Kaka, as I call him now, got wind of the fact that I could do a fair mimicry of film star, Dev Anand and till date he asks me to mimic him, whenever we meet.

Soon after the first Ranji Trophy match I was dropped from the fourteen, and it not only disappointed me but I felt rather confused. After all, I had nothing to do but field and, when there, I had taken a good running catch. This is one thing which has always foxed me. How the reserves get dropped remains a mystery. Do they suddenly become so bad after one game that they do not merit a place, even as a 'reserve'? How can one merit such treatment, even without playing?

At this time I had become a member of the Dadar Union Sporting Club, which has a tradition for excellent fielding, discipline, tenacity and ability to fight back. Dadar Union was then a dream side. Madhav Mantri had built up the team, and under his captaincy it had earned a great name for itself. When I joined Dadar Union, Madhav Mantri had retired and had taken under his wings a weaker neighbouring side full of youngsters. Vasu Paranjpen was captain of the Dadar Union. His outlook on the game was a blend of the carefree approach of the West Indians and the bulldog tenacity of the Australians. He was positively in love with Australian cricket and his dream of a tour to Australia was realised when he went there with the Cricket Club of India team in 1971-72 when I was also in Australia. Throughout his stay in Australia, Vasu wore a broad smile even when he was dumped into the swimming pool at a party. Incidentally he cannot swim, and had to be fished out! As a fielder he was magnificent and his aggressive batting won many a hopeless match for Dadar Union. His captaincy was as dynamic as his batting, and he loved a challenge. It was Vasu who gave me my nickname Sunny which has stuck to me ever since.

But more than Vasu, one man who literally carried Dadar Union on his shoulders was Vithal 'Marshall' Patil. Marshall, with his swing bowling, was almost unplayable in the first few overs and in the limited overs matches he seldom proved expensive. Besides, he also 'doubled' as secretary of the club and has done a good job. Marshall literally lives for cricket. Morning and evening he would bowl to aspiring young cricketers, find the chinks in their armour and guide them accordingly. In later years, his bowling lost its sting because the nip off the wicket was gone and the batsmen had enough time to change their strokes. However, his length never wavered. If there is one man who has taken a great deal of interest in my cricket and encouraged me at every step it is Marshall. Often he would drop in at our house late after dinner and say, 'Sunny, century tomorrow.' I think he had more confidence in my cricketing ability than I had myself.

P. K. 'Joe' Kamat is more famous as the guiding spirit behind Ajit Wadekar. I, however, remember him more for his 158 against Maharashtra at the Bombay Gymkhana ground. He just about hit the ball everywhere and almost every blade of grass must have felt the sting of his power-packed shots. A fearless hooker, he believed in going for the bowling right from the first ball. I think this adventurous spirit cost him a lot because he did not stay in the Bombay team for long. An absolutely brilliant fielder anywhere, he took amazing catches at gully. I remember the time when after splitting his palm catching a full blooded Budhi Kunderan hit, he just ran to the doctor round the corner, had his palm stitched and was back again at gully. 'Joe' can discuss cricket at length and his views are clear and arguments convincing. He is always ready to discuss any cricketing problem with you and will try to sort it out. Joe and Marshall are so deeply dedicated to cricket that they are still bachelors!

The next year I was back in the Bombay 14 though I did not play in the first two Ranji Trophy matches. However, I found a place in the eleven against the Rest of India in the annual Irani Trophy match. At the end of the match the team to tour Australia and New Zealand was to be selected. So, while everybody else was trying to get a place in the Indian team, I was the only player trying to earn a place in the Bombay side. However, I was a complete failure in my first outing for Bombay.

The wicket had the typical first morning life when we batted. Dilip Sardesai, who opened with me, was caught off the splice when a ball cocked up. My pleasure at seeing Ajit Wadekar at the other end and the dream of having a big partnership with him vanished when I was also caught at leg-slip off Chakravarty, who had earlier claimed Dilip's wicket. Ashok Mankad and Hardikar, however, took Bombay to a safe position. The wicket still had a bit of life when the Rest started batting. Ramakant Desai, who had not been selected for the earlier England tour and who was not even in the thirty called for a camp prior to the Australia-New Zealand tour, bowled with fire. With Umesh Kulkarni giving him valuable support, they bowled themselves into the team for Australia and New Zealand. In the second innings I offered no stroke to a ball and was out plumb leg-before, again to Chakravarty, for a duck.

Six Bombay players were selected for the Australia-New Zealand tour and since they were to leave within ten days, the Bombay selectors recalled Madhav Apte, among others, for the next Ranji Trophy match. Although Madhav Apte had been playing club cricket regularly he had not played first-class cricket for a number of years. Sudhir Naik was also recalled and I found myself left out of the eleven. I was quite bitter about this because I thought that I should have been given another chance, instead of Madhav Apte's being recalled. This feeling was strengthened when Apte was bowled first ball by Urmikant Mody, my Dadar Union colleague, who played for Saurashtra. However, I was thankful to the selectors because I realised I was very immature then and another failure would have demoralised me completely. Madhav Apte himself was very sympathetic and comforted me. It was, however, quite sad to see him struggling to make runs, and such is the Bombay spirit that towards the end of the tournament, especially in the knock-out stage, I wanted him to succeed in giving Bombay a good start. Madharao, as he is popularly known, had a very good series against the West Indies in 1953, but he played only a few Tests thereafter. His fielding even in 1968 was good enough for the batsmen to think twice before taking a run. He retired immediately after the end of the 1967-68 season, along with Hardikar and Baloo Gupte.

When Bapu Nadkarni also retired from first-class cricket at the end of the Australian tour, the Bombay team for 1968-69 suddenly had a lot of vacancies. Luckily, Bombay has always had reserves who are only waiting for their chance. Solkar was already an established Ranji Trophy player and Sudhir Naik, with a good season behind him, had also established himself in the team.

In the 1967-68 season I had not gone on tour with the university team as I had wanted to concentrate on my studies. The next season I became captain of the Bombay University team, but I was not included among the fourteen players for the Ranji Trophy. Ramnath Parkar had replaced me in the Bombay 14, but for the next three seasons he had to be content with being the twelfth man. I had a wonderful season otherwise, but I was still unable to find a place in the Bombay team.

Bombay University lost in the semifinal of the West Zone matches of the interuniversity tournament to Indore in a thriller. Bombay took a first innings lead of 52 runs, and on the third and final day, were required to score 202 runs to win. Meanwhile, in the other semifinal, Baroda, the hosts, had won and were awaiting the result of our match. Ours was the best side in the West Zone and to ensure a smooth final for Baroda, the local umpires started raising their fingers for practically every appeal by an Indore player. As a result, Bombay at the time were 110 for 8 and with 90 runs to make we had given up all hope. But Dilip Galvankar (a medical student) had other ideas. He played a cavalier innings of 52 and carried the side to within ten runs of victory, with about fifteen minutes left for draw of stumps. The entire crowd, which by then was pronouncedly anti-Bombay, suddenly became pro-Bombay and as our last man walked in, there was tremendous excitement in the air. Having taken a first innings lead we had only to draw the match to qualify for the final. Navin Ambulkar, a great character to have around, was playing a dogged innings and with only two runs and seven minutes to go, glanced the ball to deep fine-leg. Surprisingly, he was halfway down the wicket when he was declared out leg-before. Ambulkar was so shocked by the decision that, for

17

almost ten minutes after that he could not speak even though he tried to. In the meanwhile both the umpires had run off and had not bothered to sign the score book, as is the rule. The Indore boys also were sympathetic and our players were clearly agitated. But we wended our way back slowly to our hostel, being comforted by the fact that from a near hopeless position we had almost won, and we would have, but for those two gentlemen in white coats.

The Vizzy Trophy final against North Zone that year was played in New Delhi. I had an innings of 247 not out against South Zone, followed by an innings of 113 not out in the final against North Zone at New Delhi. Though the North Zone was strongly fancied to lift the trophy, the West finished victors for the third time in a row. Even this performance did not impress the Bombay selectors and I was not included in the team for the Ranji Trophy. This served only to make me more determined to assert my claim. In the Purshottam Shield final at Bombay, just before the team for the Ranji Trophy final was selected, I scored 301 not out. Well, it was still 'no go' as far as the selectors were concerned. They probably did not want to change a winning combination. I was, however, satisfied that the season had been a marvellous one for me.

A truly amazing part of cricket is that after a good season, the next one turns out to be a barren one. And so it happened with me. Right from the club games to the university matches, I found run-getting extremely difficult.

This time the interuniversity matches were played at Jabalpur. We got past the first round easily and in the second round, clashed with Gujarat. After being dismissed cheaply, we conceded a first innings lead to Gujarat. Then we fought back and scored 200 runs, leaving Gujarat to score 162 runs for victory. We dismissed Gujarat for 150 with just about ten minutes to spare.

Dilip Mulherkar, who was so short that he had to shout before anyone looked down at him, bowled his off and leg-spinners so effectively that the Gujarat batsmen had no clue as to what was happening. Our victory was achieved when Jayprakash Patel, Gujarat's captain, tried to swing Mulherkar out of the ground and the ball rose up at mid-off. Hemant Waingankar, not the best fielder in the side, got himself underneath and waited. I turned my face away and kept on looking at the wicketkeeper. Only when he let out a smile and a well done skip did I turn around and congratulate Mulherkar on his excellent bowling.

Somehow after his sensational start Mulherkar just went into oblivion. Perhaps his small frame was not up to the task of toiling and spinning away for hours. But he did a great job that year for Bombay University, and it was he who was mainly responsible for our winning the coveted Rohinton-Baria Trophy. We had a good team that year and all of us were keen to avenge our previous year's defeat by Indore. Indore, however, did not have its stalwarts of the previous year and our victory was an easy one.

In the all-India final we played Bangalore. It was a good match and we won mainly because everybody contributed his bit towards the victory. It was a proud moment for me when I received the Rohinton-Baria Trophy and we had a real celebration that night.

West Zone, however, lost their hold on the Vizzy Trophy that year, convincingly beaten by East in the semifinals. It was a great disappointment but also a relief to be able to get back home and to one's books.

A word about the interuniversity tournament. These are the very matches which are the stepping stones to first-class cricket. Every university in each zone gets to host the matches by rotation and the all-India final and the Vizzy Trophy matches are played at the same centre. The tournament, which is played during December-January in cold weather, can take quite a toll on one's resources. The teams are asked to stay in rooms where eight to ten boys are crammed. There is hardly any hot water to bathe and shave and the boys have to sleep on the floor in freezing weather. It's all very unhygienic apart from being terribly uncomfortable. The boys get a very nominal allowance from the university for their meals and one has to spend from one's own pocket to make up for the inadequacies. The university also does not provide sweaters and blazers. Actually, Bombay University gives blazers only to the teams that win, and that too after the tournament is over. Because of their tremendous enthusiasm, the boys overcome these handicaps and appreciate the difficulties of the host university. I feel that the participants in this prestigious tournament deserve a better deal and the basic necessities must be provided. Many schoolboy prodigies fade out when up against tougher competition, and it is seldom that they succeed in first-class cricket. It is the university lads who eventually hit the top and if they are treated better it will be an investment for the future, and also help to create a climate for the proper development of latent talent.

3

Bombay Blues

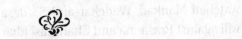

BY EARLY 1970, BOMBAY HAD MADE THEIR WAY TO THE KNOCKOUT
stage of the Ranji Trophy Tournament and I was surprised to
find my name in the team. Obviously my selection was not
prompted by my performance. In the university matches it had
been awful, and my only big score was a double century in the
intercollegiate final against a none-too-impressive attack. I had
replaced Sudhir Naik who also had a poor Ranji season. Ashok
Mankad, having earlier been asked to open for India in the
Tests against Australia, was the other opener for Bombay.

Bombay lost the toss. We, however, dismissed Mysore (as
Karnataka was then called) for 220 runs. When our turn to bat
came I requested Ashok to let me take the first strike. After
playing four balls I missed the fifth one and was plumb leg-
before wicket and out for a duck. I will never forget the booing

of the crowd that day, accusing me of coming into the side because my uncle was a member of the selection committee. Actually, I learnt much later from the other selectors that whenever my name was proposed or discussed, Mr Mantri would not take part in the discussions and would seldom venture an opinion. Yet, the public never believed it and I was the target of the crowd's displeasure every time. When I entered the dressing room there was a deathly silence and the players completely ignored me. As I was removing my leg-guards I realised what a great opportunity I had missed and thinking of the mess I had made of that shot I started laughing. Some of the players were worried and began to wonder whether I had lost my mind. But when I explained how I had missed a half-volley, which was the reason I was laughing, they relaxed. We then sat out and watched Mankad, Wadekar and Sardesai score runs almost at will against Prasanna and Chandrasekhar. In the second innings, Vishwanath, making his first appearance in Bombay after his triumphant series against Australia, scored 95 runs. He missed his hundred when he tried to cut a ball from Abdulla Ismail and was caught behind. He played a variety of strokes all round the wicket but there was one cover-drive which stands out in my memory. He stepped out to a flighted one from Rege and at the last minute, with a flick of the wrist, guided the ball between short third-man and cover-point. From my position at first slip, I had seen exactly how he had changed his shot at the last minute. Vishwanath too remembers that shot.

Brijesh Patel scored a century on that occasion and Budhi Kunderan, the Mysore captain who was retiring from first-class cricket at the end of the match and migrating to England, declared his innings to give us the last ninety minutes of batting. Of the fifth ball, again of the first over, I was dropped at leg-slip and thus avoided a pair. Both Ashok and I played out the ninety minutes and I scored 27 not out, while Mankad was beaten when he was 28. When the team for the next match against Rajasthan was announced I was expecting the axe. But the selectors had decided to give me another chance. Probably my three catches in the slips in the earlier match had influenced them. Whatever it was, I was glad to have another go, which I knew would truly be my last chance.

Rajasthan won the toss and batted first. However, Ismail and Saeed Hattea skittled them out for 217, just before close of play. In the few minutes left, I got off the mark and the next day I was lucky to see a simple snick being dropped by the wicketkeeper. After that I gave only one more chance before reaching a century. That was at 95 when a cut went through Parthasarthy Sharma's hands in the slips, to take my score to one run short of my first century in the Ranji Trophy. All this while Ashok Mankad had already notched up his century, carting Kailash Gattani repeatedly over square-leg. We struck up a good understanding and took some cheeky singles. It was with one such run of the last ball of the over before tea that I got the century. As we were returning to the pavilion, Raj Singh and Hanumant Singh came and offered their congratulations. Raj Singh said he hoped this would be first of many I would get in the Ranji Trophy. Both Ashok and I had overhauled Rajasthan's score without being separated and we broke the previous record for the opening stand for Bombay when we passed 273 runs. We were eventually separated at 279 when I was caught behind, off Salim Durrani, for 114. Ashok went on to score 171 runs. It was a great knock. We got Rajasthan out cheaply again in the second innings and, once again, I held three catches. Thus another win was registered for Bombay and I ended up with renewed confidence and hope that I could make it big.

Earlier in the season the Combined Universities had played the touring New Zealanders and I had been selected to play against the visitors. Collinge and Dayle Hadlee, their bowlers, were fast and it was the first time I had faced bowling above medium-pace. I stuck around for almost two hours and scraped 25 runs before a great piece of cricket got me out. Bryan Yuile, the left-hand bowler, induced me to go for a cut. I bottom-edged the ball on to the wicketkeeper's pads. From there it flew to Hastings at gully, who knocked it up behind him. Glenn Turner from first slip ran and dived behind Hastings to take a left-handed catch, inches from the ground. This was incredible but I was out. I was satisfied with my first encounter with pace and thought I had done a good job to see the new ball bowlers off in both the innings.

The selectors, who were watching, also must have been impressed, because they called Ramesh Nagdev and me for trials on the fourth day of the first Test against Australia at Bombay. Ramesh was then selected as twelfth man for the second Test at Kanpur. After these trials were over I had a problem because I had no pass to sit in the pavilion. Mr Chinnaswamy, probably the nicest of all the board officials, immediately gave me one.

I watched the Bombay Test being slowly grabbed by Australia. They knocked out all the Indian batsmen, and only Wadekar and Venkataraghavan were able to withstand their attack somewhat. Then Venkat was declared out, caught behind and as he didn't seem happy with the decision the crowd also showed its displeasure. Suddenly, a section of the spectators became violent and the rest is now history. The next day, when I came for the game, my gloves had been smattered with blood and the whole dressing room was in a mess.

4

Going Places

THE 1970 SEASON BEGAN WITH THE INDIAN UNIVERSITIES' TEAM going to Sri Lanka. Ashok Gandotra was the captain and I was his deputy. We had a camp in Madras, and from there flew to neighbouring Sri Lanka. Our trip was a successful one as we won all our matches. Unlike in India, Sri Lanka's university boys are not half as good as the Sri Lanka schoolboys. In the island school cricket is very competitive and people throng to watch these games.

We had an interesting match against the Sri Lanka Cricket Board XI led by Anura Tennekoon and including many other Sri Lanka players. After we won the toss Vinay Lamba and I put on 60 runs before both of us were dismissed in succession. The others followed. The Sri Lankan team took a lead of about 70 runs. While fielding at silly mid-off my

25

thumb was injured when I tried to stop a fierce drive. This prevented me from opening in the second innings. There was a bit of rain and the wicket had just that little bit of life to encourage the Sri Lanka bowlers. They had us on the hop. I went in at number seven, and, first with Kailash Gattani and then with Dilip Doshi, managed to avert a collapse. We declared, leaving the Sri Lankan team to score 130 runs in ninety minutes. They almost made it but eventually fell short by just 11 runs.

The next match was against Sri Lanka University. Jayantilal and I put on 174 runs before Jayanti was out. I went on to score 203 not out. In the last match, on a matting track, Vinay Lamba scored 150 and thus we ended the tour on a satisfactory note. Ashok Gandotra, however, did not have a successful tour and disappointed many people who had come specially to watch him.

In the meanwhile I had a cable from home informing me of my selection for the Bombay team for the first Ranji Trophy match of the season. Of course, I could not leave the tour midway and so I missed the first match. Sudhir Naik replaced me and scored 74 runs. Thus I found myself left out of the eleven for the next game against Gujarat.

Since I was not going to play in the team I did not carry my leg-guards to the nets on the days preceding the match. Seldom does a reserve player get batting at the nets because all the eleven want to have a go. So the reserve's main job is to bowl and field at the nets.

So, imagine my embarrassment when, on the morning of the match, skipper Ajit Wadekar declared himself unfit and Dilip Sardesai, deputising for him, told me that I was playing. I phoned home frantically for my leg-guards. My mother, poor thing, rushed in a taxi with the leg-guards and returned home in the same taxi after leaving the leg-guards with the doorman. One wonders why she did not stay to see me play; and thereby hangs a tale. Ever since I was out for a duck in my first Ranji Trophy match against Mysore, my mother had not watched me batting. She would refuse to come on the first day, not knowing whether we would bat or not. Then if I had finished batting, she would come the next day. If we had to field first, she would not come at all.

Meanwhile, seeing my predicament, Wadekar offered me his leg-guards since he was not playing. When I came at lunch unbeaten with 71 runs, he advised me to continue with his leg-guards instead of changing over to mine. I went on to score a century and was out soon after. My innings had lasted 160 minutes.

Saeed Hattea could not produce the same speed as in the previous year and went down with back trouble. This, together with some fielding lapses, enabled Gujarat to force a draw. Incidentally, in Gujarat's second innings, I got my first wicket in the Ranji Trophy when I clean bowled Saldhana, their opening batsman. Sudhir Naik who had opened in the first match had to bat lower down in the order in this match, in spite of his big score in the first game.

With Wadekar being fit for the next game it was a problem as to whom to drop. This was solved when Sardesai discovered he had cracked a rib and could not play. This was the match which was to prove a crucial one for me. It was always the Maharashtra-Bombay tie that decided the West Zone championship. The Poona wicket was a featherbed and there would be no reason for alarm for the batsmen. Bombay, batting first, were 322 for two at the end of the first day. Sudhir Naik, batting at number three and I added 227 runs for the second wicket. Earlier, Ashok and I had a partnership of 52 runs.

Sudhir scored 110 and I was unbeaten with 144 at the end of the day.

The next day we went for the bowling and lost wickets in the process. I was out for 176, giving me my third century in three Ranji Trophy matches after my disastrous debut against Mysore. The match ended in a dull draw as Maharashtra were just content to plod along. They achieved their aim of not giving us even the first innings lead. So we shared points.

Sardesai reported fit for the next game, but this time I was down with influenza. So, once again the ticklish problem of dropping a good player was avoided.

After this, the West Zone team against the South Zone was announced and I was surprised to find myself excluded. People sympathised with me and consoled me by predicting that I was a certainty for the forthcoming West Indies tour. Because of this, they said, the selectors had decided to watch the others. I did not derive any comfort from this, because, until then I had played only four first-class matches and I feared that my inexperience could have gone against me.

I consulted Madhav Mantri and he advised me to go ahead and lead Bombay University in the interuniversity matches to be played at Poona. He said that I should not worry unduly about team selection and should just play my natural game. I then asked him a question that was uppermost in my mind. Supposing I was selected to play in the final of the Duleep Trophy what was I to do? Should I return from the interuniversity matches? His reply was typical of him: 'You are the captain of the Bombay University. Just go and forget everything else. We'll cross that bridge when we come to it.'

Poona is just a four-hour drive from Bombay and I completely forgot about the impending selection as the boys started their usual bantering and joking in the train. As soon as we arrived

28

in Poona, we had a net practice session because we were playing the next day. In the four innings I played, my scores were 226, 99, 327 and 124. Only the last innings was really worth something because the attack was better than the rest. Incidentally, the 327 bettered Ajit Wadekar's record of 324 runs set up twelve years ago. And it came just before Ajit was selected as the captain of the Indian team to the West Indies. The university boys were happy and we went on to beat Poona University in the final to reach the all-India semifinals.

My mother had telephoned me the previous evening and said that she wanted me to do her a favour. When I asked her what it was, she replied that she wanted me to break the individual batting record of 324. I promised to try my best, but 325 was a tall order in interuniversity cricket.

How the record came about is rather interesting. Avi Karnik said to me after I was out for 226 in the first match that I should have gone on to better the record. I told him that I had not thought of it and, besides, there was hardly any time. During the innings of 327, when I was not out with 269 at tea, he came and said, 'Now there is plenty of time and so don't throw it away.' I did not, but after the boundary that gave me the record, the next ball sent my off-stump cartwheeling to the wicketkeeper, as I tried to steer it past third man. Imagine being out like that after scoring 327. All my elation vanished with this ignominious dismissal.

The team came back to Bombay before travelling to Waltair down south, for the All-India Championship. The day the team was to leave for Waltair, the Indian team for the West Indies was to be announced, so I stayed back in Bombay promising the boys that I would fly to Waltair and join them.

I remember how I spent that afternoon with Saeed Ahmed Hattea. He was also strongly tipped to make the team and both of us went to a cinema show to while away same time. However, we were not very interested in the show and walked out soon after. When we went to the Bombay Cricket Association office to inquire if the team had been announced we were told that the selection committee meeting was still on. We spent another half-an-hour and I suggested to Saeed that we better go home. The suburban train was crowded with office workers returning home. Saeed, with his long hair (quite a new fad those days), was easily recognised and many commuters 'selected' him in the team. When Saeed very politely pointed to me and asked, 'What about Mr Gavaskar?' they said, 'O.K. he will also be there', but they did not sound very convincing. We parted company wishing each other luck and promising to phone on hearing the news. When I reached home everybody was relaxed except my mother, who looked tense and asked me anxiously whether there was any news. My father and sister were, however, confident that I was 'in' and showed no signs of anxiety.

I played around a bit with my cousin and just before dinner, decided to drop the little kid home. I was hardly out of the door when the telephone rang. I waited outside the door and did not ring the bell, waiting to see if it was for me. It was! Ashok Mankad was on the line telling me that I was in the squad to tour the West Indies. I felt a tremendous surge of happiness and hugged my parents who were shedding tears of joy. I immediately went to the pooja room and prayed for the Almighty's blessings.

I was on my way to Madhav Mantri's house when the telephone call had come. I told him the good news and he embraced me and we sat down while he told me a few things. But my mind was in a whirl. I came home soon afterwards and had dinner. There was tremendous excitement in the house. The telephone did not ring again because the team had not been officially announced. But, through it all, I could not help thinking of Saeed who was not 'in'; I felt sorry for him and didn't have the heart to telephone him as I had promised.

About the same time I was asked by the Board secretary that I would go and play in two fixtures against the visiting Sri Lanka team. Earlier, I had asked for permission to continue with my interuniversity matches, which had reached the all-India stage and Bombay University were in the final. However, I was refused permission on the ground that I might get injured. At the same time, I was surprised at being asked to play against the Sri Lankan team, apparently because 'it was always nice to be in the good books of the south'. This stunned me but I had no choice, and so I went. Ashok and I decided that we would just throw our bats around. We did just that, though in both the matches my throwing the bat around fetched me quick runs and the crowd's approval.

Meanwhile, Bombay University played and lost in the final to Madras. I am sure all the boys must still be thinking that I had let them down. I hope, after reading this, they will change their minds. If I hadn't played any game at all, it would have been all right, but the reasons given as to why I should play against the Sri Lankan team were stupid because I had to play against better and quicker bowlers on matting. As it is, Jayantilal fractured his thumb, but as he was having only a slight pain, he went to the West Indies. This fracture was finally diagnosed when he had his hand x-rayed after injury to another finger just before the last Test in the West Indies.

5

Caribbean Journey

WE HAD ABOUT TEN DAYS' PRACTICE BEFORE WE LEFT FOR THE West Indies. There were the usual tour formalities, which were all new to me, to be completed. I was all at sea, but 'Mama' Karmarkar, the genial but live-wire assistant secretary of the Cricket Control Board took care of everything and asked me not to worry. I am sure the Board officials, especially the players, would feel completely lost if 'Mama' wasn't there. Everybody loved him, though he would chide the players occasionally, because he is warm hearted and genuinely anxious to help people.

Three days before we left I began to get a funny kind of pain in the middle finger of my left hand. It was as if some object had gone in. The doctor diagnosed it as a whitlow and asked me not to do any net practice. Ajit kindly excused me practice sessions. Instead, I sat and watched the others practise on the last two days. Govindraj told me that he had the same trouble a few days earlier and how he had got rid of it. At that time, I didn't pay any attention to him and only followed the doctor's advise.

The chairman of the selection committee, Mr Vijay Merchant, met the members of the Indian team before we left for the Caribb. He conveyed his good wishes to us and expressed the hope that we would acquit ourselves creditably. During his talk, Mr Merchant said that the batsmen should give our bowlers enough runs to bowl with. A hundred should only be the stepping-stone to another hundred. He said that the only player who followed this precept was Sunil Gavaskar. 'Though he is the youngest player in the team, the senior players would do well to follow his example', he added. This was very flattering indeed. It also made me aware of the high expectations, not only of the selection committee, but those who followed Indian cricket. I am glad I didn't disappoint them.

We left for London on our way to the West Indies on 1 February 1971. I had bandaged my finger to protect it from hurting myself as a result of the jostling we might get from the enthusiastic crowd that had turned up to see us off. During the flight I decided to follow Govindraj's method to reduce the pain. I asked the air hostess for some sweet lime, sliced into two. I shoved my finger into one half and kept it there for an hour or so. According to Govindraj, this would draw out the pus and the finger would heal quickly. Since the flight to London takes about nine hours, I continued the treatment until we reached our destination. We had a night's halt in London which we used for bit of sightseeing. Ashok Mankad, who had spent the previous English cricket season in Manchester, was my guide and we went around in our tropical suits, cheerfully ignoring the startled

33

Londoners in their overcoats. The finger had not started its tricks till then and I had my hand in my trouser-pocket all the time, while going around Piccadilly Circus.

The next morning we left for New York. By this time the finger was throbbing with pain, probably because the condition was aggravated by the cold of London. Hardly had the plane taken off when the pain started increasing in intensity until I couldn't even move it one way or the other. I was feeling miserable. I tried bearing the pain for a couple of hours but when I couldn't any longer, I talked to our manager, Mr Tarapore. He looked worried and he had an emergency announcement made over the aircraft's public address system, to enquire if a doctor was on board. Luckily for me, there was one and he gave me some capsules which reduced the intensity of the pain and kept me from howling in agony.

As soon as we checked into our hotel near Kennedy airport in New York, Mr Tarapore took me to a hospital. When the nurse on duty saw my finger, she turned her face away because it was badly swollen and full of puss. The doctor examined it and said he would have to operate immediately. He assured me that it would take less than ten minutes but I would be out of action for two weeks. He said, 'Thank God, you've come now. If you had delayed even by twenty-four hours, gangrene would have set in and the finger would have had to be chopped off.' The operation, which was a minor one, did not take long, and I felt very much relieved. The pain was gone. I am deeply grateful to Mr Keki Tarapore for the prompt action he took and for taking me to the hospital. Keki came to the hospital and stayed with me all the time. He comforted me, saying I would soon be well. And, when we returned to the hotel, he packed me off straight to bed as I had lost a bit of blood and a night's rest would do a lot of good to me. He was right and I woke up feeling very much refreshed, with the finger looking tender, but certainly better. While I was at the hospital, the other members of team went on a lightning tour of New York making the most of the night halt in the fabulous city.

Our flight to Jamaica from New York was short, compared to the long flight from Bombay to London and New York – sixteen hours in all. We landed at Palisades airport in Kingston where the West Indies cricket officials received us. The people were nice and friendly and began to talk to our players. Jaisimha, Sardesai, Prasanna and Durrani, who had been in the West Indies with the 1962 team, were especially sought after but nobody paid much attention to the others. While we waited for our luggage, a round of rum-punch was served. When I said I did not drink, the person serving the drink looked at me flabbergasted and said, 'What maan, you, a batsman! You can't score runs here unless you drink rum.' Still I declined and so did a few others. The welcome was friendly though naturally not over-enthusiastic after the 5-0 drubbing we received in 1962. It was frustrating for some of the players to find their kitbags misplaced as they had not arrived from New York. We had just one day before our first match against Jamaica. I, of course, was out of it all, though I earnestly wanted to get into the thick of things. I did quite a bit of running and bowled a lot to our batsmen, just to keep myself fit, especially my legs.

Just before the match against Jamaica, Vishwanath had to drop out. He had twisted his knee very badly in the South Zone vs. Central Zone final at Bombay and now it had started to trouble him. So, Dilip Sardesai who was not in the eleven for the match and was, in fact, a last-minute choice for the tour, got in. And, how he made full use of his opportunity! Even before he was selected for the tour, Dilip used to say that he

35

would score two or three centuries in the West Indies and then retire from first-class cricket. This self-confidence was justified when he slammed three centuries in the Tests, all of them under the most difficult circumstances.

In the match against Jamaica, Dilip scored 97 runs before being run out in a mix-up with Ajit Wadekar. Both Ajit and Dilip, in spite of their innumerable long partnerships for Bombay and West Zone, were terrible runners between wickets and, more often than not, the only way to get them out was through a run out. Dilip thus missed the distinction of being the first to hit a century on the tour. In a way it was good because generally those who start with a century always find runs hard to come by later on. This proved true in the case of Salim Durrani who hit a century (131) in the second innings, but failed to make any substantial contribution with the bat thereafter. Ajit had a long look at the bowling and the wicket and scored 70 runs in 240 minutes. It was Sardesai, however, who stole the show. Equally comfortable against pace and spin, his innings was an tremendous lesson to players like me.

In the second innings Durrani played as only he can. With the minimum movement of his feet he still got the maximum power behind his shots, which fairly sizzled over the grass. He hooked Dowe out of the small Sabina Park ground and then cover-drove him to the boundary. This caused excitement among the tree-top spectators, who began to jump and clap with such gusto that a branch of the tree crashed down with its human load. While some people who had fallen were dusting themselves and looking for broken bones, the others quickly scrambled back to their high perch. It was quite a sight and it shows how keen the West Indians are where cricket is concerned. The spectators in the Caribbean want to see bumpers bowled and love to see the batsmen wilt. They are annoyed if a batsman (especially Indian) hooks the bumpers for boundaries.

During this match we had our first look at Lawrence Rowe. According to one player, Rowe is in the habit of whistling while playing a shot. He clipped a few shots but was out quickly in the first innings for 19 and scored 19 not out in the second knock. We played our second match at Montego Bay against the West Indies Board President's XI. Alvin Kallicharran played in the match and got a few runs (57 not out) in the second innings. At that time he looked like a batsman ever ready to hit every ball out of sight. But, by the time he came to India in 1974-75, he had become a complete batsman, willing to wait for the loose ball, yet elegant at all times. I remember how Kalicharan was despondent when we met him at a beach party in the evening after he was out for only 6 runs in the first innings. He was apparently haunted by the fear that he would never be selected to play for the West Indies and was on the verge of tears. Vishwanath and I did our best to console him and we have been good friends ever since.

Vishwanath and I, in the meanwhile, were regular visitors to the hospital where the doctor who was treating us talked endlessly about cricket. The doctors were undecided about the condition of Vishwanath's knee. My finger now needed only cleaning and dressing, and it was getting better. Vishwanath and I would be at the hospital when the others were on the field and listening to the radio commentary on the match. We would suddenly look at each other and laugh while we really felt miserable. Imagine, two 21-year-olds in hospital! Vishwanath's leg had been shaved and it was a funny sight. I never stopped ribbing him about it, and even while in hospital, we tried to pull each other's leg.

With both of us unfit for the first two games of the tour,

the rest of the team members had more opportunity of establishing themselves. Ashok Mankad, finding it difficult to cope with livelier wickets, was struggling to get runs and was not played in the first Test. The tour selectors decided to experiment with Abid Ali who had earlier opened for India in Tests against Australia and New Zealand, both at home (1969) and in the two countries (1967).

I played my first match against the University of the West Indies, which was a one-day game played over 45 overs a side. We scored freely and I got 71 runs. The finger wound looked to have opened a bit and I was worried. But it was a minor thing and the rest I got while we played the first Test was enough for it to heal. Vishwanath also played in the match, his first on the tour, and got 50 runs. Dilip was his usual self but was run out again when he was on 55. After his third run out in three matches, Dilip swore that if he was ever run out again he would pack up and go home. In this game he got into a muddle with Salim Durrani and Salim saw to it that Dilip didn't get home. Salim and Dilip were roommates and they got on famously, and it was this that probably also prompted Durrani to throw away his wicket. We won the match fairly easily, by a wide margin of by 101 runs.

The first Test at Kingston started late, as there was a bit of rain and the first day's play was washed out. On the second day, Sobers won the toss and asked India to bat. The wicket, freshened by rain, had a lot of life which the Caribbean pace bowlers fully exploited. Shillingford sent back Jayantilal with only 10 runs on the board. Jayantilal withdrew his bat at the last moment, but the ball came back sharply, got an edge and travelled like lighting between second and third slip. There was a flash of movement and Sobers came up laughing with the ball clutched to his chest. 'What a catch!' I told somebody.

'Now all I want to see is Rohan Kanhai's falling sweep shot, and my tour is made.' Abid followed soon after, sparring at one outside the off-stump for Camacho to take an easy catch. Ajit held on grimly till he gloved an attempted hook off Holder for another easy catch. Dilip and Salim of room number 53, Flamingo Hotel, got together and added runs slowly. The spinners came on and Test debutante Barrett struck, claiming Durrani's wicket who missed a pull and was bowled by a ball that kept low. Jaisimha, my boyhood idol, came and played on to Holder and was bowled. India were 75 for five and already the radio commentators and critics were sharpening their knives. One commentator called us a club side. I don't know whether Eknath Solkar heard it, but, when he went out, Dilip met him halfway and had a word with him. With Dilip's constant encouragement, Eknath, who was playing his first Test abroad, put his head down and the pair slowly wore out the Windies' attack. They added 137 runs, a new record for the sixth wicket, and batted up to the third day before Solkar was bowled by Sobers for 61. India were 260 for eight when Prasanna joined Dilip. Those who complain that Prasanna is chicken-hearted and is afraid of a contest should have been there to see how well he stood his ground against pace and spin. In between, he played a delightful square-cut when Holder took the third new ball. The Dilip-Prasanna partnership flourished and 122 runs were added before Prasanna (25) was bowled by Holder. This was yet another wicket record in Tests against the Windies. And then, Dilip (212) was caught behind off Holder. India were all out for 387 which was a remarkable improvement on 75 for five. We were on top right through after that initial debacle. When the Windies batted, their stroke players found it difficult to score against our spinners. Only Kanhai and to some extent,

Sobers, batted comfortably. Once they were gone, the others just collapsed and the West Indies were all out for 217.

The first day's play having been washed out, we could enforce the follow-on, which we did. Incidentally this was the first time in twenty-three years that the West Indies had to do so against India. Ajit told us how the Windies were looking downcast when he went to their dressing-room to ask them to bat again. This time they played sensible cricket and Kanhai remained unbeaten with 158, Sobers scored a dazzling 93 while Clive Lloyd was run out for 57. Kanhai played his falling sweep shot in this innings which made my day. Earlier, Dilip, nursing a strained thigh muscle, came in to rest. While watching the match with Grayson Shillingford, Dilip suddenly turned round and told the West Indian bowler as he pointed to me, 'Watch him, he'll also score two hundreds against your bowling.' For a moment I was stunned and could only manage a weak smile. I had not, until then, played a first-class match in the Windies and a statement like that from somebody, who was the first to score a double century against the West Indies, was a bolt from the blue, so to speak. Dilip's thunderbolt was even faster than what Shillingford was to bowl in the two Tests I played against him!

The Test ended in a draw, and our performance had put us back in the game and salvaged a lot of our prestige. The critics turned their comments against the West Indies and their players came in for a bit of lashing.

We went to St Kitts for a three-day game against the Leeward Islands which we won by nine wickets. This was my first-class game in the West Indies and I was happy to be able to get off the mark with a score of 82, before hitting a full toss back to Willett, in the first innings. Ajit was unbeaten with a brilliant 128 and Abid was 64 not out. Left to get 57 runs in twelve mandatory overs to win, we got 60 with an over to spare. Andy Roberts played in this game and bowled with a lot of pace but he lacked direction. When we next met him in 1974-75, he had matured a lot. We found him very accurate and he had increased his pace by a couple of yards.

6

Glorious Victory

AFTER AN OVERNIGHT FLIGHT, DUE TO SOME MIX-UP, WE LANDED at Trinidad airport pretty late. The drive to Guaracara Park, about sixty miles away, was tedious and the match against Trinidad started late. Ajit won the toss and we batted, while everybody from number five downwards went to sleep to make up for the previous night. They must have slept soundly because Ashok and I were not separated until just before tea. We had scored 155 runs, Ashok contributing a strokeful 79. Durrani then clouted two mighty sixes out of the ground before he was run out for 43. I got my century (119) with Dilip as my partner. Next morning I was run out for 125 while Dilip went on to score 94 before he was out. The disappointment was Vishwanath who hooked a bumper straight to Gabriel at mid-wicket. For Trinidad, Charlie Davis scored 100, while his brother Bryan Davis contributed 61 runs. Almost all the Trinidad batsmen made runs and they totalled 338 runs. Before Ajit declared our innings at 162 for five, I got 63 runs in ninety minutes when I played a lazy shot and was caught at extra-cover. The match ended in a drab draw. After the match, the Trinidad Cricket Council presented me with a magnificent trophy, which holds a very prominent position in my house. It was terrific getting a trophy even before I had played a Test and did wonders for my confidence.

In the second Test at Port of Spain, Ashok Mankad and I came into the team. Ashok was staging a comeback after being dropped for the first Test, while I was making my debut. At dinner that night my team-mates wished me luck and I went to sleep with the thought that the next day I was going to play my first Test for my country. I don't think I slept well and as I lay tossing in bed, I could see Vishwanath fast asleep without a care in the world. He wasn't playing in the game!

Sobers again won the toss and elected to bat. Opener Fredericks was bowled off his pads off the very first delivery by Abid Ali. After that, the West Indies lost wickets at regular intervals and were all out for 214. Only Charlie Davis batted well to remain unbeaten with 74. We had about thirty minutes' batting before close of play. As I took strike, after Ashok had got three runs, I was a little afraid that I might not be up to the mark. Holder thundered down and bowled on the leg-stump. The ball struck my leg-guards and went down to fine-leg for two leg-byes. But I was surprised to see that the umpire did not make any signal, so I was off the mark with two runs when actually I shouldn't have had any. This helped me to get rid of the fear of failure, and I was soon middling the ball and clipped Holder to the square-leg fence for my first boundary in Tests. We ended the day with 22 without being separated. Ashok was on 14 with me on 8.

The next morning I was glad to see Sobers grass a low, fast edge off Holder as I tried to drive him off the back-foot. Sobers tumbled in the attempt but spilled the ball. This was a lucky break and I went on with greater confidence and got my 50 after lunch. It was a slow innings, but I was encouraged when Kanhai, fielding in the slips, said, 'Well played, son'. That gave me a terrific boost and after that I seemed to play much better. I got to 65 before I pulled a short ball from Noreiga, for Clive Lloyd, half-way to the square-leg boundary, to take a simple catch. My baptism in Test cricket was over and I hadn't done too badly. Ajit was out next ball before he had scored, but Solkar prevented the hat-trick. Dilip, in the meantime, had settled down and, with dazzling footwork, was neutralising any spin that Noreiga and Sobers were getting from the wicket. It was an abject lesson on how to play spin. Dilip made 112, before he fell to a catch off Noreiga. India were all out for 352, which gave us a lead of 138 runs. In the second innings the West Indians lost Kanhai cheaply, but Fredericks and Charlie Davis settled down. At the end of the day's play they had just about wiped out the arrears.

It was one of those freak accidents which gave us an opening. Fredericks and Davis were batting at the nets when a shot by Fredericks went through and hit Davis on the right eyebrow, splitting it. He had to be carried to hospital and Lloyd came out with Fredericks to resume the innings. Fredericks was, however, run out without any addition to his overnight score. Lloyd, after hitting an uppish shot past mid-wicket, was caught brilliantly by Ajit who had stationed himself at short mid-wicket just before the previous ball was delivered. Then Durrani bowled a prodigious break-back that went through Sobers' bat and pad and lifted the leg-bail. The way 'Uncle' Salim jumped up after this and kept on jumping was a sight worth seeing. After this, the West Indies batting collapsed though Davis came back and was unbeaten with 74. India had to get 124 runs to win with half of the fourth day's play still left. However, we finished the match that day itself and celebrated our victory on the last day. I was 67 not-out without even being aware that I had passed the 50-run mark. We had lost three wickets for 84 runs but Abid Ali, promoted by Ajit, which proved to be an intelligent move, joined me. We then required 40 runs to win and went on serenely towards the target. During our unbroken stand we were just tapping and running and in the bargain, got some bonus runs from overthrows. Though we thoroughly enjoyed ourselves, I was sure that we must have given a real fright to our colleagues in the pavilion. Victory, the first against the West Indies in twenty-three years, came fifteen minutes before the end of the fourth day's play.

As I returned to the pavilion after our historic win, Keki Tarapore came out and embraced me, followed by Ajit and the others. It was a sweet moment. Our first ever victory over the West Indies! The Windies players also trooped into our dressing room and joined in the handshaking and back-slapping. The Indians in Trinidad were thrilled and we had quite a celebration that night. A well-to-do Indian there gave us a champagne party at his fabulous estate. But we were well aware that the West Indies were smarting under defeat, and we were determined to see that our success did not make us complacent. It didn't.

I have often been asked about my feelings after my Test debut in an encounter which is a landmark in the annals of Indian cricket. Frankly, I felt satisfied with my performance even though I did not do anything outstanding. However, I had taken the first step and I had the satisfaction of having scored 132 runs in two innings, and had remained unbeaten once, to give me the very high average of 132. But to me it has always been a matter of great pride that I was able to, in my very first Test, be associated in India's maiden Test victory against the West Indies and that too in the lion's den.

7

'Sardee Maan' Tops

OUR VICTORY HAD RAISED OUR STOCK AND DILIP WITH A DOUBLE century and century in two Tests was the hero of all the West Indies. Everywhere we went, people wanted to see 'Sardee maan', as Dilip was affectionately called. Dilip was prepared to talk cricket with anybody, which made him a big hit. The department stores threw open their doors to him, and people were falling over each other to invite him to their homes for a meal.

I remember, once Dilip had charged out leaving his food which he loves, to take up cudgels against a young Indian who had said to me in Jamaica, 'Sobers will get you out, first ball, bowled behind the legs.' One of the other boys reported this to Dilip who was about to bite into his chicken; he left it and caught hold of the Indian, and nearly started a row. We stopped him but Dilip was fuming. He was touchy about what was said about the team, especially any of the younger players.

Just before the third Test we played Guyana at Georgetown, though I was included in the team, I had to drop out due to shin trouble, after the toss was over. The Guyanese captain, Rohan Kanhai, very sportingly agreed to allow the change. For India, Jaisimha (108) and Jayantilal (122 not out) batted well. The match was drawn.

The third Test was also played at Georgetown. The only change in our team was Vishwanath in place of Jaisimha. Poor Vishwanath was struggling to shrug off his knee trouble but he was so conscious of it that it hampered his game. Normally a very mobile fielder he took a longer time to turn and run for the ball. But there was never any doubt in the minds of the West Indian cricket lovers about his class. It was writ large from the moment he took strike. We shared a room after the Jamaican leg of the tour. He did not, however, come to St Kitts but went directly to Trinidad for his knee treatment. I got to know him closely then and realised what a tremendous sense of humour he has. He was miserable about his knee but in his inimitable way of speaking, he made light of it. Being about the same height as myself, he could use all my clothes and he did so nonchalantly. But I was then heavier than him and so couldn't return the compliment by using his clothes. The position was reversed, however, within a couple of years when Vishwanath put on a bit of weight. He loved his beer and when he got going he could go on and on. But he hardly drank a drop before and during Test matches.

Ajit lost the toss for the third time in the series and we went in to field on a hot and humid day. Things didn't go too well for us, as the openers Carew and Fredericks settled down. Carew swept a no-ball from Durrani to Ashok Mankad at square-leg. Not learning from experience he again swept the next ball to Ashok and was caught. Kanhai played some nice shots and then, jumping out to drive Bedi, missed and was easily stumped. Charlie Davis and Clive Lloyd then got together and pushed the score along briskly before Davis, trying to sweep Solkar, was out leg-before. Lloyd, in the meanwhile, was getting into top gear. A freak collision, however, got rid of him. He swept a ball to deep square-leg, took one run and with his eye on the ball, turned for a second and collided with Sobers. The impact was terrific.

Meanwhile Bedi's throw had come to wicketkeeper Krishnamurthy, and Lloyd was run out once again, just as he was beginning to look dangerous. Sobers was so stunned by the impact that he made a feeble attempt to cut Bedi and was caught by Venkataraghavan at slip off Krishnamurthy's pads. This was a lucky break for us and we surrounded Desmond Lewis who was making his Test debut. Lewis slashed at Bedi and was dropped by Sardesai at slip when he was only three. Dilip, who had pulled a thigh muscle, had come to stand in the slips so that he did not have to run. That was a bit of bad luck for us because Lewis went on to score 81 not out and helped West Indies recover at a respectable total of 363. Lewis and the local hero Lance Gibbs, who invariably raised a laugh with his antics but batted with purpose, added 84 runs for the ninth wicket.

India batted soon after tea on the second day. Ashok and I started cautiously against Shillingford and Boyce. When I was six I cut at a short rising ball from Shillingford and the ball flew like a bullet straight at Sobers' neck. He got his hands to it but dropped it. Later he told me that he didn't see the ball at all and it was only when it was almost on him did he realise it was coming at his face. I celebrated my luck by hooking the next ball, a predictable bouncer, for four. Ashok then opened out and we had added 78 runs when, in trying to cut Noreiga, Ashok played on to his stumps. Ajit and I played out time and when stumps were drawn I was batting with 84 and Ajit with 16.

The next day was another glorious morning and we went out to resume the innings. Ajit muttered something like 'We must stick around and score'. But he got out to a ball from Sobers that kept low without adding to his overnight score. Vishwanath joined me for his first Test innings in the West Indies, to a lot of humming among the expectant spectators. When he passed Clive Lloyd at cover there was a big laugh from the crowd because of the difference in their heights. From the beginning Vishwanath was middling the ball. With him there is no edging. He either middles it or misses and more often than not it is the sweet sound of the bat meeting the ball. We went on to add 112 runs for the third wicket. As I was nearing my first Test century, dark clouds began gathering over the ground and it started to drizzle. Play continued, however, and on 94 I survived what was probably the simplest of catches. I played forward to a flighted delivery from Noreiga. The ball spun and jumped hitting me on my glove and went to Sobers, who would have taken a dolly catch if he had been standing where he was before the ball was delivered. But Gary, anticipating my forward defensive stroke, had moved forward to try and get me. Thus he had to jump and stretch for the ball, which eluded him and in the bargain I got a run. At the end of the over, Gary stood in front of me and said: 'Maan, why are you after me, can't you find some other fielder?' He had dropped me thrice so far and this last one was the easiest of the lot. We came in because of rain when I was on 98. We resumed after a while and I duly got my first Test century.

Many people must be wondering as to how one feels when one gets a century in Tests. My own reaction was simply to think of my parents who had given me every encouragement and how they would be beaming when the news reached them. Soon we had another stoppage due to rain. When we resumed, Sobers took the new ball himself. I drove him through the covers and in trying to repeat the shot managed only to edge it to Carew at second slip who, after a lot of juggling, clasped it to his stomach. That was the end of my innings which had lasted 265 minutes and fetched me 116 runs. Keith Boyce then captured his first Test wicket bowling Vishwanath, and then Durrani was out leg-before to Sobers. Sardesai, who batted at number six because of his leg trouble, played a dour innings and with Abid hitting boldly, we overtook the West Indies total to lead them in the third successive Test.

When the Windies batted again, Eknath Solkar ripped through Fredericks' defence and had him leg-before for five. Carew was again harassed by Bishen Bedi, but he struggled gamely to score 45 runs. Lloyd and Kanhai got out early and Sobers, when he was on seven, survived a bat-pad catch appeal. I was fielding at long-on and I saw the deflection clearly and naturally jumped with joy in anticipation of our having taken the prize wicket of the great Sobers. But Gary waited and the umpire ruled not out. For once Salim Durrani lost his cool and flung down the ball in disgust. I don't blame him. He had started the tour brilliantly and was now on the verge of losing his Test place. Also, there was the England tour in the offing and he was keen to make it as he had missed the 1967 tour. The crowd reacted predictably and booed Salim. Gary then hammered us for a century (108 not out) between lunch and tea and Charlie Davis also scored a century (125 not out). Gary's innings included a six when he hit Solkar out of the ground. At this stage Sobers declared his innings, with the total at 307 for three.

We had ninety minutes' batting and Ashok (53) and I (64) put on 123 runs without being separated. My personal Test aggregate had gone up to 312 in four innings, twice not out and an average of 156. We ended the Test on a high note and went to Bridgetown for the Colony game against Barbados, followed by the fourth Test at the same venue. I was in good form and so was Ashok. Vishwanath had also played well. We were a little worried about Dilip's pulled muscle, but he was better after the intensive treatment he had received at Barbados. And how Dilip put us back in the game is now a part of India's cricketing history.

8

Deflated in Barbados

BARBADOS IS A BEAUTIFUL PLACE. IT HAS MANY LOVELY BEACHES which are invariably crowded with tourists from America, Canada and Europe. It is also the country which has given some great cricketers to the world, including the then West Indies skipper Gary Sobers. When we arrived at Bridgetown (Barbados), the customs officials wanted to see Sardesai. Asked if he had anything to declare, Dilip said with a broad smile: 'I have come here with runs, and I am going to leave Barbados with more runs.' It was a sight to see Dilip being bombarded with questions by the officials and the ready answers he had for them. Dilip was, by far, the most popular man in the Indian team. At the airport he was told that Wesley Hall had been included in the Barbados side. Dilip's reply was typical of his self-confident self. 'Ha! By the time I come to bat we will be 200 for two wickets so what is your Wes Hall going to do?' The officials loved him. He was a man after their own heart.

We were staying in a hotel on the beach and whenever we were not at the nets the boys spent their time at the beach, swimming and ogling at the bikini-clad beauties. This was, of course, a temporary respite before we got down to the real job, I mean the match against Barbados, later. Now, in Barbados, if you beat the West Indies the crowd will not feel very sorry. But if Barbados lose, then it is a national catastrophe. Nothing delights a Bajan, as Barbadians are called, as much as a Barbados victory over a touring side.

We won the toss against Barbados led by Sobers, and elected to bat. I was to take strike and saw Wes Hall go almost up to the screen for his run-up. I thought to myself, 'I'll need binoculars to know when he starts running in.' As is normally the case with me, I am always a bit apprehensive when I face a bowler for the first time. But only when he delivers the first ball. So, as Wes Hall started running up to bowl, I was expecting something like a rocket. In this event it proved to be a less dangerous delivery, which was down the leg-side and brushed my leg-guards as I let it go. And, wonder of wonders, the strap of the leg-guard was broken. However, instead of changing the leg-guard, I just tied a handkerchief round it. As it proved later it would have been a waste of time because I was out in the next over.

Jayantilal played a ball from Holder down towards square-leg. I thought we could take a quick single and I took off, expecting Jayantilal to respond. When I found he wasn't moving, I tried to stop, slipped and fell heavily. I was so stunned that I couldn't even get up as the fielder rushed past me and knocked off the bails at the bowler's end. This was the first time that I had failed in the West Indies, and I walked back to the pavilion dejected, with a zero to my name. We then collapsed and were all out for 185. When Barbados batted, Govindraj bowled a good spell which had Seymour Nurse ducking and sparring at outgoing balls. Nurse, however, survived but before he got off the mark he fell to a catch by wicketkeeper Jeejeebhoy, off Abid. However, Sobers chose this moment to get back into the century habit, with his cousin David Holford (111) to keep him company. Barbados thus ran up a mammoth total of 449.

In the second innings I was determined to score. In Hall's second over, when he bounced one at me, I played the best hook shot I've ever played. The ball went skimming to the mid-wicket boundary. I wish I could play shots like that more often. We had an opening partnership of 149 before I was bowled by a shooter from Holder for 67. After that, there was very little resistance and we were all out, leaving Barbados to score 50 runs for victory. Again Govindraj bowled well, but was positively unlucky not to get Nurse's wicket. Barbados won easily by nine wickets.

There was an incident during the Barbados match which involved Russi Jeejeebhoy and Seymour Nurse. Nurse, annoyed by Russi's constant thrusting of his pads to the ball, made a sarcastic comment that Russi had a bat to play the ball with. Russi resented the remark and walked down the wicket gesturing that he wanted to have a word with Sobers, who was then bowling. Sobers told Russi off who was so upset about it that he refused to talk to anyone in the dressing room when he returned after he was out. Dilip ribbed him a lot about this and even his room-mate Solkar did not spare him. The sight of the outraged Russi walking down the wicket to remonstrate with Sobers is one of the memorable events of the 1971 West Indies tour.

The fourth Test was to start on 1 April which was Ajit Wadekar's birthday. As if to give himself a birthday gift, Ajit won the toss for the first time in the series and elected to field. This decision was prompted by the greenish wicket and the fact that the West Indian team did not have a spin bowler to exploit the worn wicket on the last day. Lewis (88) and Kanhai (85) had a partnership of 166 runs for the second wicket before both fell. Charlie Davis and Sobers went on to score 178, in his team's total of 501 for five, before declaring on the second day. This left us with about forty minutes of batting. The West Indians had capped Uton Dowe, a fast bowler, for the Test. The fifteen thousand Barbadians were yelling their throats dry and giving Dowe just the encouragement he needed as he pounded in to bowl. He was fast, but nowhere near as frightening as he was reckoned to be. By this time dark clouds were gathering and the light was deteriorating fast. Ashok Mankad came up to me and asked me whether we should appeal against the light. I suggested that we wait for another over. Ashok appealed against the light before Dowe bowled his second over. The umpire C. Jordan, however, turned down our appeal. Off Dowe's fourth ball I was out to a simple catch by Holder at mid-wicket when I had scored only one run - my lowest score in Tests. Two balls later, Krishnamurthy, who went in as night-watchman, also appealed against the light. This time the appeal was upheld and play ended twenty minutes before time. It is amazing how the light could have deteriorated after just two deliveries, which justified the umpires calling it a day!

The next day we lost quick wickets and plunged to 70 for six, when Solkar came in to join Dilip. At this stage Dilip was batting magnificently. At 96 he played a perfect cover-drive off Sobers to reach his third century of the series. As if to prove he could do it again he repeated the shot off the next ball. This time the grass sizzled as the ball sped to the boundary. Dilip (111) and Solkar (59) resumed the innings on the morning of the fourth day and carried the total to 256, when Solkar (65) became Dowe's fourth victim. Their partnership had realised 186 runs for the seventh wicket – yet another wicket record for India. The danger of follow-on had not passed when Bedi joined Dilip for the last wicket. Bishen, though good enough to go in as night-watchman against the Australians in 1969-70, was not in his best batting form. In between some airy shots and a simple edge that wicket-keeper Lewis and Kanhai let by, he played some firm shots. With Sardesai also putting his weight behind his shots we avoided the follow-on amidst excitement. India had totalled 347 runs – the last four wickets putting on 277 runs. The last-wicket partnership between Dilip and Bedi had realised 62 priceless runs – again a new record for India.

The West Indians went on a run spree in their second knock, and Lloyd in particular hammered away as if he was having batting practice. We were expecting a declaration leaving us thirty minutes' batting, which is the kind of declaration every opening batsman dreads. But Sobers, who had other ideas, did not declare until he played an over on the last morning. That left us with a little over five hours to save the game. With no off-spinner in the West Indies side this was not going to be a tough task if we kept our wits about. That's exactly what we did and we easily saved the match. Early in our second innings Ashok Mankad fractured his right wrist in trying to fend off a delivery from Dowe. Ashok, however, did not flinch but carried on pluckily for almost an hour, playing most of the time with one hand. I had to shield him from the bowling and often I had to forget taking singles off the first few deliveries of the over, and where we could take three runs, we ran only two.

Ashok's courage in the face of physical disability was not lost on the rest of the boys and they helped me to save the match. In the process I got a century (117 not out). It was a purely defensive innings since winning was out of question. Yet, I played my shots with confidence and authority, and a hook for six off a Dowe bouncer stands out in my memory. My second century of the series somewhat compensated me for my failure in the first innings. My Test aggregate had mounted to 430 but my average had come down to just over 143.

And, so on to the last Test, secure in the knowledge that we couldn't lose the series, and there was more than an even chance of increasing our margin of victory to 2-0. It was a good augury for us that the venue of this last encounter was the Queen's Park Oval at Port of Spain, capital of Trinidad, where we had won the second Test barely a month ago. For me, the beautiful island of Trinidad has a special fascination, because it was here that I took my first bow in Test cricket. Little did I know when we were journeying back to Port of Spain that I would see my finest hour there.

9

My Finest Hour

> ... It was Gavaskar
> The real master
> Just like a wall
> We couldn't out Gavaskar at all,
> not at all
> You know the West Indies couldn't
> out *Gavaskar at all**
>
> — Lord Relator

It was sunny, hot and humid at Port of Spain. I was tired, sweaty and very, very thirsty. It was Trinidad, after all, where the climate

---

* From a calypso composed by Lord Relator in honour of the visiting Indian cricket team to the West Indies in 1971.

makes you feel as if you have just stepped out of a steam bath – particularly after a strenuous practice session at the nets. The dressing rooms at the Queen's Park Oval are some distance from the nets and, tired as I was, the prospect of having to trudge back through that seemingly endless stretch before being able to get myself a glass of cold water was not a particularly exciting one. Just then I saw a number of boys, along with Ashok Mankad who was out of the game with a fractured wrist, making their way towards us with the drinks tray. It was a very welcome sight and all of us automatically started converging on the approaching procession. My throat, by now, was really parched and instead of waiting for the water to be poured into the tumbler, I asked Ashok to pour the delightfully cold water from the jug straight into my mouth for me to gulp it down. I had to pay for this impatience of mine and how! For, along with the water, a small bit of ice also went down and got stuck in the cavity of one of my teeth. The cavity had been there for a long time, but I let it be as it had not been giving me any trouble. But after the ice melted in the cavity, the trouble started and from then on, it was sheer agomy.

I had hoped that I would get some relief at night but I was wrong. I spent the entire night moaning and, in the process, disturbed my room-mate Vishwanath, who loves his sleep. Pain killers didn't help me much. On the contrary, I became even more acutely aware of the pain and sleep just wouldn't come.

After a sleepless and agomy-filled night I went in to battle in the fifth Test at the Queen's Park Oval. To make things more difficult, Ajit won the toss and elected to bat. And, there I was, with bloodshot eyes owing to lack of sleep, to open the innings with Abid Ali as my partner.

The Test began on a note of controversy, but this did not come to public notice and no one was the wiser for it. There was a misunderstanding over the toss. Apparently, both Wadekar and Sobers believed that he had won the toss. Now, in a six-day Test, the toss is vital and Sobers showed wonderful spirit when he conceded the toss to Ajit, who promptly elected to bat.

It was obvious that Gary was a changed man in this Test, for he bowled a great spell in the morning with sustained pace, moving the ball both ways. He had Abid caught by Charlie Davis, and greeted Wadekar with a bouncer, followed by a yorker. Ajit was having a tough time, but he batted with self-confidence till he fished for a ball outside the off-stump, and Sobers dived to his left to take the catch. In the process the ball jammed between his diaphragm and hands and Sobers was off the field after lunch. When Dilip Sardesai joined me we were 70 for two wickets. Dilip, for some reason, was nervous and he flashed outside the off-stump to Dowe quite often, once escaping being caught by Carew. He, however, put his initial uncertainty behind, and was soon playing with his customary confidence. Dilip overtook me at 70, but was out soon afterwards, when he tried to flick one down the leg-side and Lewis took a good catch. However, we were able to add a substantial 122 runs for the fourth wicket.

Dilip, whenever he batted, was most careless about his appearance. If the pad-straps were loose and were hanging about, he wouldn't be bothered. After a discussion at the end of the over I told him about a strap which had come loose and asked him to tie it up. Dilip turned round and saw Clive Lloyd crossing over to the other side, and asked him in Marathi to tie up the loose pad-strap. Naturally Clive didn't understand what was wanted and Dilip realised his mistake. He then requested Clive in English to adjust the pad-strap.

In trying to hook a short ball from Sobers I missed and

was hit in the midriff, but this didn't cause so much pain as the tooth. Every run I took caused more pain as the running jarred the tooth. I've had a painful tooth before, but this was quite something. Surprisingly, however, the pain sharpened my other instincts. My reflexes were quicker and my concentration became more intense as the pain increased. Vishwanath, who had joined me, made 22 while I crawled to the nineties. Vishwanath and Jaisimha, however, got out immediately, and I eventually got my century and at the end of the day's play was 102 not out. Solkar was on three and we were a respectable 250 for five wickets. At the end of the day when we returned to the pavilion I couldn't even laugh at the jokes which Vishwanath and Dilip cracked. Above all, I couldn't even have a cold drink to quench my unquenchable thirst because of the toothache. The manager, Keki Tarapore, however, refused to let me have the tooth extracted. 'Not during the Test, and no pain killers or injections, they'll only make you drowsy', he said. I groaned, but had no alternative. Imagine bearing the severe pain for another five days, I thought to myself. Sleeping tablets helped a little. Instead of spending a totally sleepless night, I had a fitful sleep for some time around dawn. Eating was also a problem because I could not chew.

As we walked in to bat the next day, Solkar jokingly said to me, 'Watch and learn from me.' Well, he was out third ball, and I couldn't learn much as he had played and missed the earlier two deliveries. Anyway, Venkataraghavan came in with a determined look on his face. I tried to shield him from the new ball but Venkataraghavan didn't seem to like it, and to prove his point, he smote Dowe's bouncers to mid-wicket. My innings ended when I was caught by Lewis, off Holford, for 124. Venkataraghavan had scored a valuable 51 and India ended up with a fighting score of 360.

Lewis opened the West Indies innings and was lucky to see umpire Gosein negative an appeal for caught behind. He eventually went on to score 72 runs. But the most incredible decision was when Sobers was given not out, after Bishen Bedi had taken a low return catch, stumbled and then run on a bit. We didn't appeal, because we thought we didn't have to. But Sobers, who was then 34, stood his ground and the umpire turned down our appeal. After that, Gary went on to score 132 before he was bowled by Prasanna. Davis turned in another good performance, scoring 105 runs - his second Test century in the series.

I was fielding at the third-man fence when Foster was batting on 99. A spectator ran up to me and bet me that Foster wouldn't score a 100. He said he would give me a hundred dollars if Foster got that run or else I would have to give him one dollar. Well, Foster was bowled by Abid a few balls later and that chap never got his 100. After tea, I took my dollar and, when I was fielding at the boundary, I gave it to the man. Such is the kind of betting that goes on among the spectators there. In fact, there is virtually a ball to ball betting in cricket matches in the Caribbean. The West Indies innings ended on the fourth day with the total at 526, a first innings lead of 166.

When India batted again, I was feeling pretty weak, because I had not eaten well for several days and had spent many sleepless nights. Abid was out early, leg-before to Gary, a decision he didn't appreciate and quite rightly too. Ajit joined me and we had a fruitful partnership. When I had scored 51 runs I passed 1,000 runs on the tour. It was the latest of the records I was to set. At the end of the day we were 94 for one, while I was unbeaten with 57.

The next day we carried the score to 159, before Ajit was out for 54, his best score in the series. He had played some classic cover-drives off Shepherd and Sobers. Dilip came in to join me and the crowd gave him a great ovation. We still required eight runs to wipe off the West Indies lead. I took two fours off Noreiga, and moved closer to my second century in the match. Sobers tightened the field, but I eventually got my hundred (twelve fours), which I had reached in 215 minutes. This was the signal for tremendous cheering by the huge crowd, which invaded the field to congratulate me on becoming the second Indian to score a century in each innings of a Test. With this, I joined the distinguished company of Vijay Hazare, who had accomplished the feat against the Australians led by Don Bradman, about twenty-four years ago. I was naturally elated about my success, and thought how proud and happy my parents would be! However, when at the end of the fourth day, I was unbeaten with 57, I had no idea of trying to score a century in each innings. I was just content to try and get some sleep, which I needed so badly. However, I found that runs were more easy to come by than sleep. After I had got my second hundred, Dilip came up to congratulate me and offered a bit of advice. He told me, 'I know you are not sleeping well. So, go to sleep at the wicket and don't get out.' Anyway, Dilip did not stay with me long, as he fell to a return catch by Foster. In fact Foster was pleasantly surprised that he should have got the prize wicket of Dilip with an innocuous delivery. But, such are the vagaries of cricket!

Vishwanath and I then added 99 runs when Sobers with the new ball made one scoot through low to bowl him. Jaisimha, in danger of bagging a pair, stayed on till the end of the day's play. At the end of the fifth day I was unbeaten with 180, and dead tired. As I returned to the pavilion at draw of stumps the crowd gave me a big hand. The ovation still reverberates in my ears. It was fantastic. The pain wasn't.

When I woke up on the sixth, the last day of the Test it was with a sense of pleasure. It was not because I was expecting a double century, but simply because I knew that, come what may, I was going to be relieved of the pain by evening. But, pain or no pain, I had to resume my innings, with the Indian total at 324. Eventually, I reached the 200-run mark with a cover-drive off Dowe. This brought about a virtual 'explosion' in the stands. The spectators surged on to the ground in their hundreds to congratulate me. One of the Indians even shoved the Indian national flag in my hand. I was hoisted on willing shoulders, as the frenzied spectators danced around in joy. It was all very moving, and I shall never forget those few exciting moments on a foreign field far away from home. However, I was scared that in their enthusiasm my admirers might pull an arm or a leg apart because, quite honestly, the chaps were not in their senses. And, if anybody by mistake even lightly brushed my jaw I would have been in trouble. Finally, they put me down with such force that not only the bad tooth but the entire set of teeth rattled!

The pain was somewhat mitigated by the elation I felt at having scored a century in the first innings and a double century in the second. At that time I did not know that I had crossed yet another landmark when I got my double century. With this I became the second batsman in the history of cricket to score a century and a double century in the same Test. By a strange coincidence, K.D. Walters of Australia was the first to perform the feat, also against the West Indies, at Sydney in the 1968-69 series.

When things quietened, I got down to the serious business of carrying on from where I had left off. I knew that my task was not yet over. I had to carry on till the lead and time was beyond the reach of the West Indies. I was eager to get a few more runs, but I chopped a ball from Shepherd on to my stumps and was bowled for 220 which included twenty-fours.

As I walked back to the pavilion, the maestro Gary Sobers smilingly tousled my cap. I was greeted by deafening applause, which still rings in my ears. It was extremely touching to see the huge crowd give me a standing ovation.

I had begun to remove my leg-guards mechanically when I suddenly realised that now I could actually have my tooth extracted. Keki Tarapore agreed and immediately took me to the dentist, where we listened to the radio commentary, while the tooth was being extracted. I did not follow Vishwanath's advice that I should keep the tooth as a souvenir, to remind me of those six days of agony and ecstasy I had undergone in Trinidad. By the time I returned to the ground, the West Indies had lost five wickets, Abid getting Kanhai and Sobers off successive balls. The end of the match saw almost all the players breathing down the necks of the ninth-wicket pair of Lewis and Dowe. But they held on. And so the Test ended in a draw and the West Indies, who had dominated the match for most part of the game, were struggling to avoid defeat in the end. India had thus won their first series against the West Indies by virtue of the solitary victory in the second Test at Port of Spain. It had been a wonderful tour and a memorable one especially for me.

We spent an enjoyable day in Tobago where we saw some of the greatest sights underwater. On the way back home, we halted in New York, and also went to see the breathtaking Niagara Falls, and returned to a fabulous welcome in Bombay. We had expected a big crowd, but nothing like what we saw at the airport. It was terrific. We were garlanded profusely and officials were swarming around, pumping our hands in real joy.

10

Blight on Blighty

WE HAD FUNCTIONS GALORE, BUT SOON WE HAD TO GET DOWN
to prepare for the England tour. We had a new manager, the
stern but amiable Lt. Col. Hemu Adhikari. He put us through
a gruelling spell of training, during which all the excitement
of the celebrations after our triumph over the West Indies
melted away. When we finally took off for London on an Air
India Jumbo, we were fighting fit. There were three changes in
the side that had returned from West Indies a month earlier.
Durrani, Jaisimha and Jeejeebhoy were dropped. Their places
were taken by Abbas Ali Baig, Chandrasekhar and Kirmani.
Farokh Engineer was to be available only for the Tests, which
meant we were carrying two other regular keepers in Kirmani
and Krishnamurthy. Just before we left, Prof. Chandgadkar, the
secretary of the Cricket Control Board, promised a red carpet

welcome from the airport to the Brabourne Stadium, if the team was as successful in England as it had been in the Caribbean.

As we circled over London, someone in the team remarked, 'Look at the greenery around, we are in for green wickets.' We practised a few days at the Oval because the second Test between Pakistan and England was on at Lord's. However, we were to play the first match of the tour at Lord's against Middlesex. Lord's, at first sight, is not impressive. Quite frankly, I don't understand why cricketers are overawed by Lord's. The members are the stuffiest know-alls you can come across, and the ground is most uninspiring. It slopes from one end to the other. I shuddered to think of it as the Headquarters of Cricket!

We won the Middlesex match with two wickets to spare. It was exciting to start the tour so well. In the second game, however, we were brought down to earth by Essex, for whom the West Indian bowler, Keith Boyce, skittled us out cheaply in the first innings. We fought back in the second innings to make Essex bat again. They had to make 68 runs in eighteen overs, which they succeeded in doing only in the last over, winning the match by six wickets.

We then played a series of matches before we clashed with England in the first Test at Lord's. During these matches most of the batsmen scored runs. Vishwanath, Wadekar, Sardesai, Ashok Mankad and I had hit centuries, with Vishwanath leading with three hundreds. With a 109 against Hampshire just before the first Test, Ashok earned a place in the Test side. The other two openers Baig and Jayantilal had not struck form. Seeing Baig bat, we wondered if he was the same person who had scored a maiden Test century against Trueman at his best twelve years ago. Quite clearly, he had lost the appetite to face fast bowling.

For the first Test at Lord's, England fielded a strong side. They had a terrific batting line-up and the bowling was in the hands of Snow, Price and Hutton, with Gifford and Illingworth to provide the spin. Ray Illingworth, leading England for the first time against India, won the toss which wasn't surprising, as Ajit was not very lucky with the coin even for Bombay. England were, however, in for a shock as Boycott went early fishing outside his off-stump. I very much wanted to see Boycott play a long innings but was disappointed when he fell to a catch by Engineer off Abid Ali for 3. Then our spinners struck and at 71 for five England were in a virtually hopeless position. At this stage Illingworth played back to a flipper from Chandrasekhar, which skidded low and benefited from umpire David Constant negativing an appeal for leg-before wicket. Incidentally, Umpire Constant was constant in his support for England that year. So, with a spirited partner in Snow, Illingworth slowly built up the innings before he was out. Snow went on to record his highest Test score of 73. England were all out for 304.

Our innings started badly, with both Ashok and I being sent back cheaply. Ajit then played a strokeful innings to score 85. Vishwanath and Solkar chipped in with 68 and 67 respectively and we led England by 9 runs. This was the second time that India had left England behind on the first innings in a Test in England. The England second innings was a repeat of their first, despite the umpire's support to the batsmen. We were left to score 183 runs in four hours to win. Ashok and Ajit fell in quick succession and Farokh was promoted in the batting order. We had a partnership of 66, before Farokh stepped out once too often to Gifford and was easily stumped by Knott, his opposite number, for 35.

Earlier, during our partnership just before lunch, an incident, the famous Snow charge, took place involving me. Snow bowled to Farokh from the Nursery End, and Farokh trying to turn a ball to leg missed and was hit on the thigh. The ball fell near short square-leg. We set off for a quick run. From the corner of my eye I saw Snow also setting off for the ball. I would have reached 'home' safely as Snow had gone across to the other side on his follow through. However, I found to my surprise that he was level with me and with the ball nowhere near him, the hefty fast bowler gave me a violent shove which sent me sprawling. Now, Snow is a well-built bowler with strong shoulders, so poor little me had no chance! I crawled to the crease having lost my bat in the tumble. Snow came and tossed the bat back to me. He did not fling it as reported in the newspapers. In fact, after lunch he came to me and apologised. However, the England selectors dropped him from the next Test as a disciplinary measure. Snow, in any case, looked a tired man after his strenuous Australian tour and was nowhere near his best in the Lord's Test.

Vishwanath went next, given out, caught in the leg-trap with the ball coming off his pads. That was a sad blow, but the worse was yet to come. Dilip Sardesai tried to cut a straight ball from Illingworth and left his stumps open, with fatal results. I got out when a ball from Gifford kicked up from a length, hit my gloves and lobbed to Edrich in the gully. At this moment there was a slight drizzle and though play continued for a while, the players couldn't come out after tea. India then needed 38 runs for victory with two wickets in hand. Though the dice was heavily loaded in England's favour, India could also have won if play had continued. Everybody agreed that a draw was a fair result to this thrilling match.

Peter Lever, recalled to the England ranks to take John Snow's place for the second Test, would be playing on his home ground at Old Trafford, and what a game he had! Illingworth won the toss again and elected to bat on a wicket so green that, from the players' balcony, it was difficult to distinguish the pitch from the rest of the outfield.

Abid, however, gave the England batsmen a fright, knocking out three batsmen (Jameson, Edrich and Fletcher) in ten balls in his sixth and seventh overs for 25 runs. At this stage Luckhurst swept at a ball from Venkataraghavan, which got the top edge of the bat and switched away. I was fielding at leg-slip, an unusual position for me and started running for it. I almost reached it, but couldn't touch the ball. I was told later that Mankad at deep square-leg could also have gone for it, since running forward is much easier than running backward. Anyway, Luckhurst escaped and went on to score 78 runs.

As far as we were concerned, however, the turning point of the game came when Illingworth was given not out to a straightforward bat-and-pad catch by Solkar off Chandrasekhar. This was the third time in three innings that Illingworth had been given a second life by the umpires. I guess there are advantages of being an England captain in England! Illingworth went on to score 108 runs and with Peter Lever (88 not out) he added 168 valuable runs – a record for the England eighth wicket against India. When we went in to bat we had to face Price bowling very fast in the gloom of the evening. Fortunately for us, the light deteriorated and we ran into the warmth of the dressing room.

The next day was no better. Price was faster than ever. He just stood around while Lever grabbed the wickets. Actually Price was by far the quicker of the two, but, as it often happens, it was Lever who got among the wickets. The over that Price bowled to me and got my wicket was the fastest spell of bowling I've ever faced. I was out to him when the ball brushed my glove as I was removing my bat out of the way, to offer an easy catch to wicketkeeper Knott. Solkar offered some resistance and the two of us were the only Indians to score over 50 runs. Our innings ended with 212 runs on the board. With a lead of 174, England went for quick runs in their second innings. Solkar injured his hand trying to fasten on to a fierce cut from Jameson, off Abid, and had to be taken to hospital for an x-ray. I was asked to bowl my medium-pace stuff and nearly got my first Test wicket, but Farokh Engineer missed a leg-side catch off Luckhurst. To make things more difficult for us, the weather was extremely cold and our spinners could do nothing as their fingers were numb. Luckhurst helped himself to a century (101), while Edrich got 59. Illingworth declared at tea, leaving us to get 420 for victory. At the end of the day we were in a precarious position, but knowing Sardesai and Vishwanath's potential with the reliable Solkar to follow, we could have saved the game. However, it rained the whole of the last day and we spent the time reading and writing letters while some played cards with the English players. The Test, which looked ominous for us, eventually ended in a draw.

Our main problem was to find an opening partner for me. Ashok Mankad was not successful in the Tests though he was getting plenty of runs in the county games. Jayantilal was finding it tough playing in English conditions, and Abbas Ali Baig was a total disappointment. Engineer wasn't keen on opening the batting, and so we kept on with Mankad because, with his determined approach, he was the most likely to succeed.

We went to the third and final Test at the Oval, with an unchanged team, praying for rain-free days and better umpiring. Illingworth won the toss for the third time in the series, but Luckhurst was back in the pavilion in Solkar's first over. The England opener sliced a drive and was caught by me in the slips. Edrich and Jameson then had a fruitful 106-run partnership. Jameson struck some hefty blows and was rather unlucky to be run out for 182 runs. He played punishing cricket and slammed two sixes, which the crowd loved. On this occasion our spinners couldn't do a thing. Earlier, playing for Warwickshire against us he piled up 231 runs in even time. That was an unbelievable innings and left our attack in tatters. After the Jameson-Edrich partnership was broken, England suffered a slight collapse but Hutton and Knott steadied the innings. Knott made 90 and Hutton 81, and the innings ended at 355, a few minutes before the end of the day's play. It was an entertaining day's cricket for the spectators and they thoroughly enjoyed it.

The next day, the headlines in some of the English newspapers surprised us. One of the newspapers even went to the extent of saying that England could go ahead to an easy victory. Mind you, at this stage we had not even begun our batting; but the English critics were already predicting England's victory. This, more than anything else, spurred us on to do better.

The entire second day's play was washed out by rain. On the third day there was a delayed start, but Price struck the first blow when he bowled Mankad for 10. John Snow, back in the team in place of Lever, bowled me middle-stump, and we were two down for 21 runs. Just before Snow knocked out my middle-stump, a dog had strayed on to the field and play was held up for a long time. The dog came behind me, sniffed and went away. Those who know me are aware that I am mortally scared of dogs, and this one had come and stood so close to me that I was literally shivering, though I tried to make a supremely nonchalant gesture of looking the other way. In no way do I ascribe this incident for my dismissal because it was a good ball that got me. However, I am mentioning this to indicate my state of mind. Let me add that Snow had been bowling with a lot of fire. He bounced his first delivery to me and was really going flat out with his thunderbolts. Perhaps, this time he wanted to give me a shove with the ball! Ducking into one of Snow's attempted bouncers, I broke the chain I wore round my neck as the ball brushed past me. Illingworth at short-leg picked it up and returned it to me saying, 'You shouldn't be wearing gold in a Test, lad!'

Ajit and Dilip came together and played some brilliant cricket to offset the advantage that Snow and Price had given England. Dilip was at his best. He had an unproductive tour until then, and badly needed a big score. He chose this Test to mark his return to form. However, he was out after scoring 54 runs, which was marked by the usual 'raid' of the field by some over-enthusiastic spectators. An announcement was made on the public address system asking spectators not to rush to the wicket, just as Ajit was taking strike. This must have disturbed his concentration, because he played a wild slash outside his off-stump and was out for 48. Vishwanath was bowled for a duck by a ball from Illingworth which Vishwanath played over. Eknath Solkar, however, played a pretty good knock of 44 before he was out. Engineer (59) was out to the last ball of the day, when he played an overhead tennis-like shot at a bouncer from Snow and was caught at mid-on. We were in trouble again.

After the rest day, Abid and Venkataraghavan added a few runs before our innings ended, 71 runs behind England's score. When England began their second innings they were well placed to drive home the advantage. Instead, they found Chandrasekhar at his devastating best. No batsman had an answer to him and he scalped six wickets for 38, with Venkataraghavan chipping in with two for 44, and Bedi taking one for 1. Solkar held some incredible catches while Venkataraghavan also took a superb catch to get rid of Luckhurst for 33.

We had a little over two hours and the entire fifth day to

get the 171 runs required to win. I was given out leg-before to a ball from Snow, which clearly pitched outside the leg-stump and to which I offered no stroke. But then you don't question an English umpire's decision, do you? They are supposed to be the best in the world. However, I earned the distinction (?) of getting out for a duck for the first time in Tests! Ashok Mankad played determinedly and with Ajit stroking well they took the score to 37 and wore down the England pace attack. Ashok was finally out to Underwood for 11, his highest in the series. But he had stuck around and denied the pace bowlers a breakthrough. His was an insignificant score but an immense contribution to the eventual victory. Ashok has a tremendous sense of humour and constantly pulled everybody's leg. After he returned to the pavilion and had taken a shower, he remarked, 'At last I can go home and tell them what the English spinners were like.' Then when he was told that he had scored just 11 runs, he said, 'A pity the Tests are over, I was just getting into my stride and by the fifth Test I would surely have scored 25 runs.' Travelling by coach between the counties, Ashok would keep everybody in good humour with his jokes and singing. At the several official parties and receptions he had to face innumerable people who would come to him and tell him they knew his father and would talk about him and Ashok would turn around to one of us and say 'I am getting to know a lot about my father.' He would put on a typical British accent and converse with the people. He enjoyed doing that and with his power of observation he was a terrific mimic.

Well, to come back to the game, Dilip and Ajit played sensibly picking the right ball to hit. On a wicket which was yielding considerable turn, particularly to the crafty Illingworth, Dilip repeatedly stepped out and drove through the covers. To hit an off-spinner on a normal wicket through the covers is difficult but Dilip proved that he could do it even on a turning wicket. Dilip has such quick footwork that the moment the ball is flighted a couple of inches more than normal, he is down the wicket and crash goes the ball. Towards his later years he developed a cross-batted swish against the off-spinners which often sent the ball soaring over the mid-wicket boundary. On that day he employed that shot very rarely because the Oval boundary is a long one. But his stepping out to the spinners, particularly whenever Underwood threw up his slower one, was as good as ever. He was out to an amazing catch by Knott who plucked the edge almost off the bat.

Ajit was his usual calm self and realising how close at hand victory was, took the minimum risks, content to nudge the ball away for singles and twos. This was in complete contrast to his first innings knock. Then he had played some thrilling shots with supreme confidence. At the end of the fourth day we were 95 for two.

The next day we were in for an early shock when Ajit was run out, as he hesitated a little in responding to Dilip's call for a run. D'Oliveira's throw was bang on top of the wicket and Knott had only to whip off the bails. Ajit returned very depressed and after watching the game for a few minutes went off to sleep.

Vishwanath joined Dilip and Illingworth promptly crowded him with fielders. But Vishwanath was equal to the task. He was soon playing his wristy shots and the fielders, who had blocked his tiny figure from our view, were soon dispersed to the deep to stop his shots. Dilip fell to a brilliant catch by Knott after he had scored 40 and Solkar followed soon after, making a half-hearted drive which was well caught by bowler Underwood. Now the pressure was on. Farokh Engineer dealt with the situation in his own flamboyant way. He played a few risky shots, but settled down just before lunch. Illingworth brought back Snow and Price for a final fling, but Vishwanath and Farokh were unperturbed. At lunch we were only 29 runs away from victory.

During the morning session, particularly after Dilip's dismissal, I gave up watching the game and preferred to play cards with Abid who had padded up, and a couple of others. Abid too didn't want to watch the game. But, though we were playing cards, our ears were tuned to the game outside. After lunch, Farokh became more aggressive and with only four runs required for victory, Luckhurst was brought in to bowl. Vishwanath, who had played patiently so far, tried to hoist him over mid-wicket for the winning hit, but only succeeded in snicking the ball to Knott, for the wicketkeeper to take an easy catch. Abid, however, after scooping the first ball uppishly, square-cut the next for 4 and we won.

The scene that followed was unbelievable. Abid was swallowed up by the huge crowd of spectators, mostly Indians, who had rushed on to the field. Farokh, who was at the other end, had no chance of making it to the pavilion. Both the players were engulfed by the crowd and they were hoisted on willing shoulders and held high up in the air. Their trousers were stuffed with money and it was a good ten minutes before they could get to the dressing room where there were equally wild scenes. After all, this was our first ever victory in England against England and in the process we had won the rubber - also for the first time in England. The players were all shaking hands and embracing one another. Some Pakistani players were also there to congratulate us and we could see that they were really happy. A number of former England's players came in and offered their congratulations. After some time, the English players, still in their flannels, joined us in celebrating our victory with champagne. Ajit and Hemu Adhikari were on the telephone receiving congratulations and felicitations from the Prime Minister of India from New Delhi, the Indian High Commissioner in London and numerous other well-wishers. Then the crowd below wanted the players on the balcony, particularly Chandrasekhar, Wadekar and Vishwanath. They went out and acknowledged the thunderous cheers with which they were greeted. It was great stuff! Very moving indeed! The celebrations continued after the match. We were entertained to some choice Indian food at a famous Indian restaurant. The Indian High Commissioner also hosted a party for us. Actually, this was just the beginning of a chain of celebrations which followed when the team returned home.

The tour was not over and we played a few games before returning home. Just before we played Worcestershire, an English daily newspaper had published the tour averages of the Indian team. I noticed that I needed 189 runs for making thousand runs on the tour and I was determined to get those runs. Ajit won the toss against Worcestershire and elected to bat. I opened with Jayantilal, but he was out soon, and Ajit joined me. Ajit was also nearing a thousand runs and he played superbly. I survived two chances before I reached ten but was comfortable thereafter. We two added 327 runs for the second wicket. Ajit was out for 150 runs, during which he passed the thousand runs on the tour. I was 188 not out at the end of the day needing only one run to complete my thousand. I got my thousand runs and went on to score 194 when I lost my wicket in trying to push the score along. Surprisingly, the later batsmen made no attempt to score quickly. If I had known that there was no need to rush things, I could have played quietly and got my double century. However, since the instructions were to go for runs, I threw my wicket away.

In the last game, against T.N. Pearce's XI, we won a thriller by five wickets with three quarters of an hour to spare. And, so ended the tour on a triumphant note. Ashok carried his bat through in the first innings for 154 runs and I got 128 in the second innings.

It was time to go home and we heard that there were big plans on our return. The plane was to be diverted to Delhi so that the team could meet the Prime Minister. A red-carpet welcome awaited us at Bombay and numerous functions were being organised all over. But I was to miss all this. I had been invited to play a double-wicket tournament in Bermuda, for which the President of the Cricket Control Board, Mr A.N. Ghose, had given me permission. Along with me there were Intikhab Alam, Gary Sobers, Rohan Kanhai and Brian Luckhurst. Wes Hall was to arrive directly from the West Indies.

We had a fright when our aircraft was landing in Bermuda. The pilot took off again, just as he was within ten or twenty feet from the runway, which the aircraft had apparently overshot. The plane shuddered and it appeared as if it was going to break into pieces. But we lifted off again and then returned, this time for a perfect landing.

Alma 'Champ' Hunt, the President of Bermuda Cricket Association, was on hand to receive us. When we reached our hotel room, there was a basket of fruits and two bottles of Bacardi rum on the table who were also the famous rum were sponsor's of the tournament. Rohan Kanhai came and took away one of the bottles, knowing that I didn't drink, and left the other one saying, with a wink, 'That's a souvenir for you. It's rum and not water.'

The tournament was won by Intikhab Alam and his partner. We all had local partners. The highlight of the tournament was a magnificent spell of fast bowling by Hall, particularly to Luckhurst. Luckhurst had decided to share the prize money with the rest of us. This was done while Wes Hall and his partner were in the process of beating Gary Sobers and partner. When Wes was approached by Luckhurst to share his prize money in case he won, Wes flared up thinking this was cooked up by Luckhurst because Hall and his partner had beaten Sobers and his partner. And so, Luckhurst had a torrid time with Hall, who, knowing he had only three overs to bowl, put his all into each delivery.

11

On the Hop, Down Under

WHEN I RETURNED HOME FROM BERMUDA, THE SECRETARY OF THE
Cricket Control Board, Prof Chandgadkar, received me at the
airport. He told me that I had been invited to play for 'Rest of
the World' which was to tour Australia, instead of the South
Africans who had been refused entry by the Australian government.
Prof. Chandgadkar, however, asked me to keep the information
to myself because the Australian Cricket Board had still to
announce the team.

The Indian team had, meanwhile, returned from England
to a fabulous reception. At Delhi's Palam airport they were
treated to a bhangra dance; while at Bombay it looked as if
the entire city had come to receive them at Santa Cruz airport.
The team was entertained by the Prime Minister, who presented
mementoes to them. Alas, I missed all this, being away in

Bermuda. It was fascinating to hear about it all and I basked in the glory of being a hero, though at second-hand. One of my friends told me that even the Pope and Mr Khrushchev had not received such a tumultuous welcome in Bombay. Later, I saw it all on film and was very much moved by the adulation. Young and old, male and female, were in high spirits. It was terrific but I had to miss it all!

Soon after my return I had to go to Madras with my office team to play in the Buchi Babu tournament. When we reached the ground which was rather small, I couldn't believe my eyes. The crowd was simply terrific. I was told that the people had come to see me in action and I better not disappoint them. I had to be escorted by the police to the wicket, which I do not think has happened anywhere before. Still, the people would surge on to the field during the drinks interval. I will never, never forget that day and that crowd. And I am glad I did not disappoint them, for I scored 75 runs and the crowd seemed happy enough. The A.C.C. team for whom I played won the shield, easily beating the State Bank team from Bangalore.

I had to fly off that evening to Bombay to attend Milind Rage's engagement ceremony, who is like an elder brother to me. He had kept on postponing the engagement because I couldn't be in Bombay and even when he had finally fixed the date, I was away in Madras. I managed to be in Bombay later in the evening and was able to join in the festivities. Milind and I grew up together and started our cricketing career at the same time. Though I played for Bombay in the Irani Trophy, he played in the Ranji Trophy before me. In fact, when I made my debut in the Ranji Trophy, he was already an established Bombay player. Although he was selected for Bombay primarily as an off-spinner, his strokeful and aggressive batting often saved the side and also got bonus points. It was unfortunate that illness temporarily halted his first-class cricket. He has recently made a comeback in club matches with a bang, though strictly as a batsman.

A.C.C. also participated in the Moin-ud-Dowla Gold Cup Tournament at Hyderabad that year, and we lost an interesting game to the State Bank in the final. I had a good tournament though I missed my hundred in the first game against Hyderabad by just six runs. I've never been able to score a century in the Moin-ud-Dowla Tournament, though I've reached 80s and 90s almost every time that we've participated.

The Moin-ud-Dowla tournament was very popular earlier, but now interest seems to have waned a bit. The Fateh Maidan Club could do with a bit of renovation, particularly the rooms where the players stay. These are uncomfortable to say the least and the mosquito nets hardly give any protection. The toilet facilities are poor as also the food. The Hyderabad Cricket Association is not to blame as the club is apparently owned by the Andhra Pradesh government.

The tournament attracts the cream of national talent and occasionally even overseas players are invited to participate. Also, this tournament is among the first-class games of the season, which makes it an important fixture for which the facilities should be improved.

Before I left for Australia, Bombay lost the Irani Trophy to the Rest of India. For the Rest of India, Chandrasekhar bowled devastatingly to rout Bombay with all its batting array.

On our way to Australia to play for the Rest of the World team, we spent a couple of pleasant days in Singapore where we joined the rest of the players who had flown directly from England. I had met most of them, except Asif Masood and Prob Taylor. Tony Greig and Hylton Ackerman who were playing in the Currie Cup, South Africa's national championship, and the

83

Pollock brothers were to join the team from the third Test onwards in the new year.

We landed at Melbourne where Gary Sobers who had been playing club cricket in South Australia, Tony Greig and Hylton Ackerman received us at the airport. During the drive to the motel where we were to stay, we were told of a humorous incident involving Ackerman. Greig and he had flown in from South Africa, and were received at Adelaide airport by Gary Sobers and an elderly gentleman. Gary mumbled an introduction and Greig and Ackerman, both tired from the long journey, sleepily mumbled 'hello' and sat down for a cup of coffee. While waiting to go to the hotel Ackerman asked the gentleman to hold his overnight bag while he went to the toilet to freshen himself up. When he returned, he made some polite conversation and then asked the gentleman if he was connected with Australian cricket. The gentleman replied in the affirmative. Ackerman asked him if he had played cricket, to which the reply was again a yes. Since Ackerman had not caught the gentlemen's name properly, he asked him, 'What did you say your name was?' The answer was 'Don Bradman!'

Ackerman was a tremendous bloke. He was the other opener in the team besides me, and we got on famously right from the start.

My first meeting with Sir Donald Bradman was no less amusing. The Don had come to meet us at the Adelaide airport while we were in transit to Perth for the second Test. He came around asking, 'Where's that little fellow from India?' I was chatting with Bob Taylor and Sir Donald joined us. He asked me how the tour was getting on. Gary, seeing us together shouted, 'Hey, you little blokes must gang up together huh?' Sir Donald turned to me and said, 'These big blokes have the power, but we little ones have the footwork, huh?' This was said

84

with a wink, and his chàrming and modest ways bowled me over completely.

We began with a game against Victoria. I had been warned by Farokh Engineer about 'Froggie' Thomson, the Australian fast ·bowler; but when I faced him I found him to be erratic. I was meeting the ball well and found that I liked the ball coming on to the bat. In fact, I was enjoying myself when I foolishly repeated the swing off my legs to give a catch to long-leg. Earlier I had swung a similar delivery over the long-leg fence.

The match was interrupted by rain and was eventually left unfinished. The walk from the Melbourne dressing room to the wicket is the longest that I've come across. So, before I opened Farokh jokingly said: 'Don't get out for a duck. It's too long a walk back.' I didn't, but Farokh did!

We went on to play New South Wales next. After failing in the first innings, I got 95 runs in the second. I was dropped off the first ball I faced in the second innings, when the fielder at gully moved far too slowly. I had another life when a cut was deflected by the wicketkeeper; but at 95 the same fielder at gully took a brilliant catch to his left to get me out. That was to be my highest score in Australia.

We played Queensland next. Rohan Kanhai played a brilliant innings, scoring a century between lunch and tea. For Queensland, Allen Jones, a tall right-hander, played some exciting shots. But the one who impressed me most because of his correct approach was Philip Carlson. Carlson was also a good medium-pace bowler and we were certain that he would be selected to tour England in 1972. But so far he has not even got a look-in in the Australian side. In the second innings Farokh scored a century and we shared a century opening partnership. I was stumped off leg-spinner Francke who had migrated to Australia from Sri Lanka.

85

Just before we played the first 'International', there was a mild controversy regarding the preparation of the wicket. Clem Jones, who was the Lord Mayor of Brisbane as well as the President of the Queensland Cricket Association, had taken upon himself the task of preparing the wicket. It had been raining intermittently, yet the Lord Mayor was there out in the middle in his shorts, trying to get the wicket redone. However, the first day's play was washed out, and we were asked to make up for it by playing on the rest day. We refused and got a fair bit of stick from the press, who complained that we were interested in pastimes other than cricket.

Australia won the toss and elected to bat. Keith Stackpole and Bruce Francis opened. After Francis was out early, Keith and Ian Chappell settled down and slammed centuries. Stackpole enjoyed himself cutting and hooking the short stuff, while Chappell played his drives nicely. This was a great demonstration because the wicket was slow and the ball was coming up even slower, but not once did Chappell mistime his drives.

When our turn came to bat, the wicket had been rolled out to be hard, with just a hint of moisture on it. I started by cutting the first two balls from fast bowler Lillee for fours; but he had his revenge, for he bowled me with an inswinger which kept low. I made 22 runs. Zaheer Abbas was out early, and then Kanhai joined Ackerman, who had opened with me. Both of them played the lively pace of Lillee and McKenzie with relative ease and went on to score centuries.

In the second innings, Stackpole and Chappell batted well again, with Chappell scoring another century. He hit Bedi for a huge six in the mid-wicket region and showed his quick footwork against the spin of Bedi and Intikhab Alam. It was during this innings that Richard Hutton, a tremendously funny bloke, made that coarse remark to Stackpole who had hammered

Hutton's loose deliveries in the first over for a couple of boundaries. In the second over, however, Hutton struck a length and beat Stackpole thrice with perfect out-swingers. After the third time Stackpole had groped, Hutton walked up to him and said: 'Why are you pulling the slip's legs, why don't you edge one for a change?' Everytime Stackpole and Chappell hit him, Hutton would invite them to play against him on Yorkshire's green wicket, where he said, he would be able to move the ball better than on the Gabba wicket.

The match having been reduced to four days, a draw was inevitable. We had just the last two hours of the game to bat, but during that time Dennis Lillee showed what a force he would be before the rest of the series, as well as against future opponents. In a display of blistering speed and late movement off the wicket, he had both Ackerman and myself out, and gave a torrid time to the others before Ian Chappell rested him. Compared to him, McKenzie looked fast-medium, though the movement he got off the wicket was more than that of Lillee. Suddenly, with Lillee's show of speed, our boys developed a healthy respect for the Australian bowling.

I was rested from the Western Australia game at Perth. Zaheer got a brilliant hundred and another fifty in the second knock. He played some cracking shots on the off-side and his flicks to the square-leg boundaries, off his legs, went scorching off the grass to the fence. It was good to have him in form, for he is essentially an attacking player and on his good day he can tear any attack apart.

We lost the services of Ackerman before the second International match when he sprained his ankle at the nets. It was a blow to us because he had scored a century in the first International and on the Perth wicket, the fastest in Australia, he would have been an asset. Besides, he was the only other recognised opening batsman in the side. Farokh was then asked to open with me.

Ian Chappell won the toss and elected to bat. Though Stackpole got 55 and Walters and Chappell made useful contributions, the Australian innings ended at the end of the day's play for 349. The wicket played perfectly though Gary let slip an occasional quick one which whistled past the batsman's nose. One of the most unpleasant features of Perth is the number of flies that attack you while you are in the middle. We were constantly spraying ourselves with repellent every second over. In any case, I didn't give the flies much chance to disturb me, because I was caught behind, off the fourth ball from Lillee. This came up from a length, brushed my gloves and that was that! Lillee was just warming up before starting to let himself go. Farokh was not very comfortable against him and hit back a catch to Lillee. Zaheer and Kanhai tried to repair the damage, but Zaheer was run out. It was then that the collapse started. Lloyd was out, fending a short one, to be caught brilliantly by wicketkeeper Marsh on the leg-side. Gary Sobers lasted just two balls. In trying to protect his chin, he only managed a snick and was caught behind. Tony Greig retaliated in a typically aggressive fashion but after two boundaries over the slip's heads, he was caught off a fierce slash by Stackpole. Bedi didn't last long and the Rest of the World were knocked out for 59 runs, Lillee taking eight wickets for 29. It was a great spell of fast bowling. McKenzie gave him good support and got rid of the dangerous looking Kanhai. Imagine the World XI batting shot out in less than two hours!

We had to follow on and had a few minute's batting before lunch. During this time we lost Farokh again. Farokh tried new tactics against the fast bowlers, going away to the leg-side and trying to slash the ball over the slips. He didn't succeed, and all that he did was to lob a catch to Sheahan in the covers. So Farokh had the dubious distinction of having been out twice in one session. I had got off the mark off the first ball I faced from Lillee, but that was also eventful. I played the ball very wide to the right of gully where Jenner was fielding. However, he was so far back and the ball was a good fifteen yards away that I didn't even doubt a single would be difficult. But Farokh had not budged from his crease when I found myself almost facing him. In the meanwhile Jenner who had earlier relaxed in anticipation of an easy single, suddenly found that there was a run-out chance. He tried to hit the stumps as I charged back, but fortunately he missed them and off the overthrow we took three runs. The incredible part was that, though the ball was in the hands of the fielder, Farokh wanted to go for the fourth run.

After Farokh was out he came in and said he had mistimed his shot because the ball had stopped. On this wicket there was no stopping, and everybody in the team ribbed him for this statement. This, as well as an earlier statement by Farokh about the India-Pakistan War which was then going on, didn't exactly make him Mr Popular with Bishen and myself as well as the other members of the team. Farokh was reported to have told an Australian journalist that because his house in Bombay faced the sea, he was afraid about the safety of his wife and daughters and that he was going to ask them to go home to Lancashire. Bishen whose parents were in Amritsar, was rightly upset because Amritsar is close to the Pakistan border. Nevertheless, Bishen had offered no comments to the press.

The World XI players, particularly Ackerman, used the situation to imagine some really funny situations, such as Intikhab and Farokh facing each other with bayonets; myself in a fighter plane, with Asif Masood on my tail; and Bishen and Zaheer trying to run away. We had a good laugh. Though the

Australian players were careful not to joke with us on this subject, Richard Hutton came up with a typical one when he said that even if Farokh stabbed Intikhab first with his bayonet, the Pakistani player would survive as he had so much of fat to absorb the blow.

I must say that there was no tension at all between the Indians and Pakistani players despite what was happening. Almost every evening we went out for a meal to a restaurant owned by a Pakistani. The owner would hear reports from various radio news bulletins and write them down in Urdu on a paper napkin and give it to Intikhab. Intikhab would barely glance at it, crumple it up and throw it away.

Coming back to the International match, Kanhai joined me and what an innings he played! He told me just to hang on at one end while he would look after the bowlers, and he really set after them. After a rising ball from Lillee had struck him on the chest, his next shot was a hook to the mid-wicket boundary. I was with him for hundred minutes during which he was well past his 50. When I flashed outside the stumps he would come over and caution me. Watching him bat that day was an education on how to play pace bowling. I got out when I inside-edged a ball from McKenzie on to my stumps. Zaheer then joined Kanhai and together they added 107 runs before Zaheer was out. Kanhai made 118 runs. It was a brilliant innings right through. There was just a bit of resistance from Sobers, but we folded up thereafter against Lillee, who claimed four wickets. We lost by an innings and 11 runs.

We lost to South Australia in just two days, with only Greig and myself being regular batsmen in the side, since the others were either rested or injured. Clive Lloyd's injury took place during this match. Ashley Mallet drove an Intikhab leg-spinner uppishly and Hubert, as Clive is called, jumped up to his right and took the catch, falling down in the process. I think that he fell in a wrong position, and the next thing we saw was that the ball had slipped from his grasp, and Hubert was lying prone on the field. He was hardly moving. We rushed to him and he said he was in pain and couldn't move at all. A physiotherapist examined him and he was carried off the ground on a stretcher.

At the hospital it was found that he had badly injured his spine. The doctor said that the bone which was dislocated had gone even half an inch deeper, Lloyd would have been paralysed for life.

We were all very sorry for Lloyd and to cheer him up for X'mas, the Rest of the World team composed a song and booked a call to his hospital room to sing it to him. Imagine our surprise when we were told that he had gone out. Only a week before the doctors were of the opinion that he may not be able to walk! We were happy, anyway, though he was obviously not going to play on the tour anymore.

We came in for a lot of lashing from the press again for our approach to the game. Even Sobers was criticised for not practising at the nets with the team. After this, we had a meeting of the entire team and were told to be more serious to keep up our reputation.

On the eve of the New Year (1972) the Pollock brothers – Peter, better known for his fast bowling, and Graeme, the left-handed batting artist – joined us. The brothers are vastly different though obviously attached to each other. Peter who is a journalist by profession is an extrovert. He loves beer and enjoys a cigarette. He would talk about cricket endlessly showing an amazing knowledge of Indian cricket, which really surprised me.

Graeme, on the other hand, doesn't look as sturdy as his elder brother. He does not smoke and drinks beer only occasionally. He is the quiet type and would rather smile than talk. In any case, his deeds spoke for themselves. He, too, was very much interested in Indian cricket, and recalled with pleasure his association during the 1968 series with Chandrasekhar. He thought Chandrasekhar was as fascinating as his bowling.

We had tremendous celebrations on New Year's eve. At that time the Australian Open Tennis championships were on, and many of the boys had the women tennis players as their dates. The next day, however, was the start of the third International and all this celebration wasn't certainly going to do us much good. It didn't.

Gary won the toss and elected to bat which surprised many of us. This was because the Melbourne wicket had the reputation of playing unusually quick on the first morning than at any other time during a match. Besides, the history of the Sheffield Shield matches played earlier in the season had showed that the sides batting first had never scored more than 250 runs.

But there we were, Hylton Ackerman back in the side after his ankle injury, and little Sunil Gavaskar walking the long distance from the Melbourne dressing room to the middle. Ackerman looked and smelt as if he had not recovered from the earlier evening's celebration. As we walked out he made a classic comment, 'Dennis Lillee, huh, I'll take care of him.' Three balls later Dennis Lillee had taken care of Ackerman, by clean bowling him! But, I suppose, Ackerman had a good reason to be so confident. In the first international match he had scored a very good hundred and, in the second, which was Lillee's match, he was absent owing to a sprained ankle.

Zaheer Abbas also didn't stay on long. Bob Massie, who was making his debut for Australia, moved one away and Zaheer was caught behind. This brought in Graeme Pollock who had begun wearing spectacles the previous season. There was plenty of speculation in the Australian newspapers about the effect this had on his play. He played the first ball sweetly off the middle of the/blade for two and that removed doubts about his future in the game.

All this while, I was determined to stick around without bothering about the number of runs I scored. After our defeat in the Perth game, as is the practice in Australia, some of the journalists came into our dressing room. One of them pointedly asked me whether I was suffering from a Lillee complex since I was out to Dennis Lillee three out of four times. I was not only stunned by this but also I was determined to prove him wrong. Lillee, however, was bowling not only very fast but intelligently. He got the wicket of Graeme Pollock when a ball rising from a length just outside his off-stump took the edge of his bat. Graeme took a step as if to walk, but waited for the umpire's decision. There was, however, no doubt in the umpire's mind and his finger shot skyward.

As Gary walked up to the wicket I was wondering if I could have a long partnership with the great man. But Gary was out first ball: a delivery similar to the one that got Pollock out, and Gary edged it to second slip. Gary looked ruefully at the spot from where the ball had come up, smiled and walked away. The Australian were all cock-a-hoop. They crowded round Lillee with broad smiles and were joking away. The crowd too were on their feet though they must have been disappointed to see the great man out so soon. I was watching all this from the other end. Tony Greig came, smiled and said, 'Well, it's up to us.'

We built the score along steadily. Lillee was tiring now and he was replaced by 'Beatle' Watson, who had an action similar to Graham McKenzie's, but he was much slower. Greig, after blasting him through the covers for four, edged his next ball on to his pads and Greg Chappell dived forward to pick up a brilliant catch. Greig, however, had turned his back to the whole thing and pretended to be an innocent spectator of the proceedings. The Australians appealed loudly but the umpire negatived it. Greig smiled broadly at Greg Chappell, took his stance impassively and carried on with his batting. We were unseparated at lunch and, as we were returning to the pavilion, Greig kept on urging me to stick around with him. We must have looked a sight: Greig in his impressive 6 feet 7 inches and the pint-sized Gavaskar a bare 5 feet 5 inches. I was 33 not out at lunch. Lillee was brought back again, and this time it was sheer over-confidence that was my undoing. Trying to hit through the covers off the back-foot, I only managed to edge a catch to third slip. As I walked past Greg Chappell who had taken the catch, I heard him tell something to his brother, Ian, about a 'hot potato'.

Intikhab and Greig added valuable runs and both got fifties. Intikhab played some awkward-looking shots, but, as far as I was concerned, the shot of the match was played by Bishen Bedi. He put his front foot down the wicket and drove Lillee, with a full follow through, through the covers. Our dressing room erupted at that shot and it put us in a good frame of mind to get at the Aussies. We got the wickets of Watson and Stackpole quickly and there wasn't much resistance from the others except Greg Chappell.

Gerg had not played in the first two games and he hadn't been too successful in the other first-class games he had played against us. But in this game he showed us why he was soon to be acknowledged as one of the greats of the game. He started off by showing Bishen and Intikhab the sight screen and then all bowling came alike to him. He found a useful partner in Bob Massie and they added 97 invaluable runs for the ninth wicket.

Sobers, with the new ball, had Massie caught behind and greeted Dennis Lillee with a bouncer. The ball whistled past Lillee's hair and Gary told Lillee: 'We can also bowl this stuff.' Lillee was out next ball, wildly hitting into the covers to Bedi. Greg Chappell was unbeaten with 115.

We expected Lillee to open the attack. I had to face much of the bowling and I think Lillee tried too hard to bowl too fast. Unusually for him, he sprayed the ball a bit. We lost Ackerman, however, caught in the gully off Massie. Zaheer joined me and got into his stride right away. He stroked Lillee off his legs to the square-leg boundary and drove Massie to the cover fence. The Melbourne boundary is so long that often one had to run three before the ball crossed over the boundary.

Zaheer was in an attacking mood and he was severe on anything slightly loose. Sometimes he played odd-looking shots. He has a peculiar style, and lifts his bat from point, and then brings it down quickly. He doesn't seem to have a forward defensive shot, but follows through and seldom does the ball stay dead at his feet. For deliveries pitched on his legs he turns quickly and, with a flick of the wrists, sends them past square-leg. This is a remarkable shot because, more often than not, he is only showing part of the face of the bat to the ball. He has very supple and strong wrists and in spite of his seemingly incorrect technique, plays very stylishly.

The pace attack was seen off by us and the spinners came on. This was the first time in the series that I was playing an Australian spinner. In the Perth game, I had played just one ball from Jenner, got a single off it and didn't face him again. My extra-watchfulness against the speedsters came on again as Jenner tossed his leggers invitingly, which I played very watchfully. Then, in Jenner's next over, the ball hit the toes of my stretched left foot, as I played forward with my bat behind the pads, and carried to Ian Chappell at first slip. After a typical Australian appeal I was given out. I was very disappointed, as I was looking forward to playing the spinners well, after being watchful for so long. I had scored 27. Later, some of the fielders in the covers came and sympathised with me on the decision. Anyway, the damage was done. Graeme Pollock, who joined Zaheer, was careful but he also didn't stay long.

My entry into the dressing room wasn't exactly peaceful and, when I was inside, I gave full vent to my feelings. Gary, already upset by his first innings failure, was fuming because of the manner in which the Australians had done me in. As Graeme got out, Gary was padding up. At the fall of the next wicket, he picked up his bat saying 'We have to show them.' Zaheer, who was on 86, was the one who was out. Trying to cut a ball, he edged it high to Ian Chappell at slip.

The innings Gary played has been described by many, including Sir Don Bradman, as the 'greatest ever' since the war. Lillee had his tail up and, no doubt, the bouncer with which Gary had greeted him earlier was fresh in his mind. But, Lillee was an intelligent bowler. He did not pitch it in short to Gary. Instead he pitched it right up outside the maestro's off-stump but Gary was very watchful. Then, after Gary had been in for about ten minutes, Lillee bowled a bouncer. The ball was hit with such a force that it was at the fence before you could say 'Gary Sobers'. After that Gary just cut loose. Anything pitched up was driven past the bowler and anything pitched short was cut or hooked savagely. Until he reached his 50 there was, seemingly, no footwork. None of the technicalities like the front-foot near the ball, as the bat simply came down from a high back lift and ended with a classic full follow-through. It was exhilarating cricket and it was coming from the captain of our side who had been smarting under criticism. At the end of the day, Gary was unbeaten with 139, and was his usual, laughing self. Though tired he joked with us and the Australians. Peter Pollock was unbeaten with 28 and had given his skipper excellent support.

During this International, particularly in the Perth game, I was feeling a kind of lump around my right eye. I ignored it thinking it was a mosquito bite or something. On the rest day, however, I went to have it examined. It turned out to be a cyst and the doctor advised me to get it off immediately. I phoned up Bill Jacobs, our manager, who asked me to go ahead and get it off. I was advised not to play for one week.

He put a patch on my right eye and so for the day I became a one-eyed Jack. This temporary disability brought home to me the tremendous handicap under which Mansur Ali Khan Pataudi had to play. When I tried to take hold of a glass of water, I would miss it by a foot. It was the same when I tried to do anything on my right side. My admiration for Tiger Pataudi grew as a result of my experience. Every little thing I did, like eating an ice-cream cone, found me missing the cone and licking the air instead! I wondered how Tiger played fast bowling and so well too.

The next day Gary continued to hammer the bowling and with Peter Pollock defending stoutly and attacking in sudden bursts, we were really going strong. Two shots of Gary stood out. First, when he cut Massie to the point boundary, the ball beat the fielder who was posted wide just for this kind of shot, before he could move even two feet. And remember, Melbourne has the longest boundary in the world. The second one was off Dennis Lillee, when Gary went back and slammed the ball straight back past the bowler and it crashed into the fence. He also lifted O'Keefe for two successive sixes. When he returned to the pavilion the crowd rose to a man in applause.

Peter Pollock went on to score 54 before he was out. It was a disciplined knock and his stubborn resistance made it possible for Gary to launch his magnificent assault. However, his long innings didn't stop Peter Pollock from showing his mettle as a pace bowler. He worked up a lively pace and bowled the bouncer liberally. He confessed that the sight of a batsman in a green Australian cap always spurred him on to bowl that much faster. Watching him from the dressing room, with my one good eye, I admired his lovely run-up and high bowling action.

Tony Greig, who relieved Peter Pollock, bowled in his customary steady style, his action showing that he did more with the ball than in actual fact. As he was bowling, his hand brushed against his leg, resulting in the grip being loosened and the ball went through high, but slowly. Graeme Watson tried to hook it, but only succeeded in edging it on to his nose. The impact was hard, because he started bleeding from the cut and, within minutes, his shirt was soaked in blood.

Watson was brought into the dressing room and, when I went to see him, I found that the blood was spurting out of his nose at regular intervals. He was whisked away to hospital in an ambulance. We learnt later that his life was in danger and he had to be given a tremendous amount of blood. It speaks volumes for his courage that within three months he was back in the team for England.

Doug Walters played a terrific second innings. But, what surprised me most was that Gary never really tested him with any quickies. This is not to take away credit from Walter's innings – he scored 100 in two hours and that too against Bedi and Intikhab. But, I for one, felt that Peter Pollock, who had pulled a leg muscle, would have really tested him. However, we won the match by 96 runs, to level the score at one-all.

Everybody now looked forward to the fourth 'International' at Sydney. Before this, we played a game against the New South Wales County XI and another one in Canberra. These games were not much, but we remember them for our tantalising air journey. Newcastle is not very far from Sydney, so we took a shabby-looking Dakota aircraft, which really looked rather ancient. After the plane took off we were sorry that we had decided to fly in it, because it lurched and shook and it was anything but a pleasant journey. The return flight was also equally depressing and nerve-racking.

Shrugging off all this, however, Graeme Pollock scored his first century. I was his partner in a long stand and one incident stands out in my mind. Graeme uses a very heavy bat – about three pounds in weight. He played forward to a ball and I called out to him to wait. Imagine my surprise when I saw the ball speed past the mid-off fielder to the boundary. Graeme had timed it so sweetly that it had looked like a defensive push and, as he had put no power behind it, I had declined a run. I sheepishly said to him, 'Jeezus, that did go, huh?' Graeme replied modestly, 'Yeah, sometimes they do!'.

We went into the fourth International full of confidence. Ian Chappell won the toss and elected to bat. Peter Pollock was unfit and Bob Cunis was brought back in his place. The morning's play belonged to Bedi. Ian Chappell, who had started well, was lured down the wicket and, as he tried to drive, he found the ball just that much short and was bowled. Next ball, Greg Chappell was brought full stretch forward, with the ball turning sufficiently to bowl him. And, all this, during the first session of play! The crowd went wild, as Bishen bowed down to accept their greetings. After all, though he had got two of their favourite batsmen out, to the crowd Bishen was their son-in-law, having married a Sydney girl.

Our batting was, however, rocked by the swing of Bob Massie. He started by claiming the wickets of Ackerman and Zaheer, and Asif Masood came in as night watchman. The next morning Asif, playing the first over from Massie, missed five balls consecutively and, in disgust, hit the next to mid-on. I suffered from a bad decision again when I chopped a ball from Massie down into the ground and was given out caught by Stackpole in the slips. Once again, we were rescued by Greig and Intikhab, and some hilarious hitting by Bedi. He had the crowd on its feet, particularly those one on the Hill, who kept on chanting, 'Bedi, Bedi, Bedi'.

In Australia's second innings, Ian Chappell got a hundred (119), but the innings of the match was that of his younger brother Greg. Having been out first ball in the first innings, Greg was naturally cautious at the start, but then played his shots so well that he was unbeaten with 197 runs when the innings ended.

As we walked back to the pavilion applauding Greg's magnificent innings, we heard him say some harsh words to Lillee. Greg had very cleverly shielded him from Intikhab for a long time but, because of a miscalculation, he had taken a run off the sixth ball. This left Lillee to face two balls from Intikhab who bowled Lillee with the first delivery. A prize of five hundred dollars was offered to anyone who scored 200, and it was a pity that Greg missed it by three runs. When we asked Greg later in the evening whether the harsh words to Lillee were out of disappointment at missing the 200 runs and the five hundred dollars, he smiled and said: 'Hell no! I just wanted him to be rearing mad to get at you boys when he bowled.' Well, Lillee did bowl really fast for a couple of overs but suddenly slowed down his run-up. It was the beginning of the back trouble that was to keep him out of cricket for over a year.

Ackerman and I added 155 runs for the first wicket, with Ackerman as the dominant partner. I had learnt my lesson and, after the early part of the tour when I was trying to score runs off every ball and getting out in the process, I had gone to the other extreme and was hardly playing my shots. During this innings, however, I played my shots but not as recklessly as before, and the result was a good innings.

However, after Ackerman was out there was a 'mini' collapse, during which we lost Zaheer and Graeme Pollock in the same over. Then Gary Sobers was bowled by a full toss from Inverarity. At the end of the day I was left unbeaten with 68 runs, and the World XI had to survive a full day to save the match. Luckily for us down came the rain and the match had to be abandoned as a draw.

By this time I was feeling pretty homesick, though the presence of the Cricket Club of India team which was touring Australia, lessened the feeling. Since I was a member of the club and knew all the players it was nice to know from them about what had been happening at home.

The fifth International was played at Adelaide and, after my unbeaten 68, I was full of confidence and looking forward to the game. The Adelaide wicket reminded me of the Ferozeshah Kotla wicket in New Delhi. It was absolutely devoid of grass and, like the Kotla wicket, took spin from the very first day. Australia batted first and were able to reach a respectable total (311), thanks to good knocks by Greg Chappell and John Benaud. Greg Chappell scored 85 and Benaud 99, who got out flicking a short ball from Intikhab straight to me at short mid-on. I fumbled with the ball, but caught it at the second attempt and poor John missed his ton by one run. I felt sorry for him because he had played some grand shots.

The highlight of our innings was a classic 135 by Graeme

Pollock. On a turning wicket he played so well that I can't remember his being beaten even once. He hit two sixes off deliveries which were barely short of a good length. Zaheer scored 73 runs, but was the victim of sledging. Stackpole, who had been brought on to bowl, would raise his hands or say something to Zaheer after every delivery. Losing his patience and temper, Zaheer tried to hit him out of the ground and was bowled. Earlier, I had scored 18 runs, before uppishly driving O'Keefe to Walters who was substituting at mid-wicket.

In Australia's second innings Ian Chappell played a superb, attacking innings. Time and again he danced down the track to Bishen and Intikhab and drove them powerfully through the off-side. His hundred (111 not out) came after a peculiar mix-up, which almost got him run out. He was stranded in the middle but two overthrows enabled him to reach the century mark. The Australian innings ended leaving us just 146 runs to win.

Ackerman was again the dominant partner but I reached my first 50 and simultaneously the 100 of the partnership was raised. However, I was out in the same over in trying to steer wide off the slips, but instead tickled one which stuck in the leg-guards of wicketkeeper Rodney Marsh. Ackerman continued the good work and, when we won, he was unbeaten with 79 runs to his name. We won the series 2-1.

After the match, Sir Don Bradman distributed the various awards and I was thrilled to receive the award for the best fielder of the series. These awards were given on the basis of points scored in every match. Just before Lloyd's injury he was leading me by two points and he was easily the most outstanding fielder on either side, but here I, an average fielder, was walking away with the prize. The only thing in my favour was that I ran and chased the ball on those long Australian boundaries and made an honest effort to save as many runs as I could.

The teams had their usual friendly drinks, and the Australian Cricket Board officials also joined us in the dressing room. Sir Don Bradman spoke to me at length about my batting and pointed out the shortcomings which, he suggested, I should try to remove. He was most encouraging in his remarks, and I was thrilled when he said that a square-drive I had played in the South Australia match was a memorable one. It was a great compliment coming from one of the all-time greats of the game. I felt very happy that he remembered the shot I had played two months ago.

Sir Donald asked me not to be over-anxious to attack as I had been doing during the early part of the tour, or over-defensive as I had been later. He suggested that a judicious blend between attack and defence would do me good. It was super hearing 'The Greatest' giving you friendly advice and it is evergreen in my memory.

The evening before we dispersed to return to our homes we had a team dinner, to which Sir Donald Bradman was invited, since it was he who was largely responsible for organising the tour. He gave his impressions about every member of the side. He spoke in glowing terms about Sobers and Pollock, and offered great encouragement to Zaheer and myself when he said some very complimentary things about our performance. Then every member of the team talked about his individual experience during the three months we had spent in Australia. It was all very touching, and nobody really wanted the evening to end.

I said farewell to my teammates, particularly my partner, as Ackerman called me, and the Pollock brothers who were South Africans. I wasn't sure whether I would ever play with them again. The Pollocks had been extremely nice to me, and I cherish my friendship with them and with Ackerman very much.

103

I hope some day to meet Ackerman again. The Pollocks, I may mention, made sincere enquiries about Chandrasekhar, Bapu Nadkarni and Tiger Pataudi, which showed how much they cared for their friends of former years.

Sunny Days

12

Riding on Euphoria

I RETURNED HOME FROM AUSTRALIA WITH THE CRICKET CLUB OF India team and played a game for them at Singapore on the way back. It was, however, all in fun and we were all more keen to do some shopping rather than playing. Everybody took turns at batting and then went out shopping.

When I returned home there was more cricket as the knockout stage of the Ranji Trophy was still to be played. However, I immediately had to fly to Jamshedpur to play in the Duleep Trophy. Amazing, this was to be my first Duleep Trophy match. Imagine playing a Duleep Trophy game only after having played for the Rest of the World! Both Ramnath Parker and I got centuries on our first appearance, and Ashok Mankad also got a hundred. We won the game easily on the first innings.

In the final,' however, we were surprised by Central Zone. This was Salim Durrani's game. Apparently, he had promised Hanumant Singh that he would win the Duleep Trophy for Central. Durrani's superb bowling and bold hitting swung in their favour a match which looked like being in our pockets when we led by 79 runs on the first innings. This was Central Zone's first victory in the Duleep Trophy and, indeed, a deserving one.

In between these games a match was arranged between the victorious Indian XI (comprising members of the 1971 team to the West Indies and England) and the Rest of India XI. The match was to be played at New Delhi in aid of the National Defence Fund. At Jamshedpur I had verbally secured permission from the Board President to skip this N.D.F. match. However, I got frantic telephone calls from New Delhi asking me to come over. My decision to go turned out to be an important one eventually. For, during the game I was introduced by Dilip Doshi, the Bengal left-arm bowler, to Marshniel Mehrotra who, two years later, was to become my wife.

I wasn't particularly successful in this match because I was troubled by a sore leg muscle. We were due to play the knock-out and hence I didn't want to aggravate the injury. In the knock-out stage our first game was against Bihar. At the end of the first day I was 200 not out and Solkar was unbeaten with 88. The next day he got his 100 and went on to score 131. I was last out at 282, when Anand Shukla foxed me with a wrong one and bowled me. We, however, had an easy innings victory but during this game I sustained a hairline fracture of the thumb while catching Ramesh Saxena. Curiously, this didn't bother me in the semifinals against Mysore. This was probably because I didn't bother the Mysore bowlers, getting out in the first over of the match for 4 in the first innings, and for 45 runs in the second innings. I also played in Vijay Manjrekar's benefit match though the pain had increased during the match.

It was a touch and go situation as to whether I would play in the Ranji Trophy final against Bengal. Until the eve of the game I was uncertain as I was getting a pain in the injured thumb every time I played the ball. I went through a fitness Test on the morning of play and found that the pain had eased a bit. Ajit Wadekar was also keen that I should play and I eventually did.

Subroto Guha and Samir Chakravarty, one of our foremost pairs of new-ball bowlers, luckily didn't make use of the moisture on the first morning. After a slow and painful start I opened out and at the day's end was unbeaten with 139. Ajit Wadekar who scored 57 easily played the better innings and so also did Dilip Sardesai who scored a strokeful 34. Mine was a satisfying innings, however, and Bombay were in a very healthy position, being 280 for three wickets. The next day Guha bowled me middle-stump for 157. He had a fine spell with the second new ball and Bombay slumped to 377 all out.

For Bengal Gopal Bose and Ambar Roy batted well before Rege got rid of both of them within minutes of each other. Rege was again proving his usefulness to the Bombay side. Having come in primarily as an off-spinner replacement for Sharad Diwadkar, he had pulled Bombay out of trouble with his hard hitting batting many a time. His performances as a bowler were never as spectacular as Shivalkar's, but if one is to see through the score sheets, he would see that he had usually chipped in with two or three wickets. Besides, he was a tremendous fielder at gully and had a powerful throw, flat and straight on top of the bails.

In our second innings, both Parker and I got out cheaply and there was an outside chance of Bengal surprising Bombay.

But Ashok Mankad played such a terrific attacking innings that the phrase taking the bull by its horns immediately came to mind. He was unfortunately run out when he was two short of his 100, but what a grand 98 runs they were!

That was it. Bengal had no chance after that as Ismail demolished the top half of their batting and the next day they crumbled for 115 runs. Bombay had won the Ranji Trophy for the fourteenth year in a row. Thankfully the season, which started for me in September 1970, had ended in mid-April 1972. I was glad to lock my kit for a further four months before the new season began. I thought I had had enough cricket for a while and looked forward to a few weeks' rest. I really needed to relax.

The 1972-73 season began, as usual, with the Irani Trophy. Earlier, of course, was the Moin-ud-Dowla Tournament organised by the Hyderabad Cricket Association, which is traditionally the curtain-raiser to the season. The locked-up cricket kit comes out, the boots are given a new coat of white, the leg-guards are brushed, the bat is oiled, and sometimes even the limbs have to be oiled for loosening creaking joints.

Generally, when rain prevents Moin-ud-Dowla matches from being completed, the coin decides the winner. But, fortunately, the final is invariably uninterrupted. The State Bank of India team with its galaxy of Test stars, have won this Gold Cup more often than any other side. Vazir Sultan Tobacco Company sponsored a team full of youngsters with a senior cricketer as captain. Many of today's India players have played for Vazir Sultan Colts. The company deserves compliments for the way it has been encouraging cricketing talent in the country. When I was just out of school I played for the V.S.T. Colts under Tiger Pataudi. It was a great thrill to play under the Indian captain. Tiger, of course, couldn't do much by himself and the inexperienced youngsters under him exposed to rain-affected tracks, were no help. U-Foam is another company which is invited to participate and they include a number of Test players as well as Test aspirants in the side. Captained by the evergreen and shrewd Jaisimha, they have made a habit of entering the final.

Spectator-interest in this tournament in recent years has been disappointing and only the final attracts a decent crowd. The Hyderabad Cricket Association, in spite of this, continues to hold this tournament. Peter 'P. R.' Mansingh, a live-wire, is one of the leading lights of the Hyderabad Cricket Association, and he has tried hard to make Hyderabad cricket a success. He organises tours for the Hyderabad Blues whose players have proved very popular overseas.

The 1972-73 Irani Trophy tie was played at Poona. If that match proved anything it was that Ramnath Parker had arrived. Until the end of various seasons Parker had been in the reserves for Bombay. He seized his opportunity when five Bombay players went to West Indies with the 1971 Indian team and scored two centuries. He also fielded brilliantly in the covers and saved at least 30 to 40 runs. In the Irani Trophy match, however, he staked his claim as an opening batsman for India. He scored 70 runs in the first innings in just ninety-five minutes before recklessly jumping out to be stumped off Bishen Bedi. He learnt his lesson after this and scored 195 runs in the second innings before he was out following a doubtful decision. He played all shots to the distant corners of Poona's Nehru Stadium and didn't spare even Bedi, Prasanna and Venkataraghavan.

Vishwanath's reply to Parker's 195 was a classic, unbeaten 161 in the Rest of India's second innings. Whereas Ramnath, who is even shorter and slighter than Vishwanath, hit the ball with tremendous power, the Karnataka batsman seemed to caress the ball to the boundary.

Dilip Sardesai, in spite of a bruised forearm, also scored a century for Bombay. Time and again he proved he was a champion player of spin as he danced down the wicket and drove and lofted the bowlers who didn't know where to pitch the next ball.

I failed miserably in this match and the next two games of the Ranji Trophy didn't ease my worries about my poor form. I was batting reasonably well until I got 20 or 30 runs and then got out.

When I went to play for the Board President's XI against the visiting M.C.C. team, their opening match of the tour, I was hoping to strike form. Ramnath Parker opened with me and we added 100 runs before Parker was out for 59. He clinched his place in the Indian team with this innings. Though I was certain of being picked as the other opener, I wanted runs behind me before the first Test.

I thus batted slowly against the tight M.C.C. attack and was content to wait for my runs. When I was in my 70's I had an attack of cramps in the right leg. At 80 I tried to take a cheeky single but turned slowly because of the cramped right leg and was beaten by Amiss' direct hit at the stumps. It was disappointing to miss the century though I was fairly happy that I had been able to regain my usual concentration.

For the M.C.C. openers Amiss and Denness batted well and they too were trying to get acclimatised to Indian conditions. The others, however, didn't last long and we had to bat out the last session of the match when Tony Lewis declared at the tea-time score.

Tony Greig opened the M.C.C. attack and his second ball, a huge in-swinger, got me leg-before. So I was to back to square one! As I packed my kit-bag to get to Delhi for the Test, I was hoping for a break in the run-famine. I consoled myself with the thought that everything would click in the Tests.

We reached New Delhi a week before the Test started. Except for the few who were engaged in playing for their Zonal team against the tourists, everybody was there and we had a good work-out. My form at the nets was satisfactory, and I felt very much elated. Invariably when I have batted well at the nets I have batted badly in the match. If, on the other hand, I've batted badly at the nets the result is that I am able to concentrate better in the match and I find that it helps me to score runs.

Ajit Wadekar, who led India in the first Test, was lucky with the toss and Parker made his Test debut with me as my partner. This must surely be one of the rare occasions when the same players open the batting for their club, state, zonal and national teams. The wicket looked a beauty though there was a hint of moisture which is always the case at Ferozeshah Kotla. Geoff Arnold opened the attack for England while Bob Cottam bowled from the other end. England had decided to feed Ramnath Parker with short deliveries, knowing his tendency to go for the hook shot. Accordingly, Arnold trying to get more bounce overstepped the mark thrice in succession and off the third delivery had Parker caught on the deep fine-leg fence by Polock. The umpire had failed to call a no-ball on all the three occasions and, thus a wicket, which should not have fallen, had gone. Ajit Wadekar came in and, after a couple of overs, was late in coming down on the ball and had his off-stump knocked out of the ground.

At this stage what was needed was caution because Arnold was bowling well and with two wickets behind him was roaring to go. I thought if I attacked he might be taken off. So when he bowled short outside the off-stump, I went to cut, but only managed to edge the ball and saw Tony Greig leaping up at second slip to catch the ball. I doubt if anyone else in the M.C.C. team would have reached the ball, but there it was. A rank bad shot and a deserving fate. And so back to the pavilion for me.

Vishwanath and Sardesai held on till the lunch-break. At lunch Dilip, in his characteristic way, promised to make a hundred. In the West Indies and often for Bombay whenever Dilip made a promise he generally kept his word. This time, however, Arnold got through his defence and bowled him without addition to his lunch score. We were soon in trouble because Solkar also didn't stay long. Abid, however, struck back boldly to get runs and we reached a total of 173.

Now, the only way of saving the match was to get England out cheaply. Chandrasekhar bowled a terrific spell and got eight wickets, beating the England batsmen by his spin and bounce. Only Greig defied him to a certain extent and remained unbeaten with 68.

We had, however, to ensure that our batting clicked in the second innings and we got enough runs to make it a stiff target for the Englishmen. This time Parker scrupulously avoided his favourite hook shot but played some lovely shots off his legs. I was given out, caught by Greig, after the ball had come off my pads. The poor umpire got foxed by Greig and wicket-keeper Knott, who began applauding the bowler with such gusto that he declared me out. When I met Greig in our dressing room in the evening, he laughed in characteristic fashion and started pulling my leg. I, however, swallowed all the choice bad words I had thought of, because, with Greig it is a love-hate relationship. On the field he makes you hate him; but off it he is a wonderful chap who doesn't bear you any grudge. He believes that whatever happens on the field should be left there and should not be allowed to sour one's friendship.

Throughout the tour Greig made use of his knowledge of Hindi expletives which he learnt from us and the Pakistanis during the Rest of the World's tour of Australia. Often, he did not even know the meaning of what he was saying, but the rest of the members of the Indian team were certainly surprised to hear his Hindi vocabulary. His pronunciation was not perfect but the meaning was clear. More than anyone else Farokh and Ajit suffered because they often played long innings during the series. Yet, when the M.C.C. left all our players agreed that he was a likeable guy off the field.

To come back to the Delhi Test, Farokh Engineer and Eknath Solkar tried vainly to put us back in the game but, when we were finally all out, the M.C.C. were left to score only 210 runs for victory. They scored 95 of these runs, losing three wickets on the fourth evening. The last morning we had to get a breakthrough to stay in the game. Though we got Barry Wood at his overnight score of 45, Tony Greig and Tony Lewis played sensibly and England notched up their first victory of the series easily.

Ajit Wadekar said after the Test that it was a Christmas present to Tony Lewis and he hoped that Tony would give him a New Year's gift in return! The second Test was to be played at the Eden Gardens in Calcutta. The ground can accommodate about sixty-five thousand people, but with a little squeezing seventy thousand people can be crammed into the stands to enjoy their cricket. The Test, which was a real thriller right from the first morning to the last day, kept a huge crowd agog with excitement. When India won their joy knew no bounds and the scene after that had to be seen to be believed.

Ajit Wadekar must have used a lucky coin, because he won the toss again. To us, the Bombay players, it was a common sight to see Ajit come in after the toss to announce with a shrug of his shoulders that he didn't mind losing the toss so long as he won the match. Well, this time he came in to announce that we were to bat. Geoff Arnold who had set us on the road to defeat at Delhi, was unable to play due to some stomach trouble. I am sure he must have eaten some tinned food brought from England! Chris Old, making his Test debut, opened the bowling and I got off the mark with a boundary to square-leg off the first ball. I wonder what Chris Old thought of starting his Test career like that. Parker was playing well and we safely negotiated the new ball. Derek Underwood was brought on and he got my wicket immediately. A delivery popped up from a length, hit my glove and landed in the direction of silly mid-on where Chris Old diving to his left took a good catch.

Wadekar, the next man, ducked in to a short ball from Greig and had a bad crack on the ribs which compelled him to retire. Vishwanath didn't stay long and Parker after playing well was caught behind off Old for 26. Our innings was again in the doldrums. Durrani failed and so did Solkar. Engineer played a lone hand scoring 75 runs.

England fared no better and though Greig was looking dangerous we got him out and secured a lead of 36 runs. The start of our second innings was a disastrous one. I tried to put a shortish delivery from Old, missed it completely and was leg-before for two runs. Ajit was sick and so Durrani came one wicket down and began to clout the bowling. Parker in the meanwhile had been caught behind off Old. But Vishwanath played a lovely innings of 34.

Salim Durrani who had injured his leg while fielding took me as his runner. But there was precious little running I had to do for Durrani who seemed to concentrate on hitting boundaries. Once, after the crowd chanted that they wanted a six, Durrani swung a ball from Underwood into the noisiest stand at mid-wicket for a huge six. While the ball was being returned I walked from my square-leg position and congratulated Salim for the shot. I also wanted to caution him because our position was not secure as yet. Salim's reply was typical of him: 'I wanted to show him (Underwood) who is the boss.' He scored 53 before he fell to a brilliant diving catch by Fletcher in the slips. He had, however, played his part well. With useful contributions from Engineer and Abid, England were left to score 261 runs for victory.

Abid bowled Barry Wood with a lovely leg-cutter, then Bedi chipped in with three victims, and England had slumped to four for 17. Greig and Mike Denness, however, held on and towards the close both played some confident shots that set us thinking. The next morning Chandrasekhar struck. He had bowled indifferently the previous evening but, on that morning, he was right on top. Denness was out leg-before and Greig followed in the same manner, when he missed a dipping full toss. Typically, Greig stood his ground and looked unhappy for the entire world to see. After the game, however, he was again laughing and admitted that he was plumb leg-before wicket. In desperation, Alan Knott tried to swing Chandrasekhar but succeeded only in skying a catch to Durrani at mid-on. Durrani held on to the ball for dear life because he would have been in trouble if he had muffed it. Earlier in the morning, before the match started, Salim had made some gestures to the crowd under the huge scoreboard, showing his annoyance because they had booed him for dropping catches during practice. The crowd was thus properly steamed up and in spite of his earlier innings if Salim had dropped Knott, then his life would not have been worth a paisa. To relieve the tension, I went up to Salim, raised his hand, and the crowd roared back signifying that it had understood.

Chris Old put up unexpected resistance and clouted a six over long-on. He and Cottam took the score to within 28 runs of their target before Cottam padded up to a googly and was leg-before wicket. Underwood was brilliantly taken by Wadekar diving to his left. For a man running a temperature, this was truly a magnificent catch and after that our victory was a formality.

As we sprinted to the pavilion we were engulfed by the crowd which was delirious with joy. Some people had hoisted us on their shoulders. The stumps, of course, had vanished and if we had not taken the precaution of leaving our caps behind those too would have disappeared.

Long after the game was over huge crowds were waiting outside our hotel to catch a glimpse of the players. Calcutta crowds are terrific and the players are treated like heroes. The players, I feel, unnecessarily think that there is danger to them physically. True, the enthusiasm of the crowds can be a little too much but it is well meant. The enthusiasm of the Calcutta crowd is terrific and I, for one, would rather play before a Calcutta crowd than at Lord's where the applause is strictly limited to three or four claps.

Tony Lewis, remembering Ajit Wadekar's words after the first Test, said that as Ajit had wanted he had given him a New Year's present and he hoped that there were no more Indian festivals to follow. What Tony Lewis didn't know was that the Pongal celebration would be on in Madras around the same time as the third Test.

Between this and the Madras Test I got 160 runs against Gujarat in the Ranji Trophy and was quite pleased to be among the runs. My four innings in Tests had got me a meagre 40 runs: 20 in the first Test and 20 in the second.

The third Test at Madras started off with Ajit Wadekar losing the toss and Lewis had no hesitation in electing to bat. Abid Ali had been dropped and Eknath Solkar shared the new ball attack with me. The only over I bowled in the Test proved uneventful and disheartening. I tried to bounce one but the ball wouldn't get up at all. Wadekar took me off and gave the ball to Bedi and I said to Ajit, 'I had just warmed up.' But then Bedi proved his skipper right by having Wood caught. Soon, England were in serious trouble with Chandrasekhar striking repeated blows. Amiss became his hundredth victim in Tests when he snicked one to Farokh Engineer and Lewis followed when he gave an easy catch to Solkar. All the while Keith Fletcher had survived precariously against Bedi at the other end. Fletcher, always a nervous starter, kept pushing out his leg-guards along with the bat. More often than not the ball hit his pads. Slowly, however, the ball started hitting the bat with a regularity which was disconcerting to us. In spite of the uncertain start, Fletcher's knock was a classic example of how to build up an innings. Towards the end he was so confident that he smote three sixes into the stands. However, he was left stranded at 97, but his innings had saved England from utter rout. We had two overs left to play out before draw of stumps; Chetan Chauhan and I survived the overs and we were 4 for no wicket at the end of the day's play.

The next morning Chauhan, who had returned to the Indian team for the first time since 1969-70, was caught behind off Arnold for a duck. He sparred at one leaving him and paid the penalty. Chauhan's failure in Tests continues to surprise me, for he has a good technique and a voracious appetite for runs. One has to just glance at his Ranji Trophy record to see how prolific a scorer he has been. Though he doesn't have many shots, it's his determination that gets him runs. I don't believe that he lacks big-match temperament. I think he hasn't got on well at the Test level, because he has been unlucky. He has invariably fallen to a good ball or a brilliant catch. In any case, he can hardly complain for he has played five or six Tests without much success.

117

Wadekar joined me and got quickly into his stride. Arnold was bowling well as usual and Old was working up a good pace. One of his deliveries reared up from a length and he hit me on the thumb and then my shoulder. Later, I discovered that I had a hairline fracture of the thumb and also a badly bruised shoulder. Tony Greig once again got me out. I played defensively forward to Norman Gifford. The ball again went off the pads to Greig who promptly began a war dance with Knott and there was Gavaskar once more making his way back to the pavilion. I had made 20 runs and had been looking forward to many more. Wadekar scored 44 and Durrani again hit a huge six on demand from the crowd in his 38. But the innings of the Test was Pataudi's 73. Having missed two series against the West Indies and England in 1971, it was thought by many that his career as a Test player had ended. Tiger, however, got a 100 for South Zone against the M.C.C. and was picked for the Madras Test. He confessed later that he had been out second ball in the match, but the umpire had negatived the appeal for leg-before and he went on to score a century. In the Test he didn't need any such luck as he middled the ball sweetly and sent it to the far corners of the Chepauk ground. He hit three sixes and in trying to hit another, was caught on the boundary.

England's second innings was a shambles right from the start. Only Denness put up some resistance in scoring 76 before Solkar took a brilliant catch off Prasanna, who finished with a tally of four wickets. We were left to score only 86 runs to win and everybody was relaxed. Since I was nursing a bruised thumb, Farokh Engineer opened the innings with Chauhan. Chris Old, however, shattered our complacency by having Engineer leg-before wicket. Farokh who, during the series had never once played off the back-foot to the fast bowlers, as far as I can remember, was given out as he characteristically

The Indians don't call that a farce, do they? And, passing judgment from thousands of miles away is just rubbish!

The fourth Test at Kanpur ended in a draw. This was inevitable on a wicket which was perfect for batting. Batting first, Chauhan and I put on 85 runs. I finally managed to score more than 20 runs and when I reached 21, I had scored 1,000 runs in Tests. Later I came to know that it was the fastest (in 11 Tests) by an Indian batsman. But, from 774 in the first four Tests I had played in the West Indies in 1971, it had taken me seven more Tests to score 226 runs. I was eventually out for 69 being Jack Birkenshaw's first Test victim. I pulled a short ball straight to Tony Greig at square-leg, who took the ball well up. I cursed my luck for trying to clear the tallest Test cricketer. Greig had now caught me four times in four Tests. The fact that twice it was off the pads doesn't alter what's in the record books.

During my innings there was a funny incident when I survived a leg-before appeal off Arnold. Greig walking past me at the end of the over remarked, 'It was close, wasn't it?' I replied. 'Yeah, sure. But the umpire is my uncle!' Greig then asked what his name was. I said 'Gothoskar, but he had changed it, or else he would never get to be a Test umpire.' Within minutes word had gone round and I was asked with much consternation by quite a few people whether umpire Gothoskar was really my uncle.

Ajit Wadekar got to 90, before Greig got him caught by Fletcher, who had to dive to his left to reach to ball. Tiger Pataudi got 54, before being leg-before to Arnold. When England started their innings they had a new opening pair in Denness and Roope, both of whom were dismissed by Chandrasekhar. Knott batted well for his 40, and so did Fletcher who was a completely different batsman after his 97 not out in the Madras

danced down the wicket. The decision not only surprised him but all of us too for he was as far down the track that it looked as if he was going to shake hands with the bowler.

Wadekar, who followed, edged Chris Old low to Greig at second slip and was caught. Ajit, however, had missed seeing the ball and therefore had no idea of the direction the ball had travelled and he waited for the umpire's decision. To this day I can't fathom why umpire Mamsa didn't give him out there and then but had to consult the square-leg umpire. While Mamsa walked to speak to his colleague, all hell seemed to break loose. Greig ran forward with the ball in his raised right hand, Alan Knott flung his glove in the air and the other England players rushed in from where they were fielding, to confront the umpire. At this stage, Tony Lewis came in from mid-on to calm his players and asked them to get back to their position while the umpires conferred and then Mamsa declared Wadekar out. Lewis deserves full marks for the way he handled the explosive situation. Luckily, this happened in Madras where the crowds are the most disciplined and I shudder to think what would have happened if the game was at Kingston, Jamaica.

We asked Ajit Wadekar why he waited for the decision. He explained that he had not seen the ball after he edged it and then when he heard Tony Greig appealing and knowing his ways, did not walk. Whatever it was we were 10 for two!

The next morning we lost Chauhan and Durrani, who smashed 38 quick runs. During this innings he survived a confident appeal for leg-before. Gifford, the bowler said something and Durrani promptly hit the next delivery for a six. We lost Solkar too when he was caught at cover. Vishwanath was bowled by a beauty from Pocock. The ball curled between his bat and pads and took off his bails. At 72 for six, I walked in with my thumb strapped up. I had not opened the innings and when I went in I was the last recognised batsman left. However, I had to do precious little except to play out an over from Gifford. Tiger Pataudi got the runs off Pocock and the scores were level when Gifford bowled a no ball to give us victory. I was not out without scoring, and my aggregate in the fourth Test was only 20, and a total of 60 in three Tests.

I don't subscribe to the view that if we had to chase a target of 150 runs, we would have lost. I am sure that if the target had been that much the players would have batted with greater concentration. As it is, in spite of our losing wickets regularly, the atmosphere in the dressing room was relaxed knowing that victory couldn't elude us.

Just before the Test, an English journalist complained that Farokh Engineer led a chorus of forty-five thousand people when appealing. This allegation was carried in an Indian newspaper. This shut up Farokh effectively because he had to consider his prospect in English cricket, and thereafter he rarely appealed. It set me wondering that if Farokh was appealing what was Alan Knott doing? He wasn't opening his mouth as a part of the exercises he performed! As a matter of fact, Alan Knott appealed almost as much as Farokh. And it is hardly Farokh's fault that Indian crowds love their cricket so much that they take vocal part in the Tests. As I have said, I'd rather play before a vocal crowd than have the spectators sit mournfully watching a match, as they do in England.

All through the tour this English critic did nothing but criticise the conduct of the Indian players and spectators. If this was his idea of encouraging the Englishmen or lifting their drooping morale, he was sadly mistaken. As far as he was concerned, everything the Englishmen did was pardonable and the Indians were always wrong.

According to this English journalist, whenever the Indians

appealed, it was pressurising the umpires to force t a decision against England. It's funny how the En come up with all kinds of arguments to cover up team's weakness. If an Australian quick bowler ru an England team, invariably the British press will bowler as a chucker. If the bowler's action is scrup then he is accused of overstepping the bowling cre is not being no-balled by the umpires. If all else fails is accused of using abusive language towards the b in all, it is any kind of stick with which to beat thos to beat England in their own game. So much for t of English cricket writers!

In India, the complaint is not only against the our appealing, it is the condition of our wickets alleged that Indian wickets are invariably tailor spinners. True! Absolutely true! We would be fool not prepare wickets to suit our ace spinners. Whe England, we cannot distinguish the wicket from tl And, aren't English wickets prepared for the advant own bowlers? But, of course, it is all right for Eng so. The British are fair but we are not.

The M.C.C. team itself was friendly off the field a couple of players but then there will always be s apples in any group. What made the Indian players a determined was the patent bias of the English critic comments. John Snow had declined to come to India to play for a Melbourne club in Australia. From tha he had passed a judgment that it was absurd to cal India a Test, because 'the spinners come on in the and, therefore, the Test is a farce'. I suppose it wa fast bowler's lament. But then I wonder what one c in England where the spinners are seldom called upo

Test. He was confident from the start and played some crisp shots. All these innings were, however, overshadowed by Tony Lewis's maiden Test century. Showing beautiful footwork, he stepped down the wicket repeatedly and played some fine lofted shots. His confidence, I'm sure, must have increased with the knowledge that the ball wouldn't turn on this wicket. It was a very fine innings.

With India trailing by 40 in the first innings and about three hours to go, the match was doomed to be a draw. Our careless batting, however, led to an exciting finish. We had lost five wickets for only 75 runs, and still there was more than an hour of play left. Vishwanath and Solkar, however, batted sensibly and avoided an embarrassing situation. Vishwanath remained unbeaten with 75 which saved the innings. Just imagine that he was on the verge of losing his place in the side!

Towards the end, with Prasanna defending stubbornly, Chris Old bowled him five consecutive bouncers. It was a blatant attempt to injure one of our star spinners. Prasanna, who, over the years, has played bowlers faster than Chris Old returned unbeaten to the pavilion with his usual broad smile. Like all renowned bowlers, Prasanna takes his batting seriously and nothing makes him happier than a good innings. He has saved India often by resisting solidly while his partner has got the runs.

I was still being troubled by the broken thumb and so the West Zone selectors left me out of the game against the M.C.C. at Ahmedabad. Wadekar was rested and Sardesai led West Zone. He, however, did not use this last opportunity to win back his place in the Indian side. It was known that he was retiring at the end of the season. Parker also didn't enhance his chances by failing in the game.

For the fifth and final Test at Bombay, Chetan Chauhan was

dropped from the side, and Farokh was to open with me. This was my first Test before my home crowd at Bombay. But I began badly when Chris Old bowled me through the gate for only 4 runs. When I made my way back to the pavilion I was booed by the huge crowd in the C.C.I. stands. It was an unnerving experience. Farokh, however, went about merrily and Ajit, who was magnificently consistent in the series, added over 220 runs with him. Just as they looked like going on and on, Lewis brought on Birkenshaw. His second ball, a full-toss, got the wicket of Ajit who tried to hit him over mid-wicket but ended by giving a catch to the fielder there. Ajit had again missed his century this time by 13 runs. Ajit has only one Test century to his credit, having been out in the 80s or 90s on six occasions.

Farokh also got out to a Birkenshaw full-toss for 121 runs. At this stage he was getting runs off almost every ball and playing some shots which were not in the coaching manual. Before the day was out Pataudi was yorked by Underwood, and he too was booed by the crowd. Vishwanath and Durrani carried on as Wadekar and Engineer had done earlier. Salim had been dropped for the Kanpur Test, and there was a big outcry in Bombay, where posters appeared saying 'No Durrani, no Test'. The posters also condemned the chairman of the selection committee for leaving out Durrani, and there was considerable public support for his inclusion in the team for the Bombay test. Durrani did not disappoint his fans. Once again he hit a six when the crowd asked for it. Trying another one, he got out for 73.

Vishwanath, however, was a different sight. All elegance, he caressed the ball beautifully to the boundary. When he scampered for the run that got him his 100, he became the first Indian to score another 100, after making a century on test debut. Tony Greig, who has the uncanny knack of the right danced down the wicket. The decision not only surprised him but all of us too for he was as far down the track that it looked as if he was going to shake hands with the bowler.

Wadekar, who followed, edged Chris Old low to Greig at second slip and was caught. Ajit, however, had missed seeing the ball and therefore had no idea of the direction the ball had travelled and he waited for the umpire's decision. To this day I can't fathom why umpire Mamsa didn't give him out there and then but had to consult the square-leg umpire. While Mamsa walked to speak to his colleague, all hell seemed to break loose. Greig ran forward with the ball in his raised right hand, Alan Knott flung his glove in the air and the other England players rushed in from where they were fielding, to confront the umpire. At this stage, Tony Lewis came in from mid-on to calm his players and asked them to get back to their position while the umpires conferred and then Mamsa declared Wadekar out. Lewis deserves full marks for the way he handled the explosive situation. Luckily, this happened in Madras where the crowds are the most disciplined and I shudder to think what would have happened if the game was at Kingston, Jamaica.

We asked Ajit Wadekar why he waited for the decision. He explained that he had not seen the ball after he edged it and then when he heard Tony Greig appealing and knowing his ways, did not walk. Whatever it was we were 10 for two!

The next morning we lost Chauhan and Durrani, who smashed 38 quick runs. During this innings he survived a confident appeal for leg-before. Gifford, the bowler said something and Durrani promptly hit the next delivery for a six. We lost Solkar too when he was caught at cover. Vishwanath was bowled by a beauty from Pocock. The ball curled between his bat and pads and took off his bails. At 72 for six, I walked in with my thumb strapped up. I had not opened the innings and when I went in I was the last recognised batsman left. However, I had to do precious little except to play out an over from Gifford. Tiger Pataudi got the runs off Pocock and the scores were level when Gifford bowled a no ball to give us victory. I was not out without scoring, and my aggregate in the fourth Test was only 20, and a total of 60 in three Tests.

I don't subscribe to the view that if we had to chase a target of 150 runs, we would have lost. I am sure that if the target had been that much the players would have batted with greater concentration. As it is, in spite of our losing wickets regularly, the atmosphere in the dressing room was relaxed knowing that victory couldn't elude us.

Just before the Test, an English journalist complained that Farokh Engineer led a chorus of forty-five thousand people when appealing. This allegation was carried in an Indian newspaper. This shut up Farokh effectively because he had to consider his prospect in English cricket, and thereafter he rarely appealed. It set me wondering that if Farokh was appealing what was Alan Knott doing? He wasn't opening his mouth as a part of the exercises he performed! As a matter of fact, Alan Knott appealed almost as much as Farokh. And it is hardly Farokh's fault that Indian crowds love their cricket so much that they take vocal part in the Tests. As I have said, I'd rather play before a vocal crowd than have the spectators sit mournfully watching a match, as they do in England.

All through the tour this English critic did nothing but criticise the conduct of the Indian players and spectators. If this was his idea of encouraging the Englishmen or lifting their drooping morale, he was sadly mistaken. As far as he was concerned, everything the Englishmen did was pardonable and the Indians were always wrong.

According to this English journalist, whenever the Indians

appealed, it was pressurising the umpires to force them to give a decision against England. It's funny how the English critics come up with all kinds of arguments to cover up their own team's weakness. If an Australian quick bowler runs through an England team, invariably the British press will damn the bowler as a chucker. If the bowler's action is scrupulously fair, then he is accused of overstepping the bowling crease, but he is not being no-balled by the umpires. If all else fails, the bowler is accused of using abusive language towards the batsman. All in all, it is any kind of stick with which to beat those who dare to beat England in their own game. So much for the fairness of English cricket writers!

In India, the complaint is not only against the manner of our appealing, it is the condition of our wickets also. It is alleged that Indian wickets are invariably tailored for our spinners. True! Absolutely true! We would be fools if we did not prepare wickets to suit our ace spinners. When we go to England, we cannot distinguish the wicket from the outfield. And, aren't English wickets prepared for the advantage of their own bowlers? But, of course, it is all right for England to do so. The British are fair but we are not.

The M.C.C. team itself was friendly off the field except for a couple of players but then there will always be some rotten apples in any group. What made the Indian players all the more determined was the patent bias of the English critics and their comments. John Snow had declined to come to India preferring to play for a Melbourne club in Australia. From that distance he had passed a judgment that it was absurd to call a Test in India a Test, because 'the spinners come on in the third over and, therefore, the Test is a farce'. I suppose it was a typical fast bowler's lament. But then I wonder what one calls a Test in England where the spinners are seldom called upon to bowl.

The Indians don't call that a farce, do they? And, passing judgment from thousands of miles away is just rubbish!

The fourth Test at Kanpur ended in a draw. This was inevitable on a wicket which was perfect for batting. Batting first, Chauhan and I put on 85 runs. I finally managed to score more than 20 runs and when I reached 21, I had scored 1,000 runs in Tests. Later I came to know that it was the fastest (in 11 Tests) by an Indian batsman. But, from 774 in the first four Tests I had played in the West Indies in 1971, it had taken me seven more Tests to score 226 runs. I was eventually out for 69 being Jack Birkenshaw's first Test victim. I pulled a short ball straight to Tony Greig at square-leg, who took the ball well up. I cursed my luck for trying to clear the tallest Test cricketer. Greig had now caught me four times in four Tests. The fact that twice it was off the pads doesn't alter what's in the record books.

During my innings there was a funny incident when I survived a leg-before appeal off Arnold. Greig walking past me at the end of the over remarked, 'It was close, wasn't it?' I replied. 'Yeah, sure. But the umpire is my uncle!' Greig then asked what his name was. I said 'Gothoskar, but he had changed it, or else he would never get to be a Test umpire.' Within minutes word had gone round and I was asked with much consternation by quite a few people whether umpire Gothoskar was really my uncle.

Ajit Wadekar got to 90, before Greig got him caught by Fletcher, who had to dive to his left to reach to ball. Tiger Pataudi got 54, before being leg-before to Arnold. When England started their innings they had a new opening pair in Denness and Roope, both of whom were dismissed by Chandrasekhar. Knott batted well for his 40, and so did Fletcher who was a completely different batsman after his 97 not out in the Madras gesture at the right time, picked the puny Vishwanath up and rocked him like a baby. The crowd roared in laughter and clapped in wild appreciation for this sporting gesture. From that moment, Greig was the most popular member of the England team.

Tony Lewis was bowled first ball off his chest when England batted and Roope was brilliantly caught by Abid Ali at leg-slip when he hit a full-blooded shot off Chandrasekhar. So, Abid had a hand in the eventual dismissal of both the openers. Knott then played a strokeful innings to get 56, and Fletcher and Greig were left to ward off our spinners who had tasted blood. Fletcher once again showed the way to build up the innings. To the keen youngsters in the crowd, here was a fine model. He started off by pushing the ball away for singles and twos, and only after he had passed his 30s, did he venture to play his shots. Greig, on the other hand, played freely and was first to reach his hundred. At close of play, he was way ahead of Fletcher who had been dismissed in the last over of the day for 113.

The next day, however, Greig was never the same player as on the previous day and he prodded and pushed at the ball until he was dismissed for 148. Some merry hitting by Geoff Arnold and Birkenshaw took the England total to 448. When England's innings finally ended at 480, the visitors had a lead of 32 runs. We had two hours' batting before the end of the day, and we had to make certain that there was no more careless batting because there was a whole day's play left.

Farokh was confidence personified after his first innings century and went into his stride straightaway. He was lucky to see Knott fumble a stumping chance off Pocock. Pocock bowled very skilfully that evening but the bowler who spelled danger was Underwood. He had found a rough patch caused by Solkar's follow-through just on the off-stump and from there he made the ball jump, turn and at times, shoot through low. I got my 50 off one such ball which turned, took the edge and went past Fletcher at slip for a four. It was not the most satisfying way of getting a 50, but then my form in the series had been such that I was glad anyway. Farokh was unbeaten with 47 and our total at the end of the fourth day stood at 102 for no loss. The next morning both Farokh and I were out in quick succession. I was caught and bowled off a slower ball from Underwood, for 67. I drove too soon at the ball and ended up by giving a simple catch. In the next over Farokh, who had resumed with a runner, was bowled for 66. Durrani, however, was again in the mood to oblige the crowd and when they asked for a six he gave one to them. Some days, he says, he is going to write a book entitled 'Ask for a Six'.

Vishwanath not content with his first innings century was also batting well and when he was two short of 50, fell to an excellent catch down on the leg-side by Knott, off Greig. Pataudi came in for a lot of booing from the crowd for his laborious innings of 5 runs in ninety minutes. When he went in he found Underwood making the ball talk. He even survived a popped-up chance to Greig in the gully and barely survived. But the crowd whose appetite had been whetted by Durrani's big hitting couldn't understand Pataudi's crawl and started barracking him. Towards the latter half of the innings I think Tiger deliberately patted the full-tosses back to the bowler, to snub the crowd. Typically of Tiger!

Wadekar didn't declare till tea and when the curtain came down on the Test, England had lost two second innings wickets for 67 runs. Abid kept wicket, instead of the injured Farokh Engineer. Incidentally, Abid had started his career as a wicketkeeper and, though obviously not in practice, he took the unpredictable Chandrasekhar well. Interest in England's second innings centred around Chandrasekhar who required to take one more wicket to beat Vinoo Mankad's record of 34 wickets in a Test series. I am glad he got Knott's wicket with a beautifully flighted ball, and had his name inscribed in the record books! He deserves the honour.

At the end of the match the England players ran a lap of the ground and were cheered lustily by the crowd. This last gesture of theirs touched the hearts of the spectators and made the team more popular than before. Tony Lewis had done a magnificent job as captain. When he came to India he had yet to play a Test but it was apparent how much the players liked him. His charming ways also won over the crowd and went a long way in making the M.C.C. team a popular one. Tony Greig, of course, was the most popular player but Tony Lewis wasn't very far behind.

The season had not ended for us yet because the Ranji Trophy was still on. I went with the Bombay team to Indore for the quarterfinal against Madhya Pradesh. We had travelled by train and a huge crowd was waiting at Indore station to greet us. When the train stopped people swarmed all over it and some, more daring than the others, climbed on to the roof. We had no alternative but to wait inside because we just couldn't get out. Normally the train was to halt at Indore station for about twenty minutes, but this time it was well over an hour before the huge crowd could be cleared and it could steam off. Additional police reinforcements were called in before we finally got off amid much back-slapping, pushing and jostling. The enthusiasm of the crowd was truly remarkable. The cricket lovers of Indore had erected a huge bat made of concrete to commemorate India's victory over England in 1971. The names of all the players were inscribed on the bat, with the autograph of skipper Ajit Wadekar on top.

127

Looking back on that animated scene, I am reminded that when we lost to England in 1974, the same bat was smeared with tar and defaced. I suppose if we beat England in the home series in 1976, the bat will be cleaned and repaired and our image as victors will be restored!

In the Indore match I got a century against Madhya Pradesh. As I returned at the lunch interval, Syed Mushtaq Ali, one of India's all-time greats, came down the steps of the pavilion and congratulated me on my innings. This was one of my most cherished moments for I have not been so fortunate with some of the former Test greats in my own home, Bombay. And here was one of India's most popular players ever, coming down the pavilion steps to offer his felicitations! I was deeply touched by this sporting gesture. Bombay won easily. Incidentally, this was during the Holi festival and many of the players were splashed with colour every time they chased a ball to the boundary.

In the semifinal we met Hyderabad, one of the strongest sides in the tournament. With a century from me and brisk knocks by Sardesai and Wadekar, we were through to the final.

Our trip for the final against Tamil Nadu at Madras started eventfully. Sandwiched between the semifinals and the final was the Inter-Office Tournament in Bombay. This left us little time to make the journey down south by train and the Bombay Cricket Association, ever alive to the interests of the players, agreed to send the team by air to Madras. We landed at Madras with a bang, the worst I've ever experienced. At one moment the wing-tip on my side almost touched the runway and we very lucky to get out in one piece. Some of us thought that this was a good omen for us and we were destined to retain the Ranji Trophy.

The five-day final lasted just one ball bowled on the third day. On a wicket which one can only charitably call a cricket pitch, we were shot out for 151. It was obvious that if the Bombay batsmen were unable to cope with the viciously turning ball, the Tamil Nadu batsmen would do no better, particularly in view of Bombay's excellent close-in fielding. This is exactly what happened. From the overnight score of 50 for two, Madras were all out for 66. Their spinners Venkataraghavan and Kumar again bowled well to get us out for 113. As wickets were tumbling I was watching the game from the stands and the crowd around me, expecting a Tamil Nadu victory, were laughingly asking me what I thought Bombay's chances were. Poor ignorant souls! They should have, instead, been worried about Tamil Nadu's chances of pulling through. With just 171 runs to get for victory, Madras lost nine wickets for 61 runs at the end of the second day. One ball on the third day, and Bombay were the champions again – our fourteenth victory in a row.

Dilip Sardesai, who retired from first-class cricket with this match, was given the honour of leading the side back to the pavilion. The crowd gave him a standing ovation and I thought I saw tears in Dilip's eyes which showed how moved he was. Dilip had come into the side in 1958 and since then and until the 1972-73 season Bombay had never lost the Ranji Trophy. He kept on repeating this and said he hoped that Bombay would continue the same winning streak.

The long season had ended and we were looking forward to the monsoon for a period of rest and relaxation.

13

Sour Sir Lanka

THE 1973-74 SEASON ONCE AGAIN OPENED WITH THE IRANI TROPHY
game between Bombay, the Ranji Trophy Champions, and the
Rest of India. The match was played at the new stadium of the
Karnataka Cricket Association in Bangalore.

After the 1972-73 series against England, Wadekar had
once again lapsed into his usual habit of losing the toss. The
Irani Trophy match also started with Ajit calling wrongly, and
conceding first use of the wicket to the Rest of India. On a
wicket which gave no help to the bowlers, the Rest team piled
up runs. Gopal Bose got 170. Jayantilal, Vishwanath and Brijesh
Patel all got runs. Chasing a total of 444, Bombay started
disastrously. Parker was bowled by Amitava Roy for 2, Ajit fell
to Chandrasekhar and I was run out for 24 when Mankad sent
me back. I thought I had reached the crease and was most

disappointed about the decision. I confess I was so upset that I showed my disappointment and surprise by glaring at the umpire which was an absolutely silly thing to do. I realised as soon as I was in the pavilion that my action was unworthy of a sportsman. In future I only hope my frustration doesn't cloud my judgment, as it did on that occasion.

Milind Rege (67) and Sudhir Naik were the only players who resisted but we could not avoid the follow-on. In our second innings we struck the kind of form we should have had in the first innings. Parker and I put on 83 runs before Parker was out for 50. Then Naik, who had scored 58 in the first innings, was promoted to number three and I shared another fruitful partnership with him. I eventually got my first century in the Irani Trophy. Over the years, I had been consistently failing in this annual fixture and my century, though too late to be of help to Bombay, was satisfying. Naik scored another 50. He was wonderfully consistent that season.

The Indian team was due to leave for Sri Lanka for a six-week tour in early January next year (1974). It was pretty well known that our main spinners would not go to Sri Lanka as the tour to England was to follow in April. Before the team to Sri Lanka was picked, North Zone created a sensation by winning the Duleep Trophy. Wooden spooners till then, they surprised everybody by beating West Zone in the semifinal and Central Zone in the final. Central had earlier shocked South Zone, which was yet another upset in the Duleep Trophy.

Before the start of the season I was pleasantly surprised and honoured to be appointed Ajit Wadekar's deputy in the Bombay team. Ajit couldn't play two of the league games and I led Bombay for the first time.

The Deodhar Trophy for one-day limited-over games between the Zonal sides was started this year. In the final between the

West and South Zones, I had to face the most embarrassing incident of my cricketing career. Our captain Ajit Wadekar split a finger in trying to catch Jaisimha in the slips and went in for medical attention. For a minute or two there was complete confusion as to who should lead the side in his absence. Being Ajit's deputy for Bombay, I took charge and led the side for three overs before the twelfth man came in and told me that the seniormost player in the side, Ashok Mankad, was to act as captain.

Kaka, as we called Ashok, was most apologetic about it but took command. For me, however, it was most embarrassing to be told to hand over charge to another player in full view of more than twenty thousand people who must have seen the change. Even to this day I cannot help shuddering whenever I remember the incident. I feel that a vice-captain should invariably be appointed or the seniormost cricketer should be authorised to take over automatically in case something happens to the skipper. An almost similar situation occurred when I was appointed deputy to Tiger Pataudi in the Bangalore Test against the West Indies in 1974-75. Fortunately, I was told before the game that I was the vice-captain and so there was no trouble on the field once I announced that I was taking charge.

My form was atrocious and, but for the century innings in the Irani Trophy and a score of 84 against Saurashtra, I had not been among runs. Against Baroda also, I led the side in Ajit's absence. After this match a journalist from one of the national news agencies came to interview me. When he had called me up I had told him that I would only speak about our just-concluded Ranji Trophy match against Baroda. He agreed and so I invited him to our hotel. Sometime during our talks the topic turned to the forthcoming tour of Sri Lanka. He wanted to know what my team would be. I said I was not

competent enough to select a team and in any case I didn't
want to say anything on the subject. He, however, reverted to
the composition of the team to Sri Lanka again. But this time
he wanted to know my view which he assured me would be
treated as being strictly off the record. I said then that, may be,
our main spinners should be rested for the England tour and
some of the others should be given a chance. I also said that
the main batsmen should, however, be there to go to Sri Lanka.
A few days after my return to Bombay a news item appeared
in the newspapers quoting me as saying that younger spinners
should be taken to Sri Lanka, which was all right. But the
journalist had mentioned the names of some of these spinners,
which I had not done. In any case, our talk about the Sri Lanka
tour was off the record and the journalist had no business to
use it in his report.

The next thing I knew was that the President of the Cricket
Control Board wanted to see me about this matter. I explained
the position to him and he very kindly accepted my word. I was
furious anyway with the journalist. Later, I came to know that
this journalist had heard from some other friend that, at a
private dinner, I had mentioned the names of these promising
cricketers who, I thought, deserved a chance and rushed off
to make it appear as if I had personally suggested the names
of those players when he met me.

As expected, all our main spinners except Venkataraghavan,
were rested and a number of young players were selected for
the Sri Lanka tour. It was to give them a chance of staking their
claims for the England tour a few months later.

Sri Lanka had been trying to get full membership of the
International Cricket Conference for some time. In this they had
Pakistan's backing. In order to strengthen their claim for grant
of Test status, Sri Lanka were anxious to notch up a victory

133

against India. For this reason they attached a great deal of importance to the Indian team's visit. I was happy to tour Sri Lanka where I was very successful with the Universities team in 1970. I had made a few friends there and I wanted to renew those friendships.

Leo Wijesinghe, Harold de Andrado and Eddie Melder had looked after me well during my last visit and I was looking forward to meeting them again. All three of them are not only cricket-mad but also keen students of the game and we had spent a lot of time talking cricket. I also had friends in the Sri Lanka team.

We started the tour with a game against the Sri Lanka Cricket Board President's XI. Within an hour of the game an accident robbed us of the services of Vishwanath. Chasing a ball, he tripped over the boundary rope and injured his right knee again, which developed a swelling. He had to be taken off the field assisted by Salgaonkar and Madan Lal, two hefty young men who were to serve us so well on the tour. Though the knee looked bad, we were all shocked to learn that Vishwanath was going to be sent back home, apparently on instructions from the President of the Indian Cricket Control Board. The ridiculousness of the decision was apparent when Vishwanath was practising with the boys on the day of the first unofficial Test against Sri Lanka. By this time his replacement, Parthasarathy Sharma, had arrived in Sri Lanka and though the Sri Lanka Cricket Board very generously agreed to bear Vishwanath's expenses if he stayed with the team, he was asked to return.

The journey from Colombo city to the airport takes longer than the air journey from Madras to Colombo. Solkar and I went to see Vishwanath off at the airport and I've never seen the good-humoured Vishwanath so upset as on that day. As we were driving to the airport he did all the physical exercises one can think of excepting standing on his head to prove that there was nothing wrong with his knee. Vishwanath is tremendously popular and we were all disappointed that he had to go away and particularly since he was fit to carry on.

I started off the tour well with a century against the Board President's XI at the Colombo Oval. I was hoping to have as successful a tour as my earlier visit to the island with the universities team. Our first four-day Test was also at the same venue. We elected to bat on a greenish wicket and lost three wickets. Ashok Mankad held on and gave the innings some respectability. The chief wreckers were Mevan Peiris and Tony Opatha.

When Sri Lanka batted, it soon became obvious to us that it was useless asking for leg-before decisions. Anura Tennekoon, their skipper, survived even a caught behind decision off Venkataraghavan and went on to score a century. He played some lovely shots but, time and again, he was rapped on the pads by the spinners who shouted themselves hoarse appealing to the umpires. When he got his century there were a couple of our boys who didn't clap and the Sri Lanka newspapers raised a furore about it. Commenting on the appeal for caught behind, which was turned down by the umpire, the newspapers said that Tennekoon would have walked because he was a gentleman. In effect, it amounted to calling us cheats.

In our second innings, Gopal Bose and I shared an opening partnership of 194 runs, when I was out for 85 runs. Gopal went on to score a century and we saved the match easily.

In the one-day matches we beat Sri Lanka with ridiculous ease. It was rather funny that, prior to these matches, the Sri Lanka newspapers were calling their team World Champions in one-day cricket. This claim eventually turned out to be a big joke, and we proved to the hilt how ridiculous such self-praise can be. As it happened, we beat them without a bead of sweat on our brows. Our players also made no secret of their feelings. Quite frankly, the crowds and the newspapers were terribly biased and it gave us perverse pleasure in seeing the crowds go back dejected.

By this time Sri Lanka were desperate. They badly wanted to beat us to prove to the International Cricket Conference that they were good enough for official Tests. But this was not to be and their fondest hopes were shattered. In the second Test, our batsmen came into their own. Gopal Bose got 50, Ajit Wadekar who was a doubtful starter made 89, Parthasarathy and Mankad got 60 each and we piled up a total of 344. When Sri Lanka batted Salgaonkar and Madan Lal skittled them out for 121 runs. Both bowled with tremendous fire and for the first time, we were standing a good twenty yards behind the wicket in the slips. Salgaonkar, in particular, achieved great pace and what is remarkable, he sustained it throughout his long spell.

Having been asked to follow on, Sri Lanka did little better and were quickly in trouble against Salgaonkar and Madan Lal who didn't seem tired after their first innings effort. Anura Tennekoon, however, played a captain's innings. He suffered a bad blow on the elbow from Salgaonkar but he kept going with determination. At the end of the Sri Lankan innings he was unbeaten with 169, a truly magnificent innings. We should, however, have dismissed them earlier but for some atrocious umpiring decisions. I am specially reminded of one such perverse decision. Ajit deSilva popped up a catch off his gloves to the wicketkeeper, but the umpire negatived it. All this while the batsman was wringing his hand in pain and after the over, took off his gloves to inspect the damage!

As the Sri Lankan innings ended I was reported by the newspapers to have clapped the umpires to the pavilion. This

136

was yet another example of tendentious reporting because I do remember applauding our bowlers but surely not the umpires. Madan Lal was walking behind them and I applauded him as he walked along with the umpires. I read about this later somewhere and I thought that I really should have applauded the umpire for having given the last man run-out. So what if the batsman was a good two yards out of his crease as long as he was in his half of the wicket, and could have easily been given not out. But horror of horrors, the umpire actually gave him out. Surprises never cease! I should have known that the umpires were actually practising raising their fingers for the time when we would bat. True enough, I played forward to Pieris and there were the fingers sticking up its signal for me to go back. We, however, won the match in the seventeenth of the twenty mandatory overs; not because of the umpires, but in spite of them.

Right then I thought I would never tour Sri Lanka again, certainly not as a cricketer. Most of my team-mates also agreed with me after that tour. I must add, however, that the relations between the players of both the teams were excellent. In fact, all of us made a number of friends on the tour though the crowd never got used to the idea that we were the better team. One can understand their patriotism, but the spectators were positively hostile and our players were barely applauded for their cricket.

My feeling is that the Sri Lankan journalists, in their enthusiasm to secure official Test status for their country, got carried away; and the average man who read these reports got the impression that we were an unsporting bunch. And thus the hostile attitude to anything we did on the field.

From this tour Salgaonkar and Madan Lal emerged as India's new-ball hopes and Gopal Bose staked his claim for the opener's berth. The success of the tour was Ashok Mankad. He seized the opportunity afforded by Vishwanath's absence and scored heavily. Eknath Solkar was, however, a failure on the tour. But, it must be added that he suffered terribly at the umpire's hands. He was given out leg-before in almost all his innings. This prompted Vishwanath later on to remark that Eknath had gone through a pad patch and not bad patch. Parthasarathy Sharma also made runs in the few innings he played. One man for whom the tour proved a disappointment was Karsan Ghavri. He just didn't get a chance to play in the Tests.

To compensate him for this, Ghavri met his future wife on the tour and returned to Sri Lanka a year later to get married. Thus the tour was not completely futile for this hard-working and talented cricketer!

Back home, I once again plunged into cricket with the Ranji Trophy Tournament still on. In the Ranji Trophy knock-out match Bihar almost surprised us. They got us out for 200 runs and took a first innings lead of 72 runs, thanks to a century by Tilak Raj. His innings was a mixture of some superb shots and a good bit of playing and missing the ball. In our second innings we scored runs mainly through Parker, Naik and Mankad. Amid mounting excitement we got the Bihar batsmen out in the second innings and managed to scrape through to the semifinals, with a 59-run victory. Shivalkar bowled superbly, accounting for most of the wickets.

The semifinal against Karnataka started sensationally. Ismail's first ball, an out-swinger, was edged by Vijay Kumar straight to me. I fumbled with the simple catch, but luckily the ball stuck in my lap. Vishwanath let go at the next ball but off the third delivery, he played back, missed and was hit on the pads at ankle height. Surprisingly, the umpire gave him not out. Thereafter Vishwanath simply blasted our bowling all over the ground. We couldn't get him to commit a second mistake until he was 162. If ever an umpiring decision changed the complexion of a match, it was the one when Brijesh Patel was let off when he was 16. Patel went on to score a century and Vishwanath took a heavy toll of our bowling to take the Karnataka total to 385.

At one stage, Bombay were 200 for two wickets, and Wadekar and Mankad were batting untroubled against Chandrasekhar and Prasanna. Ajit, however, ran himself out and despite Naik continuing to get runs, we started losing wickets. We were all out for 320 with only a day's play left. We were out of the Ranji Trophy final for the first time in fifteen years. It was a quite a blow for Bombay. In the other semifinal there was another upset when Rajasthan got Hyderabad out cheaply in their second innings. Karnataka eventually went on to lift the glittering Ranji Trophy for the first and only time in their career. It was a proud moment for Prasanna when he received the Ranji Trophy as captain of the victorious team.

So, Ajit Wadekar as the captain of Bombay had lost the Irani Trophy, the Ranji Trophy and the Duleep Trophy. In a few months, he was to lose a Test series for the first time and concede a 3-0 victory to England!

14

Back to Blighty

THE TEAM TO ENGLAND HAD MORE OR LESS PICKED ITSELF AND THERE were no surprises. However, a mild flutter was caused by the omission of Salgaonkar, particularly after his lion-hearted bowling in Sri Lanka. The experience of English wickets would have done him a world of good. After he was left out of the team which was to tour England, a number of cricket lovers collected funds to send him to Alf Gover's Coaching School in England. Unfortunately, while in England, Salgaonkar fell ill and couldn't play much cricket. As a result, when he returned to India, he had put on a lot of weight but his stamina was the same and he could bowl for long spells. He can still work up a lot of pace and if he seriously applies himself, he can hope to play for India.

We left for London, in defence of the rubber we had won

in two successive series, after the usual round of farewell functions. As our plane circled over London in bright sunshine I told those of us who were having their first view of England, to take a good look because they might not see the sun again! As it happened, for the next month and a half, in fact right through our lightning tour, the sun came out to dispel the gloom only for a week or ten days.

The start of the tour could not have been more miserable for us. In our first match against D.H. Robins' XI at Eastbourne, John Jameson caned our attack for a century before lunch in eighty-five minutes. He was helped quite a lot by the extremely cold weather. None of the fielders dared to put their hands out to stop his hard-hit shots. It was bitterly cold for that kind of bravado! Dennis Amiss notched up 152 and the home team's total reached 402. Then, in the last hour of the evening, we lost two wickets to John Lever. However, Brijesh Patel somewhat redeemed us with a knock of 107.

That certainly wasn't the end of our troubles on that day. We were invited that evening to dinner by an Indian family. At the dinner there was a serious and furious argument between Ajit Wadekar and Bishen Singh Bedi. Without going into the rights and wrongs of that verbal battle, it is sufficient to say that for the younger members of the side, it was a terrible thing to see two of India's senior-most cricketers squabbling in an unseemly manner, specially in a house where we were guests. Sure, on a tour there are always minor disagreements but what happened on the day of our first match on the tour was more than a mere disagreement.

When we returned to our hotel, I could see that the younger members had been shocked by what they had seen. Though the whole thing was patched up by the players concerned the next day, there was a lot of tension around. This continued throughout the tour. Now, Bishen was a very popular member of the team and, Ajit also, in his own way, was liked by everyone. Besides, he was also the captain.

Ajit and Bishen are men of different stamps. Bishen is an extrovert who joked and fooled with the boys, never once letting the younger members feel that they were with a great bowler. Ajit, on the other hand, has a dry sense of humour, and is always prepared to help his junior colleagues in all their difficulties. However, towards the end of the tour I found Ajit a little more withdrawn, and he preferred to spend his time alone with his worries. To their credit, however, it must be said that whatever their differences, it did not interfere with their trying their best on the field. However, their best, as well as the team's, was just not good enough to beat England that year.

Jameson, who must be the only player in the world to rate the Indian spinners as his favourite target of attack, once again scored a whirlwind century. In the little time left Gopal Bose stroked 59 runs.

Our second game against Worcestershire proved to be an exciting one. Madan Lal, in a great spell of bowling, captured seven wickets for 95 runs. Vanburn Holder then ran through our side. He bowled real quick on that track and the light drizzle kept the pitch fresh for his seam bowling. Norman Gifford, The Pink Panther as he is called, declared Worcestershire's second innings closed, giving us 195 minutes to score 221 runs to win. It was a very sporting declaration as the mandatory twenty overs were also to be bowled in the last hour. After we had lost two wickets, Vishwanath joined me and we carried the score to 150 before Vish played on to Inchmore, off the last ball before tea. Abid and Eknath Solkar kept up the chase with me but, at 203 for six, we had to put up the shutters. I was run out for 88 when I slipped while turning for a second run. It was an exciting game mainly owing to Gifford's declaration.

The weather still wasn't getting any better. We almost always played in cloudy conditions and in terribly cold weather. However, the match against Somerset saw Brijesh in good form and it ended in a draw. We played another drawn match against Hampshire at Southampton before taking on Leicestershire.

Ajit Wadekar must rank Leicestershire's Grace Road as his favourite ground. On the 1971 tour he had got a century here and in the course of the innings, scattered the people at the bar when his sweep for a six, off Birkenshaw, crashed through the glass panes and shattered them. The section of the crowd in front of the bar was full of Indians who remembered this feat and were demanding a repeat. Ajit, however, preferred to play himself into form and he did just that with a century. He overshadowed Eknath Solkar who scored 75. A ball from Holder had struck a painful blow to me in the ribs during the Worcester game, which began to give me a lot of trouble and I found that it greatly hampered my movement. So I was rested from the Yorkshire game during which I learnt that a blood clot had formed and would require heat treatment.

The Yorkshire match was the beginning of Geoff Boycott's failures which were to climax in his eventually losing place in the England side. As if to compensate for this, the game marked Chris Old's advance as a batsman and he scored his first century in a first-class match to rescue Yorkshire. To show he was not to be ignored as a bowler, Old took five wickets to send us reeling to 102 all out. Only Madan Lal with a defiant, strokeful 48 not out, resisted him. Madan was developing into a fine all-rounder. He was playing the quick bowlers comfortably, relishing the short delivery. In the Hampshire game he had belted Andy Robert's bouncers all over the place to score an unbeaten 79. So, his subsequent failure in the tests and his repeated dismissals off the short ball came as a big surprise and we were extremely disappointed.

Boycott had fallen leg-before to Abid Ali in the first innings for 15, and Solkar got him in the second for 14. But, after losing two more wickets, Yorkshire were saved by an attacking innings from Barry Leadbeater and Peter Squires, both of whom got fifties. Set to score 265 for victory, we ended the game on 144 for five, Wadekar playing brilliantly for his 47.

We travelled to Manchester to take on Lancashire, the traditional rivals of Yorkshire. In this match we tried Solkar as my opening partner, since Gopal Bose had not been shaping well and Sudhir Naik was still recovering from a hand injury. Solkar batted well against the pace of Peter Lever, Peter Lee and Ken Shuttleworth and at lunch on the first day, I was the only batsman out with over 100 runs on the board. At lunch, Solkar who was on 48 and batting confidently, cheerfully predicted, 'You saw my technique, now see my strokes.' After the first two balls bowled on resumption, he was back in the pavilion grinning sheepishly. However, Solkar had helped Ajit put on 93 runs for the second wicket before he was out. We lost two quick wickets, those of Vishwanath and Ashok Mankad, before Wadekar and Brijesh Patel steadied the innings with a 57-run partnership, when Wadekar was out for 82. When Ajit gets going, his partner can never hope to match him. So was the case with Brijesh. After Ajit went, Brijesh took over to play some lovely shots off Lee. When he got his second century of the tour and was unbeaten with 104 runs, Wadekar declared.

For Lancashire, David Lloyd scored a century showing very good footwork against the spinners; and Clive Lloyd scored 55 runs in even time. But the innings the crowd enjoyed most was that of Frank Hayes. At times Hayes was halfway down the track to drive our spinners. He reached his century with two thrilling shots. At 91 he suddenly rushed out to loft Bedi deep into the stands at long-off for a six. Of the next ball he clouted him for another six. This time the ball kept going on and on and landed on the roof over the scorer's box. This is the longest hit sixer I've seen. Hayes didn't let up after reaching his century but went on to score 187 and eventually fell to a catch by wicketkeeper Kirmani off Bedi. All the Lancashire batsmen made merry at the expense of our attack.

Surprisingly Lancashire did not declare. Unlike Gifford whose declaration enlivened the Worcester game, David Lloyd continued to let his batsmen go on and by the time our turn came to bat, there was no hope of a positive result. At the end of the game we were 187 for no loss. I had scored my first century of the tour and was unbeaten with 104, while Eknath again showed his ability as an opener with 69. During our partnership we had to run often between the wickets because the ball just wouldn't travel on the grassy outfield. In one over from Lee we took 3, 2, 3, 1 and 3. At this stage both of us were completely out of breath. So, in order to get back my breath I pretended that my leg-guards had come loose and I took my own time to adjust it. Solkar, who was leaning heavily on his bat at the other end while I finished adjusting my pads, had not recovered his breath, so he took off his gloves and began tightening his boot laces. Peter Lee's last ball of the over was a slower half-volley, but I just didn't have the strength to put it away and patted it back to him.

Now came the mini Test against M.C.C. at Lord's. Boycott fell to Solkar again edging a drive to me at second slip. Then Eknath got Amiss caught by Patel at cover. Harry Pilling was caught by Vishwanath off Bedi. This catch went via the bat and pad to Vishwanath who would normally have taken this easily, but not being accustomed to the forward short-leg position, he had to lean forward to reach the ball. In the process he lost his balance and toppled over, but held on to the ball. We were roaring with laughter. Vishwanath calmly dusted his flannels and announced he had better lose weight by scoring runs. Mike Denness and Fletcher scored lovely centuries; Denness in particular was most impressive. Fletcher suffered in comparison, but was still very good. Greig fell in the chase for runs before the M.C.C. declared at their overnight score of 305 for eight.

Arnold got Eknath out quickly and then Edmonds picked up a flick from me, which should have gone for four runs instead of sending me back into the pavilion. Ajit Wadekar and Vishwanath counter-attacked only as they can, with stylish strokes all round the wicket. Engineer made a brisk 44.

We were all out for 231. In M.C.C's second innings Solkar got Boycott again, caught by me. As Geoff was making his way to the pavilion Solkar came running around gesturing to him how he had made the ball move away to take the edge of Boycott's bat. I dropped Amiss, off Solkar, low down to my left, just before the day's play ended.

Next day there were to be no more wickets for us for a long time. Amiss showed the kind of form that was to make him such a prolific scorer against us later in the Test.

Harry Pilling, who is as short as me, if not shorter, scored 81 not out and Edmonds, promoted just for a slog, was 29 not out. There was no question of us going for the runs, so we settled down to some batting practice. I got 57 not out and Ashok Mankad played an attacking innings to remain unbeaten with 50. He hit Edmonds for four successive fours in an over, all brilliant shots.

On the last evening of the game, we were entertained at an official dinner by the M.C.C. Ajit made a bright, humorous speech and so too did Manager Lt. Col. Adhikari, the manager.

During the dinner Bishen Bedi was collecting autographs of the great names in cricket who were present at the function. He approached Geoff Boycott who turned around and told him 'I'll give you my autograph only if you bowl me a full toss first ball.' Bishen quipped: 'Yes, provided you last out our seamers.' In a newspaper article a few days later Boycott wrote, 'Everybody's talking about the great Indian spinners and many have asked me what I think about them. But, where have I played them? I am getting out before these famous spinners come on to bowl.'

In the next game against Northamptonshire, Vishwanath struck form to get 103 not out. Against Essex in the next match, Sudhir Naik touched splendid form to score a century. Though slow at times his innings showed that he was prepared to stay at the wicket and wait for the runs to come. Again, in the second innings he played patiently to score 42 not out. Wadekar got 50 in each inning and Madan Lal scored 64 not out.

We had so far played ten matches and all of them had ended indecisively. There were only two games left before the first Test and it was essential that Farokh Engineer should strike batting form before we took on England. Unfortunately, against Surrey he failed again, rushing out to Intikhab and was stumped. I got my second century (136) of the tour, playing for the most part with one hand, particularly the seamers, as a ball from Jackman had hit me on the right thumb early on. It was a beautiful wicket and Ajit Wadekar showed his appreciation by banging ten boundaries in his score of 57.

Surrey were skittled out for 85 by Abid Ali, who took six wickets for 23 runs. On such a beautiful batting track it was great bowling by Abid, who kept the ball up, moving it both ways and had everybody in trouble. Following on, Surrey did a little better in the second innings scoring 265, Roope (64) and Intikhab Alam (56) being the main scorers. Intikhab Alam used the long handle effectively, while Roope played a patient innings. Farokh Engineer, who opened with Naik, slammed 32 out of the 37 runs needed for victory. We had finally won a match after ten drawn games.

During the Surrey match I had strained a thigh muscle badly and had not fielded in Surrey's second innings. The muscle was not responding to treatment and I had to drop out of the next game against Derbyshire, which was to be our last county fixture before the first Test.

Abid, continuing to maintain good form, bowled Lawrence Rowe first ball and went on to take five wickets. Only Brian Bolus who played as many balls with his pads as with the bat, survived. He scored a century. Farokh at last got into form with a bustling century and Ashok Mankad played a patient innings for his 66 not out. Bolus left us 155 minutes to score 197 runs to win. With Naik playing strokefully and Engineer treating the seamers with scant respect, we won the match at the cost of only two wickets. Naik with 76 and Engineer with 55 remained unbeaten.

With two victories under our belt and centuries from all our recognised batsmen, we went into the first Test with confidence. Our bowlers had also bowled well in adverse conditions. There was only one major problem and that was Ajit Wadekar's fractured finger. He had broken it while fielding in the Surrey match. I passed the fitness test on the morning of the Test and Ajit, too, decided to play. He did not, however, field in his customary position at first slip.

The Old Trafford wicket of Manchester looked green, so much so that it could not be distinguished from the rest of the field. And it was cold, really cold. Mike Denness won the toss and elected to bat. It was so cold we were swathed in four sweaters each. Boycott and Amiss began confidently. Abid opened with a wayward over, but then settled down to bowl a good length. Soon we had to turn off the field as it started raining. After the interval, Abid brought one back to trap Boycott leg-before for 10. The decision was given after due deliberation but there was no doubt about its correctness. Edrich was bowled round his legs by Abid, and Denness was bowled off Bishen's faster delivery. During the tour Bishen had practised this delivery and he got plenty of wickets trapping the batsmen either leg-before or bowling them as they expected the slower, flighted delivery.

Abid was bowling superbly and he brought one back off the seam to trap Fletcher on his back-foot. Our appeal was, however, negatived by the same umpire who had given Boycott out to an identical delivery. Boycott had been hit on the front foot as he shuffled across, but Fletcher was on his back foot and he was perhaps more palpably leg-before wicket than Boycott. May be the umpire didn't like Boycott very much! Dennis Amiss, who had survived three chances, got his 50 and then pulled Chandrasekhar straight to Madan Lal at square-leg. Underwood came in as night-watchman and survived the last few overs.

The next day Fletcher went on in his methodical way, unleashing all of a sudden a slashing cover-drive. Greig came and attacked the bowling straightaway. By this time, the weather was really turning bad and our spinners could hardly grip the ball in the cold. Chandrasekhar was constantly blowing into his palms to warm them up. In the slips we stood with our hands in our pockets till the last possible second when the ball would be delivered. There wasn't a fielder whose nose wasn't running. Fletcher and Greig, taking advantage of the situation, added 103 runs for the sixth wicket. Greig eventually fell trying to force the pace, to give Madan Lal his first Test wicket. Two balls later, Madan Lal trapped Knott leg-before. Fletcher reached his century in the company of Bob Willis who pushed his front foot down the wicket to smother the spin. Denness declared at 328 giving us half an hour's batting before close.

That season there was a new provision in the playing conditions for the series. If more than an hour's play was lost it would be made up by playing after 6.30. So we had to play till 7.30. Bob Willis worked up a good pace and Hendrick bowled well. Hendrick got a wicket with his second ball when he had Solkar taken low down by Willis in the gully. Venkataraghavan who had come in as night-watchman, was yorked by Willis and at that stage, play ended for the day with India on 26 for two.

Rain delayed start of play the next day till half an hour before lunch and we lost Ajit Wadekar during that time. Driving at a ball leaving him he was caught by Hendrick, off Chris Old. Vishwanath joined me looking like a round, white ball wearing three sweaters. Right from the start he was meeting the ball in the middle of the bat and a square-drive by him rocked to the fence at point, in spite of the heavy outfield. After lunch we carried on cautiously and Underwood, brought on to relieve the fast bowlers, got a wicket. He made a ball turn almost at right angles and knocked out Vishwanath's off-stump. It was a ball which could have got anybody out and it was Vishwanath's bad luck to get it. This was like a shot in the arm for the England bowlers, coming just when the initiative was slipping away from them. Patel opened his Test career driving a four to mid-on; but he fell to Willis who was brought on after Vishwanath's dismissal. I was doubtful if the ball had carried to Knott who was standing behind, but Brijesh walked without waiting for the umpire's verdict. Farokh Engineer came in to a grand ovation from his home crowd, who expected fireworks from him. He, however, disappointed them by being yorked by Willis for a duck. First ball after tea, Hendrick bowled Madan Lal, when his off and leg stumps were knocked down. Abid, who came in to take his place, made his intentions quite clear as he started attacking the bowling with great gusto. When Greig came on to bowl his off-spinners he was carved to mid-wicket twice in succession. As I neared my first Test century in England, Abid got his 50. Abid is a very fast runner between wickets. He loves to take singles from under the very nose of the fielders, but gets carried away and so is a poor judge of a run. What he doesn't take into account is that the other man may be a slow runner. We, however, struck a good understanding and took many singles by just tapping the ball away.

When I was on 97 the umpire wanted to know if we wanted to go in as the light was getting bad. I didn't want to, because both of us were right on top of the bowling and there was no sense giving a respite to the England bowlers. So, we opted to carry on much to the delight of the crowd which was loving the fight we were putting up.

I got my century off a ball from Underwood, which I lost sight of as it left his hand. I only saw it at the last minute pitching short outside the off-stump. I cut it away past Willis for three to get my century. It was a great moment and very satisfying to get a century under such difficult circumstances. I was engulfed by a large number of Indian spectators who swarmed on to the field. One of them put his scarf around my neck and, if Mike Denness had not put his hand through, I may have been strangled. My elation had turned to shock. Abid came and drove the crowd away.

Bob Willis was brought on by Denness in the fading light, but I was destined to be run out. After Abid hit the ball a little

151

wide off Denness, we hesitated a fraction of a second before taking the run. Denness who is an outstanding fielder, hit the stump directly, with me just failing to make the crease. Abid carried on shielding Chandrasekhar from the bowlers and was last out for a rousing 71. It was a knock which put hope into our hearts again. Abid had not only shown defiance, but also rattled the England players with his attacking batting.

This Test saw a unique record being created. I normally don't wear a cap while batting and even on this windy day, I wasn't wearing one. The breeze often blew my hair over my left eye, obstructing my vision somewhat as the bowler delivered the ball. Instead of asking for a cap, I asked umpire Dickie Bird if he had a pair of scissors with him. Dickie replied that he had a razor blade and I requested him to cut off the offending locks of hair. He was taken aback at first but then cheerfully did the job muttering, 'What things the umpire has to do these days!' Keith Fletcher who passed by during the hair-cutting operation, remarked to Dickie Bird that what he needed was not a pair of scissors but a pair of shears. Keith was no doubt influenced by my thick curly hair, which over the years had thinned considerably. I have taken to wearing a cap now while batting and the hairy problem is no longer there. I am happy to hold this unique record of a hair-cut in the midst of a Test match!

It was England's turn to bat out the last hour and Solkar got Geoff Boycott's wicket again, caught brilliantly by Engineer. It was amazing to see Boycott fish outside for such an innocuous ball. Make no mistake, Boycott is a great player. Only that morning at the nets he had shown his ability, tackling Willis and Company who were outstepping the mark and really letting the ball go. He played them all with time to spare and once contemptuously called to Willis not to bowl spinners.

However, Amiss and Edrich thwarted our spinners. There was no purchase from the wicket. The rain also saw to it that our bowlers never got a good grip on the ball. Edrich, particularly, played some lovely shots. Two of them, both lofted ones, stand out in my memory. A ferocious square-cut, off Abid, rammed into the fence. Amiss was eventually out to a beautiful piece of bowling. Bedi brought him forward twice and had him groping for the ball as it turned away from the bat. Before he bowled the next one, I was asked to move from mid-off to first slip. The next ball was a beautifully flighted delivery. It pitched on the middle-stump, lifted a bit as it turned and off the shoulder of Amiss's bat, the ball curled to me for an easy catch. Venkataraghavan, who had been fielding at slip all this while and had just moved to gully so that I could take up my position at first slip, turned around and said, 'I field here all morning and nothing comes and you turn up for one ball and end up with a catch.'

Denness came in and pushed the score along in order to declare. Edrich was exactly 100 when bad light stopped play. It was a grand comeback by John Edrich who was playing a Test after two years. Denness declared first thing next morning. No doubt he wanted more runs behind him, but the previous evening's rain had upset his plans. It was a decision which showed his boldness. He gave his bowlers a whole day to get us out. At the same time we needed just two good partnerships to win the match.

Solkar started by sending Willis' first delivery for a six over deep fine-leg. Both of us were going on well when Derek Underwood got Solkar out to a brilliant catch by Hendrick, who had to dive to his left to take it. Ajit was never very comfortable due to his fractured finger. He tended to slice his drives and in trying to cut Greig, was caught behind by Knott.

153

Vishwanath and I were then concerned in a fruitful partnership. I was past my 50 when a ball from Old stood up and lobbed off my bat gently to Hendrick in the gully. I was batting well and had hoped to get a few more runs. Vishwanath cut and flicked his way to 60 before he was declared caught behind as the ball flicked his shirtsleeve. That was the beginning of the end. Abid was caught by Boycott, who ran a good twenty yards for the catch, and Engineer fell to Hendrick. We were all out for 182, leaving England winners by 113 runs.

We could have saved the match, because we lost the game only in the thirteenth of the twenty mandatory overs. Abid and Farokh played totally irresponsible shots when the situation cried out for watchfulness. It was a good win for England but, to a large extent, we had made their task easy.

We next played at Oxford against the Combined Universities and won an exciting match in the last over. The outstanding performance of the match came from the Pakistani cricketer Imran Khan. He got a brilliant century in the universities' first innings in addition to taking four wickets. In the second, he led the counterattack which put them in a winning position, but after his dismissal there was a collapse and we won. On our side, good performances came from Solkar and Sudhir Naik, both of whom got centuries in the second innings. Bose batted well in both the innings and so did Mankad. Bose had a good match taking four wickets in the first innings with his off-spinners.

We continued our successful run against the counties by beating Gloucestershire by five wickets. Nichols and Stovold added 95 runs for the first wicket with Stovold as the dominant partner. Mike Proctor failed in the first innings being bowled by a Chandrasekhar googly. The wicket was not of much help to the South African Mike Proctor as he came bounding in and bowled off the wrong foot. He bowls sharp in-swingers and, for variety, goes round the wicket. The odd ball that goes straight through often yields a snick. That is how he got my wicket when I was 61. Abid was 54 not out to boost our score to 281, before Ajit declared the innings.

Proctor batted well in the second innings, hitting two huge sixes off Bedi in his 51. Set to score 195 runs to win, Naik and I put on 58 runs before I was declared caught by Knight, when the ball actually hit my foot as I danced down to off-spinner Graveney. Naik also played well, including an unforgettable shot, when he crashed a Proctor bouncer through the covers. Ajit Wadekar made the issue safe for us with a commanding 76. Just as in the first Test, we were going to the second Test with two successive victories.

Ajit Wadekar lost the toss which wasn't unexpected. Dennis Amiss and David Lloyd, making his Test debut, put on 116 runs before Solkar dived in front of him to catch Lloyd off Prasanna for 46. That was the only wicket to fall that day as Amiss and Edrich plundered runs on a beautiful track. Amiss played some great shots. His cover-drive was magnificent and he was 187 at the end of the day's play, with Edrich on 96. Prasanna struck a big blow for us when he got Amiss leg-before for 188. From the other end, Bedi dealt similarly with Edrich who missed his century by only four runs. His impetuosity got the better of him as he tried to pull a ball which was not short enough for the shot. Fletcher, the first Test centurion, fell to Bedi, but that was the end of our success for a long time. Mike Denness and Tony Greig scored centuries and added 202 runs. Denness walked down the track often to play the spinners, whereas Greig, with his height, did not need to do so. During the Amiss-Edrich partnership of 221 runs we had lost the services of our trump card, Chandrasekhar, who injured his thumb trying to stop a hard drive from Amiss, when he was just beginning to bowl well.

Funnily, during the massive Denness-Greig partnership, Bedi continued to flight the ball unnecessarily. The batsmen either stepped out and drove him or lay back and cut and pulled him. Ajit should have taken him off but he persisted with him and the batsmen made merry. Bishen has said that he will not stop giving the ball air just because the batsmen are attacking. However, the situation was such that he should have bowled tight. There was no question of buying the wickets and England were all out for 629, leaving us with an hour's batting.

Farokh, who had kept wicket all through the innings, opened with me and typically went on the attack. The way he batted in that last hour gave the impression that he wanted to score those 630 runs in an hour. To the crowd it was thrilling. To me it was horrifying. We survived the hour and were 51 without loss at the end of the day.

The next day Farokh reached his 50 in a flash. He was batting responsibly this time, though still playing his shots. I reached 49 and then was frustrated when Farokh refused easy singles thrice in an over. When Farokh is at the non-striker's end a quick single is out of the question. Even after the bowler has delivered the ball he is near the stumps and does not bother to back up a few yards down the wicket. For a cricketer who plays limited-overs cricket in England regularly, this is an unpardonable habit. When he is batting, he is always looking for quick singles but when he is at the non-striker's end, his attitude is one of indifference and inertia.

In my frustration, I tried to turn a ball from Old down to third man but the ball moved a fraction and I succeeded only in edging it to Knott. I was out for 49 and our partnership had yielded 131 runs. Farokh carried on, driving and pulling the

England bowlers but at 86 played too soon at Old and gave Denness at cover an easy catch. Vishwanath scored 52 and Solkar 43. The rest didn't offer much resistance and we were all out for 302. Chandrasekhar, despite his injured thumb, went in to bat, which was quite unnecessary. There was no question of avoiding the follow-on. We were only exposing our main bowler to the risk of further injury. In the one over possible after being asked to follow on we were two for no loss.

The next day we were entertained to lunch by the Lalvani brothers who are great cricket fans and always entertain visiting Indian teams and present them with wonderful souvenirs. They came to England when they were very young and are extremely successful and respected businessmen in London. During the lunch which the whole team attended, the topic was only whether we could avoid an innings defeat and force a draw. There were still two more days of play left and a draw would have been a great achievement. All this speculation was fruitless as the events of the next day were to prove.

Arnold started with two huge out-swingers, followed by an in-swinger which hit Engineer on the pads as he played forward. Farokh stands a fair bit outside the batting crease and then he had stretched forward, so it must have required tremendous eyesight to give him out. Later Farokh claimed that he had even got a faint edge. Wadekar was bowled by Old and Vishwanath was out to a beauty which Knott snapped up in front of first slip. Patel got one which lifted and brushed his glove on its way to the wicket-keeper. Eknath received a bouncer from Old, which he tried to hook but which bounced off his head. He hit the next bouncer over the deep fine-leg boundary for a six. At the end of the over, Solkar came down the wicket to ask me to stay and help him save the game. That was not to be as I was leg-before to an Arnold break-back. By the time I had removed my leg-guards, Madan and Abid had joined me in the pavilion. And before you knew it, we were all out for 42. England had won the test by an innings and 285 runs, and with that the series.

Lots of theories have been advanced about our being skittled our for a paltry 42 runs, when on that same wicket England made 629 and India 302 runs. The simple answer is that Arnold and Old bowled five good balls which got our top five batsmen out. After that there was no resistance from the tail-enders. We were skittled out before lunch, and champagne was flowing in the English dressing room to celebrate England's victory in the series.

The day after the Test we were supposed to attend the Indian High Commissioner's party. We were also invited to a party to bid farewell to the State Bank of India's London manager and to welcome his successor. Our team consisted of at least eight players who were employed in the State Bank and so we accepted the invitation for the function which we were to attend from 5.45 to 6.15 p.m. and then proceed for the High Commissioner's party. As we came down the elevator to gather in the hotel lounge before leaving, we saw our manager, Lt. Col. Adhikari, talking worriedly over the telephone. His conversation went on for about half an hour. We had no idea of the reason for his agitated look and the numerous telephone calls he made then. Finally, instead of leaving at 5 o'clock we started for the bank function at about 5.40 and reached the function around 6. But before we left the coach, we were told to stay at the function only for ten minutes and leave for the High Commissioner's party.

At the bank function a few London-based Indian journalists asked us the reasons for being out for 42 runs. When we explained that it was a game they turned round and accused us of having had fights amongst us, and of being drunk and various other misdemeanours. A few players ignored these accusations but others gave a verbal lashing to the journalists. I was watching all this quietly. I heard two of the journalists say, 'We'll see that these chaps are brought down. What do they think of themselves?' As we were leaving the bank function there was the usual cluster for group photographs and this went on for about ten minutes. The resident Indian journalists also couldn't resist the temptation of being photographed with the cricketers.

By the time we got into the bus it was already 6.30, the time we were expected to be present at the High Commissioner's party. Fortunately, the manager and treasurer, Mr B.C. Mohanty, had gone there earlier to explain to the High Commissioner that we would be a few minutes late. Normally, the distance between the venue of the bank function and the High Commissioner's residence takes about fifteen to thirty minutes by car. Our coach got delayed in the traffic and we reached the entrance of the Kensington Gardens around 7 p.m. The entrance was too narrow for the big coach to go in and all of us had to get off and rush past a few houses until we came to the High Commissioner's residence. Ajit, Venkataraghavan and Farokh had rushed in while Vishwanath and I were, as usual, last in the line. When Ajit had gone in we were still in the driveway of the house. By the time we reached the porch, Ajit was returning, crestfallen and looking grim. When we asked what the matter was, Ajit replied, 'He has asked us to get out.' We realised that Ajit was referring to the High Commissioner, so we all trooped back to the coach which was waiting outside. I will never forget the look of astonishment on the face of Derek Allen, our coach driver, who said: 'Don't tell me it's the bloody wrong address!'

There was a lot of excited conversation going on with everybody wanting to talk at the same time. It was in the coach that I learnt what had really happened. Some of the boys said that we should not go in for the party. By this time Lt. Col. Hemu Adhikari had rushed into the coach and was exhorting the boys to return to the party. Some of the senior players tried to explain that since the host had asked us to get out, there was no question of our going back. The others felt that since the captain had been insulted, nobody should go back. All this while, Ajit sat around calmly smoking a cigarette. Meanwhile, somebody from the High Commission came and said that the High Commissioner was sorry and had requested the boys to come back. None of us was, however, in the mood to comply. Lt. Col. Adhikari was in tears and he resorted to ordering the players to go back to the party. Still, no one budged. Finally, it was Venkataraghavan who said that we should go back to the party. After a few minutes everybody got up and went back. The High Commissioner embraced Ajit and apologised to him for losing his temper. This time I was among the first to get in because I didn't want to miss this part as I had missed the beginning. The resident Indian journalists were straining their ears near the High Commissioner to hear his conversation with Ajit.

Donald Carr and Tony Lewis were also at the party and the boys spoke to them more than the others around. Though very few accepted the snacks that were being served, most of us accepted something to drink. The incident was another opportunity for the Indian journalist friends to pass comments. They sent back reports that we had insulted the High Commissioner and refused to take any drinks and refreshments served at the party. I suppose, having to stay in London, they couldn't afford to write against the High Commissioner. Also, the fact that they had been snubbed by some of the players barely half an hour ago was too fresh in their minds. And hence the vengeful tirade against the Indian team.

I really wonder how we could have insulted the High Commissioner. True, we were late by about forty minutes and for that deserved a rocket, whatever the reasons for our delayed arrival. As a matter of fact, Ajit's first words to the High Commissioner were, 'We are sorry for being late.' And how can one stay at a party where the host himself asks us to get out? The High Commissioner could have given us a ticking off later on. After all, in his position he has to tackle so many problems that he ought to be able to keep cool, whatever the circumstances. Actually his blowing up came as a surprise because when he had visited us during the Manchester Test, he looked extremely mild and keen on cricket. As for the accusation that we didn't accept the drinks or snacks, it is a blatant lie. I know for a fact that almost everybody did. A lot of the boys left the party later without sipping the drinks, but the newspapers reports said that the entire team had refused refreshments.

Poor Bishen Bedi was reported to have said uncomplimentary things about the High Commissioner in the coach, while all Bishen said was that 'If we had won, and turned up late there would have been no problem. But just because we've lost, we get the stick.' All said and done, it was a sad affair and got a lot of unhealthy publicity. Later on, the players agreed that the High Commissioner was after all human and so blew his top. When we met him at another function later he was his usual jovial self and there was no tension at all between us.

What we didn't understand was why the manager kept on telephoning in spite of knowing that it was delaying our departure for the two functions. The mystery was solved the following day.

We were due to play the Indian Gymkhana in a one-day friendly game which was unfortunately washed out. During the lunch interval Lt. Col. Adhikari called us solemnly and announced that Sudhir Naik had been accused of shoplifting and he had made efforts to hush up the matter, but unfortunately it had still appeared in the evening newspapers. That was the reason why he had delayed the coach's departure for the State Bank function and the High Commissioner's reception, while he spoke to the various authorities on the telephone.

This came to us as a bolt from the blue and suddenly the reason for Sudhir's absence at the previous evening's function became clear. Some of the boys insisted that he should be sent back to India. Yet others, like myself, wanted to hear his story and then decide on what should be done. In any case, the manager had spoken to the Cricket Control Board authorities in India and was going to be told the course of action to follow.

I have known Sudhir Naik ever since we played against each other in shorts in tennis ball tournaments between teams of young boys living in the different blocks of buildings in our locality in Bombay. I was shocked and was positive that this was all a mistake. I didn't ask him at all about what had happened but later he told me his story, and I had no doubt in my mind that he was innocent.

He had gone out shopping on that fateful afternoon in London while a few of us had gone to see a movie. Some of the players had given money to buy some underwear, toilet goods and other things. Before he had gone to the Marks & Spencer department store on Oxford Street, he had bought two pairs of slacks from a boutique, and was carrying them in a paper bag with a handle. From there he went to the department store and selected about twenty pairs of socks, put these into

the paper bag and moved on to the counter to the sales girl
to pay for the socks which he gave to the girl to pack for him.
Suddenly he remembered that four of the players had asked
him to buy underwear for them. He went to another counter
to buy these items, where the sales girl put his purchases in
a paper bag and gave it to him. Now, Marks & Spencer don't
give paper bags with handles and Sudhir had to hold it in his
other free hand when he went back to the socks counter to
pay for them and take delivery of the socks. Since he couldn't
possibly hold it in both his hands, he requested the sales girl
to put the parcel of socks in the paper bag. While doing this,
the sales girl noticed a pair of socks under the slacks he had
purchased from the boutique. Sudhir told me that when he
took the socks from the shelf he had put all of them in the
bag along with the slacks, and had taken them out to put them
on the cash counter when he went to pay for the socks. In doing
this two pairs of socks had apparently slipped under the pair
of trousers and was overlooked by him. It was this pair which
he was accused of having stolen.

In any case, it is difficult to believe that a man who can
pay for twenty pairs of socks will not pay for two pairs. The
department store authorities were adamant and wouldn't listen
to his explanation. It was at this stage that Sudhir was given,
what I think, a bit of wrong advice. He was asked to plead guilty
before the Magistrate on the assurance that the case would be
over, and due care would be taken to ensure that the matter
received no publicity at all. If he pleaded 'not guilty', the case
would go on and who would bear the expenses? The attitude
of those concerned should have been, 'to hell with the expenses,
we'll go ahead and get our man a good lawyer for his defence'.
But then Sudhir was not given a chance even to think and he
was hustled to plead guilty and in the process got a black mark

which will be difficult to erase. In cases like this, the contracts which the player signs with the Cricket Control Board to keep mum is a severe handicap. There was thus no way in which Sudhir could explain the true facts through the press, though it was very sympathetic. The result of this was that he was not able to clear doubts in the minds of people in England and at home.

I asked Lt. Col. Adhikari to let me allow Sudhir to share my room for the rest of the tour. He agreed even though the practice was not to have players from the same state sharing a room. But in this case he made an exception. I intercepted a number of anonymous telephone calls to Sudhir, obviously from people who were out to give him hell. Sudhir confessed later that because of the stigma attached to his name, even though it was entirely wrong, made him contemplate taking his own life. But when he saw on television the former U.S. President, Richard Nixon, cheerfully waving after the Watergate scandal, he thought to himself, 'If this man can take so much, why can't I? Particularly because I know that I am innocent.'

It speaks volumes for Sudhir's concentration and determination that he got runs after this traumatic experience. In the game against Nottinghamshire he got 73 and 68, Vishwanath scored a century, and Mankad and Abid batted well. His consistency earned Sudhir Naik a Test cap, and Mankad was brought into the side in place of Brijesh Patel to bolster the middle-order batting for the third and last Test of the series at Edgbaston (Birmingham).

Ajit won the toss and elected to bat. However, rain washed out play on the first day but when the game got going, it began disastrously for India. Geoff Arnold's first ball to me was pitched outside the off-stump and cut back in sharply. I tried to withdraw my bat, but the ball seemed to be drawn by a magnet, hit my gloves and went to wicketkeeper Knott. For the first time I was out to the first ball in a Test match and also found a 'duck' against my name for the second time in a Test! It was an extremely disappointing way to get out.

Farokh was the only one who offered some resistance, and was 64 not out in our score of 165. Any team that bats for less than three hours doesn't deserve any piece of luck and that was the case with us.

Amiss and David Lloyd ground us down before Amiss played what appeared to be an uncharacteristic uppish drive to be caught for 79. David Lloyd and Mike Denness then rubbed the salt in with a vengeance. Lloyd remained unbeaten with 214, Denness and later Fletcher also contributed handsomely. David Lloyd swept and drove well while Denness played elegant shots off the front-foot.

I was on a 'king pair' when we had to follow on 204 runs behind England. However, I met the first ball in the second innings bang in the middle of the bat, which was reassuring. I pushed one to cover and got off the mark. It was a tremendous relief. I was, however, not destined to stay long. A ball from Chris Old moved sharply away, nicked my bat and, of course, it was useless hoping that Knott would drop such a simple catch. He didn't. I had scored four runs, three runs short of the 1,000 runs on the tour mark. I cursed my luck because this was the last first-class match of the tour and I would never make it. How unlucky can one get!

Sudhir Naik played well after an uncertain start and so did Ashok Mankad. They added 87 runs for the fifth wicket, out of which Sudhir got 77, before he was surprisingly given out leg-before. Engineer scored a defiant 33, but it was hopeless and we lost by an innings and 76 runs, to lose the three-match series 3-0.

When I was out first ball, I had gone without looking at Bill Alley, the former Australian cricketer, who was making his debut as a Test umpire. Later on, he came and jokingly scolded me for walking. 'My first Test, my first decision off the first ball, and you don't give me the opportunity to raise my finger. You walk!' He also had the distinction of giving a decision off the last ball of the Test when he declared Farokh Engineer out leg-before.

It was a totally disastrous series and the tour was one of the worst I had made. There was no such thing as team spirit. Instead there were a lot of petty squabbles, which didn't do anybody any good. The incidents which gave the team such a bad name didn't help. It was all extremely frustrating.

We had still to play two one-day international matches. In the first we scored a record 275, which England overtook losing only seven wickets. Ajit and Brijesh Patel scored fluently, after Naik and I had put on 44 runs in the first seven overs. John Edrich led the England chase with 70 runs, but his innings was nowhere as good as Brijesh's; yet, he was given the 'Man of the Match' award. In the next game we were beaten by six wickets, with Fletcher getting the Man of the Match award.

These defeats completed our tale of woes. There were reports from Bombay that Ajit's home had been stoned. This was difficult to believe as Ajit lives in an apartment on the top floor of a high building. But we were really concerned and unhappy when we learnt that the concrete bat erected in Indore following our victories in the West Indies and England in 1971 had been defaced. We sensed that the mood of the people back home would be ugly. We had left for the tour with high hopes, and cricket-lovers in the country were expecting us to do well. Fortunately nothing untoward happened on our return and we were received well by a small number of people.

15

The Windies, Again

THE WEST INDIES WERE DUE TO TOUR INDIA IN THE 1974-75 SEASON and everybody was keen to have a couple of months' rest before beginning to train and get fit for the series. I had to delay this process because I was getting ready for one of the most important events of my life. On 23 September 1974 Marshniel Mehrotra became Mrs Sunil Gavaskar and almost overnight I was properly hooked. Meanwhile, Bombay began the quest to regain the Ranji Trophy with a match against Saurashtra at Porbandar. I told the Bombay Cricket Association that I would be unavailable for the quarterfinals of the Duleep Trophy.

Unknown to me a lot of dramatic events took place during my week-long honeymoon. Firstly, Ajit Wadekar was dropped from the West Zone team for the Duleep Trophy. The reason given for this apparently was that he was not in form and didn't deserve a place. Imagine an India captain only six weeks before the new season dropped from the zonal side! One could understand the decision to strip him off his captaincy but to drop him from the side altogether was ridiculous. Ajit was among the top two batsmen in the country then, the other being Vishwanath. Understandably this was a blow to Ajit and to avoid further embarrassment he announced his retirement from first-class cricket and earned a benefit match. Actually, he had been in correspondence with the West Indies Cricket Board since 1973 for a benefit match. The 1971 team to the West Indies led by Ajit was a very popular one and the Windies Board agreed to play two one-day fixtures for Ajit Wadekar's benefit.

The mantle of captaincy for the West Zone team for the Duleep Trophy matches fell on Ashok Mankad. We won the quarterfinal against East Zone by virtue of the first innings lead. I played my first match of the season in the semifinals of the Duleep Trophy against Central Zone at Nagpur. In a low-scoring match we won by 64 runs and earned the right to clash with South Zone at Hyderabad.

The South Zone team is an extremely well-balanced side and one has to play twice as well to beat them. In this case, on a spongy wicket, Chandrasekhar, Venkataraghavan and Prasanna ran through our batting. By the time the South's turn to bat came, the wicket had improved considerably. The story was repeated in our second innings and Venkataraghavan once again won the Duleep Trophy for South Zone.

For two seasons I had been Wadekar's deputy for Bombay and I naturally expected to be asked to lead the side after Ajit announced his retirement. Imagine my shock when I learnt that I had been passed over by the same selection committee which had only a month ago appointed me vice-captain for the season. Ajit retired after playing only one game and, when the selection committee met, the chairman's casting vote put me out after there was a stalemate between the four selectors. It was hard for me to understand the logic of this decision, especially after I had led Bombay to outright victories, admittedly against comparatively weaker teams.

Captaining a Bombay side is one of the easiest things in the world. Everybody knows exactly what he is expected to do. Besides, the camaraderie that exists between the players has to be seen to be believed. Yes, there are occasions when the team is in trouble, but these instances when the captain has to really face problems are pretty rare. More importantly, most of the members of the team are captains of their respective club sides, and there is no lack of experienced players to give advice when the occasion arises.

Thinking back now, my disappointment was mainly due to the fact that I had been appointed vice-captain earlier. Of course, there have been numerous occasions when the vice-captain had been bypassed for another player. Ashok, who got the job, was more senior to me and had longer experience as a captain. I am sure he must have been disappointed when I was appointed Ajit's deputy in the first place. I have always believed that the team comes first and I did not allow my personal feelings to interfere with my batting. The important thing was to see that Bombay regained the Ranji Trophy, which we had lost the previous year after winning it for fifteen years.

The West Indies team came to India with an awesome reputation. Leading them was Clive Lloyd who had with him Andy Roberts, the fastest bowler in the world then. The visitors opened their tour with a game against West Zone at Pune. Though they lost Fredericks' on the first ball, Lloyd, Richards and Greenidge showed their appreciation of the wicket by scoring plenty of runs. Richards got a century (102 not out), while Lloyd missed his by only four runs. However, the start was electrifying. Fredericks was surprised by Salgaonkar's pace and the West Indies opener fell to a gloved catch to me at second slip. Then, Rowe was also deceived by Ghavri's pace and fell on his wicket trying to hook. Both the batsmen were out before scoring. Greenidge showed his aggression by hitting Salgaonkar for three boundaries, but when Ghavri pitched one short he skied à hook to square-leg where Solkar, running from leg-slip, failed to take the catch. He went on to score 66. We had just half an hour's batting and Andy Roberts showed his pace in his four overs. Naik, however, drove his way to 22 runs.

Next day I found the ball going sweetly off the bat. When Roberts pitched short, I hooked him for a six. This shot went almost parallel to the ground, hit the cement wall and rebounded back half way on to the ground. It was a great thrill, for everything I did clicked, right from my footwork to the timing of the shots. When Boyce bounced one at me, I was in position and again cleared the boundary, this time the ball just brushing Roberts' fingertips on the boundary. When the spinners came on, it was like butter which I love so much and in trying to get this butter, I was run out when Naik cut the ball and called for a quick single.

Kanitkar carried on in his calm, unhurried way, while Naik played some polished shots. After Naik's dismissal, Ashok Mankad picked up the threads and scored 69. In the hope of making the match interesting Ashok declared 24 runs behind the West Indies, but there was no response from Lloyd and the Windies used the time for batting practice. It was only when Naik who is not a regular bowler came on to bowl that Lloyd declared, leaving us two hours' batting. My left thigh which had been bruised by a scorcher from Roberts, prevented me from opening the innings, but Naik used the opportunity to score

68 not out after being dropped off the first ball he received. He displayed his ability to stand up to pace and score runs. It was an impressive innings.

There was a bombshell just before the selectors met to name the team for the first Test. The President of the Board of Control asked the selectors not to consider Bishen Singh Bedi for the first Test for disciplinary reasons. Bedi's offence was reportedly a television appearance in England after our team had left. Let me say quite frankly that Bishen certainly wasn't on top of my popularity chart as well as on a lot of his other teammates on the 1974 tour. His behaviour towards the captain, to put it mildly, wasn't exactly respectful. Bishen was generally impatient and intolerant with the rest of the boys. Despite this, the Board President's action was shocking. Apparently Bishen had not replied to about seventeen letters and cables sent to him to appear before the Inquiry Committee that had been set up. So, without waiting for Bishen's explanation, the President had asked the selectors not to consider him for the first Test.

This was a big letdown for Indian cricket because there is no doubt that Bishen is the best left-arm spinner in the world today. To go into the first Test of the series against such a formidable team as the West Indies without one of our ace bowlers, wasn't exactly a boost to the morale of the team. To top it all, Padmakar Shivalkar, who must be the second-best left-arm spinner in the world, was overlooked and Rajinder Goel was selected. Year after year Shivalkar has been taking an average of forty wickets in the Ranji Trophy and the only thing that stood between him and a Test cap was the presence of Bishen Bedi. However, with Bishen Bedi out of reckoning, it was expected that Shivalkar would be selected. Despite this, we went into the Test with high hopes because the Bangalore wicket was not expected to be very helpful to the West Indies fast bowlers. On the eve of the match I was told by the selectors that I was the vice-captain. But, for some reason, I was asked to keep the news confidential. This surprised me very much because I didn't understand why I should have been chosen vice-captain if the matter was kept confidential. I am afraid this cloak-and-dagger business did not make much sense to me.

At the introduction ceremony preceding the first day's play, too, I was asked to go down the line and not stand next to Tiger Pataudi, the captain, as I should have done. This hurt me because I don't believe that a vice-captain has to stand next to the captain. Yet when in the bustle of the match I did so, I was asked to go elsewhere. Frankly, Vishwanath and I love standing last in the line for the introduction ritual. We've always done that. So even though Vishwanath knew I was the vice-captain he laughed when I came and stood next to him at the end of the line. With a grin he asked me, 'Demoted?' Yes, I was, just because there was nobody with the guts to say: 'Right now, he's the vice-captain and he should stand next to the skipper.' So, there I was.

Heavy overnight rain delayed the start of the Test until twenty-two minutes before lunch. Pataudi, back in the saddle after five years, won the toss but asked the West Indies to bat. Solkar should have got a wicket in his first over, but Prasanna dropped Greenidge before he had opened his account. Fredericks retired hurt as he twisted his ankle in trying to pull a short one from Chandrasekhar. Kalicharan took his place and looked confident right from the start. Greenidge, however, had another life when Prasanna dropped a hot return catch. Both the batsmen scored a run-a-minute and batted with complete freedom until a misunderstanding between them caused Greenidge to be run out. I was fielding at short mid-on and anticipated the shot and was already starting for the ball. Seeing this Kalicharan refused to run but, expecting that the ball could still beat me, went on. Greenidge was not, however, ready and when he decided to make a dash for it, I had picked the ball up and returned it to the bowler. Greenidge failed to make it. So the first wicket fell at 177 and Greenidge missed a century in his first Test innings by only seven runs. Richards was out soon afterwards when he drove Chandrasekhar straight to Prasanna at mid-off, and this time Prasanna made no mistake. Lloyd and Kalicharan, however, carried the score to 212 for two at the end of the day.

Play began again after lunch on the second day, and Venkataraghavan and Chandrasekhar used the wicket splendidly to dismiss the West Indies for 289. Kalicharan, 64 overnight, added 60 runs out of a total of 77 runs scored. It was batting of the highest class and he fully deserved his century (124). With the ball turning and popping, Kalicharan gave us a tremendous batting lesson. The ball dropped dead at his feet when he played defensively forward. But when he hit the ball it invariably went to the boundary. A six off Chandrasekhar showed his quick reflexes. He was preparing for a defensive shot when he heard the no-ball call from the umpire and he changed his shot to swing it over the mid-wicket fence.

With seventy-five minutes of batting left, we had to face Roberts on a damp wicket, which was not a pleasant proposition at all. I got two boundaries in his first over – a cover-drive and a hook to the vacant long-leg position. In his next over Roberts made a ball rise awkwardly, hitting me very painfully on the wrist. The numbness was acute and I was not able to flex the wrist again. Anyway, I wasn't very lucky. I flicked Holder hard, the ball hitting Richards on his thigh and bouncing away, but Richards showed amazing reflexes and dived to his left to take a catch inches off the ground. The ball, after ricocheting off

173

his thigh, was almost on the other side of the wicket. I couldn't believe my eyes when Richards came up with the ball. Instead of getting four runs I had lost my wicket! That was Richards' second catch. Earlier he had caught Engineer off Roberts at the same position. Hemant Kanitkar was making his Test debut and the first ball from Andy Roberts, which was a real scorcher, hit him bang on the gloves as he played defensively. To this day I wonder how nothing happened to his fingers. The blow was sickening even to me, at the non-striker's end, but Hemant carried on as if nothing had happened. He batted really bravely in his first Test innings despite the punishment he received. When he came in, his chest was black and blue from bruises he had received. He also survived a run-out after being stranded at the same end with Vishwanath. How he beat the bowler's throw to the wicketkeeper beats me. But he was there and when he returned to the pavilion his face was as expressionless as ever.

The next day Kanitkar added 89 runs with Vishwanath who fell leg-before to Lance Gibbs for 29. Kanitkar was batting on 64 at lunch. But with the first ball after the interval Barrett had him stumped when Kanitkar went down the track to play the bowler on the half-volley. Our middle-order batting caved in after this, and only Abid with a bright 49, and Prasanna with a cheeky 23, enabled us to end 29 runs short of the West Indies total.

Murray opened with Greenidge and got a pair, being leg-before to Abid. Greenidge and Kalicharan, however, were equal to the task. Greenidge who hit Chandrasekhar for a huge six out of the ground was the dominant partner. However, Kalicharan and Richards fell in quick succession, but the turning point of the game came when Lloyd pummelled his way to a glorious 163. In spite of being an opponent, I couldn't but admire the superb batting of the tall, gangling Super Cat as he swept and swung away merrily. Greenidge also got the century he had missed in the first innings. During this partnership we lost Farokh Engineer, when he was hit above the eye by a ball from Prasanna, which bounced unexpectedly. Boyce came in with the intention of blasting our spinners but, in trying to hit Venkataraghavan, be skied the ball to Pataudi who brought off a good catch but dislocated his ring finger and had to leave the field.

I was fielding on the mid-wicket boundary at the time and I was already rushing in to congratulate Venkataraghavan for taking Boyce's wicket, when Pataudi left the field. The captain did not say whether he was coming back immediately or not; but I told Venkataraghavan that I was incharge and took over the task of setting the field. At the end of the over, Rajinder Goel came out to inform me that Tiger would not be returning immediately and that I should take charge. There were only a few minutes left before the tea break. After tea Lloyd was out to a superb catch by Eknath Solkar. Soon after, the West Indies captain declared at 356 for six, leaving us to make 386 runs in 390 minutes to win. When we began our second knock I sparred at an out-swinger from Boyce, snicked the ball to the wicketkeeper and was out for a duck. It was terrible that I should begin my career as Test skipper, even though a mere substitute, with a duck. Eknath Solkar was also out to a rash shot. And our innings ended three minutes before lunch with Engineer and Pataudi being unable to bat. Vishwanath and, to some extent, Brijesh Patel offered some resistance. Holder and Roberts were the wreckers-in-chief. We lost the test by 267 runs.

As Pataudi was unfit for the second Test I was appointed to take his place. When the news came, I was too stunned to believe it. Of course, I had ambitions of leading India but I never expected it then. Imagine me as captain! I was in a daze. Leading one's country, even if it was only for one Test! I started preparing myself mentally for a Test skipper's job which doesn't begin and end on the field. Since I had to lead India at Delhi, the country's capital, I had a lot of homework to do.

Before the Test, however, Bombay were to play Maharashtra in the Ranji Trophy Tournament at Nasik, but I was only thinking of the Delhi match. Ismail started Maharashtra's slide in the first over itself, getting Chetan Chauhan caught behind for zero. Maharashtra were 19 for four, but a fighting century by Yajuvendra Singh and a good knock by Vithal Joshi took them to 222. We had about eighty minutes batting left before the close and Pandurang Salgaonkar and Anwar Shaikh bowled some hostile overs. Salgaonkar bowled real quick, making the ball get up from the matting wicket. His direction was not so good and he wasted a lot of his energy bowling bouncers which went too high to do any damage, physical or psychological. Shaikh, on the other hand, bowled a steady length trying to make the best use of the new ball. Anwar was unlucky not to get higher honours. He is a fine bowler who can not only bowl for long spells but also one who never gives up. A fighter to the core.

I was facing Salgaonkar most of the time and, in trying to put down a ball just short of a length, I was hit on the glove when it kicked. I knew instantly that I had broken a finger and, as I crossed over for a single, I told the umpire of my injury. He wanted to know whether I wished to continue, and I said I wanted to, since there were only forty minutes left and Salgaonkar was likely to be encouraged if I retired. I held on till the end, playing with only one hand for most of the time. Luckily for me Madhu Gupte didn't bring on a spinner, which would have put me in a lot of trouble since I was playing with only one hand. The injury certainly wasn't Salgaonkar's fault. It was just my luck that my finger got jammed between the handle and the ball. After the x-ray, I rang up the Secretary of the Cricket Control Board, who asked me to come to Bombay immediately the next day. I didn't want to leave because our position was not secure. The next day Salgaonkar and Anwar didn't bowl half as well as on the previous evening, but we lost three wickets in the morning and slumped to 103 for four. Solkar batted despite high fever and Karsan Ghavri put on 156 runs for the sixth wicket. We had now taken a first innings lead. With the match safe, I left for Bombay the next morning.

My worst fears were confirmed when the doctors in Bombay told me that I couldn't play for at least three weeks. Dr Arun Samsi was very sympathetic, but he ruled out my playing in the Delhi Test. I was a little put off because Dr (Mrs) Nadkarni in Nasik had diplomatically told me not to worry and she had not given me any idea of the nature of the injury. However, they were very nice people and their prompt treatment and care helped the injury to heal very fast. But I had lost a golden opportunity of leading the country in a Test. I decided, however, to go to Delhi to watch the match. In Delhi, I couldn't get hold of any official of the Delhi & District Cricket Association and but for the fact that Sudhir Naik and Vishwanath obliged me with a ticket, I would have had to watch the match on television. When I did meet a senior official of the D.D.C.A. and told him of my predicament, he told me, 'You are famous, you don't need a complimentary ticket.' That was some consolation even if I did not get a ticket!

Before I went to Calcutta for the next Test, I had a workout session at the nets. I didn't feel too bad I went to Calcutta. There somehow I found that I couldn't even hold the bat in comfort, and I had no alternative but to rule myself out for the Calcutta Test too. During my three days' stay in Calcutta I noticed a singular lack of interest in getting my finger treated. Amalda who was, however, most helpful and turned up regularly, found that the doctors at the clinic were also busy watching the Test. I decided to return to Bombay for treatment instead of wasting my time in Calcutta. I left on the second day of the Test and so missed seeing Vishwanath's magnificent fighting century that put us on the road to victory.

I went to Madras for the fourth Test full of hopes of being fit to play. I had fielding practice on the first day and there was no trouble with the finger. Next day, the first ball I faced at the nets from Karsan Ghavri hit the same finger sickeningly and it ended my chances of playing the Test the next day. Within minutes the finger had swollen, even more than the first time when I was hurt at Nasik. Once again I had to seek medical assistance and renewed my acquaintance with Dr Ahmed who had treated me when I fractured a thumb playing against the M.C.C. at Madras. It was the ointment he gave me which enabled me to play in the Kanpur Test ten days later. And when I got runs there he sent me a cable congratulating me for playing with the bat and not with the thumb. Once again his calm, methodical manner helped me a lot as did the ointment. But I had missed three Tests. I did not want to take any more chances, so I got a special rubber padding put on the batting gloves and went to the nets. Fortunately, nothing happened at the nets and I was in the team for the Test at Bombay.

The Test was played at a new venue, the Wankhade Stadium, which had been constructed at an amazing speed and was ready in time for the big event. It was a magnificent sight when the curtains went up on the fifth Test in the New Year. The atmosphere was electric. If there is one crowd I positively love to play in front of, it's in Bombay. The average man in this home of cricket knows a lot more about the game than anywhere else in the country. This is especially true of the spectators in the north stands, occupied by Bombay's club cricketers who are always quick to appreciate and applaud a good game. For this reason, I lay great stress on the reactions of people in this particular part of the stands. Their praise or criticism is based on knowledge and experience of the game, which is of immense value to a cricketer. For the Bombay crowd good cricket is important and it does not matter whether it is from the home team or a visiting side. The applause will be there only for good cricket. At other places, there may be sections of people who will applaud only the home team but they are a minority here. Bombay crowds are also noted for their sense of humour which is not evident at other centres in India.

I was happy to be fit to play in the decisive Bombay Test. The series was level at this stage and the enthusiasm in the match was tremendous. Gerry Alexander, the West Indies manager, lodged a protest on the eve of the Test, that the wicket was under-prepared and unfit. This was a serious allegation, but some people in Bombay who were disappointed that the Brabourne Stadium was no longer the venue, were happy about the protest. I do not know how Gerry Alexander came to the conclusion about the wicket because 1,000 runs were scored after both sides had completed only one innings each.

Roy Fredericks set the tempo for the West Indies batting by blasting a century in under three hours. Unfortunately we had lost the services of Bedi within minutes of the start. Bishen had been troubled by a bad back and though he said he was fit he had to leave the field. However, when he returned, he was on the spot and got rid of Fredericks for 104. But he was not completely fit and it told on his bowling. Kalicharan made 98 before Vishwanath in the slips took a fine low catch off Ghavri. Lloyd, who was missed thrice, was unbeaten with 64 at the end of the day and the West Indies were 309 for three.

In the first over of the next morning, Solkar let a ball slip through his fingers and Lloyd got another life. Nobody could make much impression on the West Indies captain thereafter and he went on to score a double century. In the process he hit two huge sixes into the Garware Pavilion. When Clive reached his double century, an enthusiastic fan chased by a lot of policemen ran on to the field to congratulate him. The policemen caught him and handled him pretty roughly. This was the signal for the crowd to voice their protest and slogans were raised against the minions of the law. Soon tempers rose and good sense seemed to vanish as the crowd started tearing up benches and the fence. A part of the stand was set on fire which, however, was quickly brought under control.

There is no doubt that the police action against the lone enthusiast had provoked this outburst. What I can't understand is why the policemen rushed on to the field in such large numbers to apprehend a solitary intruder. In any case, there was no way he could have escaped from the stadium. The police could have waited for his return just inside the boundary. Yes, if a large number of intruders had invaded the field then, I suppose, the police would have been justified to move in to disperse them. But, in this instance, it was wholly unnecessary.

The flare-up occurred during tea and there was no prospect of any further play that day. Murray was not out with 91 and the next day his partnership with Lloyd was worth 250 runs. Lloyd remained unbeaten with 242 at the declaration which came at 604 for 6.

Farokh Engineer was out for a duck to Julien in the half hour before lunch when we batted a second time. Thereafter, Eknath Solkar batted confidently to support me in a 168-run stand. I was out for 86, with just five minutes' play left. It was an innings that gave me great satisfaction, because I had had doubts whether I should have played in the Test at all, since I hadn't played first-class cricket for about two months after my injury. Surprisingly, I had fifteen fours in my innings. I got a bit bogged down after my 50 and suffered from cramps in my left forearm after tea. Still it was good to be among runs in Test cricket.

I do not look at the scoreboard when I am batting nor do I look at the time. However, I do have a general idea about my score. On this occasion I was misled by a shout from the stands for a six and I thought that I was on 94. Being aware that there was time only for one or two overs and seeing the vacant space between extra-cover and point, I thought I had room to cut the ball through the gap, but missed and was bowled.

Eknath went on to score his first Test century the next day after giving all of us some terribly anxious moments in the 90s. Vishwanath was again among runs but was out when he was 95. With Anshuman Gaekwad unbeaten on 51, we were 373 for six wickets, needing 32 runs to avoid the follow-on. Anshuman went in the first over and Tiger struggled, but Karsan Ghavri and Bishen Bedi avoided the follow-on and we were all out for 406.

With a lead of 198 runs the West Indies unleashed some super shots and thrilled the crowd. Lloyd, in particular, played a hurricane innings of 37 and Vivian Richards played some incredible shots to score 39 in thirty minutes before Lloyd declared at 205 for three.

Our second innings started on a disastrous note with Farokh edging a ball on to his wicket to get a pair. Andy Roberts, bowling at a furious pace, got one up off a length to get me caught off the shoulder of the bat for 18. Our biggest hope, Vishwanath, was bowled by a beauty from Holder, and at close we were a hopeless 53 for three.

Seventy-five minutes after lunch the next day the West Indies won the Test to clinch the rubber. Gaekwad again batted very stubbornly for 42 runs and Brijesh Patel scored a sparkling 73 not out. Apart from Holder's bowling the only thing of interest was a girl running up to Brijesh and, in spite of his best efforts to avoid her, planting a kiss on his cheek. Brijesh had a very interesting story to tell after that, but I won't mention it here because I do not want to deny him the pleasure of recounting his story if he ever writes his autobiography. The Windies also played two one-day games before leaving for Sri Lanka and Pakistan.

I now turned to concentrate on Bombay regaining the Ranji Trophy. With the finger troubling me again, I was never in form and struggled for runs until the final against Karnataka, to whom we had lost in the previous year.

Ashok Mankad and Ramnath Parker were in top form and Ashok especially was batting superbly. Before the final he had hit three successive centuries. Prasanna, who seems to have a knack for winning tossess, chose to bat on a wicket which looked a bit green. Karsan Ghavri worked up a lively pace and only Vishwanath was able to stand up to him with confidence. I have a sneaking suspicion that Vijay Kumar was testing my ability as a slip fielder. I had caught him in the slips in almost every match we had played. This time, instead of a snick, he tried to swing Ghavri away to leg, but only gloved the ball behind the wicketkeeper, and I had to run back a few steps to catch it. Vishwanath was out the next morning without adding to his overnight score of 144. The ball had, however, gone off his thigh and was not an edge, though the umpire thought so. Karnataka's score of 240 didn't look impressive at all.

In the hour before lunch we scored 52 without loss but the last ball before lunch from Chandrasekhar was disastrous for me. It popped up from a length and struck me on the index finger which I had broken twice earlier in the season. That was enough to cause it to swell but I was fortunate that this time, I did not suffer a fracture even though the swelling was enormous and it was very painful.

I delayed going to the hospital. Within an hour we lost four wickets for 129 and I walked out to bat again. Ashok Mankad came up and said he would try and keep the strike as much as possible so that my injured thumb was not further damaged. But, at 147, he was out when he mistimed a pull and was caught at square-leg. Karsan Ghavri who followed him was most uncomfortable against Prasanna but showed great determination to stay at the wicket. We added 97 runs during which I was hit on the finger three times more, all by Chandrasekhar's googlies which were jumping off the pitch. But both Prasanna and Chandrasekhar began to tire towards the end of the day, and we ended just five short of the Karnataka total. There were innumerable interruptions during the day's play because after every boundary stroke the crowd invaded the field. This was most annoying as we required every bit of concentration against the guiles of Prasanna and Chandrasekhar.

The next day, though we lost Ghavri, Tandon and Bandiwadekar early, Abdul Ismail kept me company. Ismail has a most ungainly stance but, like all bowlers, he hates to lose his wicket and he stubbornly resisted Prasanna and Chandrasekhar. Once, after being rapped on the pads several times in one over, he swung Prasanna over mid-on for a six. Prasanna and Chandrasekhar, however, didn't have other bowlers to back them up while one of them rested. In sheer desperation, Prasanna brought on Lakshminarayan who got Ismail and Shivalkar with his leg-spinners, leaving me stranded four short of a century. Bombay were all out for 305.

When Karnataka batted again, Solkar, bowling his seamers, got rid of Vishwanath with a ball that kept low, but Brijesh Patel attacked the bowling with his usual gusto and reached 50 in as much time. At that score, Eknath Solkar, bowling spinners this time, made one pop up and turn prodigiously. Wicketkeeper Bandiwadekar took an excellent catch to dismiss him. The Karnataka batting collapsed and they were all out for 215. Set to score 115 to win, Ashok and Ajit Pai added 98 runs for their unbroken fourth wicket stand, to bring the Ranji Trophy back to Bombay. Once again the Bombay team made a happy picture holding aloft the Ranji Trophy. The new stadium at Bangalore had brought luck to Karnataka the previous year and with it the Ranji Trophy. The new stadium in Bombay had been equally lucky for us, and the Ranji Trophy was back with us for the twenty-fifth time in forty years.

In six matches I had failed to score a century and this was the second successive year that I had not reached three figures in a single game in the Ranji Trophy.

Alan Knott — Fitness fanatic, who made wicket-keeping look so easy.

Andy Roberts — The quietest fast bowler in the world.

Asif Iqbal — Swift runner between the wickets,
a charmer on the field.

Bishan Bedi — Floats like a butterfly, stings like a bee.

B.S. Chandrashekhar — "Wicked" taking arm of India.

E.A.S. Prasanna — The smiling "assassin".

Clive Lloyd — Supercat. Cricket's real gentleman.

Derek Underwood — 'Deadly' on the field, perfect gentleman off it.

Glenn Turner — Perfection combined with run-hunger.

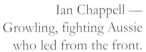

Ian Chappell —
Growling, fighting Aussie
who led from the front.

Greg Chappell — Mr. Elegance
on and off the field.

G.R. Vishwanath — The supreme stylist little man with a big heart.

(below) Ian Botham — Big, beefy and the best all-rounder in the world.

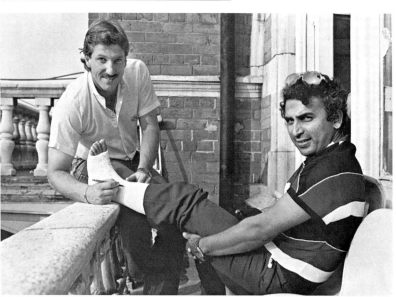

Javed Miandad — Great improviser

Jeff Thomson — Pace like lightning.

John Snow — England's hit man of the early 70s.

Kapil Dev — The most natural cricketer in the world.

Mohinder Amarnath — Courage, thy name is 'Jimmy'.

P.K. Shivalkar — Honest trier
who missed out.

Rajinder Goel —
Simply unlucky.

Richard Hadlee — New Zealand's man of steel, super all-rounder.

Syed Kirmani — Keeper of India's fortunes.

Viv Richards — Does anybody bat better than him?

Zaheer Abbas — The big hundred specialist.

16

On the Mat

MY INJURY PREVENTED ME FROM PARTICIPATING IN THE TRIAL
MATCHES for the selection the team for the first-ever Prudential
World Cup, scheduled to be played in England in June 1975.
Venkataraghavan was appointed captain and I was to be his
deputy. Since Venkataraghavan had to leave for England in April
to play for Derbyshire in the county championship, I was in
charge of the nets at the Wankhede Stadium in Bombay. We
had five days at the nets before our departure for London on
25 May. We had only six players at the nets since five members
of the team were already in England. Mohinder Amarnath,
Vishwanath and wicketkeeper Kirmani didn't report until the day
before the last day of the nets. We, however, had some help from
the local cricketers who bowled to us at the nets. Arrangements
had been made for us to stay at the Wankhede Stadium; but

Stadium; but as I was a local player, the manager allowed me to go home for the night. As Bombay was extremely hot at that time, we used to begin practice at 9 o'clock in the morning, and finish at 11, followed by a second session beginning at 3.30 in the afternoon.

One morning I turned up at the Wankhede Stadium and found the Cricket Control Board President, Mr P. M. Rungta, having breakfast with the boys. When he saw me he wanted to know whether I was staying at the stadium or going home. I told him I was going home for the night. He rebuked me saying, 'Why do you think arrangements have been made for the team to stay here? Team spirit has to be developed and you must also stay here. You are the vice-captain and you should set an example.' I replied that I had sought the manager's permission to go home at night. I don't think Mr Rungta was listening because he turned to ask Eknath Solkar whether he too was going home for the night. Eknath replied that he was staying at the stadium. This was a lie and everybody around knew that Eknath was spending the night at home. But, seeing the Board President's attitude, he did not dare tell him the truth. I do not understand why Mr G.S. Ramchand, the manager who was present, didn't accept responsibility for allowing us to go home.

Mr Rungta's argument that by staying together we were going to develop team spirit was, to say the least, laughable. There were just six of us at the camp which was held only five days before we left. According to Mr Rungta's thinking, the six of us were going to develop team spirit as never before.

Eknath defending himself by lying hurt me more because I couldn't understand the need for it. The manager had allowed us to go. Moreover, why a Test cricketer, particularly one of the calibre of Eknath Solkar, should be afraid of a mere cricket administrator, is beyond my understanding. So what, even if the administrator was the Board President himself! Eknath had the manager's permission to go home and he should have said so. This show of inaction by the manager should have made me realise that, for self-preservation, the buck would be passed on to the boys. I was to learn the lesson more bitterly in the next few days.

In London, all the teams were staying in the same hotel. On the eve of the tournament, all the participating teams were presented to the Queen at Buckingham Palace. It was terrific, especially meeting players, many of whom one had only heard of but never seen. I was keen on renewing my acquaintance with the Pakistani boys, particularly Zaheer Abbas and Asif Masood, with whom I had so much fun in Australia. The Queen and Prince Philip chatted with the players, and then we were to go to Lord's for some photographs to be taken. There everybody was less formal and mixed freely with one another.

We were to play in the inaugural match of the tournament against England at Lord's on a wicket that became slower during the day. Playing in group A of the tournament, England ran up a record total of 334 runs in sixty-three overs, with Dennis Amiss contributing 137 runs. Fletcher and Chris Old threw their bats about with purpose and England lost only four wickets in the process.

Off the second ball I faced from Geoff Arnold, I got a very faint nick in trying to cut and was surprised when nobody appealed for a catch. I mentioned this to Greig and the news must have reached Arnold. In the very next over he bowled to me, I went for a cut, missed the ball by almost a foot, and there was Arnold yelling an appeal to the umpire. John Snow, who was back in the side after a long lay-off, bowled a tight length, while Arnold, Old and Lever bowled short of length. After one cross-batted swipe I found I was unable to connect my shots.

187

England bowlers are a very professional lot and the few loose balls they bowled I hit them straight back to a fielder. At this stage a section of the crowd started banging beer cans together causing an awful din. I didn't realise then that they were showing their displeasure at my batting. I thought, may be they were just doing it for the heck of it. I was finding it difficult to play any shots and to try anything funny against the fast bowlers was inviting trouble.

At tea which was after twenty-five overs, I was asked by the manager to look for ones and twos since I was finding it difficult to score. This was in response to my question whether I should throw away my wicket. Somebody suggested that I should drop anchor at one end while others scored at the other.

The England field placing, in spite of their big score, was not very attacking, and it was not easy to pick even ones and twos. As I waited for the bowler to run up and bowl, my mind used to be made up to have a shy at the ball, but as soon as the ball was delivered, my feet would move to a position for a defensive shot. The awful noise made by the crowd didn't help my thinking; but only confused me as hell. Right from the start we knew that the chase was out of the question. Even my attempts to take a single and give the strike to the other batsman failed. There was a complete mental block as far as I was concerned.

It was by far the worst innings I have ever played. There were occasions when I felt like moving away from the stumps so that I would be bowled. This was the only way to get rid of the mental agony which I was suffering. I was dropped thrice, off fairly easy chances too. I was in a curious position. Neither I could force the pace nor get out, even when I tried to. Towards the end, I was playing mechanically. I can understand the crowd's reaction and I am genuinely sorry for spoiling their day. What

I can't understand is the accusation that I played out sixty overs to preserve my average. I also can't stomach the argument that I scored 36 runs in sixty overs. I didn't play sixty overs myself, that's obvious. Excepting Vishwanath nobody else tried to do anything much about the situation. It was ridiculous even to say that my batting dampened the approach of the other batsmen noted for their attacking batting. Admittedly, my batting wasn't in conformity with the norms of limited-overs cricket, but then even in local cricket I have sometimes found it tough going in to attack.

The manager asked me for a formal explanation for the reasons for my dismal batting, which I did. Apparently he was satisfied by my explanation, because when I sat around with him and Venkataraghavan to pick the side for the next match not a word was spoken about my earlier innings. I should have been disciplined then, if at all. But I wasn't and that was that!

Our next match was against East Africa, who were the rabbits of the tournament, and we had no difficulty in beating them by ten wickets. For a change our medium-fast bowlers, Abid Ali, Madan Lal and Mohinder Amarnath got all the wickets that fell except for one that fell to Bedi. They were all out for 120 runs in 55.3 overs. Farokh and I then made 123 runs in 29.5 overs without being separated. My personal contribution was 65 not out.

We took on New Zealand at the Old Trafford ground at Manchester for the right to enter the semifinals. Batting first, we could muster only 230 runs in sixty overs, Abid Ali top-scoring with 70 runs. It seemed a fairly respectable total which would give us a fighting chance against the Kiwis. But we had not reckoned with the gifted New Zealand opener, Glenn Turner. Spearheading the assault on the Indian bowlers, he remained unbeaten with 114 runs when New Zealand won the match in the last over. It was a near thing and we could have won but for Glenn Turner's magnificent effort. So, we failed to enter the lists to take a tilt at the World Cup in its inaugural year. As far as my own performance was concerned, I had an aggregate of 113 runs, twice not out, and an average of 113. Incidentally, I had scored the largest number of runs for India.

I had almost forgotten about my first experience of instant cricket when I just couldn't get going against England at Lord's. It was only a bad nightmare. However, I wasn't allowed to forget the episode. When I returned to India after a month's holiday in Europe I got a letter from the Cricket Control Board President, again asking me to explain my batting in the England match. It seems the manager had reported that I had deliberately played slow cricket, contrary to the interests of the team. The manager, I was told, had also reported that, when I was asked by him to go for runs, I gave some excuse and persisted in playing slow and dull cricket. This, the manager alleged, had a demoralising effect on the younger players and was also against the country's interest. It now transpired that the explanation given by me to the manager in England was not satisfactory. All this was a great shock to me.

If my explanation to the manager was not satisfactory, why didn't he say so then, and take action against me? What, however, hurt me even more was the report of the manager who accused me of not performing my duties as vice-captain, and of keeping myself aloof from the other members of the team, instead of giving them encouragement.

I can be accused of anything but least of all being aloof from my team-mates. And, as for not encouraging the players and not mixing with them, I suggested that any eight members of the fourteen-member team be called and if they said that I was aloof and didn't offer encouragement I would retire from the game.

But then that was not to be because I had already been adjudged guilty until I was able to prove my innocence. A strange way of meting out justice! And how can one call for disciplinary action for performance on the field? If that is so, if a bowler gets slogged he will have to explain his failure. Or, if a fielder drops a catch he has to explain it. What a ridiculous state of affairs! And if my performance was so poor, what about our bowlers? They should have been sent to the gallows for allowing the England batsmen to score at will to pile up a record total of 334!

Mind you, I am the first to admit that I deserved to be censured for my slow scoring to get 36. But, to say that I deliberately played slowly was not true and entirely unfair. How does one prove that I did it deliberately and how does one say that the others didn't? The whole thing made it terribly bitter, and I couldn't bring myself to really believe that such things had happened. We weren't schoolchildren to give an explanation in writing to the school master. Bishen was asked to do that after the 1974 tour and I was put on the mat after the 1975 tour.

I was told that my explanation was not satisfactory but I was given the benefit of the doubt and the proceedings against me were dropped. That was the wisest thing that could be done by the Cricket Control Board. But all this left a very bad taste in my mouth, and did precious little to spur our players to do better in future.

17

A Fruitful Season

LEAVING ALL THE PAST UNHAPPINESS BEHIND, I DECIDED TO
concentrate on the new season. I was feeling downcast and was
disinterested in almost everything. However, when I was
unanimously appointed captain of Bombay, it put new life into
me. I started practising with a will because I wanted to prove
those who were saying that the captaincy would affect my
batting, absolutely wrong. I felt really sorry for Ashok Mankad
who, in spite of winning the Ranji Trophy in the 1974-75 season,
was discarded. But then that's how the ball rolls! I knew, however,
I could depend on his cooperation and he didn't let me down.

In our first Ranji Trophy game, we had a tough time getting
Gujarat out but we eventually succeeded on the second morning
when Gujarat had scored 245 runs. In reply, we batted well; I
got a century and Sudhir Naik contributed 65 runs. We were

got a century and Sudhir Naik contributed 65 runs. We were 240 for two at the end of the day. I knew our only chance of an outright win was to take advantage of the wicket in the morning before the batting became loose and so I declared immediately after taking the first innings lead. My hunch proved correct because Gujarat were all out for 101, our seamers doing most of the damage. We had to get 99 runs to win, which we did. The victory gave me tremendous confidence as I had taken a calculated risk and our bowlers had proved me right. Besides, the captaincy made me concentrate harder while batting, and I avoided playing all or most of the seemingly dangerous shots.

The Irani Trophy match against the Rest of India at Nagpur was my next job. This was the match where Dilip Vengsarkar made his name a household one in India. He scored 110 runs in only eighty-five minutes off eighty balls, but the manner in which he hammered Bedi and Prasanna on a turning wicket was unbelievable. Young Vengsarkar started by hitting Prasanna straight over the sight screen and then didn't spare Bedi either. In all, he hit seven sixes, all of them perfectly timed. I was having a rubdown when he reached his 50, but I stopped the massage and went out to watch this young batsman hammering India's famed spin bowlers. It was a magnificent sight. There was no wild slogging, the sixes were brought off with perfect timing and the ball sped to the region from mid-off to mid-wicket. And to think that he would have been in the reserves if Eknath Solkar had been fit who had split the webbing between the thumb and forefinger and had to drop out.

Dilip Vengsarkar didn't get to bat in the first innings in the Ranji Trophy match against Gujarat, so I promoted him to one-down in the first innings of this match, while I dropped to number five in the batting order. Dilip got a good ball and was leg-before for a duck. When he came back to the pavilion he

193

was disconsolate and worried whether he had made a hash of his opportunity. I tried to reassure him by recounting the names of some great cricketers who had been out for a duck on their first-class debut, but had gone on to do great things. I told him about my own debut in the Ranji Trophy which was similar to his, and added, 'See, today I am the Bombay captain.' I don't know whether this convinced Dilip.

Dilip Vengsarkar's innings at Nagpur reminded a lot of people of the late Col. C.K. Nayudu. Dilip promptly acquired the nickname of Colonel. We have, in the Dadar Union side, a Marshal, a Major and now a Colonel!

The next Ranji Trophy match against Maharashtra saw the Colonel playing a different game. He rarely lofted the ball and played mostly along the ground. I got 190 in the match. Maharashtra always have a good opening attack and it was good to get runs against them. Without Shivalkar who was ill, we couldn't force an outright victory in spite of getting them out cheaply in the first innings.

The Sri Lanka team was in India then to play three four-day unofficial Tests. In the first Test at Hyderabad I got 203, but it was Vishwanath who made 117 runs that stole the spectators' hearts. Vishwanath had caught up with me in the 60s and we went neck to neck till the 90s when, in one over from D.S. D'Silva, I hit three boundaries through the covers to reach my hundred first. Vishwanath got his century in the next over. Often, after I played a particular shot, Vishwanath would repeat it in the next over and more elegantly. I enjoyed batting with him, especially because it was one of the rare occasions when we had a long partnership. The Sri Lanka team had no answer to Vishwanath in this mood and we added over 200 runs for the third wicket. Vishwanath then walked when he thought he was bowled by D'Silva. I was the non-striker and I know that the ball dislodged the bails only after rebounding off the wicketkeeper's pads.

All along in Hyderabad, I often got near the century mark but never got a 100, because I used to get out in the 80s or 90s. So, I had made up my mind that when I did get past my 100, I would go on to score 200. I had to fulfil the promise I had made to myself and was happy when I realised my ambition.

The Sri Lanka bowling wasn't penetrative; only Opatha operating with the new ball needed careful watching. The other bowlers were most ordinary. Much was made of D.S. D'Silva who was supposed to be Sri Lanka's Chandrasekhar, but looked mediocre. The only good point about him was his never-say-die spirit. This was the only game I played against the visitors because I was dropped for the next two Tests. Bishen jokingly told me in the evening: 'You know, Indian batsmen are not supposed to get a double century. You have scored one, and so you have been dropped!'

My good batting form continued in the Ranji Trophy and, batting at number five, I got 171 runs against Saurashtra. But, where I should have got a big score, I didn't. That was in the Duleep Trophy semifinal against North Zone. I got only 40 runs and West Zone lost to North Zone on the first innings. In the second innings on the last day of the Duleep Trophy match, I was batting with more than 50 runs to my name. While I was walking to resume my innings after tea, Chetan Chauhan told me, 'Watch out, I'm coming on to bowl.' I was 84 and looking forward to a century when Chetan was brought on. His first delivery pitched on a length and as I went forward to it, the ball went straight through to bowl me. Chetan was delighted but knowing how anxious I was to get a century in the Duleep Trophy he was most apologetic when we met in the evening.

18

Umpiring Aberrations

WE LANDED IN AUCKLAND AFTER A TIRING AIR JOURNEY AND WERE told that there would be no overnight halt, because we were to play at Napier.

We started off by coach for Napier and at about midnight, we had a flat tyre. While the driver worked to change the tyre with the help of the sleepy-eyed boys, I entertained the team with the song that had been picturised on me for the film in which I had appeared. Judging from the enthusiastic response of the boys, the song should be a hit!

The flat tyre, however, added to our woes. What we needed most was rest after the tiring air journey. Instead, we were made to travel by bus. I wish the people responsible for making travel arrangements would travel like this and find out for themselves whether it is pleasant or not. When we reached Napier in the

I had three centuries in three Ranji Trophy matches and was keen to score another in the last match of the league against Baroda. That was, however, not to be because Dilip Vengsarkar and Sudhir Naik raised a 200-run opening partnership before Vengsarkar, who got his first Ranji Trophy century, was out. Once again, I was to bat at number five and when I went in, Anshuman Gaekwad claimed the second new ball. It was a shrewd move, for the wicket was full of runs and the new ball was more likely to get wickets than the old one which the spinners were operating.

Narayan Satham, a fine bowler with the new ball and who is nippy off the wicket, rapped me on the pads from where the ball flew to second slip. I was given out caught though the Baroda players had appealed for leg-before. They were sympathetic later on but the damage was done. Anshuman Gaekwad's fighting knock saved Baroda from outright defeat.

Just before the captain was selected for the twin-tour of New Zealand and the West Indies early in 1976, there was a controversy about Bishen Bedi. Apparently Bishen had said some harsh things to the officials of the Vidarbha Cricket Association about the board and lodging arrangements made for the players at Nagpur. So, again Bishen had to appear before an Inquiry Committee to explain his conduct.

Bishen must hold the record for the number of inquiries he has had to face, on camera or otherwise. The selectors were, however, told that there was nothing that could be held against Bishen and they promptly appointed him captain for the twin-tour. If Bishen holds the record for inquiries, I must rank a close second. Perhaps by this token I was made the vice-captain of the team. And we had the battle-scarred Polly Umrigar as manager, and Balu Alaganan as treasurer.

There were only two seamers in the side, Madan Lal and

Mohinder Amarnath, with the versatile Eknath Solkar also bowl his seamers.

We assembled in Madras before leaving for Auckland, the first leg of our twin-tour of New Zealand and the W Indies. The two days there were hectic with travel arrangeme to be worked out, the outfits to be looked after, and a lot other things to attend to. It was all a mad rush, and we wish we had more time to get things organised before leaving a protracted tour covering several thousand miles.

Just before we left for the tour, I had completed my pi in a Marathi film called *Premachi Savli*. How I came to be film actor is another story. One evening, after the Bombay net Mr P.D. Reporter who is a first-class umpire, came and aske if I was interested in acting in a movie. My reaction was negativ at first, but I wanted to wait and watch further development before taking a final decision. Mr Reporter's sister, Madhumat who is a well-known dancer and has appeared frequently on the Indian screen and her husband, Manohar Deepak, were producing this film. At the time the offer came I was inactive after being dropped from the last two Tests against Sri Lanka. I had a bit of free time at my disposal. I was assured that the shooting of my part in the film wouldn't take more than three days, which induced me to accept the invitation to appear on the silver screen.

It was a novel experience for me even though I had appeared in a few commercials earlier. However, appearing in a full-length feature film was very different. I confess that I never got used to the glare from the reflectors, which made me terribly uneasy. The film, I understand, is due for release soon and I wonder how my screen debut will be taken by cinema-goers. Anyway, I am keeping my fingers crossed and am hoping for the best.

the ball dislodged the bails only after rebounding off the wicketkeeper's pads.

All along in Hyderabad, I often got near the century mark but never got a 100, because I used to get out in the 80s or 90s. So, I had made up my mind that when I did get past my 100, I would go on to score 200. I had to fulfil the promise I had made to myself and was happy when I realised my ambition.

The Sri Lanka bowling wasn't penetrative; only Opatha operating with the new ball needed careful watching. The other bowlers were most ordinary. Much was made of D.S. D'Silva who was supposed to be Sri Lanka's Chandrasekhar, but looked mediocre. The only good point about him was his never-say-die spirit. This was the only game I played against the visitors because I was dropped for the next two Tests. Bishen jokingly told me in the evening: 'You know, Indian batsmen are not supposed to get a double century. You have scored one, and so you have been dropped!'

My good batting form continued in the Ranji Trophy and, batting at number five, I got 171 runs against Saurashtra. But, where I should have got a big score, I didn't. That was in the Duleep Trophy semifinal against North Zone. I got only 40 runs and West Zone lost to North Zone on the first innings. In the second innings on the last day of the Duleep Trophy match, I was batting with more than 50 runs to my name. While I was walking to resume my innings after tea, Chetan Chauhan told me, 'Watch out, I'm coming on to bowl.' I was 84 and looking forward to a century when Chetan was brought on. His first delivery pitched on a length and as I went forward to it, the ball went straight through to bowl me. Chetan was delighted but knowing how anxious I was to get a century in the Duleep Trophy he was most apologetic when we met in the evening.

I had three centuries in three Ranji Trophy matches and was keen to score another in the last match of the league against Baroda. That was, however, not to be because Dilip Vengsarkar and Sudhir Naik raised a 200-run opening partnership before Vengsarkar, who got his first Ranji Trophy century, was out. Once again, I was to bat at number five and when I went in, Anshuman Gaekwad claimed the second new ball. It was a shrewd move, for the wicket was full of runs and the new ball was more likely to get wickets than the old one which the spinners were operating.

Narayan Satham, a fine bowler with the new ball and who is nippy off the wicket, rapped me on the pads from where the ball flew to second slip. I was given out caught though the Baroda players had appealed for leg-before. They were sympathetic later on but the damage was done. Anshuman Gaekwad's fighting knock saved Baroda from outright defeat.

Just before the captain was selected for the twin-tour of New Zealand and the West Indies early in 1976, there was a controversy about Bishen Bedi. Apparently Bishen had said some harsh things to the officials of the Vidarbha Cricket Association about the board and lodging arrangements made for the players at Nagpur. So, again Bishen had to appear before an Inquiry Committee to explain his conduct.

Bishen must hold the record for the number of inquiries he has had to face, on camera or otherwise. The selectors were, however, told that there was nothing that could be held against Bishen and they promptly appointed him captain for the twin-tour. If Bishen holds the record for inquiries, I must rank a close second. Perhaps by this token I was made the vice-captain of the team. And we had the battle-scarred Polly Umrigar as manager, and Balu Alaganan as treasurer.

There were only two seamers in the side, Madan Lal and

Mohinder Amarnath, with the versatile Eknath Solkar also to bowl his seamers.

We assembled in Madras before leaving for Auckland, on the first leg of our twin-tour of New Zealand and the West Indies. The two days there were hectic with travel arrangements to be worked out, the outfits to be looked after, and a lot of other things to attend to. It was all a mad rush, and we wished we had more time to get things organised before leaving on a protracted tour covering several thousand miles.

Just before we left for the tour, I had completed my part in a Marathi film called *Premachi Savli*. How I came to be a film actor is another story. One evening, after the Bombay nets, Mr P.D. Reporter who is a first-class umpire, came and asked if I was interested in acting in a movie. My reaction was negative at first, but I wanted to wait and watch further developments before taking a final decision. Mr Reporter's sister, Madhumati, who is a well-known dancer and has appeared frequently on the Indian screen and her husband, Manohar Deepak, were producing this film. At the time the offer came I was inactive after being dropped from the last two Tests against Sri Lanka. I had a bit of free time at my disposal. I was assured that the shooting of my part in the film wouldn't take more than three days, which induced me to accept the invitation to appear on the silver screen.

It was a novel experience for me even though I had appeared in a few commercials earlier. However, appearing in a full-length feature film was very different. I confess that I never got used to the glare from the reflectors, which made me terribly uneasy. The film, I understand, is due for release soon and I wonder how my screen debut will be taken by cinema-goers. Anyway, I am keeping my fingers crossed and am hoping for the best.

18

Umpiring Aberrations

WE LANDED IN AUCKLAND AFTER A TIRING AIR JOURNEY AND WERE told that there would be no overnight halt, because we were to play at Napier.

We started off by coach for Napier and at about midnight, we had a flat tyre. While the driver worked to change the tyre with the help of the sleepy-eyed boys, I entertained the team with the song that had been picturised on me for the film in which I had appeared. Judging from the enthusiastic response of the boys, the song should be a hit!

The flat tyre, however, added to our woes. What we needed most was rest after the tiring air journey. Instead, we were made to travel by bus. I wish the people responsible for making travel arrangements would travel like this and find out for themselves whether it is pleasant or not. When we reached Napier in the wee hours of the morning, we didn't have enough strength even to untie our shoelaces.

It rained and rained and it looked as if our first match of the tour against the Central Districts would be washed out. Luckily, on the last two days the rain stopped and though the outfield was soggy we could start the match. The Central District team was skittled out for 152. I was given out caught behind, off the second ball of our innings. The ball had hit my pads and then bounced off, when the wicketkeeper, diving forward had taken it and appealed. I was surprised at the decision but thought I had been given out leg-before wicket. I was very disappointed. Mohinder Amarnath, Parthasarathy Sharma and Brijesh Patel played well and we won the game pretty easily by six wickets. It was, after all, a good beginning.

The next game against Northern Districts, which we played at Hamilton, also ended in a victory for us by the comparatively narrow margin of 141 runs. Brijesh Patel (71) and Madan Lal (101 not out) in the first innings, and Surinder Amarnath (59) in the second, batted well. For the home team, Roberts scored an unbeaten 104 in the first innings. It was during fielding practice at the ground before the match that Bishen Bedi pulled a leg muscle badly and was ruled out for the first Test to follow at Auckland. As vice-captain I had to lead the side and found myself as the leader of a national team for the first time in my cricketing career. Though I was sorry for Bishen, I have to confess that I was happy at the honour that had come to me purely by accident.

On the eve of the Test, I went along with a couple of senior members of the team, to have a look at the wicket. The groundsman came charging at us when we tried to lift the covers to see what the pitch was like. It was a bright day with not a cloud in sight. When I requested the groundsman to allow us to look at the wicket, he ignored me and went back to his rolling. I was furious and so were the others. Surely we were entitled to have a look at the wicket on the eve of the Test! John Reid, the former New Zealand captain who was there, spoke to the groundsman and only then did he remove the covers off the wicket, but with great reluctance. The wicket looked a beauty and we reckoned our spinners would be able to turn the ball by the third day.

Dilip Vengsarkar reported a strained leg muscle in the morning and I had to wait till the doctors reported him fit for the game. In the meanwhile Glenn Turner, who was also captaining his country for the first time, had come into our dressing room to ask me to go for the toss. I requested him to wait for a few minutes. But the few minutes turned to be pretty long for me. Glenn came a number of times, but, at my request, went back again to the New Zealand dressing room.

When we finally went out to toss I said to him, 'What a way to begin a Test captaincy!' The coin rolled quite a bit after landing and it went from one end of the wicket to the other with both Glenn and I chasing after it. Glenn took one look and triumphantly said, 'Bad luck pal, I've won it.' As we returned to the pavilion I was reminded of Ajit Wadekar's dictum, 'I never mind if I lose the toss, so long as I win the Test.'

Glenn who opened the New Zealand innings with Morrison, was not successful with the bat, and in Chandrasekhar's second over he was caught by me off bat and pad. I had to dive to my right to catch it. I was fielding there because Eknath Solkar had fractured his little finger and was not playing. When I looked towards the dressing room, there was Eknath clapping in approval.

Bevan Congdon and John Morrison, however, batted sensibly thought not too confidently. Both survived confident appeals for leg before wicket, which were turned down. Incidentally, we had been warned by some of the Indian players who had toured New Zealand in 1968 not to waste our breath appealing for leg before wicket decisions. Prasanna who was one of them, shrugged and said, 'Well, we've got to bowl them out, isn't it?'

Chandrasekhar was, meanwhile, becoming unplayable and after he caught Morrison off his own bowling, a landslide started which was checked only by a partnership between wicketkeeper Wadsworth and Dayle Hadlee. Wadsworth who had survived a bat-pad catch appeal, stepped down the track again to play Prasanna and I took the edge off the pads. Wadsworth waited for a decision but was given out. He was also out of his crease when I took the catch, so I could have got him run out, too, but I was confident that this time the umpire had heard the snick. Fortunately for us, he had! New Zealand were all out for 226 runs. In the two overs left before draw of stumps we made 16 for no loss.

Dilip Vengsarkar was out in the first over of the second morning when he was trapped leg-before by Collinge. In his first Test innings Dilip was out for seven. Surinder Amarnath, another Test debutante, joined me at this stage. He started shakily, surviving a slip chance to Turner off Howarth's first ball, but settled down to play a fine attacking innings. Howarth was really unlucky because he dropped me off his own bowling twice. Having seen his catching of Ashok Mankad off his own bowling in Bombay in 1969, I counted myself very lucky indeed, to have survived. I had another life when Bevan Congdon failed to hold a return catch. Surinder also escaped being caught by Howarth when he played a ball back to the bowler. It certainly wasn't Howarth's day.

Surinder whose nickname is Tommy, reached his century daringly. At 93 he swung O'Sullivan over long-on for six and then patted the next ball and scampered for a single to reach his first 100 in Test cricket. In scoring a century on debut, Surinder had emulated his father, Lala Amarnath, who had also scored a century on his debut against England at Bombay in 1933-34. Our partnership was worth 204 runs when Surinder was out to the second new ball. He was caught behind, off Hadlee, when he had scored 124 runs. Vishwanath also fell to a catch by wicketkeeper Wadsworth off Hadlee, before he had opened his account. The ball had actually nicked his pads, but the loud appeal by Wadsworth and company was upheld.

I was in the 80s when Brijesh Patel joined me. We trudged along cautiously against the new ball. I despatched a short ball from Collinge over the square-leg fence and followed up with a cut to the third-man boundary. With these shots I had reached my century, my first against New Zealand, and in my maiden Test against the Kiwis. It was certainly not the best of innings because I had to really struggle to get the runs. This was to be expected, because my form on the tour wasn't too good before the Test and I had to fight hard to get into three figures. On the other hand, Surinder's was a free-stroking innings, thrilling, no doubt, but at the same time it was obvious that on wickets with a little more grass and movement, he would be in trouble.

Venkataraghavan came in as night-watchman. Of our spinners, he has the best credentials as a batsman and has even scored a century in the Ranji Trophy and 51 in a Test. But Venkat has never succeeded as a night-watchman, I think due to the fact that in the last overs of the days he goes for attacking shots instead of playing out time. This is exactly the opposite of what a night-watchman should do. This time too he paid the price and was out to a brilliant catch by Congdon in the gully. Then came the turning point of the match – the partnership between Mohinder Amarnath and Madan Lal. Their 93-run partnership for the seventh wicket which ended on the third day, gave us a valuable 148-run lead which was to prove decisive.

The New Zealand second innings started with Morrison being brilliantly caught by Vishwanath, jumping up at short mid-wicket; then Madan Lal, who was at mid-wicket, ran back to hold Glenn Turner. Congdon and Parker, who put on 122 runs for the third wicket, survived mainly because the umpires refused to give them out. Bat-pad catches were smilingly turned down, and leg before wicket appeals by us might have been stupid, the way the umpires looked at us. Once when I took a bat-pad catch and found it negatived, the entire team was stunned. Shouts from the stands saying 'Home rules apply, boys', didn't sound funny. At the end of the day New Zealand were 161 for two.

We were not to be denied victory, however, and Prasanna bowled superbly to shoot the New Zealand side out for 215. He captured eight wickets for 76 runs – his best performance in Tests. Chandrasekhar got two wickets and Venkataraghavan kept the batsmen in check and never allowed them to take liberties, even though he did not take a wicket. One of the incidents in this Test, which we will all remember, is the time Chandrasekhar bowled Wadsworth to terminate New Zealand's second innings. He was appealing to the umpire, who turned round and said, 'He is bowled.' I was beside Chandrasekhar at the time, trying to calm him down. The exasperated Chandrasekhar posed the classic question, 'I know he is bowled, but is he out?' That goes to show what we thought about the umpiring.

We lost two wickets in scoring the 68 runs needed for victory and champagne was waiting for us in the dressing room.

We were one-up, and it's always good to go one-up in the first Test of a series. My debut as captain had been successful. I was back among the runs too with 116 and 35 not out.

Dunedin, where we played Otago, is very *near* the South Pole but the weather made us feel as if we were *on* the South Pole. It was blisteringly cold and with the rain coming down occasionally, the climate was certainly not suitable for a cricket match. However, the interruptions allowed me to participate in a match with a rubber ball with the little boys who had come to watch the game. I became quite popular with the enthusiastic youngsters. However, I did nothing of note in the drawn match against Otago, which preceded the second Test, except to drop Glenn Turner off my own bowling. This prompted Glenn to wonder whether caught and bowled had gone out of fashion. His bowlers had let him down a few times in the first Test and that must have been fresh in his mind. Anyway, Glenn went on to score an unbeaten 121 runs. Dilip Vengsarkar cornered all the glory with the top-score of 130 runs, and Brijesh made 73, both in the first innings.

As far as I am concerned, the wicket at Christchurch for the second Test was not a Test wicket. How can one accept a wicket on which the grass is as thick as in the outfield? There were patches of grass on the wicket, which were like big tufts. Besides, the weather was, as usual, bitterly cold and raw. To make things more difficult for us, it rained and seven and a half hours' play was lost. Bedi, leading India for the first time, won the toss. And, when we decided to bat on that track, I thought it was an unnecessary risk. It was like playing into the hands of New Zealand who had three seamers backed up by Congdon.

I started off by lofting Collinge high over the vacant mid-on position and followed up with a four over slips' heads for a boundary. It certainly wasn't risky batting as I was only going for the cut when I knew that an edge would go over slips' heads. I had made 22 before an intended drive went to Burgess, off Collinge at third slip, got me out. Vishwanath played such a marvellous innings that Mohinder Amarnath's confidence increased during their partnership. Just as they looked set to pull us out of the woods, Mohinder (45) was given out leg-before to Congdon. Mohinder is tall and he had stretched his leg down the wicket. We were all surprised at the decision. Vishwanath was caught in the slips for 83 and Bishen swung his bat merrily to make 30 and boost our score.

New Zealand's batting followed the pattern of the first Test in that we became hoarse by appealing, which were generally turned down by the umpires. Glenn Turner, in particular, survived mainly on his ability to get the ball on the pads. He scored a century (117), but I honestly can't think of a single stroke worth remembering. Even his 100th run was given to him by courtesy of the umpire. When he was on 98, he turned Madan Lal to Mohinder at deep fine-leg and took one run. He was hardly out of his ground to complete the second run when wicketkeeper Kirmani had the bails off from a lovely throw-in by Mohinder. But seeing Turner turn back for his second run, hundreds of boys and girls had taken off to greet him in the middle, and the umpire did not have the heart to disappoint them! Turner got his century and everyone around was happy.

Vishwanath's innings, particularly the way he left the rising ball alone, was fresh in my mind as I embarked on my second innings. My 71 was one of my better efforts and that too because I had Vishwanath's 83 in mind. The wicket which was not mown and was freshened by rain, made the ball kick about, but our partnership lasted quite a bit and we had soon wiped out the deficit. At the end of the game everybody said we were lucky to draw the game. I don't think so, for we needed only 100 runs more and we would have skittled out New Zealand in the second innings if the umpires fingers didn't get stuck in their pockets.

The outstanding performance in the Test was by Syed Kirmani, our wicketkeeper, who equalled the world record of dismissals in an innings - six caught and one stumped - and kept superbly throughout. His catch to dismiss Glenn Turner was astonishing. Turner had turned an in-swinger off the middle of his bat and Kirmani, anticipating it, had already moved, and yet had to fling himself to his left to come up with the catch.

Madan Lal and Mohinder also were our heroes, along with Vishwanath, the former two had bowled their hearts out on this track, with Madan Lal looking particularly dangerous. We saved the match on the last morning because of a knock of 71 by me and another 79 runs scored by Vishwanath.

Two days before the third and final Test at Wellington, the capital of New Zealand, the weather was as warm as in Bombay during December/January. From the second day of the Test, however, the weather deteriorated so much that I can safely say that it must have been the coldest day in Test cricket that I have ever encountered. The match was played on the Basin Reserve pitch, which, with a lot of grass and helped by rain, gave the New Zealand bowlers the type of wicket they had been hoping for.

On the first day we were out for 220 after winning the toss, with Brijesh making a strokeful 81 and Kirmani an enterprising 49. When New Zealand batted, Bedi got Glenn Turner down the wicket and the umpire had no option but to give him out. Bevan Congdon got 52. He had got a 50 against us in all five innings he had played. He is certainly a stubborn person to get out and we were always happy to see his back. He seemed to have plenty of time and patience to play our spinners.

On the third day Bishen didn't come out to field after lunch and I led the side. Within an hour I was also off the field with a broken cheekbone. Lance Cairns, who is a big hitter, swept a ball from Prasanna which struck me on the cheek as I was fielding at bat and pad, breaking and dislocating the bone. An operation had to be performed to get the bone back in place and after a day in the hospital, I was back in the hotel with the boys. The only trouble, apart from certain food restrictions, was that it pained when I laughed. Our team was full of funny characters and to spend a day without laughing was impossible.

Prasanna, who was my roommate, was very upset after my injury but seeing me back again after twenty-four hours, cheered up. He told me later that after my injury he wandered about aimlessly in the field without even a sweater in that bitter cold. He had to captain the side after I was off, and it certainly wasn't the best of circumstances to lead one's country for the first time, even if it was a temporary assignment.

When we were to bat we noticed that the grass had not been mown. When asked, the groundsman said that he had, which means he must have used a grass-mower without blades. Bishen remarked at the end of the Test that when the New Zealand team comes to India next, it will find the wickets devoid of grass because our groundsman use lawn-mowers with blades in them! With the help of the unmown grass and a spot just short of a length, Richard Hadlee mowed us down dismissing us for 81 – the lowest total by either country in Tests against each other.

The series was thus levelled. The New Zealanders were out to win the series, and they very nearly did. However, when they found that they couldn't win they were determined to level the series. And to achieve this purpose any means was good enough. At Wellington the wicket was changed only at the last moment, to get a grassy patch just short of length. In the process, the stumps were pitched at the end of the square and the wicket was at the edge of the plot.

The decisive factor was the umpiring which was so partial that we thought we must have really played well to win the first Test. In fact, but for the umpiring decisions we would have won the first Test by an innings. Also, we were denied victory in the second Test because of the bias shown by the umpires for the home team. During the series I found that bat-and-pad appeals were absolutely futile unless the batsman himself felt some shame and walked.

It made us very unhappy to find the New Zealand press extremely biased. We never got any headlines, which were reserved for the New Zealand players. If our batsmen got runs the headline would invariably say that the New Zealand bowlers bowled badly and if the Indian bowlers were on top, the newspapers would blame their home batsmen for throwing their wickets away. The unabashed partiality of the New Zealand press was underlined by a headline in an important newspaper at the end of the series. It said: 'Indian heads Turner and Congdon in batting averages.' The newspapers, I must say, did a great job for the Kiwis, doing their best to boost their morale by their lopsided comments. After some time, we ceased to bother about what they wrote and opened the newspaper only to see the TV programmes for the day.

The weather also made us feel miserable. If what we saw was the New Zealand summer, I shudder to think what the winter would be like. The only good thing about the country was the people. They were extremely kind and friendly. They tried to make us as comfortable as possible. If only the weather was as kind and the umpires as friendly, we would not only have won the series but would also have really enjoyed the visit.

208

19

Trinidad, I Love You

THE DOCTOR HAD ADVISED ME THREE WEEKS' REST AFTER THE NEW Zealand tour and I was allowed by the manager, Polly Umrigar, to spend some time in New York and if possible, have my injury examined by a specialist. I was still suffering from the aftereffects of the fractured jaw which had, however, begun to heal. Balu Alaganan, the treasurer of the team, was with me and we spent a pleasant week in New York with Dr S. Ravindranath, Balu's family friend. He turned out to be a keen cricket fan and we talked about cricket all the time.

Meanwhile, the team had gone on to the West Indies after a thirty-hour flight from Auckland. The tour opened with matches against Windward Islands at St Vincent and against Leeward Islands at Montserrat, both of which ended in draws. Balu and I were to join the team in Barbados on the eve of the Barbados-

India match. On the way to Barbados, we spent a day at Orlando on the east coast of the United States, to see the wonders of Disney World. However, one day was too short to see everything but we had to remind ourselves that we were on a cricket tour.

When we arrived at Bridgetown, Barbados, a customs officer wanted to know if I was going to score as many runs as I had done on the 1971 tour. Of course, it was difficult to answer the question, so I could only smile and leave it there. There were others who warned me about the West Indies fast bowlers, Andy Roberts and Holding. 'That maan Roberts, he fit maan.' Another person said, 'Gaavaska, you gonna hook Roberts maan or not?' There was nothing I could say except to assure them that I would do my best.

Bishen wanted to rest before the first Test at Bridgetown, Barbados, and I had to lead the side in spite of being out of cricket for about three weeks. I began the tour on a promising note getting 62 runs before lunch in the match against Barbados and fell to Padmore when I missed a drive. Wicketkeeper David Murray also missed the ball but recovered quickly to whip the bails to stump me.

I was worried before the match whether I would be psychologically affected by my last injury. But my fears and doubts were dispelled after my innings against Barbados and I felt very confident.

When Barbados play any visiting team, the local supporters are keen to see a Barbados victory. In fact, as I have said earlier, a West Indies victory is not celebrated with as much gusto as a Barbados victory. Barbados is generally regarded as the home of West Indian cricket, and the island has always provided the bulk of the West Indies team. Of late, however, players from other parts of the Caribbean have dominated West Indies cricket, particularly those from Guyana and Trinidad.

The first Test at Bridgetown (Barbados) began on 10 March. Bishen elected to bat on a beautiful track, after winning the toss. Parthasarathy Sharma, who had shown good form in the island games was my partner, replacing Dilip Vengsarkar who had got into a bad trot. Solkar was still on the injured list and had to stand down in the match against Windward Islands. Solkar was hit while fielding at bat-pad and the ball had rebounded off his head to be caught by the bowler Venkataraghavan! When told to go for an x-ray to see if there was any damage, particularly to the brain, some of the players quipped, 'What brain?' But, Bedi's comment really raised a laugh. 'The blow has done him good. He is talking more sense now,' said the skipper. Over the years, Solkar has taken a lot of painful blows while fielding at that position. The strain is now showing and he is no longer at his best in that position as before, when he was rated as world class.

I knew that the Kensington Oval wicket at Bridgetown was a real beauty. The ball came off quickly and it helped stroke-making. I was 37 in no time, before Andy Roberts brought one back and trapped me leg-before with a ball that kept low. I was most disappointed to get out because I was seeing the ball well and what is more important, middling it all the time. We were knocked out in the first innings for 177. The West Indies, with centuries from Vivian Richards and Clive Lloyd, and 93 by Alvin Kalicharan, piled up a big score (488 for nine declared). The Richards we saw was completely different from the one in India. Then he seemed to be bent upon hitting every ball out of sight. The new Richards showed tremendous patience without cutting away any shots. Only after he got his century did he loft the ball. And he played Chandrasekhar with confidence and ease. On the Indian tour, Chandrasekhar had given Richards plenty of trouble and many anxious moments. But in 1976 Richards was calm and unhurried while facing him, and his records didn't come as a surprise.

In our second innings, I was out to a short ball from Roberts, which never came up and found me skying the ball only to be caught by Jumadeen at forward short-leg. It was an atrocious shot and that too in the first over. What the team needed most was someone to stick around and I certainly let the side down. I was very annoyed with myself and made up my mind not to go for the hook shot at all. Vishwanath, in making 62, completed 2,000 runs in test cricket and among others, only Madan Lal and Mohinder resisted. We lost the Test by an innings. It was a very bad defeat for us and a great morale-booster for the West Indies after their shattering 1-5 defeat in Australia barely a month ago. We had dropped a fair number of catches in the close-in positions which proved very costly. We were to learn that dropping Richards (of all people) was certainly not going to pay. But, during the series, Richards benefited most from our poor catching.

Throughout the tour I was finding it difficult to concentrate in matches other than Tests and I confess my attitude to these games was not right. All I did was to go out and slog. I realised this was inexcusable and it wasn't fair to the other members of the side. However, the second innings of our match against Trinidad changed all that. I had batted in the first innings like a man who knows that his time is up and is out to grab all the fun he can. My 52 runs in seventy-two minutes included three sixes and four fours. I also attempted to play the back-handed sweep shot. After batting this way, it struck me that I should have played like this in the Prudential World Cup in England. But then, Bartholomew, Julien and Gomes were certainly not up the same street as Snow, Arnold, Old and Lever!

In the second innings, however, I regained my concentration

and scored 57 runs in forty-nine minutes, with scarcely a lofted shot. There was the urge, now and then, to let myself go but I restrained myself. In terms of stroke-play, it wasn't at all a satisfying innings but in terms of concentration and determination, I was satisfied with my knock. I had avoided all the flashy, crowd-pleasing shots during this long innings. I was only hoping that I would get more runs in the next Test, because I have always been able to concentrate in Tests. Incidentally, this did not please the spectators, one of whom came and told me, 'If you's gonna bat like that for the whole day, then you's goona put us to sleep. You's better play like the first innings!' I smiled but I had made up my mind not to do anything that would endanger the prospects of the team.

One thing you can be sure of is that there is no dearth of advisers in the West Indies. A man in the street will stop you and tell you about your game and how you should have played. This is pretty common. Moreover, what they love to see is a fast bowler being hooked. Oh yes! they love that shot in the West Indies.

In 1971, I had given them plenty of the hook shot, thanks to Uton Dowe who was bumper-happy. But, over the years, I had learnt to be discreet about this shot and I try to avoid it as much as I can.

The first day's play in the second Test at Port of Spain, Trinidad, was washed out by rain. However, when the match eventually got under way on the second, it was Vivian Richards who cornered all the glory. Coming in to bat after Roy Fredericks was bowled second ball by Madan Lal, he played so well that it looked as if it would be impossible to get him out. However, we had the West Indies on the hop as Mohinder bowled Lawrence Rowe in his first over. Kalicharan was caught at deep square-leg off Bedi; Lloyd was bowled by Chandrasekhar's loop ball. Murray, who always seems to thrive in such situations, helped Richards to add valuable runs as Chandrasekhar was tired. Richards at 83, who went out to drive Venkataraghavan, missed and was resigned to being stumped, got a reprieve when wicket-keeper Kirmani fumbled with the ball, and Richards walked back to the crease casually. Eventually, he was out for 130 and Murray was out in the second over after lunch, caught by Kirmani off Bedi. After batting so well, this was an unexpected end. But Julien played a fine attacking innings before Madan Lal dived to his right to stop the ball off his own bowling and then threw down the wicket with Julien trying to scramble back. This was magnificent cricket. The West Indies innings ended at 241.

Our innings was also off to a stumbling start. Dilip Vengsarkar, trying to hook Roberts' second ball, gloved it to the wicketkeeper and was out. Mohinder Amarnath, who went in one-down, took such a long time to come out that, if Clive Lloyd had appealed he would have been justified. Apparently Mohinder had not even padded up and was having a rubdown when Dilip was out. He sure had a lot of confidence in the opening pair! However, he was not his ambling self while batting but very alert. He played some crisp shots before an ambitious late-cut off Jumadeen ended in his dismissal. Vishwanath was just settling down when he was caught behind, off Holding. A good ball and a good batsman out! Surinder Amarnath played one rousing square-cut off Holding, the ball crashing into the fence, but lost patience against Jumadeen and gave an easy catch to Rowe at mid-wicket, as he tried a lofted shot. Brijesh Patel was aware that this was his chance to make good, so we decided to concentrate on taking singles to upset the field. And, as we knew, the West Indies fielders trying to stem the flow of runs through singles, tried to throw us out, giving us plenty of extra runs in the process. I was 90 at the end of the day, with Brijesh on 42. I was ten short of my century which would be the third successive 100 on the same ground.

The last ball before tea that day, when I was on 49, I was nearly bowled by Roberts. The ball pitched pretty wide off the off-stump, but cut back amazingly and missed my off-stump by a whisker. Trinidad is certainly not a fast bowler's dream wicket and for Roberts to bowl such a ball, when more than forty overs had already been bowled, was truly remarkable.

The next day Brijesh prospered along with me and I struck up a good understanding, picking up many singles. It was with one such single that I reached my century, the third in successive innings at Port of Spain's Queen's Park Oval - a record for the ground. Knowing that the team wanted more runs we carried on and were still together at lunch. Michael Holding bowled a good spell after lunch, and he got me out to a ball that left me for a catch to the wicketkeeper when I was on 156. Brijesh and I had added 204 runs for the fifth wicket, which gave us a lead of 89 runs over the West Indies. I was looking for runs and was taking a few risks at that stage to make the scoreboard move faster. Brijesh and Madan Lal continued where I had left off. Brijesh was understandably slow as he approached his first Test century, and Madal Lal took some time to settle down. Madan Lal, however, played one tremendous straight drive off Andy Roberts, which was a real beauty. When Bedi declared at 402 for five, Brijesh was 115 not out and Madan Lal 33 not out. The declaration left the West Indies the last session of play, with a first innings deficit of 161. In that session, we got the wicket of Fredericks. Rowe batted well the next day, but was out to an ugly cross-batted swipe off Venkataraghavan for 47.

On the morning of the last day, the Richards incident occurred. Richards had been off the field for quite some time when we batted the previous day because of a strained leg muscle. When he was batting the next day, he slipped and fell while flicking a ball to leg from Bedi. This seemed to have aggravated the injury because he went up to Bedi and sought his permission to retire. Bishen agreed to give him a runner instead, but he said that, if Richards wanted to retire, Bedi would exercise his right to dictate when he could bat again. This was not acceptable to Richards who didn't want a runner but wanted to retire. The umpires were brought into the discussion and the West Indies captain, Clive Lloyd, also joined in. Richards eventually retired and, as the next wicket fell, he came in to bat. Bishen's reasons for allowing him to bat at the fall of the fourth wicket was to try and get him out, since our bowlers were on top then.

Luckily for us Richards and Lloyd had a misunderstanding, as a result of which Richards was run out. The decision didn't go well with Richards or may be he was just unhappy at losing his wicket. However, his gestures, as he left the field, incited the crowd and as we came in at the tea interval, umpire Gosein was booed by a section of the spectators seated in front of the pavilion.

I was a little late in joining the team after the tea interval and I ran on to the field with the batsmen, Lloyd and Murray. As I walked along with them, I (naturally) walked next to Murray since he is not much taller than me. I jocularly asked Clive Lloyd, 'When is the declaration coming, skipper?' I wasn't aware that Clive Lloyd was annoyed with Bishen about the Richards incident, and was surprised when Lloyd replied with some heat, 'You want me to declare when your captain won't let my batsman retire? If he is such a stickler for the rules, I could have been too! I didn't appeal when Mohinder Amarnath took more than two minutes to appear for batting! And you want to know when I am going to declare?'

Clive Lloyd had, of course, underestimated us. Within half an hour, the West Indies had lost three more wickets and, when the mandatory overs started, they were just 228 runs ahead. Before this Roberts had played back to Chandrasekhar and survived what must have been the plumbest leg-before decision in cricket. In the third mandatory over Roberts again survived a bat-pad catch appeal which was disallowed by umpire Gosein. After the Richards run-out when the crowd gave vent to its anger, umpire Gosein wasn't going to give anybody out. Oh no! He wanted to live to see the next day. He didn't dare to take any risk because the crowd was already after his blood. Yet we tried to get Julien and Roberts out. It was only when six overs remained and the West Indies had run up a lead of 54 runs, that we gave up the attempt. When the match ended, the West Indies were 215 for eight. The statistics may show a drawn game, but never can statistics be so wrong as in this case. India had morally won the match!

India would still have won the Test had a catch of Lloyd not been spilled because of a collision between Solkar and Patel. It is difficult to pin the blame on anybody since both are excellent fielders. At the same time, I feel that Patel should have left the catch to Solkar because he has a larger pair of hands than Brijesh. The morale of the team suddenly dropped and one could feel the change. And then came those Gosein decisions! So, we had missed the bus.

When we landed at Georgetown in Guyana, it started raining ceaselessly. The Bourda Oval where we had to play Guyana, was flooded and the match was called off.

We had our moments of fun though. On April 1, All Fools Day, we sent our manager, Polly Umrigar, and treasurer, Balu Alaganan, running to the Indian High Commission. Bishen arranged a phone call to be made to Polly Umrigar in the morning, to tell him that the Indian High Commission in Trinidad had reported to the Indian High Commission in Guyana that the team's behaviour during the last session of the second Test and generally off the field was bad. The Indian High Commission was disapproving and would the manager please come and explain the matter. Polly was in a flutter and rushed to Bishen's room to tell him of the telephone call. When Polly entered the room Bishen nearly gave the game away by laughing, but he somehow controlled himself and kept his face averted by doing some backbending exercises. Polly said he didn't even have Guyanese currency for the taxi fare. Bishen, however, asked him to go and find out and not to worry. Polly carried with him a letter from the New Zealand Cricket Council which had praised the Indian team's behaviour in glowing terms, to show to the High Commissioner.

On his way to the High Commission in the taxi, Balu Alaganan realised that it could be an April Fools' joke. His initial reaction was that only I could play such a joke and they should take me along to the High Commission. Umrigar, however, wanted to go and finish off the matter. So they went and to their great relief discovered it was a joke. Polly and Balu both took it most sportingly and we all had a good laugh about it. This was unlike Dicky Rutnagar, a London-based Indian journalist covering the tour, who was very much upset by the joke played on him so much so that his relations with Bedi were spoilt.

Dicky got a call, supposedly from the Guyanese External Affairs Ministry, asking him to explain an article he had written supporting South Africa's policy of racial discrimination. The caller said that the Guyana government's policy about apartheid in South Africa was well known and so Dicky should come and explain. Dicky tried to explain that he had never written an article on South Africa, nor had he visited that country. But the caller insisted that there was a clipping of the article in the government file and he must come over to the ministry prepared to explain his conduct. Dicky realised, after going to the External Affairs Ministry, that it was a hoax and he was furious. For one who liked to pull everybody's leg, his reaction was most unsporting. Dicky tried to take it out on Bishen on several occasions and by the end of the tour, their relations were very much strained.

The rain at Georgetown didn't look like stopping and during this time a visit was organised to an army camp in the interior of Guyana. I went in the coach with the team to the airfield, but one look at the aircraft and at the clouds which looked pretty menacing, I flatly refused to fly on the plane. I knew there were others who wanted to stay put instead of flying in the inclement weather, especially in a small aircraft like the one placed at our disposal, but they all put on a brave front and decided to go along. Every member of the team (there were four others, besides me, who decided to stay back) shook hands with us solemnly before they boarded the aircraft. As the plane took off wobbling a bit while being airborne, I wondered if we would lose the series because only five players remained in Georgetown.

We were, however, destined to win, and the boys arrived safely back, smiling broadly and giving me looks that suggested, 'You worry unnecessarily'. I didn't miss the message but I wasn't going to set foot in a plane like that, especially in foul weather. After all, I had become a father while the team was in New Zealand and I wasn't going to do anything that was likely to stop me from seeing my first born!

Because of the rain, the venue of the third Test was shifted to Port of Spain and we were back in Trinidad. If people saw me smiling broadly it wasn't an illusion. I had always done well in Trinidad and my lowest score was 65. I was hoping to keep the record straight.

The Queen's Park Oval at Port of Spain in Trinidad certainly is my favourite ground in the world. When I walk out to bat there I feel quite certain that I am going to score runs. It is just a feeling I have and it has been proved right. Before the 1976 tour, my scores there were 65 and 67 not out, and 124 and 220. Besides, in the game against Trinidad at Guarcara Park I had scored 125 and 63. The crowd has a lot of people of Indian origin and so the feeling is more like playing at home than on a 'foreign field'.

I knew that a Calypso had been composed about me after our 1971 tour and so, when I went in to bat in the first innings of the match against Trinidad in 1976, I was a little tense. I didn't concentrate enough but I timed my shots well and was happy to see yet another 50 against my name at the Queen's Park Oval. It was a short innings and in the evening a West Indian came and told me, 'We wanna see you bat the whole day maan, not just for an hour.' This made me feel real good.

But to get back to the beginning of this fantastic battle at Port of Spain and the spectacular victory we eventually earned to level the series. Clive Lloyd won the toss and elected to bat. Vivian Richards, who had been a thorn in the flesh for us during the earlier Tests, showed his appreciation of the Queen's Park Oval wicket. He blasted 177 runs, which was magnificent batting. Indeed, one could see that his transformation from a slap-bang cricketer to a run-hungry batsman was complete. Clive Lloyd gave him wonderful support, with a hard-hit 68. We were worried when, at the end of the first day, West Indies had scored 320 for five, with Richards still there at 151.

Bishen Bedi spun out the remaining batsmen, and the West

Indians were all out for 359. Richards, after lofting Bedi for a huge six, attempted to repeat the shot and was caught on the boundary. This was the signal for a collapse and the remaining wickets fell in a heap.

When we batted, Anshuman Gaekwad was out to a dubious decision off Julien for only 6, but Mohinder Amarnath this time did not delay in the dressing room and, as usual, looked completely at ease against the new ball.

Michael Holding always seemed to relish bowling after lunch, and he produced a sizzling spell and got me out for 26 – the only time at Port of Spain I had been out for under 50 runs. A sharp in-cutter found me palpably in front of the wicket but I was surprised to find the umpire not responding to the united appeal of the West Indians. It was the plumbest leg-before appeal I have survived. I didn't stay long, however, to enjoy my luck. One ball later Holding struck me inside my right pad with a yorker and this time the appeal for leg-before was upheld. I thought this was a doubtful decision since the ball had been delivered from the edge of the wicket and I had hardly moved from my guard. Well, I suppose it is this way that umpiring decisions tend to even out in the long run.

There was added pain as the pad had shifted and I was hit directly on the shin. I limped off wondering whether this was the end of my big scoring in Trinidad.

Now, in Trinidad, the crowds always gather near the dressing room and the players readily mix with them. I had to listen to complaints of a large number of disgruntled people who told me they had lost bets, which they had laid on my scoring another hundred.

We were eventually out for 228 conceding a lead of 131 runs to the West Indies. We naturally thought that, with so many runs behind them, the West Indies batsmen would go on a run riot but, surprisingly, the openers Fredericks and Rowe played so slowly that, at the end of fifteen overs, they had scored only 30 runs. The booing from the crowd didn't have much effect. Madan Lal and Mohinder bowled well. When Chandrasekhar came on he had Fredericks caught by Solkar, and Venkataraghavan got rid of Rowe. Richards struck two fours imperiously and we thought that we were due for another leather-hunt. Fortunately, Venkataraghavan had tied him up and made one turn sharply go off the edge of the bat to Solkar, who took his fiftieth Test catch.

In the first innings Kalicharan had watched a ball from Chandrasekhar roll off his defensive bat on to the wicket dislodging the bails even before he had opened his account. In the second innings a similar thing happened. This time, however, the bails didn't fall off and Kalicharan looked up to the heavens to say his thanks. There was already a demand for his exclusion from the team as there was a feeling that, since he was of Indian origin, he had deliberately thrown his wicket away. Kalicharan is a professional and though he is very friendly with our team, he certainly wasn't going to sell his wicket cheaply. Taking advantage of this bit of luck and to prove his critics wrong Kalicharan hammered his eighth century.

We had still to contend with Clive Lloyd, the danger man, and we needed his wicket badly. Vishwanath did the trick when diving to his left, he brought off a superb catch to dismiss him, off Chandrasekhar. Though Murray tried to push the score along he wasn't very successful. The declaration came on the fourth day after lunch when Kalicharan had got his century and Holding had hammered two successive sixes. We were left to score 403 runs in the fourth innings of the match, and on the last day.

I was confident that we could save the game because the

wicket was still good; but the thought of winning never entered my mind.

When we batted a second time, things shaped out better. Anshuman Gaekwad and I put on 69 runs for the first wicket before Gaekwad fell to a catch by Kalicharan, off Jumadeen. Right from the beginning I was middling the ball, with Mohinder Amarnath playing with equal confidence.

On this twin tour Mohinder Amarnath had developed so well as a batsman that the tour selection committee decided to ask him to bat at number three. His complete assurance against the spinners made him look like a class player. The only thing that went against him was that he seemed to lose concentration when he got into the 30s and 40s and, with the bowlers at his mercy, he would get out. In this innings he played with so much maturity and responsibility that I was doubly sure that we could save the Test! I kept playing as it came and had twelve fours in my 86 not out at close of play. I particularly remember a cover-drive off Julien and an on-drive off Holding. These shots gave me a lot of pleasure as the ball went sweetly off the meat of the bat. We were 134 for one at close of play.

The Trinidadians had taken a century by me for granted because, at the end of the day, when I was batting on 86, they were telling me as we left the ground that they were coming the next day to watch me score a double century.

I was unusually bogged down the next day. I wasn't timing the ball well and was restrained by the bowling. It took me almost an hour to complete my century. The century came off a lucky shot. As Padmore bowled on the leg-stump I tried to play a one-handed sweep and lobbed the ball past a lunging Fredericks to get the two runs needed for my century. But my glory was shortlived, as two runs later I was out in attempting to drive Jumadeen. I missed the ball completely and was stumped by Murray. I was declared out caught behind, but actually I had not snicked the ball, but was stumped by Murray. Since there was still no thought of winning but only of saving the game, I thought I had let the side down at a crucial stage.

I must, however, mention the manner in which the spectators spurred me on as I batted on that eventful day, which brought me my fourth century at the Queen's Park Oval. The calypso song composed about my performances on the 1971 tour was audible right from the morning and until the evening. Though the tune is catchy even I was a little tired of hearing it.

This time when I got my century – the fourth on the ground – there were no invasions of the field, and I was grateful for that simply because these interruptions are no good for your concentration. In the evening there were hundreds of people to congratulate me, and there was the inevitable wise guy who shook my hand with the remark: 'Maan the calypso right, you just like a wall.' They don't speak the Queen's English there. It's difficult to understand them in the beginning, but once you do it's great fun. The people of Trinidad are different. They are not like the Jamaicans or the Barbadians, who are extremely partial and bloodthirsty. The Trinidadians also love good cricket. The Indians are popular in Trinidad because of their large number. They identify themselves with the Indian team and are India's staunch supporters.

Vishwanath took my place and with Mohinder Amarnath, carried on from where I had left off. The new ball was due at this stage but Lloyd didn't take it. Instead he continued with his spinners. When he did take the new ball, Vishwanath was firmly entrenched and there was no way of getting him out unless he became over-ambitious. When Holding bounced once, he got on his toes and square-cut the ball viciously to the boundary. The new ball only increased the flow of runs and suddenly, at tea, victory became a distinct possibility. Mohinder was batting with a lot of patience and this was surprising since he loves to thump the ball, but he kept the scoreboard ticking by taking singles to give Vishwanath the strike.

Within minutes after tea Vishwanath had neared his century. A cracking cover-drive and he got his first Test century abroad. Only a misunderstanding with Amarnath found him stranded in the middle, to be run out. That was the only way he looked like getting out. But then he had put victory within our reach and, when the mandatory overs started, we needed only 65 runs for victory. Brijesh's robust batting brought us victory in the eleventh over. It was the highest score ever made in the fourth innings victory. Out of the four wickets we had lost, two were run-out. Mohinder was run out attempting a single and Lloyd threw down the wicket at the bowler's end. He had batted more than four hundred minutes for his 85. He kept one end up ensuring that there was no pressure on the others, who went for their shots.

We had never dreamt of scoring 402 runs for victory, but were confident of saving the game. So the victory came as a tremendous morale booster. We were absolutely overjoyed since not only had we levelled the series, we had created a record for winning on the fourth innings score. The champagne really flowed and it was a memorable evening after a truly memorable day. This was undoubtedly India's greatest Test victory. Cables arrived from the President and the Prime Minister of India and other dignitaries. The change in venue had proved lucky after all. Now we were set for the last encounter for Test honours.

Yes, the Queen's Park Oval at Port of Spain has been a happy hunting ground for me. After my last innings there, a number of letters appeared in the newspapers suggesting that, after my sequence of scores at the Queen's Park Oval, the name of the ground should be changed to 'Gavaskar Oval'. My scores there were 65 and 57 not out (second Test, 1971, my debut in Test cricket), 124 and 226 (fifth Test, 1971), 156 (second Test, 1976), and 26 and 102 (3rd Test, 1976). Oh yes, I'd like to take that wicket with me everywhere but my kitbag is not big enough. And, what about that super crowd? Where would I pack them? The crowd which loves its cricket in its typically crazy way. Like the man who had a bet with me when I was playing there in 1971. I was fielding on the third-man boundary then and he was prepared to give me a hundred Trinidad dollars in return for one dollar if Maurice Foster scored a century. Foster was batting with 99 then! He won the bet, because Foster was out playing on to Abid Ali for 99! After the interval I went and gave him his dollar. He took my autograph on it. When we met again in 1976, he took another dollar from me when he bet that India would score the required 402 runs for victory. That's Trinidad for you. Trinidad, I love you!

20

Barbarism at Kingston

AFTER OUR HISTORIC VICTORY IN THE THIRD TEST IN TRINIDAD
WE travelled to Kingston to play against Jamaica. Bishen Bedi
rested for this match and I had to lead the side. The game was
the prelude to the fourth and last Test - also at Kingston which
would decide the fate of the rubber.

The Sabina Park wicket at Kingston is supposed to be the
quickest in the West Indies. It is hard and has a lot of bounce,
which is intended to help the West Indies pace bowlers. The
game against Jamaica, however, ended in a draw. My chin was
giving me trouble and it was extremely sore, so I was off the
field for most of Jamaica's first innings. Batting first, the home
team put on 299. In reply, our batting floundered a bit. Batting
at number nine, I was able to save the situation with the help
of Madan Lal. To make the game interesting, I declared after

throwing my wicket away in the chase for runs. I was not only surprised but annoyed when Foster, the Jamaica captain, refused to respond to the declaration and continued batting. I felt cheated because I had declared in good faith hoping that a response would provide an interesting finish to the game. I surely wouldn't have thrown my wicket away if I had known Foster's intentions earlier. Maybe he was scared of losing after our fantastic victory in the last Test in Trinidad.

To show my disapproval I bowled slow full tosses. Still Foster didn't respond. He surely had a safe score and there was no way he could have lost. He declared only towards the end, leaving us just two hours' batting in which to get 350 runs. He made a complete mockery of the game. And they say the West Indies love bright cricket! The Jamaica game should have warned us of the frustration and desperation of the West Indies team. They had gone to Australia to battle for the so-called World Championship and had been beaten to a pulp. On their return they found that, leave aside being World Champions, they were on the edge of being classed a cellar team. Of the team's potential there was no doubt, there was doubt only about its performance.

The fourth and final Test of the series began at Kingston's Sabina Park on 21 April. Surprisingly, Lloyd, after winning the toss, elected to field. This decision was apparently based on the assumption that the first morning's wicket would give his quick bowlers the necessary assistance to demolish the Indian batting. It did help the bowlers and the wicket was really bouncy. Holding, in particular, was making the ball bounce from a shade short of a good length. Anshuman Gaekwad survived a dropped chance in the slips. When I was on 24, I turned Holding off my toes to find Holder dropping a hot chance. At lunch we were 60 for no loss with me on 33. In the first over after lunch I hit a full toss hard back, which landed at bowler Jullien's feet. However, he dropped it because it would have required outstanding reflexes to pick up a catch going the other way on the bowling follow-through.

When Holding was brought from the Radio Commentators' Box end, I was surprised to hear the umpire say that he was going to bowl round the wicket. His first over made his intention very clear. There were three bouncers to Gaekwad.

When I faced Holding, I received four bouncers in an over and a beamer which Holding pretended had slipped from his fingers. I wasn't bothered at this stage because I thought that Holding was wasting his energy. However, the next over from him was the same and when he again said the beamer had slipped, I understood that this was a strategy to intimidate us. Lloyd, fearing that his future as captain was at stake, though he had already been appointed skipper for the team to tour England, had given us first knock, only to find us 98 for no loss. He was not only desperate but utterly frustrated. Obviously, this was the reason why he didn't do anything to stop Holding from bowling so many bumpers. Maybe he himself had asked Holding to bowl four bouncers and a beamer in an over.

When Holding pretended to be wiping his fingers to show that the ball had really slipped, it was difficult to believe. After one over, during which all I could do was to keep my head out of the way of the speeding ball, I walked up to umpire Gosein to ask him the definition of intimidatory bowling. It was during the drinks interval at the end of an over from Holding and as I approached the umpire, I realised that this was the man who had given those decisions in the second Test under pressure from the crowd, and there was no hope of my getting a satisfactory response from him. So I asked Anshuman Gaekwad to stick around and concentrate even harder.

To call the crowd a crowd in Jamaica is a misnomer. It should be called a mob. The way they shrieked and howled every time Holding bowled was positively horrible. They encouraged him with shouts of 'Kill him, Maan!', 'Hit him Maan!', 'Knock his head off, Mike!'

Their partisan attitude was even more evident when they did not applaud any shots we played. At one stage I even demanded claps for a boundary shot off Daniel. All I got was laughter from the section, which certainly hadn't graduated from the trees where they belonged. The whole thing was not cricket. The intention certainly wasn't to get a batsman out, but to knock him out.

Next morning while we were having a workout, Tony Cozier, the most respected cricket writer in the West Indies, passed by and laughingly asked me, 'Expecting applause from a Jamaican crowd?' The query speaks for itself and should give one an idea of the character of the so-called cricket-lovers in the island.

I was bowled after lunch by a yorker from Holding, which I deflected on to my wicket, for 66. The opening partnership was worth 136 runs – an Indian record for first wicket against the West Indies. Mohinder Amarnath who joined Gaekwad was unruffled and so was Anshuman. The two youngsters struck it out and no more wickets fell by draw of stumps. We were then 178 for one. The newspapers next day called it 'dull batting'. Of course, the journalists ignored the fact that only sixty-seven overs were bowled during the day and in the last thirty overs, there was no question of the ball being hit by the bat, thanks to the tactics applied by Michael Holding and Wayne Daniel.

The new ball which Lloyd took the next day was just the missile Holding needed for his lethal deliveries. He slipped one out to Mohinder, who was caught by Jullien when he deflected a delivery trying to defend his head getting knocked off! The first ball to Vishwanath must have been the most frightening delivery he has ever faced. It almost took his head with it. A similar delivery after some time crushed Vishwanath's finger as he defended his face, and Jullien again took an easy catch.

On the dot of lunch, Anshuman who had taken many blows on the body and his hands, was hit just behind the left ear. It was yet another short ball and it went like a guided missile knocking Anshuman's spectacles off. And, can one guess the crowd's reaction? They were stamping their legs, clapping and jumping with joy. The only word I can think of to describe the behaviour of the crowd is barbarian. Here was a man seriously injured and these barbarians were thirsting for more blood instead of expressing sympathy, as any civilised and sporting crowd would have done.

Anshuman Gaekwad represented the splendid fighting spirit of our team. When he was forced to retire, much against his wish, our will to fight also got knocked out.

In the pavilion there was nobody to attend to him though an Indian doctor examined him. There was nobody who wanted to take him to the hospital. The Jamaican ricket authorities showed absolutely no regard for the seriousness of the injury and their responsibility to provide medical aid. Only when I insisted that Balu Alaganan, the team's treasurer, should go and talk to the Jamaican cricket authorities, was there some action and Anshu taken to the hospital for treatment. The whole thing was sickening. Never have I seen such cold-blooded and positively indifferent behaviour of cricket officials, and the spectators, to put it mildly, were positively inhuman.

Manager Umrigar was already in the hospital having taken Vishwanath for treatment when Balu Alaganan joined him with Anshuman Gaekwad. Soon there was a third casualty when Brijesh Patel took his eyes off a ball from Holder and had his upper lip cut open. So, he too had to go to the hospital and had to shave part of his new-grown moustache to get his lip stitched. When we were 306 for six Bishen declared, primarily because he did not want to risk any more injuries, especially to our bowlers.

When the West Indies batted Fredericks found himself plumb in front of the stumps, but was relieved to find that umpire Gosein was still in no mood to lift his finger. The West Indies openers thus prospered; and Rowe, being the local hero, was immune to any appeals from us. It was only when he stepped out to Bishen, missed the ball completely and was out by a few yards that he was given out, stumped by Kirmani. Even then, if Rowe had showed some displeasure the umpire would have given him not out. But Lawrence is a nice guy and he smilingly walked away.

Richards got two lives. Bishen failed to hold a hot caught-and-bowled chance, which aggravated his finger injury. Off Bedi's next ball Kirmani dropped Richards behind the wicket. A lot of people had begun to call Kirmani, Richards' brother, for Kirmani had let him off a few times earlier in the series! The West Indies series was disappointing for Kirmani after his marvellous showing in New Zealand, but there is no doubt about his ability behind the stumps.

A further problem was created for us when Chandrasekhar injured his left thumb in an attempt to catch Lloyd off his own bowling. Later, it was found to be a fracture. He bowled gallantly, nevertheless, and got rid of the troublesome Richards with a googly.

Deryck Murray found an able partner in Holding and the two added valuable runs. Holding also got his first half century in tests, which prompted the crowd to storm on to the field and mob him. The West Indies were all out for 391 – a lead of 85 runs.

With just three batsmen in the team fit to bat, there was no hope of India making a fight of it and we closed our second innings at 97 for five. Mohinder Amarnath played a gallant innings to score 59 runs while Vengsarkar contributed 20. It wasn't a declaration but the termination of the innings since none of the others was fit to hold a bat. This left the West Indies to get 12 runs to win the Test and clinch the rubber.

Madan Lal was starting to bowl at the West Indian opening batsmen. Madan's bouncers would have caused much more damage to the West Indians, but I wanted him to bowl a beamer and then pretend as if the ball had slipped from his fingers. This was just to show Holding and company that we were not suckers to fall for that ruse. Balls, particularly beamers, don't slip from the fingers of Test bowlers and, surely, not in every over. All our seventeen players had been on the field some time or the other during the match, when Surinder Amarnath, the twelfth man, had to be rushed to hospital for an emergency appendicitis operation on the last day.

There has been a lot of comment from every quarter about the press conference that was called by our manager, Polly Umrigar, to protest against the intimidatory tactics of the West Indies bowlers. Clive Lloyd retorted by asking if we expected half-volleys to be hit for fours. May be Clive's lenses got fogged but we had hit deliveries, other than half-volleys, for fours! Clive also said that, in Australia, they got similar treatment from Lillee and Thomson but they didn't complain. True, but all through our tour we heard West Indian players moaning about the Australian umpires letting Thomson bowl from eighteen yards, and never calling him even once for overstepping.

Clyde Walcott made a statement that we must learn to play fast bowling and our complaint about intimidatory bowling was not justified. Imagine Clyde Walcott telling us what is right and wrong. As the wicketkeeper of the West Indies team in India during the 1948-49 season, he walked to the boundary, not once but time and again, to retrieve the ball thereby wasting time in order to deprive India of victory in a Test. Well, if Walcott could stoop to that level in 1948, no wonder the West Indians under Clive Lloyd touched a new low in a desperate effort to win by having all our eleven players hospitalised! So, for God's sake let's not have any more moralising, and should stop trying to teach others how to play.

The West Indies tour ended on a very sour note not because we lost the four-match series by two matches to one; but because of the patently unsporting manner in which the series was won. I am sure if umpire Gosein is honest, he will admit that a 2-all draw would have been a fair result!

The find of the twin-tour, if you can call a player who made his Test debut in 1969 as such, was Mohinder Amarnath. He is, without doubt, the most technically accomplished batsman in the side today. He needs to develop his temperament to play a long innings and when he does, he will be a force to reckon with in international cricket. This applies equally to Dilip Vengsarkar. He also needs a lot of hard work to earn a permanent place in our Test teams because he is richly endowed with talent.

Mohinder and Dilip are still very young and in the years to come, they will be the mainstay of India's batting. Our spinners are not getting any younger and this is one department where we may find a big gap after the present crop of world-class spinners retire. The wicketkeeping is safe in the hands of Kirmani who is a fair batsman as well. He must have learnt quite a lot from the West Indies series and with his willingness to train hard he should improve. These are the players of the future, though there are a few others who are established and will also be in the team.

Never before have I looked forward to returning home as keenly as this time. I was literally counting days when I would get to see my son who was already two months old. As soon as I learnt that I had had a son (I was in New Zealand at that time), I decided to name him Rohan after Rohan Kanhai, the West Indies cricketer whom I admire so much. He had helped me and given me sound advice during the Rest of the World team's tour of Australia. I am also a great admirer of M.L. Jaisimha who was my idol when I was a schoolboy. One of the shrewdest cricketing brains in the country, Jaisimha nursed me on my first tour with the Indian team to the West Indies in 1971.

Vishwanath and I first met during the Moin-ud-Dowla Gold Cup Tournament in Hyderabad. Our friendship had developed over the years so much that he is like an elder brother and a member of our family.

So, little wonder then that I should name my son Rohan Jaivishwa. He will certainly have a lot to live up to when he grows up!

I don't know what the future holds out for me. After this long twin-tour, I am not sure whether I would like to be out of the country for such a long time again. It will involve deep thinking, but right now I am concentrating on leading Bombay to victory in the Ranji Trophy. I am also looking forward to battle with the Kiwis and the Pommies, who will be visiting in the winter of 1976.

Over the years, Indian cricket-lovers have showered so much affection on me that I owe them a run-treat. So come on, ye Kiwis and Pommies!

21

Pleasures and Pains
of Touring

ONE OF THE MOST FREQUENT QUESTIONS I AM ASKED IS ABOUT THE treatment meted out to Indian cricketers abroad and life in the countries I have toured. The general impression seems to be that going on tour is a lot of fun. This is only partly true because, apart from the pleasure one undoubtedly gets, there is the negative aspect also.

The immediate problems when you go to another country is the language and the food. Not everybody in the Indian team can speak English fluently and by the time one gets used to the foreign accent, almost half the tour is over. For example, in the West Indies, the average man speaks terrible English. The grammar is all wrong and it's a very difficult job trying to understand what they are saying.

Food is another problem. The food abroad is so insipid and tasteless that all our boys find it tough to get something to fill their tummies. The south Indians in the team long for rice and the north Indians for spicy food. Luckily in England one finds plenty of Indian restaurants to eat and also some families who invite the boys for meals.

On the recent trip to New Zealand most of the boys were entertained by resident Indian families so often that the boys longed to have some typical New Zealand food. This was a bit of a problem in New Zealand where restaurants close down early, and it is not always possible to go and eat that early. The south Indians patronise Chinese restaurants for the rice and the north Indians empty the chillie sauce bottles onto their food.

Weather is another element which takes a long time for one to get used to. However, the players from the north adjust far more easily to the cold weather than those from the west and south where there is no real winter as such. Playing with four pullovers is certainly not the most convenient way of playing cricket, and keeping your hands in your pockets till the last possible second before the ball is bowled doesn't ensure good catching. Hard hits often are very cleverly avoided and so also sharp close-in catches, especially in extreme cold weather. It's also difficult to get a proper grip on the ball in such a weather. I know a few players who catch a cold in the plane, just thinking of the cold weather ahead.

Travelling can often be tedious. In England, particularly, it can be really weary. The boys have to check out of the hotel on the last morning of a match and the coach is ready in the evening outside the ground from where the team leaves for the place where they have to play the next match. Because the stay in the county is restricted to two days and departure is on the third morning, few boys bother to unpack their suitcases. Sometimes the team reaches the next county well after midnight and, by the time one is allotted a room, it is pretty nearly dawn.

On the 1971 tour of the West Indies, we flew in from St Kitts to Trinidad in the morning and then we had to drive forty miles to play. Everybody was barely awake, but fortunately Ajit Wadekar won the toss and elected to bat. As Ashok Mankad and I went out to open the innings, there were instructions to bat as long as we could so that the others could sleep. Salim Durrani, who was to bat at number three, told us, 'Bat as long as you can but please play shots, otherwise I will go to sleep with my pads on.'

Travelling by coach, though tiring, is often entertaining. The boys often conduct mock interviews. Farokh used to interview most of the players and the one with Eknath Solkar used to be the most humorous. Bawdy songs are sung and the card addicts sit down to fleece the newcomers in the team.

Touring with the Bombay team is the easiest. Time really flies with funsters like Solkar, Mankad and Abdul Ismail around. The long journey is hardly felt! The camaraderie of the Bombay team is unbelievable. The shy newcomer feels at home immediately and his nervousness is soon dispelled. The Bombay team has a Sunday Club, where everybody gathers around in the evening for a couple of hours to have a good time. There is a chairman for the meeting and he appoints two assistants who have to look after the refreshments for the rest of the team. The advantage of the Sunday Club is that it not only gets the team together, but also shows the youngsters and newcomers that the senior members are, after all, just like them. More importantly, it enables them to get to know their teammates better.

The tensions of the game as well as the success and failures are forgotten at this meeting. The player who has been dismissed for a duck has no time to brood over his failure. Fines are imposed for not adhering to the dress specified by the chairman. These fines are normally evenly imposed on everybody so that the evening's expenses and also future expenses are, to a large extent, taken care of. The Rest of the World team in Australia also has a Sunday Club. One club meeting required the players to attend wearing just a tie and an underwear. And no one was allowed to come to the meeting in a dressing gown. Everyone had to come all the way from their rooms to the meeting room in the specified uniform. There were a couple of boys who were not on the same floor as the room where the meeting was held, and it was a problem for them to get there without attracting attention. Thus, they had to use the staircase instead of the lift.

When the meeting began the chairman observed that Tony Greig and Hylton Ackerman were not wearing ties and would have to be fined. Greig, however, got up and said he was in fact wearing a tie. To prove this, he lowered his underpants to show that he was wearing the tie around his waist! His argument was that the chairman had not specified how and where exactly the tie was to be worn! Zaheer Abbas, who was the chairman, was hilarious. He wanted Rohan Kanhai to down his drink in a gulp, so he ordered, 'Mr Kanhai, I want you to do bottoms up!' Rohan, taking him literally, put *his* bottom up.

Yes, touring can be fun. There are some incidents which are incredibly funny. One of our boys, after a late night, was caught by the manager as he was returning to his room in the early hours of the morning. The manager had just opened the door of his room for the morning paper when the lift door opened and in walked our hero after a merry night. Though taken aback, he calmly wished the manager 'good morning'! The manager asked him, 'Where have you been so early in the morning?' Prompt came the reply, 'For an early morning walk.' Surprisingly, the manager believed it, without trying to find out how somebody could go for an early morning walk wearing a suit and the hair and tie dishevelled!

Then, there was another manager who clamped on a strict curfew, and would wait opposite the entrance of the hotel, usually behind a tree or a pillar, to catch the latecomers. One evening a few of us decided to surprise him. This time he was trying to stand inconspicuously at a bus-stop which was just opposite the hotel entrance. We were in time for our deadline and so decided to deliberately stroll there. When we reached the bus-stop we stopped and exclaimed, 'Good evening, Sir. Going out for a late night?' He stammered a reply saying that he was just out for some fresh air after a heavy dinner. Indeed!

On yet another occasion three of us decided to go out sightseeing. All of us were not playing in the next day's game so we weren't worried about having a late night. As we walked we talked of what we would do if the manager bumped into us around the corner. We had hardly said this when, rounding the corner, we actually ran into our manager. He immediately looked at his watch and asked where we were going. One of us replied, 'You know Sunny (as I am called), how he likes ties. He was taking us to show some ties that have caught his eye.' This manager was shrewd so he said he also wanted to buy ties for friends and he would walk with us to see the ties that I was supposed to have liked. With that went our hopes of sightseeing.

Fortunately, this schoolboyish treatment of the Indian cricketers is over and the managers now realise that a late night, now and then, helps, rather than having the boys in bed by ten every night. After all, during the Tests nobody really wants to have a late night. Everybody is aware of his responsibilities and will never try to bring about his own downfall.

On a long tour one tends to get homesick. There are days when there is no news from home either by letter or telephone. I know of one cricketer who had booked a call to his girlfriend every night of the twin-tour and got it only once, and that too the day before we left for home. Apparently the international telephone operators had never heard of this place in India, and their Indian counterparts always reported that the line was out of order.

The best part of a tour is the friends one makes in the countries one visits. More often than not one becomes more friendly with one from the opposite team. There are also the girls who add colour to the flannelled background.

The West Indies tour is a high-risk tour for bachelors. In 1953 Subhash Gupte got married to a girl from Trinidad. On the 1962 tour Dicky Rutnagur, who was covering the tour for a newspaper, got married to a Trinidadian; and in 1971, Govindraj met a Guyanese girl and married her on his return to India. In 1976, too, one player had got hooked, though whether wedding bells will ring, it is difficult to say.

During our 1976 tour in Guyana I got a very rare and interesting offer. Early one morning I got a telephone call from a girl who said she was in the foyer and wanted to see me. I asked her to wait and added it would take me a long time to come down. She said she was prepared to wait. When I eventually went down around lunch time, I had quite forgotten about her and was astonished to still find her waiting. She came and explained that she wanted to be a film actress in India and asked me to help her to get to India. I said that I didn't see any problem about her going to India because all one needed was a passport and an air ticket. She told me that her father had run away and so there was nobody who could sign her application for a passport. In that case, I asked, how was I going to help.

She hedged about a bit and then said there was one way I could help her and that was to marry her and take her as my wife! She assured me that once she reached India, she would go her own way. I told her I was already married, and there were a few bachelors in the team, so why pick on me? 'Well', she said, 'you're the most famous, that's why.' But, that was not the end of the story. After she was convinced that there was no way I could have gone down the wicket and got stumped by her, she asked me to forgive her for the bother and think of her as a sister!

This is one of the hazards of touring. Maybe after reading this, the Cricket Control Board will include another clause in the contract that the players have to sign before a tour, prohibiting a player entering into a matrimonial alliance while on tour!

22

Bombay, My Bombay

IT USED TO BE ONCE SAID THAT INDIAN CRICKET WAS 'BOMBAY cricket'. Those were the days when Bombay players accounted for half the Indian teams. In fact, on one occasion, nine of the eleven Test players were from Bombay. And not just playing in the side, but making a distinct contribution to the team's performance. Today, there are not more than four or five Bombay players in the Indian reckoning.

There is a misconception that the Bombay cricketer is proud and arrogant. This is not true, even though a Bombay cricketer will not suffer fools gladly. He is more often the one who is the friendliest. On the 1974 tour to England a member of the team from outside Bombay admitted to me that he was terribly mistaken about the boys from Bombay. He said, 'Where I come from, I was told that I must watch out for the Bombay boys. But I find boys. But I find that they are the ones who are the friendliest and who do not form groups.'

Yes, Bombay's contribution to Indian cricket has been tremendous; except in the matter of creating dissensions. That has been reduced to a fine art by a few officials outside Bombay. It is really unfortunate that the average cricketer is in awe of a Bombay cricketer. This often results in an inferiority complex, which, in turn, results in jealousy and envy. I know for a fact that Bombay cricketers go out of their way to make friends in the opposite camp. On the field they may be snarling, but off the field they are a mild lot.

The Bombay cricketer knows that he is what he is entirely due to hard work and his own efforts, unlike a few others who have come into Tests with backing from their states. This is the reason one finds most of the one-Test men from other states, while the number of one-Test cricketers from Bombay are negligible.

Cricket in Bombay, at all levels, is tough and no quarter is given and none asked for. Even a friendly fixture is played grimly and with seriousness. Right from his schooldays, the Bombay cricketer is aware that he has to be twice as good as the others, to be considered for higher honours. Besides, Bombay's cricket is organised so efficiently that there is nothing to complain about. The schoolboy cricketer, who rubs shoulders with Test heroes while playing in the Kanga League and other tournaments, is seldom bothered about reputations. Having played with Test stars, he is aware of the hard work they've put in and strives to emulate them. Competition is very keen and there are plenty of cricketers who have played in just one Ranji Trophy game, failed and never again got a look-in. There are always others waiting to occupy the places of those who cannot make good. This keeps the established players on their toes and they can never afford to be complacent and take their place in the team for granted.

Of all the tournaments in Bombay there are two which occupy pride of place: the H.D. Kanga League and the Times of India Shield. The Kanga League is the only tournament that is conducted by the Bombay Cricket Association. It is open only to clubs affiliated to the B.C.A. and has seven divisions, each with fourteen teams. The matches are played during the monsoon and as a result, many of the games played in July are washed out. The wickets are uncovered and are often exposed to rain. A cricketer's batting on these wickets helps to develop the instinct for survival, and the capacity to take punishment. This is strictly a tournament for bowlers and they invariably reap a rich harvest. A cricketer's batting ability is tested to the full and often technique is thrown overboard in favour of clean cross-batted heaves.

The outfield, which is not mown, makes the lofted shot a *must* in every batsman's repertoire of shots, because a full-blooded drive will often result only in a single due to the very slow outfield. Since the matches are spread over all available pitches, one often finds the square-leg position of one match and the cover-point position of another facing each other. Sometimes a mid-on of one match becomes the third-slip of another game being played alongside. I myself have contributed to the dismissal of a batsman in another game at the third slip position. Actually, I was at deep mid-on in our match. This put me next to the second slip of the game being played on the adjoining plot. An edge from the batsman hit me on the thigh and was gleefully caught by the second slip on the rebound. The batsman went away cursing his luck and I was profusely thanked by the fielding side for helping to get rid of a troublesome batsman.

Cricket matches are spread all over the city and there are occasions when a game in one area is completely washed out because of rain; while in the other area bright sunshine makes a full day's game possible.

Form can never be forecast and the weaker side often springs surprises on the stronger side. Towards the end of the Kanga League, when the rainy season ends, batsmen come into their own and there are fewer outright victories. This is the most tense stage when seemingly easy winners are left behind by unexpected opposition. The club of which I am captain, Dadar Union Sporting, has been winning the A Division pennant for the last four years. The pair of opening bowlers we have, V.S. Patil and Urani Mody, are unplayable. And, even when we have been dismissed for 60 runs, we have won the match comfortably, thanks to these two seamers. Dadar Union also boasts of the best all-round fielding side in the league, and some of the catches that the boys take are truly unbelievable.

The club house is unpretentious but the Dadar Union's contribution to Bombay cricket is enormous. Cricketers like Madhav Mantri, R.B. Kenny, N.S. Tamhane, the Amladi brothers, P.K. Kamath, V.S. Patil and V.J. Paranjape, among others, have played for Bombay and some for India. The present Dadar Union side contains almost all first-class players.

Right from the time of Madhav Mantri, discipline has been the Dadar Union's keynote and this has earned a great deal of respect, not only for the club but for the players as well.

The other important tournament in Bombay is the Times of India Shield. It is an interoffice tournament in which more than 260 office teams take part. All the matches, except those in the A Division, are knockout matches, played over the weekend. The A Division is divided into two groups and matches are played on a league basis. The winners of the two groups play the final for the coveted Times of India Shied. The competition has led to a lot of commercial organisations employing cricketers specially for playing in the tournament. An average cricketer is, thereby, assured of a job and it is up to him whether he makes use of his opportunity. The last date for joining an organisation to qualify for playing in the tournament is 1 September and in July and August hectic efforts are made to persuade a player to leave one organisation and join another. The matches are played over three days and are always keenly fought. There are some impressive performances and many cricketers get a chance to play in the Ranji Trophy on the strength of their performances in the Times Shield.

The only sore point is the poor standard of umpiring particularly in the A Division. Many interesting matches are ruined by umpiring errors. Admittedly the top umpires, being themselves employed, cannot stand for these matches as they are often played on weekdays. I feel that only those on the Ranji Trophy panel should be asked to umpire the A Division matches, thereby eliminating palpable mistakes.

This is the tournament where young boys can watch talent from practically all over the country. Almost every side in the A Division has about five Ranji Trophy players and even some Test stalwarts. When I was in school I used to watch these games and stand next to the sight-screen and try and learn from the Test players in action. I was once caught trying to cross the local railway track since I was in a hurry to get to the match and this was the quickest way to the ground. I was let off after a great deal of harassment by a railway sentry, and had to pay a fine for my offence. My regret is not that I had to pay a fine but that I missed the batting of Ajit Wadekar and Hanumant Singh, because their team had declared the innings closed even while I was pleading with tears in my eyes with the railway policeman to let me go.

These, and a host of other competitions, prepare the Bombay lad to face all kinds of situations. In the process he becomes a hard-boiled cricketer and a tough nut to crack. This is the stuff of which champions are made and is, perhaps, the reason why Bombay have been Ranji Trophy champions for so long.

A band of smiling officials who are always prepared to listen to the players, try to understand their point of view, and show utmost consideration to the players, also keeps the Bombay team happy. In all these years I don't think there has ever been a conflict between Bombay cricket officials and the players. This complete harmony makes Bombay what it is - the champions of Indian cricket. In fact, I can say without reservation that whatever I am in the game today is due, in a very large measure, to the fact that I have been nursed in the cradle of cricket, that is Bombay.

23

Men and Memories

'HELL, IS THAT MR DILIP SARDESAI SPEAKING? I AM AN ADMIRER OF his and I want to speak to him.'

'I am sorry, Dilip Sardesai is not in please.'

'Do you have any idea what time he will be back? I want to present him with a tape-recorder. By the way, who am I speaking to?'

'This is Salim Durrani, his roommate.'

'Oh, Mr Durrani, you are the one who took Gary Sobers' wicket and also Lloyd's, and got rid of these two to make India's victory easy. Oh, I am so happy to speak to you. I have got another tape-recorder for you. Please come and collect it and also the one for Sardesai. I am waiting in the foyer please.'

Salim Durrani was in his shorts when the telephone call came through, but he changed into respectable clothes and put on the India tie and came down to the foyer. Looking around he couldn't find anybody waiting with two tape-recorders. He made enquiries at the reception counter and went back to his room and changed back into his shorts again. Just then the telephone rang, and the caller said, 'Mr Durrani, I am waiting for you, aren't you coming down?' Salim replied: 'I had gone down, but I couldn't find you anywhere.'

'Oh, I had gone to the swimming pool to see a friend, but do please come down, I'll be waiting opposite the reception counter.'

So, Salim got back into his clothes once again, knotted his tie, smoothed back his hair and walked down the two floors to the reception counter.

Well, there was nobody waiting for him. He again asked the receptionist, went to the swimming pool and back again to the reception counter. Suddenly, a voice behind him said, 'So you want a tape-recorder, huh?' and, from behind a pillar, stepped out Dilip Sardesai who himself had made those calls to Salim. It was so funny that Salim himself started laughing, forgetting the trouble he had taken to dress up and come down to the reception counter twice in quest of a tape-recorder which just wasn't there.

The joke was on Salim this time, but he himself is capable of some terrific side-splitters. Ask him to tell you the one about the spin of the coin at Hyderabad. If that doesn't make you double-up with laughter, nothing will.

Salim, Uncle to all of us, and Prince Salim to his contemporaries of the sixties, is a unique character. I can't think of any left-hander who had as much grace on the cricket field as Salim. The crowds simply love him. During the 1972-73 series against England he was known for his ability to give the crowd a six on demand. The crowd only had to ask and he obliged by banging the ball into the stands. He has a readymade title for his book, *Ask for a Six* I don't know if he will ever write it, but I do hope he does.

Salim has been a much misunderstood man. He has been called moody and this stigma has stuck to him. But this is not a correct estimate of the man. He treats a Test match as he would treat a club game. He is a crowd-puller, first and last. He is often accused of not taking Test cricket seriously. This is equally untrue. I recall, during the 1971 West Indies tour when Salim was failing with the bat after a dazzling beginning, how upset he was about his form. He very badly wanted to make the England trip later on, especially because he had missed the 1959 and 1967 tours. Eventually he was not selected for the 1971 tour to England, but he came back with a vengeance in 1972, winning the Duleep Trophy single-handed for the Central Zone.

Salim is not much of a believer in a workout at the nets, and this has probably earned him the moody tag.

Money is a commodity which Salim will never be able to keep. He is so generous and warm-hearted that he will go out of his way to help anybody. Just before we left for the 1971 tour of the West Indies, Salim and a few others, including myself, were invited to play against the visiting Sri Lanka team. We had travelled by air from Bombay to Madras but, from Guntur to Madras, on our return journey, we had to travel by train which involved an overnight journey. Salim, with his customary charm, had organised a bed-roll for himself. Having travelled by air I had no bedding for the train journey and the cold wintry night made sleeping a problem. When Salim saw my predicament he promptly gave me his blanket and a sheet to cover myself. He was chatting away with some passengers and so wasn't prepared to sleep yet.

251

When I woke up the next morning I saw Salim fast asleep, all huddled up, to keep himself warm. I couldn't believe it. An established Test cricketer and a hero had given his only blanket and sheet to a young, unknown Ranji Trophy player. This overwhelmingly generous and totally unselfish side to Salim's personality is not known to many who only point out his faults. From that day Salim became uncle to me. His attitude towards the younger cricketers is so generous that they forget their nervousness and discuss their problems with him without inhibitions. He is always there to advise young players and give them every encouragement.

People call him a wayward genius. I don't know about his being wayward but he is certainly a genius. A genius whom the authorities have never bothered to understand.

Cricket-lovers all over the world know Farokh Engineer as a wicketkeeper of the highest class. When they watch him behind or in front of the stumps, they immediately realise that here is a man who obviously enjoys his cricket and is willing to give, in turn, enjoyment to the playing public. His acrobatic dramatics behind the wickets always keeps the crowd in good humour. Not only the crowd, but he keeps even the fielders on their toes with his chatter. Hardly is a ball bowled without Farokh saying something either to the batsmen or the fielders. It doesn't have to be cricket, of course. It can be anything. And with the Indian team he has to speak in Gujarati, very seldom in English.

In the slips he would turn round and ask a silly thing like, 'Why don't you talk? After reading *Playboy* last night you aren't talking much.' 'Dr Hill, ask Eknath how much does 37 and 19 make?' All nonsense and nothing to do with the game, but just to keep you awake and not get bored. Once he stumped a batsman out and asked him politely if he was in a hurry to catch a train home. You can be assured that with Farokh an evening can never be dull. Even if it is a team meeting, Farokh puts his points across humorously.

At a team meeting in Madras, on the eve of the fourth Test against the West Indies, electricity failed for quite a long time. Venkataraghavan had not come for the meeting for some reason, and the meeting went on without him even after the electricity failed. When the meeting was over, it was still dark and, as Prasanna was about to take everybody's leave, Farokh quipped: 'Be careful, Venky might be hiding outside.' The tensions of the serious matters that the team had discussed just faded away after this remark.

On the Rest of the World team's tour of Australia, he was always teasing Intikhab and Bob Cunis about their bulk. One day both of them challenged him to a hundred metres race. Farokh kept on postponing the event for some reason or the other. Finally, with everybody fit, it was decided to have the race during the Tasmania match. Bill Jacobs, the manager, was the starter and Tony Greig and Norman Gifford the judges. Farokh came last!

When war broke out between India and Pakistan, Farokh was always practising how to 'bayonet' Intikhab Alam with his bat and ended up by commenting that he would need a really sharp bayonet to pierce through the Pakistani player's bulk.

Farokh's favourite leg-pull is when he goes in his car to the ground for a match in England. He would tell the person with him that he had forgotten how to get to the ground and would stop the car near a passer-by. Naturally, the person with him would request the man on the road for directions to go to the ground. Just as the man started answering, Farokh would accelerate the car and drive away a laugh since he already knew the way to the ground. It was a sight to watch the sheepish face of his co-passenger person next to him. Farokh did that to Ajit Wadekar once and Ajit was so startled by the sudden acceleration that he didn't know what was happening. His expression was worth recording for future laughs!

In spite of his ready wit and humorous ways, Farokh is not liked in international cricket. Cricketers of other countries think that he is tricky. A serious allegation indeed and Farokh's reply is that all is fair in love and war, and Test cricket nowadays is more akin to a war between twenty-two players.

Even among members of the Indian team he is not particularly popular. This is basically because, in order to hide his own failures, he will put the blame on others. If he has dropped a catch his general gestures will be to show to the crowd that it wasn't really a catch, but a deflection off the pad or some such thing. He has got away with it often. During the 1972-73 series against England he missed twelve chances until the Madras Test and only three were reported by the press. It is well known that Farokh will go to the journalists in the evening and explain that it wasn't a chance at all, just the excitement made the fielders throw up their arms.

The bowler who shows his anguish at a dropped catch is ticked off for his theatrics. One such remark produced one of the ugliest dressing room scenes I have ever seen. This was between Farokh and Abid Ali during the Prudential World Cup match against East Africa at Leeds. On the field, too, one noticed both saying things to each other heatedly. As soon as the team came in for lunch the fireworks started. It was more like a bout between Mohammad Ali and Joe Frazier, the difference being that both threatened each other with bats. Unfortunately for the bat manufacturers, the stronger bat was never found out, because the other members of the team intervened and stopped the quarrel from proceeding further.

254

Yet it was horrible while it lasted. The manager, Mr G.S. Ramchand, completely forgot about this incident in his report. Of course, he was engrossed in reporting other players to the Board!

Yet, one cannot deny that Farokh Engineer is a player whom the crowds come to watch and team-mates rely upon. He has been India's saviour often and for that Indian cricket owes him a lot. He has truly been one of cricket's rare characters, a man whom the crowds call King Farokh.

In recent years no Indian tour has taken place without Ekki Solkar. At his peak in 1971 he was known as Mr Reliable and Mr Dependable. Now, on his own admission, he is not so reliable and dependable. But from 1971 to 1976, Ekki has remained the same. Incredibly funny and truly a great bloke to have around on a tour. A spirited cricketer, he thrives in tense situations which he has found by the dozen from 1969 to 1974, not only in the Tests but also for Bombay, though much less than in the Tests. If a popularity poll was taken among Indian cricketers Ekki would certainly top the list along with Vishwanath. His spontaneous and infectious smile, even during failures, has made even the most hardened players sympathise with him. And his attitude during the good times has been that of a man who would like to share it with the others.

He has been the target of many leg-pulls and many a joke has been attributed to Ekki, though he may not even be aware of it. Not very proficient in English, he still manages to get his message across in his own way, leaving the others in the team doubling up with laughter.

He loves a fight out in the middle. A tense situation brings out the best in him. In other situations he tends to relax and pays for his lack of concentration. Dilip Sardesai and he rallied India so often in the 1971 series against the West Indies that some West Indian spectators called theirs the Laurel and Hardy act. In the Barbados Test, Ekki had stayed at the wicket by sheer determination. He played and missed often but stuck to his task. While their partnership was on, the ball lost shape and had to be changed. Ekki asked to have a look at the changed ball, at which Gary Sobers remarked, 'It won't make any difference since you are going to play and miss anyway!' Ekki's retort was: 'You play your way, let me play my way.'

Also in 1971, after we were introduced to the Queen at tea on the first day of the first Test, Ekki said a hello to Geoff Boycott. Boycott, still smarting from his cheap dismissal in the morning, mistook the smile for a derisive smile and said 'The next ... innings I will be batting with a hundred at this time and then you won't ... smile.' Now, Ekki never likes to lose in a battle of words and he was replying even before Boycott had finished, 'You bloody wait, next bloody innings I will take you out bloody.' He didn't, but in 1974 he did get Boycott out four times and the last time was the last Test innings of Geoff Boycott till today. The result was that Boycott did not give him his benefit tie, which he had earlier said he would give Ekki.

Ekki is a marvellous mimic. One has to see and hear him mime to believe that if he hadn't been a cricketer he would certainly have made a great mimic. When he mimed Durrani, Engineer (whom he calls Dikra Farokh), Pataudi, Jaisimha and Wadekar, among the Indians, and Sobers, Fredericks and Kalicharan one can get a stomachache laughing. He also mimics Indian film stars very well. I do suspect that Ekki's secret ambition is to act in a film and, I am sure, the Indian team can vouch for his acting ability.

Ekki has come up from very humble beginnings. His performances as a cricketer are, therefore, of greater merit when one considers the odds he has had to overcome. Today

Ekki is such a devoted family man that he doesn't even want to stay in the dressing room once the game is over, being always in a rush to get back home.

Shopping on a tour abroad with Ekki is great fun. He can never make up his mind about anything and is always hesitant before he finally buys something. Very fond of beer, his reason being that it will help him to put on weight. He is an extremely poor eater but still manages to do some wonderful, strenuous exercises.

In New Zealand he found he was getting persistent headaches and had difficulty in breathing. The doctor who examined him advised him to forget his beer for some time. Ekki, however, was found sneaking a peg of whisky to his room. The next day, when confronted with this, he explained that he had not touched the whisky, only kept it under his bed in case he found it difficult to sleep! A unique sleeping dose, but typically like Ekki, for he himself is a unique character.

People who are used to watching Vishwanath and Farokh Engineer standing next to each other behind the wicket will only see Farokh joking with his customary gestures. Vishwanath is always the silent observer. But, enter the privacy of the dressing room and suddenly Vishwanath will be dispelling tensions with a funny remark made with a straight face. He is quick at cutting jokes and looking at him, no one would suspect what a tremendous fund of humour he has. If you hear laughter and a mini-riot inside, you can be sure the cause is Vishwanath and the target, in all probability, Eknath Solkar.

I think Vishwanath's ability at wisecracking can be matched only by Richard Hutton. Vishwanath's Hindi will horrify the purist from the north, but his accent and delivery are extremely humorous. When he finds himself stuck for a word, his hands speak a lot more than his tongue. He observes people keenly

257

and notes everything about them, storing away some important characteristic in his mind for future use. Often, he surprises you by recounting something you may have said at your first meeting with him.

Totally unassuming, in spite of his excellent international record, he is averse to giving advice to other team members unless he is specifically asked. Nevertheless he remains a popular man in the team. For sheer popularity in India nobody can touch him. All over India the crowds go wild over him and he has very seldom disappointed them. In Bangalore he is King but then the Bombay and Calcutta crowds love him no less. The applause when he walks in to bat is to be heard to be believed. He is aware of this tremendous affection that people have for him and he is always striving to give the crowd a lot of pleasure by his batting. Even a brief innings from Vishwanath is enough, though such an innings is disastrous, as far as the Indian team is concerned. His batting is an education for young aspiring cricketers. In fact, Vishwanath's entire demeanour on the cricket field is exemplary. He is always in control of his emotions, except once, when I remember he showed a trace of annoyance. This was in the second Test at Christchurch against New Zealand (1976). Glenn Turner had survived yet another appeal for leg-before and Vishwanath turned to me in the slips and said, 'If we get the same consideration we will score double centuries in every game.'

I am reminded of a funny incident associated with Vishwanath when he and a few others were invited by 'Tiger' Pataudi to play a match in Bhopal. On the rest day they decided to go on a shikar. They had hardly entered the jungle when suddenly they were surrounded by dacoits who fired a few shots from their rifles in the air, warning them not to try anything funny. Vishwanath, Prasanna and the other members of the party were asked to get down from the jeeps and hand over their belongings. When one of the men accompanying them tried to run, he was shot down by the dacoit leader. Vishwanath and Prasanna were told that they were being held to ransom. The petrified Vishwanath, who was tied to a tree, started weeping and explaining that he was an Indian Test cricketer and the country needed his services. The dacoits had never heard of cricket and weren't in the least bit impressed. They were eventually released when the ransom was supposedly paid to the dacoits and Vishwanath breathed a sigh of relief.

Only later did they come to know that the dacoits were, in fact, Tiger Pataudi's servants and the whole incident was staged as a big hoax! Prasanna knew this because Tiger had told him earlier, but poor Vishwanath to this day doesn't believe that it was a make-believe hold-up, and cannot help shivering in fright when reminded of it. Even the man who was supposedly shot down by the dacoits was not enough to convince Vishwanath that he was the victim of a practical joke. The experience was too much for him.

He took all this in his stride, as he takes every dig at him phlegmatically. He may pull people's legs but it is his ability to laugh at himself that makes him so well-liked, unlike Farokh Engineer who only wants to make fun of others and can't take a joke at his expense in the right spirit.

Another character in the Indian cricket scene is Ashok Mankad. Called Kaka, because it also happens to be the nickname of the film star Rajesh Khanna of whom he is a great admirer, Ashok is a great story-teller. His recounting of various incidents, with just the right mixture of spice and exaggeration, enlivens the evening on a tour. His ability to make people laugh makes him a great asset on a tour when one is feeling low. He loves to play cards and comes out with an incredible variation of runs. On all the tours I have been with him, I have never seen him lose except on rare occasions. Long train journeys are never tedious when Kaka is around. His winnings at cards at others' expense are adequate remuneration for the constant entertainment he provides.

The 1971 tour of England was not a memorable one for Ashok. He just couldn't get going in the Tests, though he scored heavily in the county games. Yet, he never lost his sense of humour. At the end of the series when he had got into double figures in the last innings, he was telling the English players that they should count themselves lucky that the series was confined to only three Tests. He told them he was just getting into form and would certainly have got 25 runs in the fifth Test!

Kaka is an avid cinema-goer and whenever there is a good scene in a film he is watching, he would invariably stand up and applaud. This can be pretty embarrassing for the others who are with him, but Kaka just doesn't bother and he will not change his habit. After seeing the movie *Cromwell*, the way he talked to the cab-driver must have made the poor cabby wonder where he had picked up his passengers! The poor cabby, who couldn't understand English beyond a few words, was bombarded with such phrases as, 'In the name of the Lord, I beseech you to take us to the CCI', and 'I beseech you to drive more slowly.' But, how can one blame the cabby for trying to drive fast so that he could be rid of his mad fare as quickly as possible!

Richard Hutton, son of the fabulous (Sir) Len Hutton of England, is the wittiest cricketer I have come across. My first impression of him was of a cocky Englishman whose only good point was that he had a famous last name. Certainly, he didn't look impressive in the first Test at Lord's in 1971. I didn't very much like his remarks, as I took runs off his bowling. Every time I played a shot off my legs he would remark, as I turned for the second run, 'Why don't you play where my field is?' The next time he said it, I told him to bowl to his field so, may be, I could play where his field was. This chattering went on nonstop, particularly when a batsman took runs off him. He would be waiting for you at the end of his follow-through, with his hands on his hips and the usual question on his lips. We didn't find him amusing at all. After I returned from Australia, I told the others that he was an extremely peculiar person, but I wasn't believed.

Despite Hutton's peculiarity, the Australian tour by the Rest of the World team was thoroughly enjoyable, thanks to Richard Hutton. I realised on this tour that talking to the batsmen is a habit with Richard. Perhaps he feels his bowling ability is inadequate to get a batsman out and so he likes to have a verbal weapon in his armoury. In the Brisbane Test, Hutton was hit all over the place by Stackpole when he bowled his first over. In the second over, Richard found his length and beat Stackpole thrice on the forward stroke. Walking down the pitch he asked Stackpole in all seriousness, 'Why are you pulling the fielder's legs, why don't you edge one for a change?' Every time he was whacked by an Australian batsman, he would throw out a challenge, 'Just you come down to Sheffield or Leeds, on a green wicket, and I'll see you.' Of course, nobody took him seriously. The day before the Test at Perth, we had gone to see the wicket. Richard threw a ball on the wicket and when it bounced back, he quipped, 'Eh, it came back. At Leeds it would have got stuck.'

Rohan Kanhai was, yet again, hit on the chest during the Perth Test. When he came back after an x-ray, he was greeted by Richard with the remark, 'Don't come near me, with all the x-rays you've had taken so far, you must be radioactive.' To Clive Lloyd who was having black coffee, Richard remarked,

'Don't be racial, Hubert, have some milk too.' But, by far, his best quip on the Australian tour was when he was asked at a cocktail party, 'How are the Australian girls treating you?' Richard who, till then, hadn't exactly had a roaring time, replied, 'Well, it looks like the Australian birds are a good deal colder than the weather.'

Richard Hutton loved to go sunbathing in Australia and was forever looking for an opportunity to slip down to the beach. By January he had a terrific tan and he was telling us how he was going to show his tan off to the Londoners in the cold month of February. Richard was a terrific chairman of the Sunday Club. The standard he set at the first meeting could never be touched by subsequent meetings, and by popular demand he was again voted chairman of the last Sunday Club before our dispersal and his farewell gifts to the players brought out delighted howls from the members. Our manager on that tour, Bill Jacobs, called him the funniest man he'd ever met. He was not only that, but a good bowler too, only when he bowled to his field, of course!

Centuries (30)

282	vs. Bihar, at Bombay, 1971-72
220	vs. West Indies, at Port of Spain, 1970-71 (2nd innings)
203	vs. Sri Lanka, at Hyderabad, 1975-76
194	vs. Worcestershire, at Worcester, 1971
190	vs. Maharashtra, at Bombay, 1975-76
176	vs. Maharashtra, at Poona, 1970-71
171	vs. Saurashtra, at Bombay, 1975-76
165	vs. Leicestershire, at Leicester, 1971
160	vs. Gujarat, at Bombay, 1972-73
157	vs. Bengal, at Bombay, 1971-72
156*	vs. Karnataka, at Ahmedabad, 1974-75 (Irani Cup)
156	vs. West Indies, at Port of Spain (II Test), 1975-76
136	vs. Surrey, at The Oval, 1974
135˙	vs. Madhya Pradesh, at Indore, 1972-73

134	vs. Hyderabad, at Bombay, 1972-73
128	vs. T.N. Pearse's XI, at Scarborough, 1971
125	vs. Trinidad, at Port of Spain, 1970-71
124	vs. West Indies, at Port of Spain (1st innings), 1970-71
117*	vs. West Indies, at Bridgetown, 1970-71
116	vs. West Indies, at Georgetown, 1970-71
116	vs. New Zealand, at Auckland, 1975-76
114	vs. Rajasthan, at Bombay, 1969-70
112	vs. Gujarat, at Bulsar, 1975-76
108	vs. Rest of India, at Bangalore, 1973-74 (Irani Cup)
104*	vs. Lancashire, at Manchester, 1974
104	vs. Gujarat, at Bombay, 1970-71
104	vs. Sri Lanka Board's President's XI, at Colombo, 1973-74
102	vs. West Indies, at Port of Spain, 1975-76 (III Test)
101	vs. England, at Old Trafford, 1974
101	vs. East Zone, at Calcutta, 1971-72

* Indicates not out

Career Highlights

1. Playing in his first Test series against West Indies in the West Indies, scored 774 runs, averaging 154.80 in four tests. It is the highest aggregate for a player making his debut. This included four centuries, with two separate hundreds, 124 & 220, in the last test at Port of Spain. He is the second Indian to score two separate hundreds in a Test, and the only one to score a century and double century in the same Test.

2. He 'carried his bat' through an innings for Bombay against Karnataka, in the Irani Cup match, 1974-75, for 156 runs.

3. His best bowling figures in an innings are three for 43 in the Ranji Centenary match, 1972-73, and two for 8 vs. Hampshire, in England, 1971.

4. His aggregate of 1,169 runs on the 1970-71 tour of the West Indies and 1,141 runs on the 1971 tour of England are the highest by an Indian on West Indies tour and a short tour of England.

5. Was a member of the Rest of the World team which toured Australia in 1971-72. Participated in Double Wicket Tournament at Barbados, 1971; and was also invited to participate in the Garfield Sobers' Benefit Fund match at Barbados in 1972.

6. Was appointed captain of India vs. West Indies in the second Test at Delhi, 1974-75, but could not play owing to injury. Led India in the first test against New Zealand, at Auckland, 1975-76, and scored 116. India won the match by six wickets.

7. Has captained Bombay in the Ranji Trophy, and West Zone in the Duleep Trophy and Irani Cup matches.

8. During 1965-66 Harris Shield matches in the Senior Interschools Tournament, Bombay, Gavaskar hit four hundreds and, in the All-India Schools Tournament for the Cooch-Bihar Trophy, scored 760, averaging 152.00 with scores of – 33 & 7 not out vs. Gujarat, 158 vs. Baroda, 246 not out vs. Central Zone, 222 vs. East Zone and 85 & 9 in the final against North Zone. Created record for the All-India Schools Tournament for the first-wicket partnership when he (246 not out) and Anwar Quereshi (203) added 421 runs.

9. Gavaskar (209) and Ramesh Nagdev (349), for St. Xavier's College, Bombay, put on 472 for a record first-wicket partnership, against the Institute of Science, in the Inter-Collegiate Tournament, Bombay.

10. Holds the highest individual record in the Inter-University Tournament, with a score of 327 for Bombay against Gujarat, 1970-71; and also for the Vizzy Trophy Tournament for Inter-University Zonal matches, with a score of 247 not out against South Zone Universities, 1968-69.

11. Making his debut in the Inter-University Tournament for the Rohinton-Baria Trophy in 1966-67, he scored 106 for Bombay against Jabalpur; and 139 not out in the next match against Baroda.

12. Was the recipient of the 'Chhatrapati Shivaji Award' in 1971-72 as the outstanding Sportsman of the Year. Has won the top prize given by the P.J. Hindu Gymkhana, Bombay, to the outstanding cricketer in the country; one of the two cricketers to win the L.R. Tairsee Gold Medal twice – in 1970-71 and 1975-76 – and was awarded the S.V. Rajadhyaksha Prize as the best fielder in the country in 1972-73, when he took sixteen catches in the Ranji Trophy matches during the season. In 1970-71, the Bombay Cricket Association awarded him the Justice Tendulkar Trophy as the Best Senior Cricketer of the Year.

SUNIL GAVASKAR IN FIRST-CLASS CRICKET
Compiled by Anandji Dossa

TESTS

	Year	M	I	N.O.	H.S.	Runs	Avge	100's	Bowling Runs	W	Fielding Avge	Ct.
vs. West Indies	1970-71	4	8	3	220	774	154.80	4	9	0	-	1
vs. England	1971	3	6	0	57	144	24.00	-	42	0	-	5
vs. England	1972-73	5	10	1	69	224	23.88	-	7	0	-	2
vs. England	1974	3	6	0	101	217	36.16	1	5	0	-	1
vs. West Indies	1974-75	2	4	0	86	108	27.00	-				1
vs. New Zealand	1975-76	3	5	1	116	266	66.50	1				5
vs. West Indies	1975-76	4	7	0	156	390	57.14	2				2
Total		24	46	5	220	2123	51.77	8	63	0		17

UNOFFICIAL TESTS

	Year	M	I	N.O.	H.S.	Runs	Avge	100's	Bowling Runs	W	Fielding Avge	Ct.
vs. Australia	1971-72	5	10	1	68*	257	28.55	-				5
vs. Sri Lanka	1973-74	2	4	0	85	106	26.50	-	1	0		4
vs. Sri Lanka	1975-76	1	2	0	203	238	119.0	1	8	0		1
Total		8	16	1	203	601	40.06	1	9	0		10

* Indicates not out

IRANI CUP

	Year	M	I	N.O.	H.S.	Runs	Avge	100's	Bowling		Fielding	
									Runs	W	Avge	Ct.
For Bombay	1967-68	1	2	0	5	5	2.50	-	-	-	-	0
	1970-71	1	2	1	46*	58	58.00	-	-	-	-	2
	1971-72	1	2	0	48	71	35.50	-	5	0	-	0
	1972-73	1	2	0	6	6	3.00	-	-	-	-	3
	1973-74	1	2	0	108	132	66.00	1	5	0	-	0
For Rest of India	1974-75	1	1	1	156*	156	156.00	1	12	0	-	0
For Bombay	1975-76	1	1	0	47	47	47.00	-	-	-	-	0
	Total	7	12	2	156*	475	47.50	2	22	0	-	5

AGAINST VISITING SIDES

	Year	M	I	N.O.	H.S.	Runs	Avge	100's	Bowling		Fielding	
									Runs	W	Avge	Ct.
86 & 0	1972-73 for Board President's XI vs. M.C.C.											2
81	1974-75 for West Zone vs. West Indies											3
29	1975-76 for West Zone vs. Sri Lanka											1
	Total	3	4	0	86	196	49.00				-	6

* Indicates not out

RANJI TROPHY

Year	M	I	N.O.	H.S.	Runs	Avge	100's	Bowling Runs	W	Fielding Avge	Ct.
1969-70	2	3	1	114	141	70.51	1			-	6
1970-71	2	3	0	176	307	102.33	2	19	1	19.00	0
1971-72	3	5	0	282	494	98.80	2	21	0	-	8
1972-73	7	12	2	160	579	57.90	3	0	1	06.00	16
1973-74	6	9	1	84	248	31.00	-	-	-	-	11
1974-75	5	6	2	96*	203	50.75	-	6	0	-	4
1975-76	4	5	1	190	510	127.50	3	4	0	-	5
Total	29	43	7	282	2482	68.97	11	50	2	25.00	50

DULEEP TROPHY

Year	M	I	N.O.	H.S.	Runs	Avge	100's	Bowling Runs	W	Fielding Avge	Ct.
1971-72	2	3	0	101	138	46.00	1	17	0	-	2
1972-73	2	3	1	55	65	32.50	-	-	-	-	2
1973-74	1	2	1	53*	65	65.00	-	-	-	-	0
1974-75	2	4	0	41	76	19.00	-	-	-	-	3
1975-76	1	2	0	84	124	62.00	-	37	0	-	0
Total	8	14	2	101	468	39.00	1	54	0	-	7

* Indicates not out

TOURS

	Year	M	I	N.O.	H.S.	Runs	Avge	100's	Bowling Runs	W	Fielding Avge	Ct.
West Indies	1970-71	8	16	4	220	1169	97.41	5	62	0	-	2
England	1971	15	27	1	194	1141	43.88	3	190	4	47.50	10
Australia	1971-72	11	20	2	95	559	31.05	-	4	0	-	9
Sri Lanka	1973-74	4	8	1	104	316	45.14	1	1	0	-	7
England	1974	14	26	2	136	993	41.37	3	60	2	30.00	6
New Zealand	1975-76	6	11	1	116	313	31.30	1	40	0	-	7
West Indies	1975-76	7	12	0	156	608	50.66	2	53	1	53.00	5

OTHER FIRST-CLASS MATCHES

	Year		100's	Bowling Runs	W	Fielding Avge	Ct.
39 & 38*	1971-72	Indian XI vs. Rest of India	-	20	0	-	0
34 & 6	1972-73	Board's President's XI vs. Ranji XI		43	3	14.33	0
12	1973-74	Indian XI vs. Rest of India (Karmarkar Benefit)	-			-	0
Total	3	5	1	39	129	32.25	-	63	3	31.00	0

271

* Indicates not out

SUMMARY
(Up to the end of the 1975-76 season)

Year	M	I	N.O.	H.S.	Runs	Avge	100's	Bowling Runs	W	Fielding Avge	Ct.
Ranji Trophy	29	43	7	282	2483	68.97	11	50	2	25.00	50
Tests	24	46	5	220	2123	51.77	8	63	0	-	17
Duleep Trophy	8	14	2	101	468	39.00	1	54	0	-	7
Irani Cup	7	12	2	156*	475	47.00	2	22	0	-	5
Unofficial Tests	8	16	1	203	601	40.06	1	9	0	-	10
Visiting Sides	3	4	0	86	196	49.00	-	-	-	-	6
Tours	65	120	11	220	5099	46.77	15	410	7	58.57	46
Other First-Class Matches	3	5	1	39	129	32.25	-	63	3	21.00	0

* Indicates not out

272

IDOLS

1

Alan Knott

ALAN KNOTT IS THE FINEST WICKETKEEPER I HAVE SEEN. HE
came into the England team in 1968-69 when he was picked
as an understudy to Jim Parks for the tour of the West Indies.
Midway through the tour, he was included in the XI and played
two determined innings which saved England from defeat.
Thereafter, he was a regular member of the team until the
Packer affair. He has an incredible record in Tests behind him,
both as a wicketkeeper and a batsman.

I first saw Alan Knott in 1971 when the Indian team toured
England and the match against Kent was played at Canterbury.
Knott kept wickets brilliantly and took balls, going down the leg
side, with so much ease and that too with his right hand that
it was more than obvious that here was a wicketkeeper of
extraordinary quality.

His batting was always dangerous and though he did not score many runs in that game against the Indians, we knew that he was a very dangerous player, coming at No. 7 and capable of turning the match with his totally unorthodox batting.

In Tests that summer, he kept wickets brilliantly, hardly conceding any byes, and he was such a livewire that he used to inspire the rest of the team with his performance. That was the time when spinners were more in use and his "keeping to the spinners" was of the highest order. I still remember the catch he took in the Oval Test to dismiss Dilip Sardesai off Underwood. It was an edge and the ball would have normally gone away between the wicketkeeper and the first slip, but Knott was quick enough to reach his right hand out and catch that snick. The ball would not have carried to a slip fielder. That dismissal was crucial because Sardesai was batting beautifully and looked in control of the situation.

Of course, for the quick bowlers he was absolutely magnificent. His diving was superb and the effortless triumphant way in which he came up with the ball in his gloves had be seen to be believed. His joy was infectious and spread quickly to the rest of the team as soon as the wicket had fallen and he would be the first to rush to the bowler to congratulate him on capturing a wicket.

In 1974 he took two catches, one to dismiss Brijesh Patel in the Lord's Test and the other to dismiss Ashok Mankad, diving both the times between the first and the second slips and picking up the ball which was going to fall short of the slip fielders. Someone like Knott behind the wickets meant that England actually had a sharp edge to it and that nothing would be missed. In fact, when Knott was keeping wickets, the first slip would stand a little wider and so would the leg slip. Some of the finest leg glances would be covered by Knott's agility.

His batting was generally unorthodox, although he played

straight most of the time. It was only when the spinners came on the scene that he used his reflexes and eyesight and played shots which many a top batsman would not even dream of. His shots were not in the M.C.C. coaching book and, certainly, cannot be recommended to the young aspirant trying to learn the art of batting. These were all typical Knott shots and they came through because he had great ability and confidence in his batting. His sweeping was precise and he would sweep the ball from outside the off-stump anywhere between mid-wicket and the finest of the fine-leg. Similarly, short balls from pacemen would be regularly cut over the slips' heads for four runs. In a way, this was more frustrating to the quick bowlers because to be cut over the slips' heads regularly is very, very annoying, as most of the fast bowlers would testify.

Later, after having played fast bowlers on the Packer circuit, he changed his grip and was able to fend off the short, rising deliveries and play them down instead of sending them up in the air. This meant that he practically lost the drive from his batting armoury and had to rely mainly on cuts and deflections to score most of the runs. He was always a good cutter and with his ability to push and run singles, he was seldom kept in check and only bowlers like Bishen Bedi and Chandrasekhar could bowl to him and earn his respect. This eventually led to his famous sweep shots from anywhere, even outside the off-stump. To score over 4,000 Test runs is ample proof of his batting ability and that too against the best bowlers in the world.

When he came to India with the England team in 1976, England had perhaps decided as part of their strategy, to appeal for anything and everything and go running to the umpires. To a great extent, they succeeded in the first two Tests when, for every strong appeal, they found the umpires responding in their favour. Alan Knott was one of the players who led the appeals and he used to throw the ball in the air even if the batsman had missed it by the width of a foot or two. This happened in Delhi where Underwood was turning the ball appreciably. After this had happened more than once I turned to Knotty and said, "Well, I hope you will be able to finish what you have started, because if we boys start appealing, you have no chance." Thereafter, Knotty was a little less exuberant in his appeals, though the rest of the slip fielders, including Fletcher, Underwood and Tony Greig, continued to appeal.

However, their appealing lost strength considerably since Knott was not that willing a partner in their tactics. But, then, wicketkeepers all over the world have a tendency to appeal because that's the way the bowlers all over the world want them to act. The bowlers believe that if there is no support from the wicketkeeper in appealing, umpires generally tend to ignore the appeal. If a wicketkeeper chips in with the appeal, then the umpire gives it serious consideration. But that does not mean that Knott was a cheat. He was one of the nicest persons you could ever come across. Off the field, he was always smiling, always willing to exchange a word with you and to wicketkeepers all over the world, he was always available for any tips on their technique, on physical fitness or any other mattter concerning wicketkeeping.

He was a physical-fitness freak and that could be seen by the number of exercises he did even while waiting for the bowler to go back to his bowling mark. These exercises, he explained, were necessary to loosen up his joints which were rather stiff. He was a health fanatic also and very carefully chose his diet. For example, when he came on his first tour of India in 1972-73, he brought along with him a lot of canned food. He decided to eat plenty of fruits and did not take anything else. When he was signing autographs, he reportedly used his own pen and did not use those offered by the cricket fans. I do not know how far this is true, but it goes to show how careful he was about his health. It may seem as if it was a bit much, but then he had to ensure that nothing endangered his professional career. I remember sitting with him at a lunch table in New York when we had gone to America for the Rest of the World match against the All Americans. I was simply amazed at how carefully he chose his food and how meticulously he chewed every morsel, almost according to doctor's orders, and took such a long time in finishing his meal. But then he has shown time and again that he is one of the fittest persons in the world playing cricket, thus enjoying the game to the fullest.

He is still the best wicketkeeper in the world and will remain so for some time. Now that he has decided not to be available for any future England tours, England will be poorer to that extent. Because not only is he a great wicketkeeper, he is also a fairly good batsman at No. 7 that England needs to take it out of many a tight situation, which it often is in

Like most sportsmen in England he has gone into the sporting goods business and it is mainly to develop this that he has opted out of winter tours for England. I am given to understand that his business is doing rather well, which is not really surprising. Alan Knott is not just good behind the wickets but has proved equally efficient behind the counter.

2

Andy Roberts

THE CUSTOMS AND IMMIGRATION OFFICER AT ST KITT'S AIRPORT
shouted out loudly, "Hey man, 'Sardi' man. Come over here."
Dilip Sardesai, after his double hundred in the first Test, strode
over very confidently towards this official. And the official took
his hand and pumped it vigorously, congratulating "Sardi man"
on his double hundred. But then, with a wicked look in his eyes,
he said, "Now you watch out for this Roberts fella. He gonna
knock your head off."

To which, Dilip, cocky as ever, replied, "Well, I don't know
if he's going to knock my head off because I'm not playing in
this game. But you better tell that to this little fella behind me."

There I was, wide-eyed, taking everything in with awe on my
first trip. The officer had a look at me, saw a person who had
barely begun to shave and did not know what touring was all

about. As I came to his counter he asked me my name and then asked me what I did. When I said I was the opening batsman he burst into a typical West Indian laugh in which the whole body bends forward, backward, sideways and the hands slap the thighs vigorously.

He then proceeded to tell me. "This fella, Andy Roberts, he faster than Wes Hall, man. He the best fast bowler West Indies ever had. He got two bouncers like missiles that come at your head and knock it down. You better watch that head of yours, man. Because this fella Roberts, he already hit so many people on the head in Antigua. In cricket nobody wanna face him."

Well, that I thought was a very warm welcome indeed in Antigua. When the match started there wasn't any disappointment about Roberts's speed because we won the toss and went in to bat. And sure enough, when Roberts bowled, the ball hit your bat faster than at any other time.

Andy Roberts wasn't very successful in that game. But, he's come a long way since then. In that game, my memory of Andy Roberts is just the fact that he was trying to bowl too short and trying to frighten you more with his speed than get you out. The transformation from the erratic and inaccurate bowler to one of the most deadly and accurate bowlers was complete in barely a couple of years. He had also learnt that the short ball should be used more as a surprise weapon than to try to frighten Test batsmen.

I think that Andy is the finest fast bowler I have ever faced. That is perhaps because I have played more longer innings against him than I have played against Dennis Lillee. And, therefore, having not played any long innings against Lillee it is difficult to compare the two, though Dennis is universally acknowledged to be the best fast bowler of our generation. I'm not disputing that fact; I'm just saying that because I did not play any long innings against Dennis Lillee I could not judge the variation that Lillee had in his repertoire as I could when Andy bowled against me.

I will never forget how Andy – when I was well past a hundred and the ball, a tattered sixty overs old – brought so many balls back from outside the off-stump, literally cutting them viciously over the middle stump. He followed that with two perfectly pitched leg cutters in the next over and I marvelled at the versatility of this man.

I had heard a great deal about the calypso record made by Lord Relator about our 1971 tour to the West Indies but I had never actually heard the numbers in that record. Andy Roberts was the first man who got me the cassette when we played Hampshire in 1974. He was then playing for Hampshire in the county championships and by the time we arrived he had already become a feared fast bowler. His accuracy by then was absolutely frightening and his speed was unbelievable even on the sluggish English wickets.

He had knocked no less a person than Colin Cowdrey out with his bouncer and Cowdrey, even when he was past thirty, was still a very good judge of the short ball.

Well, Andy came up to me at lunch time and wanted me to listen to that tape because I had told him in the morning that I had not heard the calypso at all. He let me take it back to the hotel so that we could all listen to it. Andy, in those days, always used to have his taperecorder with him like most of the West Indian players, who all love music and carry their own music and musical equipment on tours. Andy was no different, and his love was West Indian music, the throbbing, pulsating music that makes your feet tap. One could say the same thing about Andy's bowling, except that it made the batsman's feet not tap but dance a different rhythm altogether, a rhythm more to try and see that the ball did not hit him on the body.

Andy had already played his first Test against England the previous winter in the West Indies and though he wasn't among the wickets he impressed one and all with his lively speed and his willingness to bowl long spells.

Hampshire had signed him up at that stage and that season in England in 1974 really sharpened his bowling talents. That's where he learnt accuracy. Along with his speed, accuracy was his forte and it was very, very seldom thereafter that Andy bowled a ball which you didn't have to play. Ninety-five per cent of the deliveries he sent down you had to play and that was the greatness of Andy Roberts.

He came down to India with an established reputation in English county cricket. In his first season he had captured over a hundred wickets and so when he came to India people were really looking forward to Andy Roberts' speed. They were not disappointed because Andy really bowled quick and struck like a tornado in the Madras Test when he captured seven wickets. He was generally a very, difficult bowler to face.

The thing about Andy's bowling was that he had bouncers of different speeds. There was the bouncer that came not as quick as one expected and which one could not only avoid easily but even score runs off. And there was the other bouncer with hardly any apparent change of action or urgency in the run-up, but which really came at you like a rocket and you barely had time to get out of its path, leave aside contemplating an attacking shot off that ball.

This, coupled with a very good outswinger when the ball was new and when it had lost its hardness and shine, and the ability to bring the ball back were the strong points of Andy Roberts. The only thing one could say about Andy was that he did not have a very good yorker – not as good a yorker as Michael Holding or Jeff Thomson or Joel Garner. That was perhaps his drawback because after he had bowled those two quick bouncers the batsman would be expecting another good one and if he had as good a yorker as the other three players have, his striking power would have been even more tremendous.

Be that as it may, Andy Roberts carried the tour of India before him. He captured 32 wickets – which was more than what Wes Hall and the others had done when they had come to tour India – and that too on wickets which were generally unresponsive to his speed. The only wicket which helped him a little bit was the Madras wicket which has traditionally been a harder wicket than the others in India and therefore gives the bowlers, particularly in the earlier stages of the match, a fair amount of help.

Yet, Andy had thirty-two wickets and that spoke of his accuracy and ability to get wickets. He would come back late in the day and still bowl devastatingly fast as he had done in the earlier session.

I missed out on three of the five Test matches owing to an injury to my finger which had broken twice in two months. However, I was around for most of the Test matches and saw Andy bowl everywhere except in the Calcutta Test.

In the first Test at Bangalore, on a rain-affected track he made the ball fizz around and made life uncomfortable for all our players. Similarly in Delhi on a wicket which had been affected by rain, and the game started half an hour before lunch when it could well have started after lunch, Andy just ran through us and made life miserable for us again.

In Calcutta he delivered a blow by taking a wicket off the first delivery of the match when he had Sudhir Naik caught behind by Deryck Murray. And he just kept coming on and getting wickets almost at will. I think Andy Roberts's bowling and the batting of Clive Lloyd and Vishwanath were the highlights of the series. The duel between Andy and Vishwanath at Chepauk on a bouncy track, where Vishy scored 97 of the best runs one could ever see, was a delight. The only way Andy could keep Vishy quiet was to bowl a bouncer, and Vishy would then duck under it. That was also the only way Andy Roberts could see that Vishy did not get a run off the last ball when Vishy with only the last three batsmen to support him was trying to keep the strike by taking a run off the last ball.

Clive Lloyd had two fielders, one deep point and one deep third man, yet Vishy managed to bisect both these fielders regularly with his square cuts.

Both those were the outstanding performances of the match – the seven wickets that Andy took and Vishy's 97 not out – and were truly memorable efforts which people who were fortunate to witness will always remember.

Thereafter, Andy got a little sick of playing continuous cricket. He was playing cricket during the English summer and when that was over he was playing Test cricket for the West Indies or playing on a tour somewhere. That took the competitive edge off him and in England where country captains used him more as a stock bowler rather than a strike bowler, he just seemed to have lost his rhythm. There were only very few matches in which he came up with the old speed, although he had it all there and he produced it regularly whenever the West Indies were playing.

The 1975-76 Australia-West Indies series, which was billed as the World Championship series, had outstanding quick bowlers on both sides – Lillee, Thomson and Gilmour for Australia, and Roberts, Holding and Julien for the West Indies. That was a series in which Andy really bowled well. Michael Holding was just coming up at that time and perhaps a year later the tables could have been turned on the Australians, so quickly did Michael Holding develop into a front line fast bowler.

Andy, till then - till the arrival of Croft, till the arrival of Holding, till the arrival of Garner - was shouldering the burden of being the main wicket-taker of the West Indies very bravely, though even that began to tell on him because pressure does tell on every player and Andy was no exception.

The burden of county cricket and the burden of bowling flat out for the West Indies took its toll and he quit county cricket for Hampshire midway through their season although he came back and played mid-week games for Leicestershire in the county championships.

In 1976 when we played a series against the West Indies in the West Indies they had just arrived from Australia, and having lost, were in no mood to take things lightly against us. Roberts and Holding ran through us in the first Test. Although Holford took the main wickets in the first innings, it was Roberts and Holding who were dangerous. Roberts, right from the first over, was firing off and some of his deliveries were awkward, to say the least. Similarly, when the next Test at Trinidad was played, Andy was the man who was causing our batsmen all the trouble, although we managed to run up a score of over 400. One could never relax against him, because he was always trying something. From that short run-up of his, he generated extreme pace. The little hop before delivery, the falling away of the left shoulder and then the arm coming down was exciting to watch. There were quite a few Indian players who tried to copy Andy Roberts's run-up and action, but sadly not with much success.

After that Test Andy was rested because the West Indies team was due to have a full tour of England immediately after we had left and so they wanted to rest their main strike bowler and get him fit for the tour to follow. That tour, of course, was dominated more by Michael Holding, but Andy Roberts also got the wickets. Andy fell just one short of Holding's tally. Holding got twenty-eight wickets and Andy twenty-seven.

Out of Holding's twenty-eight wickets fourteen were taken in the last Test at the Oval which was a remarkable performance on that flat wicket. But Andy was the bowler who had the Englishmen in trouble right through the series because he kept on chipping in with his three wickets which were always the vital wickets.

Thereafter, all the West Indian players joined the World Series Cricket and Andy was therefore lost to Test cricket for a couple of years. One must realise that in the West Indies cricket is hardly a paying profession and therefore most of the West Indian cricketers come down to England to play county cricket or league cricket and if they get an offer, they go down to Australia and play there. It is the only way they can make money and one must also remember that since a cricketer's career is a short one, he must make a little money while the going is good. Therefore, Andy was no exception when Kerry Packer came forward with his offer and along with the entire West Indies team he signed up for the World Series Cricket.

They had many exciting matches over there and always the WSC West Indies side versus the WSC Australian side was a match very well fought, and though those were not, and still are not, being recognised by the authorities as Tests, the matches were very, very keenly contested. And nobody who played those games will ever believe that they were exhibition matches or matches which were played light-heartedly.

After that Andy Roberts began to decline, though decline is a harsh word to use as far as a fast bowler is concerned because Andy had the reserves to come back. Although he could not now generate the same kind of pace he was intelligent enough to add variation to his bowling and with his unfailing accuracy he was always a difficult bowler to play.

By this time he had become a fairly respectable batsman and who could, at No. 9, add useful runs for the West Indies. In fact, when many a match was thought to have slipped out of the West Indies' hands, Andy with his batting came to the rescue. When the England team was there in 1980 he hit Botham for four sixes in one over, all clouted over mid-wicket, and reached his 50 in no time. Andy has got a couple of useful scores in Test cricket and it was Andy Roberts who, in the summer of 1980 in England, won the first Test of that series very narrowly for the West Indies with just two wickets to spare.

It was Roberts who saved the match. He came down and instead of plodding around when the ball was moving he decided that attack was the best policy. That's what he did; every time Botham pitched the ball up he just carted him over mid-wicket for 4 runs. That's how he did away with pressure and won the Test for the West Indies when they looked to have made things very difficult for themselves by rather indifferent batting in the morning. They should really thank Andy Roberts for the way he turned the match for them and won it when it looked lost.

As a fielder he is a good, safe fielder in the deep with a very powerful arm, though not as good a return as Keith Boyce had. Nevertheless, batsmen dare not take the second run when the ball goes to him at deep fine leg or deep third man where he normally fields.

He is quiet by nature and does not speak too much and is more immersed in his music than in conversation. If you speak with him, all he will do is nod. His eyes are a little hooded when he does that and one doesn't really get to know the man, however much one may try to make conversation with him. This is a pity because I think this has led to him being misunderstood by a lot of players. I don't think Andy has ever been an arrogant person. I think he is one of the nicest persons who came, just played his cricket and did not want to enter into any controversies or make a nuisance of himself.

I well remember how when my wife and I were going out during the 1979 World Cup - all the teams were in the same hotel - we saw four big men walking ahead of us. They were walking so slowly and so casually that one would not have given them a second look. But we knew who they were and my wife said, "Look, how innocent, quiet and harmless these four look, don't they? But give them a ball in their hands and they turn really very dangerous."

Well, those four people ahead of us were Andy Roberts, Michael Holding, Joel Garner and Colin Croft. Theirs is an attack which has become the most feared attack in world cricket today and the leader of the pack is Andy Roberts.

3

Asif Iqbal

ONE OF PAKISTAN'S GREATEST CRICKETERS AND ONE OF THE
most attractive batsman in the world was Asif Iqbal. After the
retirement of Gary Sobers in 1973, he was the undisputed best
No. 6 batsman in the world. He came to Pakistan's rescue on
a number of occasions when they were down in the dumps. His
batting is something only found in fairy tales. His first defiant
rescue act came in 1967 when Pakistan were in danger of an
innings defeat. The England players had checked out of their
hotels and it was expected that the match would be over soon.
But Asif Iqbal and Intikhab Alam had other ideas. They added
190 runs for the eighth wicket, out of which Asif scored 146
runs. These runs were scored at almost a run a minute and Asif
Iqbal was finally out jumping out to a ball, missing it and Alan
Knott doing the rest. So pleased was Colin Cowdrey, the England

captain, with Asif that he offered him a county contract with Kent, the then county champions, which Asif accepted. In 1980-81 Asif was appointed the Kent captain.

Asif began his early cricket in Hyderabad (India), along with Jaisimha, Abbas Ali Baig and others, and when his family decided to migrate to Pakistan, Asif went there and started his cricket. He was quickly noticed for his performances and in those days he was only known as a medium-pace bowler. Soon he was selected to play for Pakistan, but mainly as a new-ball bowler. Although he had some important victims to his credit, he began to take batting a lot more seriously and concentrated on becoming an all-rounder. In those days even Majid Khan used to open the bowling for Pakistan, before an injury laid him low and made him concentrate on batting.

Gradually, Asif developed into a batsman and his batting continued to flower, with the result that he rarely bowled later in his career, but when he bowled he was not to be taken lightly. From the early seventies for almost a decade, the Pakistan batting line-up was their strongest. Asif Iqbal was the man who in the lower order saw to it that an early collapse was taken care of. He always came to Pakistan's rescue when the chips were down and his team required nothing less than a hundred from him. He has got ten Test centuries, which is ample testimony to his batting abilities, and he has scored more than 3000 runs. Apart from that, he was the quickest runner between the wickets and as a fielder he was brilliant anywhere, but particularly in covers. Pakistan has produced some of the most brilliant fielders in this region and Asif has had to move away to mid-off or in the slips where too he distinguished himself. He was able to guide the bowler with necessary encouragement from these positions. In 1976-77 Asif was the main scorer in Australia with two centuries and he batted with determination and concentration when Lillee was threatening to make short work of the Pakistan team. It was because of one of these centuries that Pakistan was able to win at Sydney and then Imran bowled his devastating spell to do the rest.

Thereafter, the West Indies tour that followed was not so successful for Asif. But he redeemed Pakistan's prestige with a brilliant 100 in the last Test. At the end of this Test, he announced his retirement because he wanted to give youngsters a chance and also because he thought that there was no real hope of playing against India. However, when the Indian tour of Pakistan was announced for 1978, Asif came back from retirement because it was his cherished dream to play against India, the country of his birth. Before that, like all leading Pakistani cricketers, he had joined the World Series Cricket and became its most active participant and its coordinator. He was also instrumental in getting a lot of Pakistani cricketers signed up for the WSC. In 1978, he scored a hundred on his first appearance against India in the second innings till he was bowled by Surinder Amarnath. But his most cherished moments in that series were when he and Zaheer Abbas clinched victory in the second Test against India and one could see the jubilation on Asif's face as he came to the pavilion waving his bat. The next Test saw Javed and Asif snatch victory from a just about hopeless position. They started the fireworks and then Imran came on the scene to scatter the attack and win the match for Pakistan. Asif and Javed picked runs almost at will by their clever running between the wickets. Asif, who gave to Javed about twelve to thirteen years in age, was running almost as fast as him. That was a tribute to his skill, his fitness, and his determination to succeed.

It was during this series that he asked some of us to play in the World Series Cricket and was damned by just about everybody for having done so. But being a coordinator for the WSC, it was his duty to get as many leading players for the WSC as possible. He was only doing his bit professionally to recruit talent and it was left to the individual to accept or reject the offer. To damn Asif Iqbal for that was totally uncalled for. He had discussions with most of us and then their managing director, Lynton Taylor, flew in from London to talk to the boys in the presence of Asif Iqbal, who was there to allay any fears and answer any queries. The fact is that none of the Indian players joined because the World Series Cricket ceased to exist from 1979. The Indian cricketers had decided that they would join only after 1979. But Asif's role in that is something the Indians have not forgotten. Therefore he has earned the notoriety of being a mercenary. That in itself is not a bad thing. Asif realises that few in this world look after a sportsman after his days are over. How many of the people, who come to watch cricket or write about it, come to the help of a sportsman when he is in need? That is why Asif realised that, if anything had to be done in this respect, it had to be done in the active playing days.

In 1979-80, he was a surprise choice as captain for the tour of India because many people felt that Mushtaq, who had done a good job as captain in the 1978 series, should have been the choice. Asif Iqbal continued as captain in the 1979 Prudential World Cup and then came to India as captain of the team. In the Prudential Cup Asif was not at his best and the Pakistan team, a strong line-up, put up a valiant fight against the West Indies before losing. When Asif came to India, the Pakistan team was rated as almost the equal of the West Indies team. That they did not do well in our country was mainly due to the fantastic effort of Kapil Dev. He produced extra bursts of speed to demolish their batting. Our meetings to chalk out the overall weaknesses of the Pakistani batsmen, particularly the bowlers bowling to a plan and with determination, led India to emerge victorious in that series. Asif had a score of 50 in the first Test, following it with another fifty plus in the second Test. But then he almost went into decline. He was always a dangerous player and going at No. 6, he had the opportunity to study the attack and play his innings. So many times when we were right on top, he took the advantage away from us by his attacking batting or often forcing the withdrawal of a particular bowler from the firing line. But, somehow, he did not produce the big effort of a hundred that was required of him. He seemed to be particularly upset when Dilip Doshi was brought in to bowl and later he said that anyone who takes that long to bowl an over, being a spinner, should be fired. We put that to good use and every time Asif came, Dilip was brought in to bowl and Asif gave us the impression that he wanted to hit Dilip out of the ground in almost every delivery.

With that kind of psychological advantage, Asif never recovered his poise. And although he made his bit of effort, he could never produce a match-winning knock.

As a captain, he was a superb diplomat off the field with his natural charm and all-round ability to get his boys together. On the field, however, one got the impression that there were quite a few disgruntled people in the Pakistan side who did not like the way Asif was leading. But these were basically Asif's problems and I am sure he solved them in his own manner and style. In the fifth Test that disgruntled attitude was absent and there seemed to be a new resolve in the Pakistan side. Asif retired after the Calcutta Test and it was a retirement he would probably remember because eighty thousand people gave him a standing ovation. He was run out, and what a way to go on one's farewell appearance for one who was reputed to be the fastest runner between the wickets! Let me add here that he was run out because he slipped while trying to return to his crease.

Asif, thereafter, concentrated on making a little money for himself. He played for Kent in the county championships, though he was out much of the time in 1980 because of an injury. He was one of the lynchpins of the Kent side and always a very popular man all round Kent and in England. Lately, he has been in the forefront of the Cricketers Benefit Fund under the stewardship of Abdul Rehman Bukhatir and he is the one who is coordinating the efforts among the Indian and Pakistani players. These matches continue to be a success and benefit all cricketers from the subcontinent. At the moment, every year, one current and one former cricketer from each country has a benefit in the UAE and Asif has a major role in getting this off the ground. It is beneficial to a lot of cricketers and will benefit plenty more in the years to come. He is one of those cricketers who make good administrators after their playing days are over. And I hope that his cricketing experience is put to good use by the authorities in Pakistan. He is a dear friend now, particularly after the 1979-80 series when we were rival captains, and I have a lot of regard for this ever-smiling cricketer, who has rendered yeoman's service to cricket and particularly to Pakistan cricket.

4

Bishen Singh Bedi

THE GREATEST LEFT-ARM BOWLER I HAVE SEEN IS BISHEN SINGH Bedi. Certainly, Sir Gary Sobers was more versatile because he could bowl left-arm pace, swing the ball, bowl cutters with the old ball, bowl left-arm unorthodox spin and bowl chinamen and googlies. In that respect, Sir Gary Sobers was perhaps the most versatile of them all. But quite simply, the greatest left-arm bowler was Bishen Bedi.

Bedi first came into prominence in 1966, playing in Delhi against the West Indies for the President's IX. It was during this match that a national selector saw him and was much impressed. He then urged the chairman of the selection committee to include Bedi in the fourteen to play in the second Test against the West Indies at Calcutta, which was to start on 31 December, 1966. The team for this Test had already been selected, but the chairman decided to include Bishen Bedi on the advice of his colleague and when Tiger Pataudi saw him in the nets, he too was convinced that this young Sikh had all the makings of a Test bowler. And Bishen Singh Bedi has proved it to the hilt by becoming India's highest wicket-taker, with 267 wickets, at a very impressive average, in a career that spanned thirteen years.

There at Calcutta on the New Years' Day in 1967, a career was launched, a career which gave immense delight to those who were bemoaning the lost art of spin bowling, which gladdened the heart of the connoisseurs of the game and which caused plenty of havoc to batsmen all over the world.

That particular Test match was not highly successful for Bishen but it was enough to convince the selectors that this youngster not only had the potential to become a world class bowler but also had the temperament to be pitchforked into a Test match without any notice and still perform without any signs of nervousness.

The next match at Madras would probably have been won by India had Rusi Surti taken a catch at backward short leg off the bowling of Bishen when the great Gary Sobers had just scored a few runs. Sobers, in partnership with Charlie Griffith, went on to save the match and thus India had a wait for another four years before registering a victory over the West Indies. In 1971, even in this victory Test, Bishen played his part and, with his impeccable line and length, saw to it that the stranglehold, which had been achieved after Abid Ali had given an early breakthrough, was never really released.

Immediately after the 1967 West Indies tour of India, the Indian team went to England and Bishen was in the team. He was an instant success with the media there because the boys in Fleet Street were only too delighted to write about a man who came on the ground in different turbans for different sessions of the game and who was able to bring back for them memories of Wilfred Rhodes and Hedley Verity and other great English bowlers of the past. In those days, Bishen used to wear the turban and not the *patka* which most Sikhs now wear while playing and I am pretty certain that the turban could not have been all that comfortable while bowling, although it must have helped keep the cold away.

On the 1967 tour of England the weather did play an important part and there were lots of matches which were washed-out and there were plenty of days when the sun never came out at all. Nonetheless, after the beating that India received, the team was off to Australia and again Bishen was in the team. He was not a great success on this trip, though off the field he met an Australian girl who was in a couple of years to become his wife.

It was in New Zealand after the Australian tour that Bishen came into his own and along with Bapu Nadkarni formed a partnership that was deadly enough to keep the batsmen under control while Prasanna made inroads into the batting line-up, bowling his off-spinners at the other end. This was the first time that the Indian team won a series abroad beating New Zealand by a 2-1 margin and thus a new spin combination was formed on that tour.

When the New Zealanders were playing their first Test match in Bombay in 1969, all eyes were on the Sikh. He hadn't been among the wickets in the first innings and the cricket-lovers of Bombay were wondering what was so outstanding about this left-arm bowler and why he was preferred to Bapu Nadkarni in 1967. Bishen showed them precisely what stuff he was made of in the second innings when he captured six New Zealand wickets to take India to a comfortable victory. That was Bombay's first sight of Bishen whom they were going to admire not only as a cricketer but also as a presence on the field. People like him are very rare. It is players like Bishen, Derek Randall, Tony Greig and Sandeep Patil, to name just a few, who spring to mind and they are the ones who not only give the crowd value for money by their cricketing ability but also by their very presence and their ability to communicate with the crowd and involve them in the match.

Ever since that time when Bishen took six wickets and led India to victory, he has been a very popular figure with the Bombay crowd. True, the Bombay crowd has given him a bit of a stick. He, being a Sikh, has added to that, but then Bishen has very sportingly taken it all and perhaps that is one of the reasons why he is so much more popular than other cricketers who do not seem to be able to take it.

Later that season Bishen recorded his best figures when he took seven wickets in the Calcutta Test against the Australians. Ian Chappell played a superlative innings of 99 on a wicket that was truly helping the spinners. But apart from him, there was little resistance to Bishen and he ended up with seven wickets in that particular innings. This performance came immediately after his wedding and naturally he was teased a great deal not only by the team members but also by others who seemed to be unanimous in their opinion that marriage had helped him get a better grip on the ball. India lost that series to Australia because of their superior pace bowling and the fact that India's middle order had not come to terms with itself and also because India had not solved the opening batsman problem. This meant that the Australians could strike early and keep the pressure on the later batsmen. Bishen, Pras and Venkat performed admirably and they were helped by the induction of some youngsters like Vishwanath, Eknath Solkar and Ashok Mankad into the team, boys who made their debut in the series and went on to serve India for a long time afterwards.

The next series that the Indians played was against the West Indies. That was the first time that I met Bishen when we were attending a training camp in Bombay prior to our departure. What impressed me about him at that time was his willingness to bowl endlessly to all the batsmen and still find the energy to go round for a training run. This is something which marks Bishen out from the other spin bowlers of the era. Because, while the other spin bowlers were perfectly happy to rely on their talent and ability, Bishen worked hard at it. Bishen never took things for granted. He trained hard and one could always see that he was trying to put in an effort. Probably, he needed to train harder than the others because he had a body which was more susceptible to stresses and strains and many times later in his career he suffered from muscle injuries that handicapped him to a great extent.

Bishen on that trip was again a force to reckon with and the West Indians truly loved what they saw. Here was a bowler coming from just a few yards away, weaving magic spells and making great players like Sobers and Kanhai look like novices at times. Sobers, of course, came into his own later in the series when he slammed three consecutive centuries but unfortunately for the West Indies, Kanhai never displayed the form that he had in the first Test when he scored a brilliant 150 not out to save the West Indies. Part of it was due to the fact that the Indian spinners got into a magnificent rhythm which meant that the West Indies were really hard put to score runs. Not too many world class spinners were around at that time but the few that were, were fortunately playing for India, Bishen the foremost among them.

Bishen kept on teasing and bowling a tantalising length and Venkat was the one who ran away with the wickets because he very intelligently capitalised on the fact that while Bishen bowled his left-arm spinners, going away from the right-handers most of the time, the ball coming in to the batsmen was the one the batsmen chose to attack. Thus, Venkat kept a very tight control over his direction and ended up with the wickets. This was, of course, intelligent bowling.

Much of the credit on the West Indies tour was given to the spinners for taking us to the position from where we could afford to dominate the West Indian bowlers. I did not get to know Bishen on this trip because this was my first tour with the Indian team and I was wide-eyed about everything and dutifully went around looking at tourist spots, etc. However, a surprise, not just a surprise but a great honour was in store for me at the end of the tour during the last Test after I had scored a hundred in the second innings following a hundred in the first innings. Bishen decided to name his son, who was born during that Test, after me. Bishen's son was christened Gavasinder Singh, and that was a tremendous honour for me, particularly because I was on my first tour. I didn't even know the man well enough, and he had paid his tribute in this unique way and a tribute coming from one of the greatest spinners of the world is something that I really cherish and am very proud of.

The tour to England that followed was even more of a trial for Chandra, who was recalled to the Indian team, than Bishen. Bishen, with his flight and beautiful action, captivated the hearts of the English critics and spectators, resulting in his being offered a contract by Northamptonshire to play in the county championship. Towards the end of that tour, three of us – Bishen, Engineer and myself – were invited to the Rest of the World team. Bishen left earlier for Australia because his wife is Australian and thus we met him at Melbourne when the team assembled there. Bishen's magic moment on that tour was when he clean bowled both the Chappell brothers in the Sydney Test. Ian, coming out to drive, was beaten in the flight and was bowled. Greg played the first ball he received down the wrong line and the ball turned sufficiently around the edge to knock his bails off. This was great bowling and enabled us to come in the match very strongly. In the last Test, it was again Bishen and Intikhab who spun the Australians out and bowled us to victory. This was the tour in which one came to know more about Bishen because on the earlier tours to the West Indies and England, he was with his own circle of friends and it was not possible to get to know him at all apart from the playing days when he was in the dressing room.

On the 1972 tour of Australia, we would meet in the evenings and Bishen spent a great deal of time with the Pakistani players and us and thus I came to know him a little more. Of course, in Melbourne he kept quite busy, with his wife's side of the family.

The following year when the England team came to India, Bishen completed his hundred wickets and that too in front of his Delhi home crowd, and it was indeed a great moment. Chandra, Pras and of course, Venkat were there to take us to a very comfortable victory and thus Ajit Wadekar, the captain of the team, was able to complete a hat trick of victories in the first three series in which he led the side. These victories were welcomed by an enthusiastic response from the cricket-loving people of India but the joy was short-lived and soon forgotten when the Indian team lost to England very badly in the summer of 1974. That was a wet and windy summer and most uncomfortable to play cricket. That was a tour which is best forgotten because there were plenty of incidents on the tour which did not at all bring credit to the Indian team and did poor justice to its strength.

Ajit Wadekar lost his place in the West Zone team and announced his retirement and thus paved the way for Mansur

Ali Khan Pataudi to stage a comeback and lead the side against the West Indies. Bishen was in good form and Pras and Chandra bowled very well to bring India back into the series after having lost the first two Tests. It was during this particular year that the controversies surrounding Bishen came to the surface. He was dropped from the first Test against the West Indies on the ground that he had breached his tour contract. He had given an interview to British TV and the Board president gave a directive to the selection committee not to consider him for the first Test. However, Bishen could not be dropped from the second Test, not because the second Test was to be played in Delhi, but because a bowler of Bishen's calibre could not be easily found and though Rajinder Goel was selected in the fourteen, he was not eventually included in the final eleven and he missed the only opportunity of playing in a Test.

It was Bishen who kept such a talented bowler like Goel out of the Test team and it is the misfortune of Indian cricket that two outstanding left-arm spinners like Goel and Shivalkar were unable to play Tests for India. This was due to the fact that Bishen was just that little bit better than the other two bowlers. He had more variety than either Goel or Shivalkar. Goel and Shivalkar were absolutely unplayable on wickets that afforded only a little help and were very difficult to score off on good batting tracks. Bishen's strength was that on good batting wickets also he was able to get the batsmen out because he had more variety. His loop and his armer were bowled with such guile that they troubled the batsmen all the time.

By the time this series ended, Tiger Pataudi announced his retirement and a new captain had to be chosen for the World Cup in 1975. The selectors chose Venkat because of his experience and for being a regular participant in the one-day matches and county championship for Derbyshire. But when the team was picked to go to New Zealand and the West Indies in 1976, Bishen was an automatic choice for the captaincy. He was fortunate to have a very good side, a side which comprised cricketers who were in top form, a side full of youngsters and a lot of experience. The series against New Zealand was drawn 1-1 and the series against the West Indies saw India make a record score of 406 in the third Test to win the Test and level the series score with one match to go.

It was during the last Test match at Sabina Park that Bishen got into another controversy when he declared India's innings closed with only five wickets down. Bishen's reasoning was very simple. He had three batsmen who were unable to bat owing to injuries and with only himself and Chandra left to bat he saw no point in continuing the innings. His own batting calibre as well as that of Chandra was well-known and the two would not have been able to score many runs, since India were only 13 ahead at that time. Perhaps, what was wrong on his part was not coming out to field as the West Indians could have scored those runs in just one or two overs. Thus Bishen got himself involved in another bit of controversy.

When the England team came in 1976 there was yet another and bigger controversy when he accused John Lever of having used vaseline to keep the shine on the ball. This in effect is the reason mentioned in many quarters for his losing the contract with Northamptonshire in the county championship. The disappointing thing was that in spite of Bishen's great service to the country, not many people came forward to support him when the allegation was made. Whatever may be the truth of the allegation, it should have been examined thoroughly and Bishen should not have been blamed completely for his part in the episode. The English cricketers over the years have been known to pressurise the umpires, sometimes blatantly, to win matches by using every trick in the book and so Bishen's allegation should not have been ignored at that stage.

Bishen then led the team to Australia in 1977-78, which turned out to be a classic series much like the 1974-75 series against the West Indies when all the five Test matches were decisive. It was Bishen's excellent bowling in the first two Tests that got the Indians so close to victory. Somehow, we fell at the last hurdle when victory was in our grasp. It must have been very disappointing for Bishen, for he bowled very well, and yet the victories eluded him in the first two Tests. India came back strongly to win the next two Tests only to lose the last one at Adelaide.

In 1978 we went to Pakistan and this was the series in which our quarter of spinners was hit out of Test cricket, although Bishen and Chandra made a comeback and Venkat also four years later. Zaheer Abbas, Asif Iqbal, Javed Miandad and Mushtaq Mohammad played very well on those perfect batting pitches. There was very little that the spinners could do and we lost the series 2-0. Many still claim that it was the one over that Bishen bowled in the Karachi Test when Imran Khan took 19 runs, including two huge sixes, that cost India the match and Bishen the captaincy. As soon as the team landed in India, Bishen was told that he had been given the sack.

By the time the West Indies arrived in India in 1978-79, Bishen had lost that little bit of extra nip and perhaps the hammering that he received in Pakistan had hastened his slide downhill. He was not the same bowler that he was before. And it was amply proved when a second string West Indian team could score runs against him without being unduly perturbed by his spin. Bishen's strong point was that he deceived the batsmen in the air but the ball after pitching still went off the pitch quickly enough not to let the batsman change his mind on the shot. However, in that series against the West Indies, it was this particular characteristic of Bishen which was missing and even if he could beat the batsman in the air he could still go backward and change his shot at the last moment. This is what hastened Bishen's exit from the Test scene.

It was my unpleasant duty as the captain of the Indian cricket team to break the news to him that he was dropped from the side for the fourth Test against the West Indies at Madras. I suggested in the selection committee meeting that for cricketing reasons somebody should accompany me, preferably the chairman of the selection committee, to break the news to him. For the kind of service he had rendered to Indian cricket, it was proper courtesy to tell him on our own rather than him being told by a third party. So Ghulam Ahmed, who was the then secretary of the Board, and I went to his room to break the news. Bishen was lying down having a rub from a masseur. He took the news sportingly and said that these things do happen and he had quite expected it. He wished the team luck for the next series. This was very magnanimous on his part and we left the room in a very sad mood to continue with the selection committee deliberations.

He made a comeback when he was picked for the team to go to England in 1979 but he was not very successful. The wickets that he picked were those of tail-enders when they were going for declarations and were under instructions to hit out against the spinners. Kapil Dev was the most successful bowler on that tour and Bishen and Venkat got only tail-end wickets.

Bishen lost his place in the Test team and has not played Test cricket since, although he ended up as India's highest-ever wicket-taker with 267 wickets. It was by any consideration a fantastic performance to have been able to play that many Tests and get that many wickets, because it works out to a tremendous average. Not many bowlers can maintain that kind of average and Bishen has done it. He has shown the world what a great spinner he was. There have been many left-arm spinners but none good enough to replace Bishen, although Dilip Doshi in his first three or four seasons was outstanding and captured many wickets. But Dilip was more of a defensive bowler, while Bishen was always an attacking one.

Bishen as a person has been a very forthright man, a man not afraid to speak his mind and let the others know exactly what he thinks of them. I do not believe when people suggest that he had got an article written insinuating that it was I who was responsible for getting him dropped from the Indian team. This is far from the truth, for the simple reason that if Bishen thought that I was responsible for it, he would have told me to my face and not made someone else write about it. Bishen is not a person to fire a gun from someone else's shoulder. Any other person may have tried that.

I have been privileged to play with Bishen and I am proud of his performance in the Indian cricket team. He took Indian cricket to a height which would not have been possible without him, and he instilled in each member of the team confidence in his ability. This was his greatest contribution as a captain. It was he who was instrumental in getting the Cricketers Association of India launched during his tenure as captain and, though Bishen did not want to be actively associated with it in any official capacity, he was always there behind the scene encouraging and giving valuable advice to the cricketers.

He is now a member of the selection committee and the secretary of the Delhi and District Cricket Association. Thus, he shoulders a great responsibility. As a former cricketer, he has shown that cricketers do make good and able administrators and as a selection committee member he has even a greater responsibility ensuring that the heights the Indian cricket team reached since winning the World Cup are up held.

Bishen is perfectly capable of achieving all this but in doing so he might hurt a few people because of his forthrightness. One does not come across people like Bishen very often in one's lifetime. It was not just an honour and privilege but a great pleasure to have enjoyed the friendship of Bishen during his active playing career and to continue to do that now when he is serving cricket in a different category altogether.

5

B.S. Chandrasekhar

THE CLOSE-IN FIELDERS MADE THE BATSMAN TENSE, A SHIVER
going down his spine as he took guard, a crowd of almost eighty
thousand howling "booo... wled" to a man as the bowler ran up
to bowl. The batsman became pale. The bowler was B.S.
Chandrasekhar and every time he bowled in Calcutta, the crowd
would give him this terrific support. I dare say that the crowds
of Calcutta have got him a few wickets by simply making the
batsman nervous by their rhythmic shouts of "booo...wled" as he
ran up to bowl.

Calcutta is one place where it is great fun to be successful,
because the stadium itself can accommodate a hundred thousand
people and when a hundred thousand supporters are backing
you, it is an almost top-of-the-world feeling. That's why to score
runs and get wickets, one must do it in Calcutta to really savour

309

the appreciation of the huge crowd that converges on the stadium. Chandra is Calcutta's favourite player and seldom has he let them down.

Chandra's debut was in 1964 against England against Mike Smith's team and with his fastish leg-breaks and googlies Chandra was the bowler who was very difficult to read and not so easy to score runs off.

Later in the same season, when the Australians visited India for a short trip, the ball with which Chandra bowled Peter Burge in the second innings is memorable. It pitched about leg and middle stumps and turned enough to bowl his off-stump as the batsman came forward for defence. Earlier in the first innings, he had latched on to a terrific catch when Peter Burge had swept at a ball from Bapu Nadkarni and the ball was travelling at a speed of ninety miles per hour. Chandra was near the square-leg umpire and he struck out both his hands to the right and came out with a real blinder.

As Chandra got confidence, and realised that he was making a permanent place for himself in the Indian side, the world began to sit up and take notice of this bowler, whom they called a "freak" bowler. In fact, there was nothing "freaky" about him at all, the only thing was that his right arm was affected by polio and with which he really could not do much except bowl. He would throw with his left hand and use his left hand for most purposes.

Chandra thus worked in tandem with Venkataraghavan when the New Zealanders came in 1965, the year before the Indian team was to face the West Indians. That was an eagerly awaited battle because people wanted to find out how far Chandra would be successful against great players like Sobers, Kanhai, Butcher and Nurse. Chandra bowled superlatively and was always a bowler whom the West Indians respected. They tried to hit him off the ground but did not succeed and, therefore, decided to play as he came, rather than plan anything against Chandra. To plan anything against Chandra was, in fact, to invite disaster. His bowling was something which you really could not predict.

The 1967 tour of England by his standards was not a successful one for him and the reason could be that Chandra found it difficult to grip the ball in the cold English weather. It was a miserable summer in 1967 and as a result Chandra tended to bowl too short and bowl loose deliveries more often than before.

Thereafter followed a lean period in Chandra's career because midway through the Australian tour in 1967-68, he was sent back home for an injury though doubts were raised as to why he was really sent back. The questions were not really answered because Chandra is not a man for controversy and would not provide the media with any material.

He went into a bit of decline after that for the simple reason that he suffered a scooter accident which meant that when the New Zealanders and the Australians came in 1969, he was not fit enough to play against them. Many people had then written Chandra off, because with Bedi, Prasanna and Venkataraghavan holding fort as spinners on the Indian side, they felt that there was no need for Chandra. Chandra missed the 1971 tour of the West Indies, but the selectors showed rare wisdom and insight in selecting him for the tour of England later that year. And what he did at the Oval is now history. After that Chandra has seldom looked back. In fact, in the 1972-73 series at home against England, he lowered the mark set by Vinoo Mankad for the highest number of wickets against England in the series by capturing thirty-five wickets. His favourite batsman seemed to be Keith Fletcher whom he could dismiss almost at will. When Keith Fletcher was finally able to unravel Chandra's mystery, he slammed a brilliant innings and then followed it up with a century in Bombay.

The 1974 trip to England was again not so successful for Chandra. The summer was cold and he had the same problem of gripping the ball. An injury added to his miseries. He broke his thumb and was unable to play midway through the second Test also missing the third Test.

However, he was fit once again when the West Indians came down that winter and amongst his prized scalps was Vivian Richards playing his first Test match - he got him out in both the innings. But Viv Richards came back with a vengeance in the second Test at Delhi scoring 192 not out and thereafter, although Viv was not as successful as expected, he had somehow managed to get out of Chandra's grip.

In New Zealand and West Indies in 1976, Chandra was not his usual devastating self, bowling some tremendous spells but generally looking off colour. The problem perhaps was that he was bowling long spells and his arm got tired and thus he took a lot of stick and once Chandra took stick, he seemed to lose confidence in his bowling. Confidence was his big asset and if he lost that, he was a bowler not to be feared. In fact, one could then pick runs with relative ease.

After this tour, which wasn't all that great by his standards, but where he had the great Viv Richards in many a difficulty, Chandra concentrated on the home season in India and bowled remarkably well against the New Zealanders and then the Englishmen. The Englishmen, and particularly Tony Greig, had found a new way to play him by standing upright. This put Chandra off to a great extent because as he ran in to bowl, Greig would suddenly stand up, which, Chandra thought then, was Greig withdrawing from the crease. With his concentration affected, Chandra was not able to bowl with the same venom as he had bowled earlier in the first Test. Also the practice of some English players to swear at him while taking a run upset Chandra who was not one to retaliate. He thus lost his concentration and was not the same bowler that he was against the New Zealanders.

The trip to Australia in 1977-78 saw both Bishen and Chandra bowl excellently. Australia had lost many players to the World Series Cricket. Bobby Simpson had been recalled to lead the side and he was the one man whom Chandra troubled the most. Simpson's habit of going on the back foot and trying to work the ball away on the leg side found him often in front of the wicket but thanks to the kindness of the Australian umpires, Simpson continued to bat and thus got out of many an awkward situation the Australian team found itself in.

Bishen got about thirty-one wickets, but Chandra was not very much behind with twenty-nine wickets in that series. Both of them bowled absolutely tops and it was a great sight and delight to be able to field in the close-in positions and watch the confrontation between them and the Aussie batsmen. Nobody seemed to have any clue to their guiles except Peter Toohey and Bobby Simpson, to some extent.

The following season came India's visit to Pakistan after eighteen long years and it was the series the subcontinent had its eyes on. The series, in fact, turned out to be one that should be easily forgotten for our spinners, because they got absolutely nothing over there on those wickets, instead had plenty of runs against their names for their labours. Zaheer Abbas was in irresistible form and with Javed Miandad chipping in two hundreds and everybody scoring runs, it was embarrassing to read the figures of the three great bowlers. The Pakistanis are exceptionally adept at playing spinners. By using their feet, by dancing down the wicket and even not being afraid to loft, they demoralised the spinners and the figures that you read against the names of Prasanna, Chandra and Bedi are the figures you read against the names of ordinary spin bowlers. Not that they had lost their ability, but they had met players who were not afraid to go down the track and in the process, the effectiveness of our spinners was considerably reduced.

Midway through the series that followed against the West Indies in 1978-79, Chandra found himself out of the Indian side. But he forced himself back into the team for the last Test and also found a place in the Indian team that went to England in 1979. However, in the first Test, Chandra was not supposed to play, because he had an ankle injury. On the morning of the match, Bedi reported unfit with a stiff neck. Then the selection committee requested Chandra to go on and play. He was not fully recovered from his injury and just could not get the turn and the nip off the plumb Edgbaston wicket and ended up with no wickets, while England had piled up a huge total of 600 runs. There was no disgrace in not getting a wicket, for the only bowler who was amongst the wickets was young Kapil Dev. None of the others got anything as England declared with five wickets down.

That was the last Test Chandra played, because in 1979-80, he was not picked against the Australians, nor was he picked against the Pakistanis and thereafter never considered for any matches.

Chandra retired in 1981 and was awarded a benefit and whatever he got by way of his benefit somehow was not really commensurate with the efforts he had put in for India, despite his handicap. Still the benefit was the sign of affection that the people had for Chandra. He was a totally uncontroversial man, a man who went about his own ways without getting involved in any controversies on cricket and was quite happy to be himself. He was often misunderstood for keeping aloof, but he was a very simple person, a very likeable man and one you could rely upon to be your friend. I was fortunate to share rooms with him. I shared a room with him when he bowled us to victory in 1971 and it was always he who got up early in the morning, made a cup of tea and passed it across to me. Also at times, when I was not batting well, he was around to give me confidence, to speak just those couple of words and knowing Chandra, those words were always sincerely meant and were a great help to regain confidence in your own ability.

Chandra was a great fan of Mukesh, the singer. To start with, this led to their meeting and becoming very good friends and it was a big blow to Chandra when Mukesh died suddenly on a concert trip to America. Chandra, who hates flying, then flew down to Bombay for his funeral. He used to call me "Sun" and it was a name he used with affection and I am privileged to be his friend. I still look forward to going to Bangalore and every time I go, it's great fun to be able to sit with this greatest of spinners and chat about our yesteryears.

6

Clive Lloyd

WHEN THE WEST INDIES TEAM CAME TO INDIA IN 1966 THE INDIAN cricket-loving public were excited because the West Indies has always been a team which has played attractive cricket wherever it has gone. The team's record in India had been tremendous; it had yet to lose a Test match to India and had carried everything before it in the earlier series.

People were discussing what kind of mayhem Rohan Kanhai, Gary Sobers, Conrad Hunte and Seymour Nurse were going to cause to the Indian bowlers. And also, the topic of discussion lingered around what Charlie Griffith, Wesley Hall and Lester King would do to our batsmen.

As usual, in the West Indies team there were one or two newcomers about whom nobody had much idea and they were expected to be used to play in the first class games when the big stars could take a break from the tensions of Test cricket. Nobody had ever thought that at the end of the tour a young man who wore glasses and walked with his neck seemingly ahead of the rest of his body, shoulders hunched together but who was greased lightning on the field would emerge as the hero of the tour. The young man's name was Clive Lloyd and he really carried everything before him in the series that was played.

Before the first Test started Lloyd had done nothing outstanding and it was expected that he would be in the reserves. But an injury to Seymour Nurse resulted in Lloyd being asked to play along with stalwarts like Hunte, Kanhai, Sobers, Griffith, Hall and Lance Gibbs. This young man was also a cousin of Lance Gibbs and so, perhaps, it was fortunate that his cousin was there on hand to give him any advice or to ease his tension a bit. Not that he needed it after his first innings in Test cricket.

Bapu Nadkarni holds the record for the most maidens bowled, and for that remarkable bowling analysis of 29 overs, 26 maidens, 3 runs and no wicket. Yet, I've never seen Bapu Nadkarni annihilated as Clive Lloyd did in the Bombay Test. On a wicket which was a dream wicket for the batsman, where the ball came on very nicely on to the bat, Lloyd just plonked his foot down and hammered everything. He was lucky that before he could get the hang of Chandrasekhar a mix-up enabled him to get a life when he was on 9. But he never looked back thereafter, and his 82 was awesome for the manner in which the ball thudded into the boundary fence. The power that he generated from that loose, easy pick-up of his was unbelievable. People who had seen Clyde Walcott belt the ball off the back foot and thought that there could be nobody who could hit the ball harder than Walcott off the back foot, had to think again after that demonstration by Clive Lloyd.

Poor Bapu Nadkarni. His career was set back after that assault on him, though, to be fair, one must say that none of the Indian bowlers escaped Lloyd's assault. Everybody was dealt with equally harshly, perhaps with the exception of Chandrasekhar. And then, apart from his batting, the crowd just wondered at the man's agility on the field. It was simply incredible. The number of times he picked up and threw the stumps down on the run or on the turn were numerous and the crowd went wild cheering this young man. He had stolen the limelight away completely from the established stars like Sobers, Kanhai, Hall and Griffith.

In the second innings too, he played his part with an unbeaten 78 which helped Gary Sobers finish off the match in a frenzy because Gary wanted to go to the races in Bombay. It looked like a target which would take well past tea time to attain, but Sobers and Lloyd just hammered around, tapped a few singles and cruised to it even before tea so that Gary could go and attend the races.

The youngster with 82 and 78 not out in his first Test had certainly arrived and everybody in the world sat up to take notice of this phenomenon. The only person who may have been dejected was Seymour Nurse because it was his place in the team which was in danger now with the arrival of this giant from Guyana.

Lloyd carried on the good work in the second and third Tests as well and apart from his explosive batting and quick-silver fielding, another facet of this cricketer was evident to the Indian cricket-loving public, and that was his ability to bowl leg spinners. In the Calcutta Test he bowled Chandu Borde who scored centuries in the first and third Tests but failed in this one. He bowled him round his legs, trying to sweep and managed to get even more turn than Lance Gibbs had on that track.

Clive Lloyd

I don't know why Clive stopped bowling his leg spinners, but he did for a while and reverted to medium pacers. Perhaps he got a little bit of pasting in the Lancashire league with his leg spinners and thought it better to resort to his seamer style which he uses today, though he doesn't bowl as much as he used to.

Thereafter, I followed his career with interest because I felt an affinity with the man who had made his debut in India and done it in such a brilliant fashion.

He had a fairly useful tour of Pakistan after the Indian tour and then in his first Test at home against the English team he scored a century. He didn't do extraordinarily well thereafter, though he followed it up with a hundred in his first appearance against Australia when the West Indies went there in 1967-68. There the Australians seemed to have noticed some weakness and they exploited that to ensure that Clive Lloyd didn't trouble them too much. But after that, Lloyd was destined for greater things. He practised hard and thought about his weaknesses – the very thinking which has got him the captaincy of the West Indies, a job which he has done extremely successfully over the last ten years.

Seymour Nurse retired from Test cricket after the 1968-69 tour of Australia and New Zealand and that meant that Clive Lloyd was assured of a place in the team and didn't need to worry about losing his place. Thereafter, Lloyd went steadily from strength to strength. He was always a person whose wicket the opposition was after, whose bowling was treated with respect and when the ball went to him the batsman throught not once or twice but thrice before embarking on a run. His reputation as a fielder perhaps got him more publicity than the sheer power of his batting and this was in a way unfortunate because his batting was always very dangerous for the opposition.

When the Indian team went to the West Indies in 1971, Lloyd was under a bit of a cloud because he hadn't had a very successful series. There were rumours going around that if he didn't do well in the first couple of Test matches his place would go to Kalicharan or Lawrence Rowe among the younger players who were knocking on the doors of Test cricket. Well, that didn't happen, because though Lloyd didn't get a century against us he certainly got his share of runs, getting his 40s and 50s fairly regularly. Although he wasn't a spectacular success, he was quite consistent and that's what was needed in the series in which most of the West Indies batsmen didn't seem to do themselves any justice against an Indian spin attack which was just coming into its own before being rated as the best spin attack in the world.

In the first Test, Lloyd was run out in a mix-up and that happened again in the second innings and also in the Test at Guyana where he collided with Gary Sobers. He had to be assisted off the field after being run out just when he looked in sight of his hundred.

The last Test in Port of Spain was the one where the West Indians were desperate to try to even the score but that was not to be. Having set a target in the second innings which they could have achieved if Kanhai and Sobers had survived along with Lloyd, they lost Sobers and Kanhai quickly which left Lloyd to do the holding-up operation instead of the attacking one which he loved so much.

In any case his innings of 64 was one which saved the West Indies from losing that Test which at one stage they looked all set to win. This was a very responsible innings and although we were defensive to start with, Ajit Wadekar quickly switched to attack when he sensed victory and it was only Lloyd with his long front foot coming down the track on a wicket which was beginning to turn that prevented our spinners from running through the side. The West Indians barely survived by the skin of their teeth, being eight wickets down and many runs away from the victory target when the last of the mandatory overs was bowled.

That winter owing to the withdrawal of the invitation to the South African team a Rest of the World team was formed and Clive Lloyd happened to be a part of that trip. The two members of the team who really made that trip memorable were Clive Lloyd and Richard Hutton. Both had a tremendous sense of humour and while Richard said everything with a straight face, Lloyd, the moment he cracked a joke, would double up with laughter his entire body shaking, with everybody joining in.

In the first Test at Brisbane, Lloyd didn't have to do too much but in the second Test he found Lillee's pace a bit difficult to handle as most of us did. That was the last of the Test he played in Australia before the unfortunate accident took place which put a question mark on his future as a cricketer. Fortunately, he came out of it and cricket-lovers all over the world are thankful that he was saved from serious injury and continued to play cricket. What happened was that Ashley Mallet drove a ball uppishly from Intikhab Alam in the game against South Australia at the Adelaide Oval and Lloyd jumped up to his right to take the catch at extra cover. He lost his balance and fell on his back rather awkwardly and the ball slipped out of his fingers, thereby giving Ashley Mallet a life. We were surprised when he wouldn't get up after the fall. Most of us thought that it was simply out of disappointment at missing the catch that he wasn't getting up. It was only when Tony Greig, who was at cover point, noticed the agony on Clive's face that the seriousness of his injury was realised. Clive couldn't move his arms and was partially paralysed. A stretcher had to be brought on to take him away to the hospital. X-rays and examinations at the hospital revealed a spinal injury and the doctors said that if a bone which had protruded had gone in another half or three-quarters of an inch, Clive would have been a paraplegic for the rest of his life. In any case, with his injury being serious he was out of the running for the side and had to stay back in Adelaide while the rest of the team went ahead with the programme. But there was so much of team spirit that we rang up Clive regularly in his hospital to cheer him up.

For Christmas the team had even composed a song and we decided to sing it over the telephone from Melbourne to Lloyd in Adelaide and we were all geared up with our throats lubricated properly, having rehearsed for some time before the call was put through. We were all waiting anxiously for Clive Lloyd to come on to the phone only to be not just disappointed but simply amazed when told that Lloyd was not in the hospital but had gone out on a date. Well, we didn't know if the date was for certain, but for a man who was so badly injured just a week ago and who one feared would have to spend the rest of his life in a wheelchair if that bone had gone in a little further, we were simply amazed to find that that man had recovered so fast. We were, of course, delighted that Hubert, as everybody called him, had recovered so quickly, though we knew that he wouldn't be participating any more on the tour. We missed him because his sense of humour was very infectious. He always kept the team's spirit up with a timely remark, a timely joke, and he always had a very cheerful view of life which was evident in the way he played his cricket.

The thing I remember most about Clive is the way he was always eager to discuss cricketing problems with me and to try and help me out with what he thought was going wrong. During that time in Australia when things were not going too well with me, I talked to a lot of people and amongst the people I can think of who were most sincere in their help were Rohan Kanhai and Clive Lloyd. They tried their best to help me, because they had seen me play in the West Indies in 1971. Also while we were in England they had watched me on television in the Test matches when India played England, and so they were in a better position to tell me what was going wrong with my batting. I am grateful to both of them for the interest they took and for what they told me about how to get over that weak moment in my career.

During that tour we would invariably end up having breakfast together because Lloyd and Farokh would be at their breakfast when I joined them and it was fun with these two fellows with their nonstop array of jokes flying between them. It was difficult to swallow your breakfast because they made you laugh so much.

I also remember one remark of Lloyd when he was asked by the waiter in Australia whether he would like any milk in his coffee. Clive said: "Yes, please, I'm not racial." That puzzled the waiter a bit, though I must say that racial overtones in Australia are perhaps the least one encounters elsewhere in the world where one has gone and played cricket.

Another incident from that trip which is memorable is the firing that the receptionist of our hotel in Melbourne gave Clive for trying to fool with her daughter. It so happened that the daughter and the mother shared the duty of the reception desk and during the time when the mother was away one of the team members tried to fool around with the daughter and this was reported to the mother by one of the staff who said that it was "one curly-haired man" who was fooling around with her daughter. The obvious one to pick was Clive Lloyd because the mother thought that Gary Sobers would never resort to such a thing and Clive Lloyd was the only other curly-haired fellow in the side. Lloyd thought that it was me, but I pointed out to him that I didn't have curly hair and both of us, for the next one week, were trying to tell each other that it was the other who had been fooling around with the receptionist's daughter.

This was even funnier because it happened when Clive was recuperating and had come to Melbourne before he flew off to join his family. He was obviously in no position to have been mischievous and the firing was, therefore, totally uncalled for.

It was good to hear that he made his comeback in a couple of months against the New Zealanders and cracked a brilliant hundred against them in the Guyana Test. This was because players of the ability of Lloyd don't come too often into the Test cricket scene and so his recovery, although it would cause a lot of problems to the Indian cricket team when it played against the West Indies, was welcome. One should look at it from a broader point of view rather than a selfish one and therefore most cricket-lovers, including Indians, were happy that Clive Lloyd had recovered completely from that injury and was back in Test cricket.

I met Lloyd thereafter in 1974 when he was playing for Lancashire in the county championships and as usual, Lloyd was great fun and it was nice to spend some time with him. I've always enjoyed Lloyd's company. For one thing, he never talks cricket unless you want to talk cricket, which means that you can get away without having your ears filled with more cricket talk, as most cricketers tend to do nothing else but talk cricket. There are plenty of topics that Clive can talk on; he's a good conversationalist and always with that underlying humour of his one can see the funny side of just about everything that he talks about.

During that tour of England in 1974 it was anticipated that Lloyd would captain the team to India if Rohan Kanhai was not available. It turned out that Kanhai was available but the selection committee had decided at that stage to drop him and look for fresh blood. Therefore, Clive Lloyd was appointed captain of the team to tour India.

That team consisted of a lot of youngsters. Lloyd himself was one of the stars along with Lance Gibbs and one of the most explosive newcomers, Andy Roberts, who had done so well in the English county championship at that stage. Lloyd's team came down to India and became tremendously popular wherever it went. Not only did they play a brand of cricket which was typically West Indian, full of aggressive shots, aggressive bowling and brilliant fielding all through, but the team's behaviour off the field was impeccable and it was all due to the captain, Clive Lloyd, who did so much to mould the team into a fighting unit.

They got a bit of a shock when, after having won the first two Tests in a canter, they were knocked back in the third and fourth Tests on wickets which were not the best. Vishwanath's brilliant innings in both these Test matches put a seal on the West Indians' fate. Vishy literally counterattacked the West Indian pace attack and therefore set his side's totals from which our spinners could weave their magic over the impatient West Indian batsmen. During that time one noticed that if things weren't going too well for the West Indian team they tended to panic and tried to hit their way out of trouble, instead of playing a more patient game. Lloyd failed in both these Tests and that perhaps is an indicator of why the team lost. They did not have somebody of the calm and experience of Lloyd to stay around and guide the rest of the inexperienced players during the tough periods of batting.

When the fifth Test came up at the newly-laid Wankhede Stadium doubts were raised about the quality of the wicket even before the Test started. The West Indian manager took photographs of the wicket and there was general doubt not just about whether the wicket would last for three days but whether the stadium would stay up during the Test. The stadium had been completed in a rush, in less than a year's time, and therefore there were doubts as to how strong the structure was. Well, on both counts, those who worried were proved wrong, because not only did the wicket last – and would have lasted for another ten days – but the stadium has now lasted for nearly ten years without looking in any danger whatsoever.

During that Test the West Indians piled up 604 runs, out of which Clive scored a massive 242 not out and perhaps could have gone on and scored innumerable runs had he not decided to take the side's interest into account and declared so as to try and get us out twice in the Test match.

Unfortunately his plans were set back a little when there was a hold-up of play after tea on the second day when the police beat up an enthusiast who had come on to the field to congratulate Lloyd for having scored 200 runs. Lloyd became the first person to score a double century at the Wankhede Stadium, though the honour to get the first century at the Wankhede went to the West Indian opener, Roy Fredericks, who slammed a brilliant hundred in no time, thereby setting the stage for Lloyd's attack Lloyd which was to follow.

In that innings Lloyd was simply magnificent. He just flogged the bowling about and hit Bedi twice deep into the Garware stand. By this time it was common knowledge that Clive Lloyd used a bat which was almost three pounds in weight, perhaps the heaviest one ever used, and with six or seven grips around the handle which really made it a thick handle. Lots of things have been written about Clive's bat – the weight, the balance, etc – but I can't think of a better bat than this one that Clive used because the sound when the ball was hit was so sweet that it was taken for granted that it was four runs. On many occasions Lloyd did not have to exert any power at all but he merely seemed to caress the ball, particularly when he played the shots on the on side, and the ball thudded into the boundary post at the Wankhede Stadium.

It was truly an unforgettable innings which was spoilt only by that one incident when the police had to face the wrath of the crowd for beating up an enthusiast and there was no play possible in spite of repeated appeals by a lot of VIPs. Lloyd's team won that Test although over a thousand runs were scored before the first innings was completed. But then Lloyd and Viv Richards went into the attack in the second innings and hammered our attack away. They set us a stiff target and while we could have survived, it was Vanburn Holder's magnificent bowling that saw to it that we were skittled away. We lost that Test and therefore the series by a margin of 3-2.

At the end of that series Clive Lloyd had established himself as the captain of the West Indies team for years to come. It was apparent that the side respected him not only as a captain but as a player and they were prepared to do anything that Lloyd asked. On numerous occasions when he asked Andy Roberts to bowl a couple of more overs in the heat of Madras and in Bombay, Roberts never refused to bowl for Lloyd. That goes to show how much respect Lloyd had from the team, how much the team respected his ability, his views and his judgement. The West Indian team thus was in the process of being moulded into one of the strongest outfits ever to be seen from that part of the world.

The old truth that a captain is only as good as the performance of the rest of his team-mates, was aptly proved the following summer when the West Indians were thrashed 5-1 by the Australians in Australia in the series which was billed as the World Championship for Test cricket. The tour had been arranged after the Australian Board had withdrawn the invitation to the South African team, and so the West Indian tour was arranged very hurriedly.

Before that tour, however, the first World Cup Championship was held in England and it was Clive Lloyd who won the first ever World Cup for the West Indies team with a brilliant hundred in the finals which was played in front of packed galleries at Lord's. When the West Indian captain came in to bat things were not looking very bright for his team and it was greatly due to the magic of Rohan Kanhai and the influence he had on the bowling, that Lloyd could get into his stride and slam that brilliant hundred. That hundred was really the one that turned the tables, because he slammed the Aussie pace bowlers all over the field and this was something which the English crowds were stunned to witness because just a few months before, their team had been destroyed by Lillee and Thomson in the Ashes series in Australia.

Lloyd then led the side astutely making very clever bowling changes to see that the advantage that his century had got to his team was never lost. Although it was a thriller to the end and the Australians lost by 17 runs only, it was apparent that the West Indians were the champion side. When Clive hoisted the Cup, after receiving it from Prince Philip, high over his head, the West Indian population in the crowd went berserk and all kinds of sounds were heard - the typical West Indian music, the banging, the screaming, the shouting, the jostling, and the laughing which is so typically West Indian; all this in as staid a place as Lord's. I'm sure Lord's has never really recovered from that and it's a good thing because participation by the spectators is so important for the players to give their best. However, if it becomes excessive in the form of intrusions into the field, it can upset players more than anything else that they encounter in a day's play.

So the West Indians, having beaten the Australians by a narrow margin, were looked upon as the world champions. Having received the title of world champions of limited overs cricket it was but natural that when they went over to Australia later in the year that the Test series would be labelled as the world championship. In reality that would have been true because the West Indians and the Australians were the strongest sides in the world at the time and they really looked as if they would produce sparkling cricket.

Well, there was a lot of sparkling cricket but the West Indians, in trying to play too much sparkling cricket, lost that series by the sorry margin of five against one.

Australia at that stage were captained by Greg Chappell who had taken over from his brother Ian who retired after the tour of England in 1975, and Chappell celebrated his appointment as captain by hitting a century in each innings of his first Test. He thereafter left his stamp on the series by scoring over 700 runs and completely dominated the series with his authoritative batting. The West Indians had problems; they could never find a suitable opening partner for Roy Fredericks and although Fredericks himself played a brilliant innings of 169 in Perth, he was never as consistent as the West Indians would have liked. Eventually, Viv Richards was pushed in to fill the slot of the opening batsman and he did a magnificent job. It was as an opening batsman that Viv's upward stride as the world's best batsman began.

But this particular series was a blow to Clive Lloyd and when they returned to the West Indies they had to play the

Indian team. Talking to them one got the impression that Lillee and Thomson must have been frighteningly quick. For the West Indians to admit that Thomson was greased lightning really means something because they themselves have genuine pace bowlers in every nook and corner of their islands. Holding was establishing himself as one of the finest fast bowlers the world had seen, Andy Roberts was reaching his peak and Bernard Julien was there to offer variety by way of his left-hand swing.

It was understandable therefore that the West Indians took the field in the first Test against the Indians at Barbados with murder in their eyes because they had to beat India in a very convincing manner to rub off the shame which had fallen upon them after their defeat by the Australians by that margin. And they did that, beating us in a very convincing manner in the first Test in which Lloyd came back to form with a brilliant hundred. It was a superb innings full of sparkling shots and as usual it was an innings which was played in a very short time.

Viv Richards came in and made a hundred and it was the beginning of a very high-scoring time for him. He never really looked back after that innings against us. Lloyd was very happy to have won that Test in three days. At that time the Indian team was really down in the dumps because we had lost two consecutive Tests, the third and the last one in New Zealand and then as soon as we landed in the West Indies, the first Test in merely three days. Morale at that time in the Indian team was pretty low and what we needed was some good thinking and plenty of determination to see that the series just did not go downhill. That determination came to the fore in the second Test which we almost won and this was where Clive Lloyd got a little jumpy. Only Viv Richards was scoring runs and the rest of the team was not contributing runs as it should have. Lloyd began to get nervous about his side's performance and also because there was talk going round that he should be replaced as captain.

The second Test was saved barely by the skin of the teeth by the West Indians. For the West Indians, the Port of Spain venue against the Indians has not been a very lucky one. The wicket hasn't been quite what their pacers would like; on the first day it has always been unpredictable and there is more turn on it than on any other West Indian wicket. Therefore the West Indians weren't exactly very happy with their performance and more so because Bishen had refused a runner for Viv Richards during the second innings when Viv had pulled a leg muscle and was not in a position to run. This angered Clive Lloyd and there was a big discussion on the rule with the umpires and between Clive and Bishen. Eventually Bishen was told that he was right though Bishen very graciously allowed Richards to come in at the fall of the next wicket. But the damage· had been done, because Clive was not the same man again. He resented what Bishen had done in the first place because he thought that that was not done in cricket. The West Indians, just about having survived that one, were to play in Guyana and with that game against the island having been washed out and the rains hardly looking like stopping, the match was transferred to Trinidad which is a bigger ground with a larger capacity. Lloyd had a frown on his face when he came to know that.

It is now history that we put in 400 runs in the second innings to record the biggest total in the second innings for a victory and thereby levelled the series one-all. Lloyd was very upset at this, though it was hardly any fault of his that his bowlers could not get us out in a day and a half. I think it was just that we batted better than at any time in the series and every one of us seemed to have clicked at the same time.

331

Not many would have given us a chance to last out the day, leave aside scoring the runs required to win. But that's what we did and Clive was very upset about it. No captain likes to lose, and Clive was no exception. Therefore, when the Kingston Test came Clive wanted to take advantage of the early life and the early moisture in the wicket and sent us in to bat. His bowlers did not bowl as well as they should have and at the end of the tea session we had put in almost a hundred runs without being separated. Before that, however, in a sheer move of desperation, Lloyd thought that the bowlers should come round the wicket and have us fending off the short deliveries. While this was a good tactical ploy it got out of hand when the bowlers got carried away and started bouncing almost every delivery round our heads.

No batsman, not even the West Indian batsman, would like this kind of bowling because it is hardly cricket and besides the hook shot is not the only shot in the game, though the West Indian crowd likes to see the ball whizz past the ear or hooked off fast bowlers.

That was a Test which saw a lot of injuries and eventually the West Indians won that, having been required to score only a few runs to win. That was perhaps a bitter note on which to end the series and while what happened on the field was unfortunate, let there be no doubt that relationships between the players of both the teams were anything but cordial. And for this, credit is due to Clive Lloyd who, in spite of all the tensions of having to play a home series and being under pressure till the last Test, kept his sense of humour. He handled the side well and was always very friendly and approachable even to the opposition.

Thereafter, it has been one long victory march for Clive Lloyd and his band excepting the series in New Zealand which they lost 1-0 two years ago and which was also a very bitter series due to the fact that the West Indians were not very happy with the New Zealand umpiring and there were shows of defiance by their players.

Under Clive, the team has gone from strength to strength. It has got plenty of great players, the best batsman in the world today, Viv Richards, and the most fearsome fast bowling attack of Croft, Holding, Roberts and Garner with Marshall and Clarke waiting in the wings to take over when one of their people gets injured or retires. They've got a very good opening pair in Greenidge and Haynes, though the spinner hasn't played a very prominent role in the West Indian bowling attack over the last few years. Otherwise it has been a very complete West Indian side. Perhaps the only problem has been that they haven't had a regular wicketkeeper. Deryck Murray has been there with David Murray but neither of them has attained very high standards. Clive, however, has built up a tremendous spirit in this team; the members in his team respect him a great deal and one can see that he's very popular with them. With his easy-going attitude off the field, and with his sense of humour it is obvious why people like him. Also, it is easy to understand that with his attacking cricket on the field he's such a favourite of the crowds.

He has only recently become the father of a boy and when I talked to him in England last year he seemed very relieved about the fact because he'd had two daughters earlier on. In 1976 I got the news that I had become the father of a boy. Just before the Barbados Test Suresh Saraiya and Ravi Chaturvedi who had come down from India had brought along an album of pictures of Rohan who was born while I was away in New Zealand. While I was looking at the pictures at a party Clive came up to me and wanted to know what I was looking at.

When I told him he just shrugged his shoulders and said: "Well, you know how to do it the right way, don't you?" This was said because he had two daughters and I had a son.

When I met him last in England I congratulated him on the birth of a son to which his reply was typically Clive. He said: "Well, at last I got the right turn of the screw!"

That's Clive Lloyd for you - not just a great cricketer and a great captain, but a person who has always looked at the funnier side of life and given so much enjoyment to cricket-lovers all over the world.

I get a little disappointed when people say that Clive is going to quit because the cricket world needs players like Clive Lloyd more than at any other time, now that the world of cricket is going through many crises which seem to crop up out of nowhere. Clive, I just hope you keep on playing. We need you - cricketers and cricket-lovers need you more than you can imagine.

7

Dennis Lillee

DENNIS LILLEE IS THE GREATEST FAST BOWLER IN CRICKETING history. Old-timers will surely dispute this statement. They would talk about other fast bowlers and Fred Trueman may object to that as well, but look at Lillee's record. In just 65 Tests, he has taken 335 wickets and when you take into consideration the fact that he missed out Test cricket for three seasons owing to his association with the World Series Cricket, and his absence from many Tests on account of his recurring back injuries, then he must have surely missed out on 70 to 100 wickets, which would have taken his tally of wickets to over 400 by now. You can thus gauge the class of this speedster. That would have been an all-time record which would have taken a long time to overhaul. Even now he could achieve this mark, but he is obviously coming to the end of his career. Yet he will leave behind his mark as the greatest fast bowler the world has seen.

Our first sight of Lillee was in 1971 in Brisbane and we had heard about him being a slippery customer. When I was taking strike and Lillee thundered in to bowl - he has in recent years modified that run-up - he kept up the movement of his arms. He now runs to the bare minimum. At that time his arms would move about, pump around vigorously and that must have caused additional strain on his back which was to give him recurring trouble later on.

Well, there he was bowling the first ball of the over to me and I steered it to the left of gully for a boundary. The next ball was short and I cut it across past gully for another boundary. Throughout that World XI series, he troubled me. In the first innings, after I had made 22, an inswinger from him kept a little low and nicked in between my bat and pad and bowled me. It was in the second innings of that Test that I decided to have second thoughts on hooking short balls. Till that time, I used to go for the hook whenever a fast bowler pitched short, because that was a challenge and I wanted to accept it. In the second innings which was of no consequence, because the match was petering out into a tame draw, we were given just ninety minutes in the post-tea session to chase an impossible target after Ian Chappell had scored a century in each innings and declared his side's innings.

This was the time to get some batting practice, some confidence against the Australian fast bowlers. Lillee came in and pitched the ball short and I went for the hook. I was in perfect position to hook the ball, but as I brought my bat down to hit the ball, I found that it had already thudded in Rodney Marsh's gloves. If that wasn't the quickest delivery I have ever seen, then I haven't seen many quick deliveries. It was at this stage that I decided that it is safer to get under the delivery pitched short or sway inside or outside the line of the ball. That was the year Lillee reigned as the fastest bowler in the world, as he was to prove in the next Test.

The Australians were all out by the end of the first day's play and our innings was to start the next day. The wicket looked good, a typical Perth wicket, hard, bouncy and obviously the new ball would have caused problems. It was important that the opening batsmen, Engineer and I, got a good start so that the stroke players, Lloyd, Sobers and Kanhai, could capitalise on it. Ackerman was already out of the team with an ankle injury. The fourth ball of the first over was a shortish delivery and as I tried to defend it, the ball brushed the glove and Marsh took an easy catch. That was the start of the slide, because in just a hundred minutes, the entire side was knocked out for a paltry 59 runs and players of the calibre of Sobers and Lloyd perished just the same way, defending the ball off their chins and only managing to edge it to the wicketkeeper or to the slips. As if that was not enough, in the ten minutes we had to bat before the lunch interval, we lost another wicket, when Engineer lofted a catch to Paul Sheahan in the covers. So Lillee had taken nine wickets in that session and the greatest fast bowler-to-be in the world had really arrived.

In the fifth Test he couldn't play owing to an injury, but in the fourth Test, he had given enough indication of the kind of menace he was going to pose to the leading batsmen in the world. Someone like Gary Sobers was out to him twice, the first ball, defending the ball off the chin, to be caught behind. And I am sure in the 100-plus innings that Gary has played, he had never been out in this manner, defending the ball off his chin in such an abject manner. Every time Lillee pitched short, Gary was in a position to hook it, but Lillee had that little bit of extra pace that forced the great man on the defence.

When Lillee went to England in 1972, he bowled some of the quickest stuff one had seen for a long, long time. Those who watched the Manchester Test believe that his spell was quite frightening. It was only bad batting that cost the Australians the match. But it was Massie's bowling at Lord's which brought the Australians back in the series and level it at two wins each. Lillee finished that series with thirty-one wickets and his reputation at that stage was second to none. Even in this series, he was showing himself to be a great competitor, aggressive, to the point of being offensive and he was not afraid to exchange a word or two with the batsman and let him know exactly what he thought of his ability.

But then there was a setback when he went to the West Indies in 1973. He found to his dismay that he was getting a pain in the back and was not able to pound in and bend his back as much as he would have liked. It was diagnosed as stress fracture in the vertebra, which meant at that stage that Lillee's cricketing career was almost finished. But those who thought so did not reckon with his fighting spirit. He underwent strenuous physical tests, hard exercises and really slogged and sweated to get back to into peak condition.

So when the 1974 season began, in Australia, doubts were expressed about Lillee's ability to bowl with the same kind of speed. In the first Sheffield Shield match, he did not impress and did not get wickets and to a battery of TV cameras and the rest of the media, he just looked an average medium pacer. But the Australian selectors knew that the Englishmen would be under psychological pressure if Lillee was included in the first Test. So Lillee and another young fast bowler, Jeff Thomson, were picked to have a go at the Englishmen.

It was obvious that Lillee had been playing a game with the TV and media by not bowling at his regular pace and perhaps his most sensible explanation was that he was building himself up to full pace gradually so as not to damage his back once again. To many Lillee appeared a little slow but it was due to the fact that Thomson was quicker than Lillee and in fact was so quick that bowling against the wind, he looked quicker than Lillee. By the end of the fifth Test, they had together annihilated the Englishmen and their batsmen were shell-shocked, to say the least, with the exception of Tony Greig who went on gustily taunting the fearsome duo and getting away with it. The Englishmen, and particularly the press, accused Lillee and Thomson of being bouncer-happy. It was only Ian Chappell's retort that it was Peter Lever and Bob Willis who had really started it off that silenced them to some extent. Ian Chappell proved the point that it was the Englishmen who had started the bouncer war, knowing fully well that Australia had the better artillery.

There was this very humorous story about David Lloyd who was writing a letter to his mother and he started off by saying, "Dear Mom, today I played a ball pitched in my half of the wicket." That goes to show that neither Lillee nor Thomson bowled well-pitched-up deliveries. But I would like to believe that with their extra pace, and particularly when they played the Englishmen, they always tried to add a yard or two to their pace and managed to get that extra steep bounce from just short of a length, which was perhaps mistaken by the Englishmen for short deliveries.

So the duo came to England in 1975 and their activities were followed with great interest. The media was fully after them, ignoring the rest of the Australian players. That was the inaugural year of the World Cup competition and, contrary to expectations, the Australians reached the final. Just when everyone had given up hopes of them making a recovery in the final against the West Indies, it was Lillee and Thomson who made the recovery possible with a last wicket partnership that brought the Australians within 17 runs of the target before a misunderstanding caused Thomson to be run out.

This fighting spirit was evident in the four-Test series that followed during which for the first time one saw in England wickets which were whitish in appearance and devoid of any grass. The Indian team never had any good quick bowlers, with the result that the wickets were thick with grass, obviously prepared to suit the attack of the Englishmen.

I was fortunate to watch the first Test and what I saw was unbelievable. Yet, Lillee managed to extract pace and bounce from the first few overs and then switched over to either cutting the ball or moving it off the wicket. Thomson, on the contrary, found it a bit difficult since he relied entirely on sheer speed and since the wicket was devoid of any grass, he could not get much bounce or movement off the pitch.

Lillee's greatness came to his rescue then and one saw why he was so highly rated by everybody. By varying his pace and using the crease and cutting the ball off the wicket Lillee exploited whatever the wicket had to offer and ran through half of the England side. Only a bold, aggressive innings by Tony Greig and David Steele, who played with his front foot down the wicket, helped England to a respectable score. John Snow then ripped through the Australian side as he had done in 1970, but here again Lillee showed tremendous fighting spirit and smashed everybody, including John Snow, to knock off 73 runs, which is his highest score in Test cricket. He seemed to be really enjoying himself and played on the front foot knowing well that no one would pitch short stuff against him.

However, the Australians did not do well and also looked pretty ineffective in the next Test. Moreover when the match was well poised, it was spoiled by vandals digging up the wicket and spraying it with oil. What would have been the finest last day's play in a Test was thus ruined.

The Oval Test also provided a docile track and there was not much that Lillee could do, but at the end of that series, he had come down a peg from his standing, but by no means disgraced. He was aggressive and sincere in his efforts but the wickets did not help him.

When the West Indians went to Australia in 1975-76, Lillee had kept himself trim, ready to have a go at them. Both the teams had a battery of fast bowlers and the series was awaited with bated breath by the connoisseurs of the game. Despite the West Indies having a fairly good, well-balanced side, Lillee and Thomson destroyed the West Indians and won the series 5-1. Most of the West Indian batsmen were caught on the bigger Australian grounds while hooking short-pitched deliveries. They could not resist the temptation of hooking and fell an easy prey to the wiles of the duo.

The following season, a short series against Pakistan was drawn owing to the magnificent bowling by Imran Khan in the Sydney Test when he took twelve wickets and which prompted the Australian skipper Greg Chappell to say that, at times Imran bowled as quick as Lillee. At that time it was the highest praise that could have been showered on a bowler and it goes to show that even in 1976, Lillee was considered the greatest fast bowler in the world.

Next year, there was the Centenary Test between England and Australia. It was dramatic right from the start. Rick McCosker's jaw was broken by a rising delivery from Bob Willis when he tried to hook and ended up by pulling the ball on his jaw, in the process hitting the wicket and getting out as well. This Test will be remembered for two reasons; Derek Randall's brilliant innings of 174 and the magnificent bowling by Dennis Lillee on a wicket which helped the bowler on the first day but was easier as the match progressed. He captured ten wickets in this match and was quite simply the major difference between the two sides, which were till then fairly evenly matched. It was Lillee's bowling that swung the match in Australia's favour.

At one stage, it looked as if England were going to pile up the highest ever fourth innings score in a Test match. That they ended up only 45 runs short, is proof enough of the closeness of the match. By coincidence the margin of victory in the first-ever Test between the two countries in 1877 was also 45 runs. It was Lillee who claimed Alan Knott leg before to give Australia the victory in 1977.

This was followed by a series in England in 1977. The euphoria of winning the Centenary Test was sweeping through Australia because Lillee had demolished the Pommies single-handedly but it was soon forgotten when Lillee announced that he would not be able to tour England because his back was causing him trouble once again. This announcement produced shock waves throughout the cricketing world. Lillee's partner Thomson too was a doubtful starter, having fractured a collarbone earlier in the season. Thomson was not too sure of giving his best. Lillee decided to rest his back as much as possible with a view to making himself available in a fully-fit condition when the Australian season started. With their main strike force not available, the Australian selectors were in a quandary.

Thomson passed the fitness test and went on the tour much to everyone's relief but he was not a success on that tour. As the team prepared to go to England came the news that the majority of the Australian players had signed up for the WSC cricket. It was a very busy season for Australia in 1977, with

342

the Centenary Test, the emergence of the WSC cricket and then the England tour. Off-the-field activities were more in news rather than cricket. Many people jumped to the conclusion that Lillee was resting to keep himself fit for the Packer series. These people did not know Dennis Lillee at all, because he would never withdraw from a cricket match, particularly where Australia was concerned, unless he was really unfit. It was rather unfortunate for him that just before this tour of England the announcement about the WSC signing up star cricketers from the cricketing world for the WSC series was made.

With the International Cricket Conference deciding to ban cricketers participating in the Packer series from official Test cricket series, Lillee was out of Test cricket for three years till a compromise was reached between the Australian Cricket Board and the WSC management in 1979. He missed quite a few Tests during this period and if he had played those Tests he would have had 400 Test wickets to his name instead of 335 which he has today. This would have been really possible because the fifty-odd wickets he took in the World Series Cricket during those years were those of some of the world's best batsmen, from England, the West Indies and other countries. Lillee thinks that he has already four hundred Test wickets in his bag; but since these matches were not official, one cannot quite accept that. But he is still capable of achieving the four-hundred wicket mark, if he keeps going for a few more years.

The 1979 season in Australia, after the team was revamped when the WSC compromise formula was accepted by the authorities, was very gruelling. Australia lost all three Tests against the West Indies and won all three against England; thus all six matches were decisive. Lillee's performance in these six Tests was once again outstanding. Against the West Indians, he troubled every batsman except Vivian Richards who was in terrific form that season with his lowest score in five Test innings being 70. Lillee was in his element against the old enemy, England, and was firing off all cylinders. In the last Test at Melbourne, which was not a very good track for fast bowlers, his cutters were described by the English captain, Mike Brearley, as the best piece of fast bowling he had ever seen. To induce a great judge of fast bowling like Geoff Boycott to shoulder arms and then knock his off-stump back was a great achievement. And Lillee just did that, much to Boycott's annoyance and discomfiture.

After that, Australia visited England for the solitary Centenary Test. And here too Lillee made his presence felt, though not with the same degree of success he is known for.

The following season he made his first appearance against India, Down Under. It is a pity that Lillee, who made his debut in Tests in 1970, had to wait for ten long years to play against India. When India toured Australia in 1977-78 and when Australia returned the visit in 1979, Lillee was with the WSC and was not selected for the Australian team. So this was the series which was eagerly looked forward to by both the sides and perhaps by Lillee too.

We first met in the one-day match at Melbourne. He was bowling to me and his first ball was short but it had enough bounce. It hit me on the glove, then my ribs and went to deep fine leg for a single. As we crossed for that run, Lillee, after his follow-through, kept glaring at me, and I said to myself he is a dragon all right. In that series, Lillee, though fiery on the field, was the mildest of persons in the dressing room.

In the first Test, I won the toss and elected to bat, a decision which was much criticised by critics who did not even bother to go to the wicket and inspect the moisture and dampness. Given the choice I would do the same thing again since we might be able to do better. In the first hour our team had lost my wicket, caught behind for a duck, and Chetan and Dilip were playing Lillee, Thomson and Pascoe with care and a degree of comfort though the ball was moving around on the Sydney track, which is normally a hard track much like the one we have in Madras.

It was in the second hour that wickets began to fall and it was mainly due to careless batting rather than good bowling by the Australians that they bundled us out for 204 and Australia followed it up with a 400-plus score. In the second innings also we scored 204 and it beats me how people can say that we would have done well to bat second in this Test when we could not score more runs than in the first innings even in the second knock.

It is now an established fact that the Indians never seem to do well in the first Test when they tour other countries and wait to gauge the strength of the opposition and their bowling. It is always after the first Test that they come into their own. Most of the time on tours the Indians have lost the first Test and performed badly or have not played to their full abilities. And so it was in this Test.

The second Test was remarkable because we scored 400 runs after chasing a 500-plus total. This was mainly due to Sandeep Patil's brilliant innings of 174 and a fine knock of 97 by Chetan Chauhan. It was that man Lillee who deprived Chetan of his first century in Test cricket. He beat him with a cleverly concealed slow leg-cutter.

And then came our memorable victory at Melbourne but before that there was the unfortunate incident when I wanted to take the side off the field along with Chetan, which would have meant that the Test would have been won by Australia as we were still short of the target. But the background of that incident needs to be told to the readers to give them a clearer picture.

I was batting well and for the first time in the series I was middling the ball well. It looked like I would get a few runs when a ball from Lillee kept low and as I played it with the inside edge of the bat it went on to hit the pad. After that a typical Lillee appeal for leg before followed as he danced down the track, eventually winning the appeal. At this stage, I must say that the umpiring of Mr. Whitehead had disappointed us, for he gave a lot of decisions that went against us. It was getting to a stage where the team-mates were saying that I must do something about it, or else it wouldn't do good to Indian cricket. For example, the previous day when Allan Border was bowled while trying to sweep Shivlal Yadav, the umpires had to confer with each other to give that decision.

Then Kirmani had told me that if the umpire had given Border not out he would have walked off. I remember having told him that whatever might be the decision, we had to abide by it. But perhaps that word walk-out was imprinted in the back of my mind, so the next day when Lillee's appeal was upheld I was furious against the umpire for having given that decision.

When the umpire did not reverse his decision a lot of anger was boiling within me but still the idea of walking off did not strike me. When I walked past Chetan, I heard friend Lillee utter one of his profanities which was a very delayed action from him and it was then I lost my balance of mind and told Chetan to walk off with me.

That is one of the most regrettable incidents in my life. Whatever may be the provocation and whatever the reason, there was no justification for my action and I now realise that I did not behave the way a captain and sportsman should. I take all the blame and responsibility for my action. I think that

Lillee in his own way forced me to take that action by uttering those words. I was walking back to the dressing room and the most that could have happened would have been that the bench on which I was sitting would have come under the impact of my bat or the locker where I kept my clothes and kit would have been knocked about. I do not fully blame Lillee because whatever may be the provocation, I should have kept my cool and allowed the anger to die down. I should have shown my disappointment in the dressing room and not on the field of play. That was Lillee on the field.

Then there was Dennis Lillee shaking our hands and wishing us well after the Test was over and hoping to come to India some day. I remember a dinner where some Indian and Australian players were invited. Also present were Sir Don Bradman and Lady Bradman. There were Dennis Lillee, Doug Walters, Karsan Ghavri, Vishwanath, Kapil Dev and myself. Kapil asked Dennis why he uttered so much abuse on the cricket field and Dennis replied, "It's because I am a fast bowler and when I bowl a bad ball or see the batsman edge without result, my frustrations come out in the open. Because there is so much effort to be put in fast bowling than you medium-pacers are required to do." That sums up the man's attitude, the man's characteristics and goes to show why he has become the greatest fast bowler in the world. He is a very, very tough competitor. He will not smile at you or give an inch. He always tries to get you out and whether he has a cricket ball in hand or a verbal missile, he never leaves you in doubt as to his intention, which is to get you back to the pavilion as quickly as possible.

Off the field he is a perfect gentleman, a man who likes to be by himself. He would spend his time in one corner. He likes to remain incognito and spends his free time with his family and dear friends. Yet, while Dennis Lillee is playing cricket, and getting wickets by dozens, the anonymity which he seeks will remain elusive. And this is something which he has to bear with or else, as most batsmen would wish, stop getting wickets in Test cricket.

8

Derek Underwood

IT IS A PITY THAT DEREK UNDERWOOD DID NOT COMPLETE HIS BAG of three hundred wickets during the England team's winter tour of India and Sri Lanka in 1981-82. He is very close to that magic figure which only three bowlers have reached so far. It is not certain that he would be picked in the England team for the future Tests and so it is a pity that he may not join the ranks of those three-hunred-plus wicket-takers in the history of the game.

On the previous tour of India in 1976, Underwood took twenty-nine wickets. He was the most successful of the English bowlers, although it was the English pace bowlers who had done most of the damage and succeeded in getting rid of the Indian middle-order batting during that series. On the last tour in 1981-82, Underwood was just a shadow of his former self

349

and though the old determination, the nagging accuracy, and the old miserliness, as far as giving away runs, was still there, the vital nip off the wicket was often missing and, therefore, he was not as successful in India as one expected him to be from his previous performances.

Derek Underwood is one of the nicest chaps you can ever come across. He wants to give the impression of being very tough on the field of play but his inborn niceness prevents him from doing so. Even though he might not like to exchange a word with others on the field lest that could relieve a little pressure or tension on the batsman, his friendliness comes to the fore and he is always there with a greeting and it is always a pleasure to play against this great left-arm bowler. He runs a little farther away than most of the left-arm spinners do. Perhaps it is not really fair to level him off as a spinner, as he is so much quicker than a normal spinner. But then, similarly, Chandrasekhar could not be called a spinner because he was so much quicker than a normal leg spinner. But Underwood has been known as a spinner so we shall go by what the world knows him as and treat him as a spinner.

With a little longer run-up than other spinners and a diagonal run-up he bowls at a quickish pace. On a wicket which is slightly soft or offers a little bit of help, he is practically unplayable, because at that pace there is hardly any chance for a batsman to use his feet against him and try and convert a good ball into a driveable ball. His accuracy is well known and more important is his ability to exploit a batsman's weakness as soon as he has seen him in action for some·time. With that legendary accuracy, he would pin a batsman down until he was fed up and tried an attacking shot and got out. Because of Underwood's accuracy, a lot of other bowlers at the other end got wickets. Having got tired of being tied down, they would try to break free at the other end and lose their wickets.

I first knew about a bowler called Underwood when a commercial firm came out with a miniature set of photographs of top cricketers in the world sometime in 1966 and there was a photograph of Underwood. After that time, whenever I followed the scores of county cricket in England, the name Underwood caught the eye and after I had seen the photograph, I came to identify the exploits of this man called Underwood in the English county matches. He soon became a Test bowler and having played Tests he did not look back. He has since become a household name in cricketing circles. He has had his ups and downs and in the earlier part of his career he was not able to keep a regular place in the England squad. For example, Norman Gifford was preferred to him during 1971 and 1972 by Ray Illingworth for reasons only Illingworth would be able to give. Perhaps, it was that Gifford was an orthodox left-arm spinner, while Underwood needed a helpful track to get his wickets. But that is something of a reputation which he had acquired and which does not really do him justice. Underwood is perfectly capable of bowling well and getting his wickets on most tracks. He does not actually need a helping track to do so.

I have got out to him many times and I think the most regular way to get out to him was the caught and bowled variety, where he has deceived me with his flight, the result being my playing the shot too early, enabling him to fasten on to the catch. I have been out to him, caught at forward short-leg, on a couple of occasions and on the opposite side at silly point as well. I think his best delivery to me was the one during the recent Calcutta Test when I played down the wrong line and was bowled by a ball that went straight through. The earlier two deliveries he had bowled just outside the leg-stump so that when the third ball was about to be delivered, my left foot automatically went down in the direction of the leg-stump and the ball which was pitched on the off-stump saw me going on the wrong line completely and hit my off-stump. That was very, very good bowling by Underwood, because this ball was also delivered a little slower than the earlier two deliveries. Apart from his normal pace, he has got a ball which comes in and is quicker than his normal delivery. This is the ball which has got him a lot of leg-before-the-wicket decisions as the batsmen have been completely beaten by the sheer speed of the ball and before their bat can come down they are trapped leg before the wicket.

As a batsman too, he has been a stubborn customer and many times he has gone in as a night-watchman and done a very commendable job of not only seeing the day through, but also taking the sting out of the attack when play would resume the next day. He is very, very proud to be playing for England. Unfortunately, joining the Packer series meant missing three very important and vital series for England. God alone knows how many more wickets he would have taken, if he had been around then. Certainly, he would have reached the 350-wicket mark, if not more. One also remembers the ball he bowled in the 1974 Test to Vishwanath when Vishy was looking good. It pitched on the leg-stump and turned enough to knock back the off-stump. A gem of a delivery and it broke a promising partnership which was on at that moment. It virtually meant England got the breakthrough to go on and win that Test match.

The other delivery which is memorable is the one he bowled to Brijesh Patel in the Madras Test in 1976. Till that time, the ball had not turned much. Though there was a lot of bounce Bob Willis was able to get off this wicket, the spinners were not able to turn the ball much and this one from Underwood again pitched somewhere on the middle and leg stumps, turned and went off with rocket-like speed to knock back Brijesh's off-stump. That was a delivery which would have foxed most of the batsmen in the world, so quickly did it move after pitching and so big was the turn. As he turned round after being congratulated by the rest of the team, he remarked that a few more like this and "we would be in business". Well, he certainly was in business in the second innings when the wicket started turning appreciably and with the bounce having not lessened, he was almost unplayable. India were knocked out for a paltry 83, which meant that England not only won that Test but also the series. Well, I hope Underwood gets a few more deliveries like that so that he can reach the magic figure of three hunred Test wickets, because no one deserves it more than this likeable, genuinely dedicated professional English cricketer.

9

E.A.S. Prasanna

ERAPALLI PRASANNA PLAYED HIS FIRST TEST MATCH IN 1960-61 against the Englishmen, went to the West Indies in 1962 and then, after a gap of four years, he was back in the Indian team. This gap of four years was necessary for completing his engineering studies and obtaining a degree. That was what his father had insisted.

In those days playing cricket did not offer as much monetary advantage as it does now. Of course, the glamour of being a Test cricketer has always been there, but it was only in the mid-seventies, particularly after Kerry Packer paraded the world's best cricketers in his series, that cricketers have been able to earn a decent living. Thus, Prasanna's father was right to ask the young lad to continue with his studies so that his engineering degree along with his cricketing ability would stand him in good stead in getting a job.

It is very difficult to make a comeback into a Test team and particularly so after a lapse of four years. For that one needs, apart from the resolve, ability, lots of fighting spirit, guts, hard work, determination and, of course, that element of luck. Pras, as he is lovingly called, had all these qualities and having acquired a taste for Test cricket earlier, he was not going to give up easily.

Recalled against the mighty West Indians in the mini-series in 1966-67, he spun a web around their batsmen and along with Bishen Bedi, who was making his debut in the series, they made life pretty uncomfortable for the West Indies batsmen. That the West Indies still managed to win the series is a tribute to the depth of their batting and just goes to show how strong they were that year.

They had come from a very successful tour of England and with Gary Sobers in fine form and the up-and-coming Clive Lloyd around, the Indians had a tough time. Among those who came out with credit after this series was Prasanna. After this performance, he was a certainty for the tour of England in 1967 that was to follow the West Indies tour of India. Before that tour, however, one witnessed the duo of Chandrasekhar and Prasanna against Wadekar and Sardesai when Bombay met Mysore (now Karnataka) in the Ranji Trophy Championship. Ajit Wadekar mercilessly scored 323 runs, while Sardesai scored a hundred, but the initial period, when both Wadekar and Sardesai were trying to find their feet, was fascinating to watch. It was a great sight for a student like me who was trying to get into cricket. Two outstanding players of spin bowling and two outstanding spin bowlers were trying to get on top of each other. Pras was all his crafty self as he went on making it appear that he had an ace up his sleeve and was going to produce it during his next delivery and Ajit, grim, bending over his bat, concentrating very hard to see that Pras was not going to slip one between his bat and pad.

Dilip Sardesai was happier against Prasanna because Dilip used his feet well. Whenever Pras tossed the ball up a shade more Dilip was down the track and, taking advantage of the flight, scored some runs. Chandra, on the other hand, was a different kind of bowler. His flight was unpredi-ctable, his length too was unpredictable and so Dilip was not as keen to play Chandra. Ajit, on the other hand, played Chandra well because the latter found it difficult bowling to left-handers, and Ajit was making full use of the short-pitched deliveries that Chandra used to bowl. The result was a massive partnership and it was as good a contest between the bat and the ball as one could have hoped to see.

Pras went off after some time complaining of a pulled muscle and it gave rise to idle gossip that Pras had chickened out. But Pras had continuous trouble with his leg muscles as his engineering job was such that he did not get enough time for training and exercising. Thus, he tended to put on a bit of weight and that made it more difficult for him to be supple and agile. This was one of the things that let Pras down when Venkat was around because the latter was trimmer and more agile. When two batsmen were completely dominating, Venkat would peg away and try to restrict the scoring with his tidy length. His superior physical fitness made him a bowler whom most captains would have liked to have in their teams.

The tour of England in 1967, though not extremely successful for Pras, still helped him establish his place in the side over Venkat and so when the tour of Australia and New Zealand came in 1967-68, Pras was able to get into the team. That was Pras' most successful trip. He took forty-nine wickets in eight Tests, twenty-five in Australia and twenty-four in New Zealand.

It was a remarkable performance and he had most of the Australian batsmen in a quandary. Many Australian batsmen rated Pras as the best off-spinner they had faced, rating him over someone like Lance Gibbs who had 300-plus wickets in Test cricket. When the Australian and New Zealand teams returned the visits in 1969, Pras was there, but this time it was Bishen Bedi who dominated the series with his left-arm spin and took the most wickets. They formed a deadly combination: Bishen, coming in easily, gliding in, while Pras coming in just a bit quicker but making the ball do exactly the opposite of what the left-armer did. And to top it all there was Chandrasekhar who would come on and bowl. Just when the batsmen thought that they were let off the cunning flight of Bishen and Pras, they were confronted with Chandra who also was a spinner but a much quicker spinner than the other two. While these bowlers were on, life was not easy for batsmen and particularly in India where the wickets tended to help them almost from the word go. It set India's new ball bowlers a difficult task because unless a new ball bowler could bat like Abid Ali, it was always impossible for him to be picked for the Indian team.

When the Indian team went to the West Indies in 1971, Pras was in the team along with Venkataraghavan who by now had been made vice-captain. The surprise omission was that of Chandrasekhar. Two other spinners in the team were Bishen Bedi and Salim Durrani. Durrani, of course, was more of an all-rounder. We thus had four bowlers who were all successful at Test level, plus Eknath Solkar who could bowl a bit of left-hand spin, and Ashok Mankad whose off-spin had picked up wickets for Bombay and West Zone in first class matches. And to bowl with the new bat were Abid, Govindraj and Solkar, who had started very recently to seam the ball. It was a fairly well-balanced side and the only question was how our batsmen would face the West Indies' quickies on their tracks.

Apart from Sardesai, Jaisimha, Pras and Salim Durrani, no one among us had been to the West Indies before and so these were the men on whom Ajit Wadekar had to rely the most on this tour. I was fortunate to have players like Salim Durrani, Jaisimha and Prasanna to help me out. This was my first trip and before this tour, I had come across these players in domestic first class matches. I had made friends with them easily and was fortunate to have encouragement from these players plus, of course, Ajit Wadekar. If I am not mistaken, Jai and Pras were room-mates and I spent most of my evenings with them. It was usual for Vishy, Eknath and me to go to their rooms and listen to them and get some cricketing knowledge and education as well. It was in the first Test itself that Pras damaged his finger. He tried to stop a drive in his follow-through and the non-striker accidentally put his foot on his palm as Pras bent down to stop the ball. The non-striker was trying to get back to his crease. This accident meant that Pras was out of that Test and also the next one. That gave Venkat just the opening he needed. Venkat bowled well, took wickets and was always an asset with his close-to-the-wicket fielding. So Pras found himself sitting on the sidelines more than he would have thought before the team took off.

Thereafter Pras was always under pressure; for one thing, Venkat, being the vice-captain, was sure of his place. And so Pras was always struggling. He had not only to take wickets but had to take them in plenty which put additional pressure on him. Thus Pras found himself out of the team and it was only when England came in 1972-73, that he was back in it. And the smile was back on his face.

The following season was one of ups and downs for Pras.

But even during that lean period, he led Karnataka to their maiden triumph in the Ranji Trophy Championship. Karnataka beat Bombay convincingly in Bangalore in the semifinals and then went on to beat Rajasthan in the final. The Karnataka team was undergoing a great transfor-mation at that stage. The team had just begun to believe in its ability to take on all comers. Pras was already a world class spinner. Chandra had stunned everybody with his devastating bowling. Vishwanath was acknowledged as the best batsman India was going to have for the next ten years and Brijesh Patel and Syed Kirmani were coming up with plenty of promise and potential. With these players as his lieutenants, Pras had no difficulty in winning the Ranji Trophy.

Pras' greatest moment as a bowler, however, was yet to come. That was on the tour of New Zealand and the West Indies in 1976. In the first Test at Auckland, Pras spun New Zealand to their doom taking eight wickets and paving the way for India's victory. It was off-spin bowling at its best. The flight, the variety, the quicker ones, were all there. But when Pras found a turning wicket, his greatest joy was not in getting the batsman caught off the inside edge at forward short-leg or backward short-leg, as most off-spinners do, but the great off-spinner that he was, was to get the batsman out bowled trying to drive him through the covers and the ball sneaking in between the bat and the pad. The ball would pitch outside the off-stump, appearing to the batsman as a desirable half-volley. As the batsman went for it and found it just a little bit short for a drive, the ball would sneak in to bowl him. The other mode of dismissal that gave Prasanna the most thrill, particularly on a turning track, was getting the batsman out caught and bowled. Players would go for the cover-drive only to find the ball turn and Prasanna waiting to snap up the return catch. These, to him, were the best methods of dismissal on a turning track. It showed that he was not just using the turning track to get the batsman out, but he was using his talent, his flight and his guile. After the first Test against New Zealand in 1976, they saw to it that he didn't get any wickets without thick grass on the wicket. So Pras and other bowlers found it difficult to get going. Pras seemed to fade away somewhat after that and although he made another tour of Australia in 1977-78 and Pakistan in 1978, he was not quite the same bowler he was before. By that time the new technique of the batsmen to play more with the pads rather than the bat had been developed and that certainly frustrated Pras. It really was not cricket when batsmen tried to place the pad as the first line of defence and the bat as the second line. It was all against the technique of the game we were taught at school and Pras belonging to the old school wasn't able to quite adjust himself to that and so he went out of Test cricket.

And it was a big disappointment for us, for it's not easy to lose first class players like Pras.

Pras was not only a world class player but also first class company off the field. We missed him running up to bowl to the batsman, beating him and then walking backwards, up to his bowling mark, with a smile on his face, which was probably another irritant to the batsman, particularly if Pras had beaten him. Pras would then jump up throwing his hands on the top of his head and showing surprise at the survival of the batsman and then go backwards to his mark.

Another notable characteristic of Pras on the field was that every time he got a wicket, he would run back to his old comrade-in-arms, Bishen Bedi, who would normally be at mid-off or mid-on position, embrace him, and both of them would have a hearty laugh as if to show what a great joke they had played on the batsman. This was a very familiar sight, one which was a source of great joy for us.

This sense of enjoyment, of life was what Pras infected all of us with. It was great fun to be with Pras on tours as well as on the same side in domestic cricket. He was always smiling and looking at the brighter side of everything and whenever you needed advice he was always there to give it.

Pras did a splendid job for India, something he can be very proud of. He has an enviable record and it was sheer bad luck that prevented him from completing two hundred wickets in Tests. In fact, he and Venkat with their off-spinners have set such a high standard that other off-spinners who are striving hard to get into the Indian team are finding it difficult to do so. The new aspirants are invariably compared to Venkat and Prasanna but are found wanting. In that sense their greatness has been a bit of disadvantage for the new off-spinners who would much more certainly have loved to follow in the footsteps find it difficult to do so. It is a gap which will take a long time to fill and even if it is filled, I have no doubt in my mind that there cannot be another bowler like Prasanna.

10

Geoffrey Boycott

NO OTHER TEST CRICKETER, PERHAPS NOT EVEN SIR DONALD Bradman, nor Harold Larwood, has been so much in the news as Geoffrey Boycott. Ever since his arrival at the Test level, he has been in the news in some form or the other and his actions on and off the field have attracted the attention of the media. He's been good copy for the press, radio and television.

What has been forgotten amidst the complicated controversies Boycott has got into, is his ability to play near-perfect against all kinds of bowling and on all kinds of wickets. There cannot be a better technician than Geoff Boycott. People of the earlier generation talk about Sir Len Hutton and his technique; they also talk about Wally Hammond; they also talk about, Vijay Merchant and his technique; but the technique of this man is simply unbelievable.

The only problem seems to be that, while he has geared himself up to meet every possible good ball delivered by a bowler, it is the bad ball that has got him out too often because he has not thought what he should do with it. And having preoccupied himself with the thought of shutting out bowlers and their good deliveries, whenever a bad ball comes, he is not ready to take care of it and gets into trouble. Along with technique is his unflagging concentration and superb physical fitness. He seems to go on and on and his appetite for runs is increasing day by day, as he grows older.

On the recent tour of India, he showed complete dedication by trying to have a net even during the lunch interval when the rest of the team were having lunch. He even had nets during the tea interval of twenty minutes to have a little warm-up session. This is something which has been his constant source of strength because he seems to be immersed in constant batting practice and nothing else seems to exist for him.

Boycott started off as a middle-order batsman and seeing his aptitude and dedication to play the moving ball, the captain of the Yorkshire team brought him up to open the innings. Thereafter, he set himself up to be as good an opening batsman as there ever was and he practised, saw films of himself, talked to people who mattered and sought their advice, repaired the various chinks in his armour and built up a reputation of being not satisfied with anything less than a hundred.

His Test debut against the Australians was not outstanding but neither was it disappointing for him or for the England selectors. He batted solidly, gave support to the others and generally made it known that his was the wicket that the bowlers would have to earn and which would never be gifted away. I cannot recall Boycott having gifted away his wicket even when the chase for runs was on. Every time a bowler got Boycott's wicket it was solidly and sweatfully earned.

Unfortunately, he has also been dogged by injuries which means that he has missed out on a number of Tests. It is staggering to think what his total aggregate and average would have been if he was physically fit to play all those matches he missed out.

There have been three phases of his absence from Test cricket. First, owing to injuries. Then there was his self-imposed exile, and, thirdly, when he was censured by the selectors for slow scoring and dropped from the next Test match as a disciplinary measure.

In a career spanning from 1968, he has played in over a hundred Test matches. He has scored over hundred first class centuries and holds the record for over 8,000 aggregate runs in Tests. He is also a record holder for a host of other things. He has taken a few wickets with his medium-paced inswingers and has become a useful bowler in limited-overs cricket. He has done a bit of bowling and helped in terminating many a good partnership when it has threatened to look very dangerous. But it is as a great batsman that Boycott is known.

People for ever will call him names. There are people who will never be able to ignore him either. You either love him or hate him. There is no in-between as far as Boycott is concerned. That about sums up the conflicting emotions this person arouses in other people. I cannot think of a better opening batsman than Geoff Boycott. Though Barry Richards came very close to that with almost a copybook defence, he did not allow his defence to get the better of his attacking strokes. Defence was used only to tackle the good balls and when the bad balls came around (sometimes even good balls) Barry Richards would hit. And his batting was always exhilarating to watch. But Geoff Boycott, perhaps, thinks the other way. He was trying to carry the England batting on his shoulders when their batting was not always sound and, in recent years, giving problems. Boycott had therefore decided to play the role of a sheet-anchor. While the other young England players went there and played their shots, he always remained rooted there in support, seeing that no wickets fell from his end. This is perhaps a good attitude but he carries it too far and sometimes ends up with the result that a new batsman feels the pressure and that brings the bowlers on top. While Boycott, in earlier years, looked as if he could rotate the strike by taking well-placed singles, today he has lost that art of keeping the scoreboard moving.

There is so much you can learn from Boycott's game: right from the stance which is correct, sideways, facing the bowler, with the elbow pointing towards the bowler and the head still, not moving and very little preliminary movement. The feet are placed just the right distance apart to stand comfortably together, not too close together, not too wide apart and the bat, though placed just around the right toe, still coming down straight, although it is picked up towards third man before the ball is delivered. When it comes down, it comes down straight which is the most important thing. While the bat comes down straight, the foot is almost in perfect position in the direction in which the ball is intended to be hit and, therefore, the body is, if the ball is to be hit on the off-side, kept rigidly sideways which is what this game is all about, being sideways in batting and sideways in bowling. He has kept to those rigid fundamentals and therefore even at the age of forty-plus he is a most difficult batsman to get out. However, he gives the impression that he is more of a bottom-hand player and this can be seen by the way the bottom hand slides down the handle of the bat just before the bowler has delivered the ball, although when he takes stance the hands on the bat handle are very close to each other. This is perhaps the reason why he is not such a good driver of the ball and prefers to nudge and cut the ball away for his runs rather than drive it off the front foot. He is also predominantly a front-foot player.

When he bats, and particularly when he plays forward, the meaning of the old saying, "smelling the ball", comes through very clearly. So low does Boycott play off the front foot. In fact, a little lower and he would be really "smelling the ball". One of the reasons why he has got a lot of injuries is the fact that he tends to go forward to everything that is bowled. Some of the more serious injuries he has received were because of this, for example, when Graham McKenzie broke his left wrist when he went forward and the ball kicked up from just short of a length.

He now wears a chest protector and also extra padding round his lower gloves which get rapped when he plays forward and low. There are more risks to his fingers getting injured when the bounce is a little more than expected. Because of his backlift which is not very high, and since his hands do not come together on the bat handle, he is not one of the removed hookers of the ball. But one must say that he is one of the best leavers of the short ball I have seen. He just lifts his head and allows the ball to pass on either side. He never seems to be in any way affected by the short ball. I have also seen him drop his wrists most magnificently when the ball climbs up suddenly and leave the ball alone. Also the way he has taken knocks on his shoulders from deliveries when he has been pinned down is something extraordinary and only a player with courage and correct technique would be able to do that. Most batsmen will try to fend it off and would be caught round the corner or gully. It is sheer luck if the ball falls harmlessly but Boycott seems to be leaving such balls easily and getting out of such situations.

His one stroke which always thrills me is the square-cut. Vishwanath plays it magnificently but Boycott plays it with such ease and correctness that it is a joy to watch him play it. The right foot moves parallel to the crease and just the right distance before the bat comes down with a heavy chopping action, the ball scuttling away to the third man boundary. Another shot of Boycott's I would love to watch is the one he plays side-ways forward.

Another aspect of Boycott is the superb way he carries himself on the field. There is just a touch of arrogance about him as he walks. He is the cynosure of almost everybody's eyes. Knowing that the eyes of the spectators are on him he carries himself superbly the field. He is always well dressed, and you will never find him in untidy and dirty clothes. He is always spick and span and with just the right amount of crease on his trousers. His whole appearance in the field is how it should be. The old saying comes to one's mind: If you are not a cricketer, at least look like one. Boycott is not only a great cricketer but he also looks every inch a cricketer. His sense of dress he carries off the field too and not for him is the culture of jeans and other casual dress as is so common with cricketers nowadays.

Boycott might not be everybody's idea of a perfect cricketer but he has many fans as can be seen from the various conflicts he has got into with the authorities. There are people who have gone with him, supported him, in their endeavours to fight the authorities, whether it was the Test and County Cricket Board, the Yorkshire Committee or the Yorkshire players.

People have called him selfish because he tends to look more towards his individual runs rather than the team runs. And that is the reason he is reportedly not liked by his team-mates.

On the 1974 tour of England, he used to be a regular visitor to our dressing room. In 1979 too he visited our dressing room almost daily to get autograph books and cricket bats signed by our players. During that time, he was a welcome visitor, because he always had a joke or two to crack, either about his team or on the situation prevailing at that time. We thought that he was quite a likeable chap. In fact, even when he came down to India in 1981-82, he was more often to be found with our players at functions in the evenings and also during the day's play. This might be due to the reason that his team-mates did not seem to have time for him with their different attitudes and different ways of life.

He was most welcome in our dressing room whenever he came but I am not too sure if he will be very welcome after his remarks on the conditions in India on the last tour, after having been forced to go back before the tour was over.

He has been a complex individual in many ways. In 1974, after Eknath Solkar got him a couple of times, he refused to participate in the last Test and the three Tests against Pakistan that followed. Then followed his refusal to go on the tour of Australia in 1974-75 and again two years later. He made his comeback in 1977 against the Australians at home, led by Greg Chappell. He had his own reasons but they did not go down well with his colleagues in the England team. Thereafter, he has been a regular member of the England team, as it should have been, as their best player and runs have always been around when the England team has needed them most. He was also in the middle of a controversy with the Yorkshire manager, Ray Illingworth, and before that when he was sacked as the captain of Yorkshire by the Yorkshire Committee. Well, he seems to have been involved in one controversy after the other and hardly had the Illingworth controversy died down, he departed from India under circumstances which were unusual, to say the least. He was playing golf when he should have been assisting the England team in the field at Calcutta. The management of the England team rightly thought so but the reasons they gave were that he was keeping indifferent health, which did not give a proper perspective to things as they really were.

Then he was a prime mover in getting a team to South Africa and it appears now that with this particular tour and with this particular act, Boycott's Test career has ended. He has the highest aggregate runs, 8,000-plus, in Test cricket, with about twenty-one centuries, which is fantastic by any standards and it speaks highly of the man's talent and his application and dedication towards batting.

11

Glenn Turner

THE BEST BATSMAN THE NEW ZEALANDERS HAVE EVER produced is undoubtedly Glenn Turner. His records in Tests prove that and also his scores in first class cricket show that he has been one of the top run-getters in the world. The fact that he had the highest aggregate runs in the 1970s and thereafter just goes to show his appetite for runs.

It is a pity that because of differences with the New Zealand Cricket Council, he hasn't been able to play as many Test matches as his supporters would have liked him to play. It is also a pity that the New Zealand Cricket Council and the New Zealand team do not have his services. The New Zealand bowling strength is not much to write home about, apart from Richard Hadlee, while the batting revolves round Geoff Howarth.

New Zealand would be a far more formidable side than it

is today if Glenn Turner played for them regularly. Today, Turner has got more than a hundred centuries to his credit in first class cricket and in spite of requests, he refused to play in domestic cricket for New Zealand. He decided to have a complete break from cricket after a strenuous season in English county cricket.

The Indians first saw Glenn Turner in 1969 when the New Zealand team came here after its tour of England to play three Tests. Turner looked a frail person and since then has not put on much.

The first match of that tour was against the Combined Universities and it was my first match against a touring Test side. Turner did not get too many runs, but he was instrumental in cutting short my first innings. I had played for over two hours and it was the first time I was facing pace bowlers of that quality and was wondering why I was getting the balls more on the gloves than the middle of the bat. For one thing, Richard Collinge was a big man and his deliveries bounced more than the others'. Dayle Hadlee, Richard's elder brother, was genuinely quick before back trouble put him out of Test cricket. For a long while, I played the new ball and was hoping to get some runs against the New Zealand spinners who weren't so impressive. I tried to cut a short delivery from Brian Yuile and just managed to nick it. Barry Millburn, the wicketkeeper, muffed up the catch. It bounced off his gloves and went to the gully fielder. The gully fielder was too close and he could just get his hands to the ball which was falling by his side when Glenn Turner, who was in the first slip, dived across and literally caught the ball inches from the ground in his left hand. It was a truly remarkable catch and would rank even higher than the catch Viv Richards took in 1974 to dismiss me against the West Indies.

The first Test was to be played at Ahmedabad, but because of riots it was shifted to Bombay at the eleventh hour and India coasted to a comfortable victory with Bishen Bedi running through the New Zealand side. New Zealand won the next Test at Nagpur on a turning track and looked set to win the third at Hyderabad before the rains came in their way and ruined their chance.

Glenn Turner did not do anything outstanding on that trip to India, though he had come with a reputation of being a difficult man to dislodge. He had carried his bat through the innings at Lord's when England won the game scoring 40-odd runs. Even in the first innings he had scored some runs while there was another New Zealand batting collapse. So his tour of India wasn't successful, but he went back to county cricket and slowly began to acquire a reputation of scoring hundreds. He was not satisfied with a hundred and went on to score double centuries.

The 1972 tour of the West Indies by New Zealand was a personal triumph for Glenn Turner. He scored over 650 runs with two double centuries, once again carrying his bat through the innings, and with a personal best of 259. In another first class game, he scored another double century and got over 1,000 runs on the tour. So Glenn Turner had arrived on the Test scene with a bang. He was now the man most teams wanted to dismiss to get the opposition out.

He continued getting thousands of runs in the county championship and when New Zealand went to England in the first half of the 1973 summer, he became one of those rare cricketers who scored a thousand runs before June. Not many players have performed this feat. The last one to have done so was Sir Donald Bradman in 1938. He was the first New Zealander to do it and achieved it against Northamptonshire on the last day in May and that too with a square-driven boundary off his friend Bishen Bedi. Unfortunately, scoring a thousand runs before June had taken a heavy toll of his concentration and when the Tests started, Turner had only one innings of above 50 in six Test innings. The result was that there was too much pressure on the other batsmen to score runs, though the New Zealand batsmen rose to the task magnificently and almost won the first Test, chasing a total of about 480 runs and failing by 30-odd runs. Thus New Zealand's successes in this series were limited and the main reason would most certainly be the failure of Glenn Turner to strike any sort of form in the Tests.

When the New Zealanders went home they had a series against Australia. Glenn was unfortunate to break a finger and did not participate in the Tests. But when Australia returned the visit, Glenn was in magnificent form and scored a century in each innings of the first Test which New Zealand won. He was then involved in a controversy with Ian Chappell. One of the New Zealanders had hit the ball over the in-fielders. The umpire, following the crowd's noise, had signalled a six, but Glenn was at the non-striker's end and he was explaining to the umpire that it was not a six. Ian Chappell came running down from the slips, being very agitated that the umpire had signalled a six, and got into an argument with the umpire and Glenn Turner which resulted in Glenn saying that he would never share the same dressing room with Ian Chappell. The incident made headlines all over the world and this was just one more incident in Ian Chappell's colourful career.

In the 1975 Prudential Cup, he was instrumental in leading the New Zealand recovery against India and then piloting a victory. However, New Zealand lost to England in the semi-finals but did not disgrace themselves at all in the World Cup by performing creditably in all their matches.

In 1976, the Indian team went on a tour of New Zealand and drew the series. Glenn Turner was the captain of New Zealand while Bishen Bedi captained India. In the first Test, I led the side as Bishen pulled a muscle just on the eve of the Test in a practice session. This was the first chance of my career to lead the country. I walked to the toss very nervously and when Glenn tossed the coin up and I called, it was an odd sight with both the captains running after the coin because it rolled almost half the length of the pitch before coming to rest. I had lost the toss in my first Test as captain and that happened throughout the rest of my career as captain in Tests. Glenn had no hesitation in choosing to bat. That Test was a memorable one for me because I got a hundred and we also won.

Bishen was back in the team for the second Test and so we had to make a change in the team. We were confident that with Bishen in the team we would be sitting pretty. But Glenn had other ideas. We won the toss and decided to bat on a greenish wicket under overcast conditions. The ball was moving around alarmingly but having the kind of spinners on our side, the decision to bat first was made so that we could take advantage of any wear and tear of the wicket. Vishy played a brilliant innings and Glenn handled his side well, shuffling around his bowlers - Richard Hadlee, Dayle Hadlee and Richard Collinge - in an impressive manner. Richard Hadlee was playing his first Test of the series then. The attack was handled most astutely by Turner and when New Zealand batted, Glenn scored a hundred but he should have been run out when he was going for his hundredth run. There was no doubt about his class. He middled the ball right from the beginning. He kept the scoreboard moving in a very professional manner, tucking the ball neatly off his legs.

We saved that game through another brilliant innings by

Vishwanath and went to the third Test at Wellington with confidence that we could not lose the series. But the wicket at Wellington was something else. I have never seen so much grass on a wicket. The groundsmen had not even bothered to prepare a wicket as such. Only light mowing was done and the wicket was left untended. And on that wicket, pace bowlers Richard Hadlee and Richard Collinge made the ball talk. Glenn was batting well once again. He was well on his way to another hundred when he stepped out to drive Bishen and was stumped for 64. We lost the Test and New Zealand squared the series.

Glenn must have been a happy man because after losing the first Test he came back to win the third. He led by personal example. He was well-respected by the New Zealand players for his individual performances. He had a flair for leadership and could extract the best out of his boys. He had a very good sense of humour also, and would enjoy a joke even at his own expense.

I remember at Otago, when the sides were exchanged, Glenn gave Bishen a list with only the nicknames of the players. So it became difficult for Bishen to know who was who. But that was Glenn and the two captains got on very well. When both captains get on well, it is good for the game, the disgruntled elements in the team can be effectively subdued, and the harmony between the two sides is maintained. The fact that Glenn married a Sikh girl from Bombay, whom he had met on the 1969 tour of India, must have been one of the reasons for Glenn's close friendship with Bishen.

The New Zealanders returned the visit after the English summer in October that year (1976) and played three Tests. The weather was uncertain with threats of rain and the series went easily India's way. In Bombay, New Zealand collapsed in the second innings without any reason and India emerged easy winners. In the second Test, they barely managed to survive, though Glenn scored a hundred and showed his displeasure when he was given out, as he thought the ball had gone off his boots. At this stage, the New Zealand batsmen's gestures of displeasure on being given out, made our boys angry, because earlier in the year, on our tour of New Zealand, they were never given the benefit of doubt. So when the New Zealanders started making complaints about our umpiring our players naturally got upset about it. Quite a few harsh words were exchanged between the players during that series. In the last Test, Chandra ran through the side and the series was won fairly easily by India by a margin of 2-0. Glenn, apart from scoring that century in the Kanpur Test, wasn't among the run getters. He was obviously the player we had to dismiss to get through the core of the New Zealand batting and it was so true that every time India got Glenn's wicket cheaply, the New Zealand batting collapsed.

Unfortunately, that series is remembered because of the behaviour of the New Zealand players with regard to umpiring in India.

After that Glenn did not play as often for New Zealand as one would expect because of his battle with the authorities. He was a professional player and wanted to have somewhat better terms for himself than the others. The other players were all amateurs and he was justified in asking for more but the dispute got wide publicity and that was not a very pleasant thing. The two sides were not ready to budge an inch and so New Zealand lost the services of one of their outstanding batsmen. As a result, the New Zealand side became weaker. The differences, however, were patched up and he agreed to play for the team in the 1979 Prudential World Cup and was ready to advise the captain with his vast experience. New Zealand once again reached the semifinals.

When the West Indies came to New Zealand in 1980, Glenn

once again decided not to play in Tests and accepted a TV offer to comment on the Tests. The New Zealand public did not like this idea at all. They would have loved to have him out there in the middle rather than remain behind the scene of action. Be that as it may, it was rather unfortunate because Glenn is a world-class player and is one of the finest batsmen the world has seen. Ever since limited overs cricket began, he adjusted to the situation and turned into an attacking batsman from an entirely defence-oriented one. There have been instances in recent years when he has scored centuries even before lunch. Technically, he has always been correct, the bat coming down in perfect line and the bat and the pad coming close together with perfect judgement, to play swing, although he has been guilty of playing and missing more than any other player of his class that I have seen. But the determination is still there, the concentration is there in abundance and the greed for runs does not seem to be getting any less. I hope he patches up his differences with the New Zealand Cricket Council and makes himself available to play Test cricket once again.

12

Greg Chappell

AUSTRALIA WERE DOWN IN THE DUMPS ON THE FAST BOUNCY TRACK of Perth against the formidable John Snow. This was also the first-ever Test match on the ground of the Western Australia Cricket Association and so the Australians were doubly keen to do well in this Test match. And at this moment of crisis, in strode a tall, pencil-slim young player to commence his Test career. John Snow had made life miserable for the Australians in the first Test and here he was threatening destruction once again. Only Ian Redpath of the old reliable guard remained and, obviously, the young man walking to the wicket showed a little sign of nervousness. After having been immediately greeted with a bouncer, he pushed the ball off his legs and started a career which has placed Gregory Stephen Chappell as the second highest run-getter among the Australians so far, with only Sir Donald Bradman leading the field with almost 7,000 runs.

Before the day's play ended, the cricketing world knew that a future star had arrived on the Test scene. With Ian Redpath giving him company and encouragement, Greg Chappell scored a hundred and saved Australia from a disaster, and what a hundred it was! It was full of strokes, hardly a trace of nervousness, and, most importantly, the confidence with which he tackled John Snow was amazing. John Snow had become something of an ogre in the minds of the Australian batsmen, but the performance of this young batsman must have surely caused a lot of heart-searching in the minds of the earlier Australian batsmen and must have showed them that if a boy making his debut can deal with John Snow so imperiously, then so could they. Ian Redpath scored 170 runs and Greg Chappell joined the band of those select few who had scored a century on their debut in the first innings. That was in 1971.

Many people thought that Greg should have gone to India and South Africa in 1969-70. But it was a blessing in disguise that Greg did not have to make his debut in international cricket under conditions which were foreign to him. Not that his career story would have been different, but to make a debut in India would have been difficult, because the crowds here can unnerve most foreign players and one has to be a really hardened veteran in Test matches to ignore the noise and din of the vociferous crowds.

After the Indian leg of the tour, the Australians went to South Africa where they were given a right royal hammering. The South Africans were thirsty for Test cricket and when they got it they really grabbed it and won the series 4-0. In that series, a batsman as accomplished as Ian Chappell had failed miserably and so had Doug Walters, a man who had a tremendous Test record till then.

The omission of Greg from the tour of India and South Africa only acted as a spur for Greg to stake his claim when the season in Australia began. The tour of India and South Africa had exposed the weakness of some of the Australian batsmen and there were obviously places in the team for the asking which Greg was well aware of. With fine performances in the Sheffield Shield, he got into the Australian side and was brought into the second Test at Perth. For him it must have been a daunting prospect to follow in the footsteps of his grandfather Victor Richardson and elder brother Ian Chappell, who was already being talked of as the future captain. But there was no trace of nervousness on the face of Greg Chappell as he went and launched his Test career.

The shrewd English professionals, however, marked his preference for the on side and completely blocked him in the other Tests to such an extent that he could only score one fifty in the series thereafter and one was beginning to think that his earlier century was a mere flash in the pan. The Australian selectors must have believed that Greg had a lot to do before he could establish himself in the Australian team, because when the South African tour of Australia was cancelled, and the Rest of the World team came over, Greg Chappell did not find a place in the team for the first two Tests or internationals as one would like to call them. In the first Test, one noticed Greg sitting under the sun on a deck chair, doing his twelfth man's duty, reading a novel. A thing like that, if it were to happen in India, would have created an unimaginable furore, but in countries like England and Australia, it is the cricketing talent that really counts and not anything else the cricketer does.

In any case Greg was well aware of what was going on in the field and was alive to the needs of the Australian team when they were on the field. One could see a certain nonchalance about the person; one could also see the confidence with which he worked, the way he carried himself; as if he knew that his time was round the corner. By the way, now Greg Chappell sports a beard because the sun apparently affect his skin which has become sensitive. This obviously is a far cry from the young player who sat in the deck chair reading a thriller.

It was New Year's day in 1972 when the third Test began. Australia were already one-up in the series, having won the Perth Test. The Rest of the World were thirsting for revenge and the World XI had made a couple of changes in their batting line-up. Greg Chappell turned out to be highly successful in this Test because he scored a hundred and stopped the Australian side from collapsing. Against the spin attack of Bedi and Intikhab Alam supported by Gary Sobers, he batted confidently and his 100 was classic. There were drives on either side of the wicket which in our team meeting the previous day, we could not believe he could play. The Englishmen, who had seen him the previous year, had said that he was predominantly an on-side player and, therefore, his one weakness could be to the ball pitched on and around the off-stump and leaving him. Frankly, this particular thing about the ball pitched on and around the off-stump and leaving the batsman being a chink in his armour amuses me because it is there in each and every batsman. If everyone could judge such balls perfectly the bowlers would have packed up and gone home.

In any case, that weakness was neither apparent nor exploited by our bowlers. Perhaps Greg did not give them a chance. Most of the time he was at the crease, the spinners were on, as it were they who had struck for us. Later, when Peter Pollock, the great burly South African, was given the bowling, he was not shy to whistle a few down Greg's ears. But Greg emerged with flying colours. The shot he played off Bishen Bedi dancing down the track and lofting it in the direction of the straight sightscreen was tremendous, because the wicket was turning. Here was a man who came down the wicket and could play the shot with so much confidence. He wasn't afraid to use his feet to the spinners. But this effort of his was overshadowed by that superlative 254 not out by Gary Sobers and a lot of enthusiasm was generated by Doug Walters's century in the second innings. Yet we knew when we sat down to plan on the eve of the fourth Test that we had more top class players to reckon with and whom we would have to plan to get out very quickly.

In that match Greg came in to bat after Ian Chappell was comprehensively bowled by Bishen Bedi. Having scored a century in the previous Test, he was full of confidence and looked around with that arrogance which has now come to be associated with him after batting all over the world. But he was bowled by the first delivery from Bishen, a gem of a ball which was well flighted and, as Greg came down, he turned slightly and saw his off-stump uprooted. I will never forget it, nor, I am sure, will Bishen Bedi or Greg Chappell. So we had both the Chappell brothers out in two deliveries and we were really on top at that stage. Greg avenged himself in the second innings when he got himself 197 and that too unbeaten. Towards the end of the innings, Dennis Lillee, who had no great batting pretensions at that stage of his career, was around and gave him staunch support by blocking a ball or two which Greg allowed him very shrewdly, while dominating the strike. This also showed that here was a man who thought about cricket and would surely lead the side one day. Eventually there was an over which Lillee had to face from Intikhab. The latter fed Lillee with a quick top spinner and got rid of him. This left Greg with three runs short of what would have been a magnificent double century.

As one was walking back from the field to pad up, Greg was heard lambasting Lillee for not being able to play one ball and was really and truly giving him a piece of his mind. At that stage it was felt that Greg was over-reacting to his missing a double century. Only later he explained why he was doing that. It was only to get Lillee sufficiently riled up for him to bowl fast at us. Well, the aim was certainly achieved because Lillee gave us a very uncomfortable time and it was all due to Greg needling him for getting out. This also showed a keen sense of appreciation of the psychology of cricket and fast bowlers. Not surprising, because his grandfather Victor Richardson was considered to be a very good captain and so was Ian Chappell, who was captaining Australia at that time.

Greg scored 85 in the next match on his home ground, Adelaide. He looked set for his third hundred when Intikhab managed to turn a ball sharply to get an edge off his forward defensive stroke which carried. He ended that series in a blaze of glory and the man who had been reading a book sitting on a deck chair, getting himself a tan, was the first man to be selected in the Australian team to tour England later that year.

There too he had a magnificent tour, scoring a hundred at Lord's and smacking another hundred at the Oval when both he and his brother shared a giant partnership and both of them scored their hundreds. It must have been a gratifying moment for their parents who had come up from Australia to watch that Test. Trevor Chappell was then playing in the Lancashire League and he was also present which must have made the entire family happy.

The next stage was the series against the West Indies. Again Australia won this series through the batting of the brothers and the fast bowling of Lillee, Thomson and Max Walker. Greg scored two centuries in that series and often came to the rescue of Australia when they needed his batting most.

Then followed the Ashes series and once again Greg batted magnificently and it was he who the opposition wanted to dismiss. Before that he had set a unique record scoring a century and a double century and making the most runs in a Test when Australia played New Zealand. The aggregate in the two innings is the highest scored by a batsman in a single Test. He simply massacred the New Zealand bowling which at that stage was pretty poor, with Richard Hadlee still a comparative newcomer and not quite the bowler he is today.

The Ashes series was completely dominated in Australia by Lillee and Thomson. That was a very good Australian team. Besides Lillee and Thomson, there was Max Walker to support them. Then there were Ian Redpath, Rodney Marsh and others and people for a moment forgot the deeds of Greg Chappell, though he scored over 600 runs in that series.

In the inaugural World Cup, Australia reached the final, but it was generally believed that they were not cut out for one-day competitions because there was practically none of this type of cricket on their calendar. But they surprised everyone by their versatility. The Australians then played four Tests in England and here Greg went through the worst patch of his career. He totalled just 108 runs in Test matches with 70-odd in the second Test being his highest score. But Ian Chappell scored a brilliant 192 in the last Test and decided to step down from the captaincy of the Australian cricket team. That paved the way for Greg to take over the leadership. There was also talk about his indifferent form in England, on account of which Ian Redpath was expected to take over the captaincy. It was believed that Greg would recover his form and then take over the captaincy in another series. But the Australian selectors had great faith in Greg's ability and they appointed him captain. He justified that faith by hammering a century in each innings in the first Test he captained and by winning that Test. This was a great feat as one's debut as a captain. He suffered very few setbacks as the captain of the Australia team thereafter.

The West Indies in 1975-76 were a great team and their clash with Australia was billed as the World Championship clash between the two teams. Both the sides had a battery of fast bowlers, free-stroking batsmen and possessed fielding of the highest order. This was enough to fill the grounds to capacity. Greg had an excellent series aggregating over 700 runs with 182 as his highest score in the deciding fourth Test. He led the side very well, judiciously using his bowlers, Lillee, Thomson and Walker and spinner Ashley Mallet when the West Indies threatened to recover. That was a disappointing series from the West Indies' point of view and they lost 1-5 in a series which should have been more closely fought.

The Pakistanis came the next season and they surprised Australia in the third Test by levelling the series. It was mainly due to the inspired bowling performance of Imran Khan, who only then had discovered his real potential. He had begun to believe in himself and his ability to bowl fast. Greg did not have a very successful series, though Pakistan seemed to be his favourite team for scoring plenty of runs against.

Before the Australian team went to England for the Ashes series, they played the Centenary Test against England in Melbourne to celebrate 100 years of Test cricket. Though the two teams did not score many runs in the first innings and Greg also did not score runs, his medium-pace bowling brought him some wickets and his slip catching was of the highest order. The Australians won that Test by an identical margin of 45 runs, the margin by which their predecessors had won a hundred years ago.

385

It was immediately after this match that the Packer bombshell burst on the unsuspecting cricketing world and turned the official international cricket topsy-turvy for the next couple of seasons. Greg had signed up with the majority of the Australians for that tour and so there seemed to be an atmosphere of distrust between those who had signed and those who had not. There were accusations that those who had not signed had not been given their due and this was due to a lack of team spirit. It was, therefore, no surprise that they lost that series 1-3 and surrendered the Ashes which were with them for quite some time. Greg's performance in this series was not in keeping with his high standards, with just one hundred in the Manchester Test, which Australia lost as well. This was his last notable innings for some time. The Australian Cricket Board had decided that the WSC players would not be selected, as they were not available to play in the Sheffield Shield matches, the performance in which was the criteria for selection to the Australian team.

He was therefore lost to official Test cricket for the next couple of seasons and had to play the World Series Cricket before crowds which were sometimes hostile, as they were not the regular cricket watching crowd. The WSC cricket was very tough. High standards were expected from every player with emphasis on physical fitness, as the players were professionals and were getting good fees for their efforts. Greg had an outstanding season. He played against the Rest of the World as well as against the West Indies and he had to play under Ian Chappell who had staged a comeback for the WSC.

It was a couple of years before a compromise was reached between the WSC and the Australian cricket officials and Test cricket could be resumed. During this period Greg put up fine performances in the WSC. When we visited Australia in 1977-

78 we saw four of his centuries on television. Greg scored 246, which is considered to be his best against an attack which was really sharp and hostile and fielding which was of the highest class. This innings came after fielding for over 600 runs. It was an amazing performance and set to rest any doubts anybody had about Greg's batting.

He scored tons of runs on his favourite West Indies wickets when the Australian team visited the Caribbeans and again proved to the world that he was still the best batsman. Meanwhile, he had some health problems. Just before the WSC Australians went to the West Indies, he had trouble with his left eye and fears were expressed at one stage that he would lose sight in it. Fortunately for the cricketing world and for Greg himself, nothing untoward happened and he was back to normal in a short time. He has these problems often and though he is a very healthy man, he is prone to viruses which are floating around. But this does not for a moment mean that Greg is not a fit person and that there is no power in his strokes. He can play a long six-to-eight-hour innings as well as anybody, as well as Boycott, and he will probably score double the runs made by Boycott in that time.

In 1980 the Australians went on a short tour of Pakistan and there Greg scored a marvellous 235 at Faisalabad to show once again that he loves the Pakistan attack more than anything in the world.

Thereafter, it was India's turn to visit Australia in the new set-up which came about due to the compromise between the WSC and the Australian Board, so that the two teams would simultaneously tour Australia in a season. In the first season after the settlement, the West Indies and England toured Australia and in the next, we were there along with New Zealand. Each played three Test matches along with a number of one-day internationals for the Benson and Hedges Cup.

The first match was the one-day international against Australia in Melbourne and India won it surprising the Australians and the Indians themselves. After the game, Greg came over to the dressing room along with his Australian colleagues as is the practice and had a word with me about the Melbourne wicket. He had been writing a lot about the deterioration in the quality of the Melbourne wicket and he wondered if I would support him on that. I told him that though I supported him to the extent that a better wicket should have been provided for this game, I could not pass any judgement on the present wicket, having played only one game. This was possibly due to the fact that I did not want the other matches to be shifted from this venue to other grounds, because a wicket where the ball did not bounce much would have been in the interest of the Indian team, when the Aussies had three or four fast bowlers at their command. While I made a comment about the wicket for that game I was not too enthusiastic about making a protest that Greg wanted me to make.

When we played the Australians we found that Greg Chappell was the lynchpin around whom the Australian side was built, although they had Kim Hughes, Allan Border and Graham Wood as their main players and had brought back Doug Walters. So if Greg got a big score, the Australians piled up a big score as a team. This was, of course, proved subsequently when Greg failed in the Melbourne Test for a duck in the second innings and the side collapsed with barely 83 runs. During the first Test, while we went out to toss, we had a very interesting discussion on the dressing rooms being as far off as they are in Sydney. Greg spoke about the dressing rooms at Lord's where one has to walk long to get to the other dressing room. And as we walked back after the toss and reached our dressing room, I realised that both of us had failed to exchange the teams. I think the thought must have simultaneously occurred in Greg's mind because he came running from his dressing room and we met midway in the Long Room, where the members normally sit, and we told each other who the twelfth men were. Greg had a marvellous Test. He scored a double hundred, despite being unfit with a virus infection. Halfway through that innings, he asked me if he could have some water and I told him, only if he had some Scotch in it. He was hammering our attack and the only way to get him out was to get him intoxicated enough to try an overambitious shot.

There were stories in some of the tabloids during this Test that the reason for Greg's sickness was a drinking spree the previous evening and not anything else. It was not correct because Greg is hardly a hard-drinks man. This shows the kind of pressure he was under at that time and why he prefers to take a break at times from cricket. While the papers went to town pinpointing the reason for his sickness no one gave him credit for that double century. In that condition, how many players would have had the energy and the determination the next day to go out and score a double hundred? - and that also when he had only a slice of toast to eat the whole day. But then that is what happens to famous personalities and it is tougher if one happens to be the Australian captain. Now I understand why Ian Chappell gave it away, and why Greg wants to take a break now and then. The pressure on him, his family, his children is tremendous and Greg therefore wisely takes time off cricket, and goes to his family to forget the pressures of being a captain and the leading batsman of his team.

The next year Greg did not have a good series when the West Indies and Pakistan were around although he got a double hundred against the Pakistanis. He did not do well in the other matches. By far his worst patch after the 1975 series against

England was in that season of 1981-82. He came back with a brilliant hundred against the New Zealanders just when Richard Hadlee threatened to make life difficult for the Australians and one hopes that Greg comes back to his normal run-getting form because there are few finer sights in cricket than Greg Chappell in strong form.

Along with his cricket contacts, he has developed other business interests. He is a very successful man in this sphere too. He owns a hotel, is a director for some insurance companies and is generally doing very well out of these ventures. For an Australian, he is a rare phenomenon in that he has continued to play at an age when most of the Australians look to their business career than their cricketing one. Having established himself in the business career, Greg wants to go on playing cricket and only the pull of the family will make him quit the game. That will be a tremendous loss for the entire cricketing world.

His batting has thrilled cricket-lovers all over the world. Although he hasn't played in India, he may be surprised to know that he has a larger number of fans here than in any other part of the world. To youngsters his batting is a terrific example of how to play correctly and also without losing one's ability to play shots. He is a superb batting model. As a sportsman he has carried himself through all controversies and tough and tense situations with dignity and he has shown that he is very much in control of his emotions. That, I think, is his greatest contribution to budding cricketers.

13

G.R. Vishwanath

THE YEAR WAS 1968, THE VENUE HYDERABAD, FOR THE MOIN-UD-Dowla Gold Cup Cricket Tournament. A young slim boy was in the nets, facing everything that was bowled at him. The nets weren't very good because it had rained earlier and the wicket was damp. The ball was climbing up, but at no stage did this youngster look in any sort of trouble. The ball that came up to his chin was played down firmly. He held the bat high above his head to let the ball pass safely above the stumps. Watching that performance in the nets were some of the Test stars: Jaisimha, Pataudi, Abbas Ali Baig and Abid Ali. That little performance was an indication that here was talent above the ordinary and very soon this talent would delight cricket-lovers all over the world. The young lad was none other than Gundappa Vishwanath and that exhibition is still fresh in my memory.

The youngster had already attracted attention, scoring 230 runs in the Ranji Trophy cricket the previous year on his debut and was included in the powerful State Bank of India team to play in the Moin-ud-Dowla Tournament. In those days, the State Bank team included Ajit Wadekar, Hanumant Singh, Sharad Diwadkar, Ambar Roy and other eminent cricketers. For a youngster like Vishwanath to find a place in the team was signal enough of the tremendous natural talent that he possessed. The selection committee of the State Bank team had confidence in him. That confidence has not been belied and Vishwanath has proved himself to be the best batsman India produced in the 1970s.

Soon after, Vishwanath was selected to represent the South Zone in the Duleep Trophy and he scored a 50 on a turning track which had found stalwarts like Jaisimha, Pataudi and Baig. This performance brought him very quickly into the Indian fourteen. When the New Zealanders came in 1969, he was selected for the Board President's XI and he scored a neat 68. In the company of Chandu Borde he rescued the side just when the New Zealanders were threatening to do some more damage. Vishwanath had started hesitantly, but Borde gave him confidence and encouragement. Vishwanath flowered and began to play his shots off his own. That season, the selection committee, chaired by no less a person than Vijay Merchant, plumped for young talent which brought to the fore players like Solkar and Vishwanath, to name just a couple, and both of them were included in the team to play New Zealand.

While Solkar made his debut in the last Test against New Zealand, "Vishy", as he is affectionately called all over the cricketing world, had to wait till the second Test against Australia, who visited India later that season, which was the fifth Test of the season. It is now history that he failed in the first innings, being caught off Allan Connolly off bat and pad for a duck, and then coming back and scoring a glorious 137, including no less than twenty-five boundaries, to join a select band of Indian cricketers, scoring a century on their Test debut. With that Vishwanath's place in the Indian side for the next decade or so was almost assured. One hundred was not enough. There were two other innings of 50s, on wickets which were not ideal for batting, that proved Vishy's class and at the end of the series, he was the find and toast of Indian cricket.

The spinners dominated the series against Australia, but among the batsmen, it was Vishwanath and Pataudi who carried the battle to the enemy camp. Vishwanath, with his adventurous play, won the hearts of the crowd.

There was a little setback for Vishy in the Duleep Trophy match in Bombay on the eve of the West Indies tour, when he twisted his knee and there was a bit of a problem. This resulted in his missing two Test matches on the 1971 tour to the West Indies. He was back in the team only in the third Test. His replacement, Dilip Sardesai, grabbed the opportunity with both hands and scored a double hundred in the first Test itself and thus it was Jaisimha who had to make way for Vishy to play his first Test against the West Indies. A 50 in that innings was not the kind of an innings Vishy was known to play, but considering that it was his first big match of the tour, it was understandable. He took his own time to gauge the West Indies attack and then prepared himself for a bigger innings. However, in that series, the big innings did not come. He scored 20s and 30s and when he looked set to be on the top of the bowling, he lost his wicket either to a good delivery or to a brilliant catch. This affliction of getting out early seemed to dog him for quite some time. When the England team came here in 1972-73, he was almost dropped, till he scored a brilliant 75 not out at

Kanpur which is his lucky ground and thus kept his place in the team.

Earlier on the tour of England, in 1971, he had become the first Indian to score a century on the tour and it was his calm, methodical type of batting that got us out of the tight situation that Illingworth had created for us at the time of our first ever victory over England in England. A score of 180 was all that India were asked to make, thanks to Chandra's marvellous bowling effort, but this target looked distant when we lost a couple of quick wickets. On the final morning, we lost skipper Wadekar, run out. But Sardesai was a fine player of spin bowling and Vishwanath steadied his bat and slowly and steadily took us to the victory target. With only four runs required for victory, Vishy played an uncharacteristic swish off the irregular bowler Brian Luckhurst and ended by giving a catch to Alan Knott. Later, when he was asked why he went for that swish, he said that he wanted to score the winning hit over the fielder's head. Unfortunately, he did not succeed and it was left to Abid Ali to score the winning run.

The 1972-73 series was a period of downs for Vishwanath. He was not getting runs although he seemed to be in no trouble at all. He was at the crease, but did not get 50 till the Kanpur Test. He was dropped from the side by the selection committee which had met before the Test was over but far from being discouraged, Vishy went on to score 75 not out and thus was reinstated in the team. He went on to score a century in the last Test at Bombay and became the first Indian to score a century on his debut and then score another. That hundred was the last by an Indian at the Brabourne Stadium because, thereafter, the venue for Test matches was shifted to the Wankhede Stadium which was constructed in record time.

The next engagement for the Indian team was the tour of

England in 1974. It was a disastrous tour, but Vishy came out of it with credit because he batted very well in all the matches. His performance, particularly in the first Test on a green top at Manchester, was superb and the way he negotiated the quick bowling was an example to budding cricketers and a great morale-booster to the batsmen who followed.

When the West Indies team came down in 1974-75, they threatened to sweep us 5-0, having won the first two Tests fairly easily, and were looking like winning the third Test and the series, at Calcutta. But Vishwanath had different ideas. He scored a scorching 139 and, in partnership with Karsan Ghavri, added runs which put pressure on the West Indies batsmen, batting last. Chandra and Bishen then spun them out and India came fighting back in that series.

In the next Test at Madras, India, at 91 for seven, looked like crashing into another defeat. Andy Roberts was bowling with such speed that he had to put on the brakes to stop in his follow-through. Such was his rhythm, such was his pace, that wickets came his way rather easily. He was stopped by our man Vishwanath. His 97 not out is the finest Test match innings I was privileged to see. That attack is the best form of defence was amply proved in this innings. From 91 for seven, Vishy helped carry the score to 191 and in the end missed his hundred by just three runs when the last man in, Chandrasekhar, who had defended dourly, surrendered his wicket to Roberts. Vishy's strokes in that innings were unbelievable. His square-cutting meant that Clive Lloyd had to keep two fielders on the third man boundary and the way Roberts was bowling that day, it is a tribute to the quality of Vishy's batsmanship. The moment Roberts bowled on the leg side, Vishy flicked him past square-leg and past mid-wicket and the moment there was an over-pitched delivery, he drove it through the covers with elegance.

When the innings ended, and both the batsmen came in, it was Chandra who looked the more disappointed for having deprived his mate of a well-deserved century. The knock raised the spirit of the Indian team and the spinners bowled us to victory to level the series at two-all.

The deciding match was to be played at the newly-laid wicket of the Wankhede Stadium. Before a ball was bowled, the West Indian manager, Gerry Alexander, complained about the quality of the wicket but the fact that more than 1,000 runs were scored in the first innings proved his apprehensions to be wrong. Vishy, though he scored 98 in the first innings, was not at his best as seen against the previous two Tests. Obviously, he was mentally and physically tired. But such was his form that in spite of committing more mistakes, he still managed to score 95, before edging a ball from Lance Gibbs into the hands of short leg. This tendency of getting out in the 90s stopped Vishy from scoring more centuries in Test cricket than he has at the moment.

The 1976 tour of New Zealand and the West Indies was very successful for Vishwanath. At Christchurch he scored a superb 83 and 79 on a green-top wicket which was helping seamers a great deal. It was an exhibition of masterful batting. When the ball pitched in line with the stumps, Vishy just let the ball go, so that the ball went above the stumps and when the ball was pitched up, he drove it. When the ball was pitched shorter, Vishy cut it and the judgement of leaving the good length balls alone which then sailed harmlessly past the stumps, or just above the stumps, was an unbelievable sight. Most present-day cricketers would have definitely played these balls and surrendered their wickets. But Vishy's judgement was absolutely correct and he didn't make a mistake at all till he got out. With the match drawn, and India having won the previous Test, the New Zealanders decided on another strategy. They left even more grass on the wicket at Wellington than they had at Christchurch. And with Richard Hadlee fulfilling the promise and potential he had shown earlier in this Test, New Zealand won it easily.

When the team arrived in Barbados to play the first Test in Bridgetown, it was Vishy who stemmed the rot by scoring 62 runs. However, the West Indies won that Test and again looked as if they would run through the Indian side. But the fortunes of the Indian team changed in the next Test at Port of Spain. When the third Test was switched over to the same venue, the Queen's Park Oval, because of continuous rain in Guyana, it was Vishy who, after scoring a brilliant 112, brought India, chasing a target of 406 runs, the remarkable victory. When the last day's play commenced in this Test, the policy of the team was to hang on and play for a draw. By mid-afternoon, thanks to Vishwanath's strokeplay, visions of a victory were raised. These visions turned into a reality when Brijesh Patel cut the ball to short third man to bring about that historic triumph. Two strokes of Vishwanath in that innings stood out. He stood on tip-toe and square cut two deliveries which were rising deliveries, to the point boundary and thus took the sting out of Holding's bowling. He showed that the new ball held no terrors for the Indian side. These two strokes were really marvellous and brought victory to us, for, if Michael Holding had got a wicket with the new ball, our chances of a victory would have diminished. Those two strokes took away Holding's confidence.

In the last Test, Holding, however, had his revenge when on a very quick wicket at Kingston he had Vishy fending at a short delivery and the resultant catch was not perhaps as painful as the fracture that Vishwanath sustained while playing that defensive stroke. He fractured his middle finger of the right hand and, at one stage, it was feared that an operation would be necessary to set the bone right. But luckily that was not required and thus in the second innings Vishy did not bat at all. Luckily, the next series on our programme was five to six months away against New Zealand, and so Vishy did not miss Test series. Vishwanath again dominated this series and on a rain-affected Madras track he demonstrated once again what a technically perfect batsman he was.

There was a bit of a slump as far as Vishy's batting was concerned after this series. The series against England did not find him getting many runs. But Vishy came into his own on the tour of Australia next year and aggregated about 500 runs to head the batting averages. He played Thomson on fast wickets giving an exhibition of the highest class. It proved to the world, if any proof was needed, that India may not play fast bowling at home regularly but when it comes to counter-attacking the fast bowling, they have as good a batsman as the best in the world.

India went to Pakistan in 1978. At Faisalabad, which was a new Test centre, Vishy became the first Indian to score centuries amongst all Test-playing visitors. Although he could not maintain that form later in the tour, he had already become a popular and respected figure in Pakistan on the strength of that innings.

Later, when the West Indies team came to India in 1978-79, he scored his highest in Test cricket so far, 179. And this was achieved at his favourite ground, Kanpur. It is difficult to say what fascination Vishy had with Kanpur, for most of his electrifying innings have been played there. There isn't a match staged in Kanpur where he has failed. The only exception that comes to my mind is the Test against the Australians in 1979 when he failed to get a score of even 50.

It was around this time that the WSC controversy surfaced and Vishy, who had been approached in Pakistan, was noncommittal about it. This is Vishy's greatest strength; he cannot be easily swayed by others' opinion. He takes his own time to think and decide on all matters. The WSC offer was one such proposal and he was a little cautious, because he had a semigovernment job and his priorities lay with India and Indian cricket. And though it was made known to him that there would be no clash with his commitments for Indian cricket, it had still generated enough storm in Vishy's mind to make him postpone taking a decision.

The Indian Cricket Board rewarded him with the vice-captaincy on the tour of England, under the captaincy of Venkataraghavan. I have failed to understand why people say that Vishy would not have made a good captain. He was as tough as any other cricketer and his knowledge of the game was second to none. Also, he was the most popular of the Indian cricketers and the other members would have done anything to help Vishy out. These factors were in his favour, but the media had somehow given him the image of a man who was reticent and one who did not enjoy captaincy. This was far from truth and in fact, I am sure that if Vishy had gained the captaincy, he would have proved to be a good captain for India.

The two Test matches he captained for India were the ones where the Indian team was mentally and physically tired and thus not in a position to give their best. People have probably judged Vishy on those performances. But then Vishy should have been made vice-captain under Pataudi and Bedi, before I was made so. Not only was he a senior player, but he was also a much respected and popular player.

In that series against England, Vishy was very successful, although he did not score as many runs as he was capable of after that Lord's Test century. That was another rescue effort as far as the Indian team was concerned and he and Vengsarkar both played magnificently to save India from an embarrassing situation. India were bowled out for 96 in the first innings and looked certain to lose this Test match, but the determined efforts of Vishy and Dilip saw to it that not only was the match saved but the team gained in confidence thereafter. Many people believe that India would have won the last Test at the Oval if Vishy had been sent at his usual batting order, instead of promoting Kapil Dev to that position. This, of course, is a matter of conjecture and this proves that cricket is a great game of 'ifs.' It is easy to criticise, particularly after the event. Venkat was criticised for not sending Vishy earlier, but if Kapil Dev, who is a reputed stroke player, had succeeded in winning the match for us, then Venkat would have been hailed as a genius,. But all this a captain has to bear and the final responsibility is his. Very seldom does he get the credit for a good decision and it's always easy to be wiser after the event.

When the team returned to India in September, the Australians were already in India and the first Test in Madras was played under sultry and humid conditions. Facing a total of 400-plus, Vishwanath once again steered India out of trouble. His century in Delhi was a fine innings and right through the first half hour of that knock, it looked as if Vishy would get out any time. Vishy's hallmark is that he very seldom plays and misses the ball, but in this particular innings he was often rapped on the pads. He played and missed on a number of occasions and it looked as if he was out of touch with himself. But as soon as the half hour was over, Vishy was back to his dazzling best and dominated the Australian bowling to score a scintillating 100.

Against the Pakistanis, he was not at his best and did not score many runs befitting his reputation as India's top batsman.

Vishwanath's next glorious moment was when he scored a hundred against Australia at Melbourne and India won that Test. The amazing part of Vishwanath's career is that every time he has scored a century, India has either won the Test or has come out of it with flying colours. India has yet to lose a Test match in which Vishwanath scores a hundred.

The 1981-82 season was perhaps his best season. On the verge of being dropped in the third Test against England, he came back to score another delightful hundred in Delhi and followed it up with his highest Test score of 222 in Madras, sacrificing his wicket on the dot of lunch in order to see that quick runs were scored. He could have gone on and on had it not been for the needs of the team. This again has been a recurrent trend in Vishy's cricket. He has always played for the side. When there was a need for attacking cricket, he has done that keeping the crowd in good humour, giving them their money's worth. It is, therefore, unfair to judge him on the number of centuries he had scored because if one looks back, one will see that he has got out very often in the 80s and 90s trying to play the shots which would have got the crowd to its feet. It has been his single aim to entertain, at the same time enjoying himself during a well-played innings. This is the reason why he has been such a popular cricketer.

He was very much missed in the last series against the West Indies and in the Prudential Cup. But he has not given up hopes of a comeback. He is practising hard and I am pretty certain that India will have to bring back this man, a genius with the bat.

He is a man who has a very good sense of humour. He always comes out with a rib-tickler when things are tense in the dressing room and his sense of repartee is well-known among the cricketing fraternity. His popularity, just not amongst cricketers, but also with our crowds, particularly in Calcutta, is legendary and I am waiting to see whether he will come back against the West Indies and perform brilliantly in front of that magnificent crowd of Calcutta. Calcutta, with its fanatical love of sports, deserves a cricketer like Vishwanath and with a bit of luck, I'm sure that Vishy will be able to come back to the Indian team and delight not just his fans in Calcutta but all over India with his wristy stroke play once more.

14

Ian Botham

IAN BOTHAM IS THE CRAZIEST CRICKETER I HAVE KNOWN. Well, when a fellow scores a hundred at breakneck speed, hitting a few deliveries into the crowd and out of the ground at times, rushes in and bowls at a quick pace and takes five wickets during which a few deliveries have whistled past the batsman's ears, dives around and comes up with incredible catches, and still has energy in the dressing room to dip his teaspoon in the tea pot and try to cause burns to the man sitting next to him, you have got to call him crazy. That crazy fellow happens to be England's No. 1 all-rounder and the cricketer who really brings in the crowds whenever England plays Test matches at home.

It is cricketers like him who really get the crowd's pulse stirring, and excitement runs high while players like Ian Botham

403

are on the scene. If the above suggests that success and popularity must have gone to his head, let me assure readers that it is not so, because, in spite of all these achievements that Botham has to his credit, he is a singularly modest man. He is a man who does not care much for statistics and who thoroughly enjoys the game and conveys his enjoyment to the people. That is why he is so enormously popular with the crowds wherever he goes.

The story of Botham's meteoric rise to fame is well chronicled in cricket magazines and the many books written on him. Therefore, I shall not dwell on how he started hitting cricket headlines and how he came to be the cricketer he is today. But it would be of interest to know that when Botham started playing cricket, he played just the same way as he is doing now. The responsibility of playing Test cricket or the pressures and tension of Test cricket do not seem to have mattered to him, not even when he was the captain of the side. He played in exactly the same manner as he did when he shot to fame on the national scene in 1976.

It was just a matter of time before he was picked to play for England and his chance came in 1977 against the Australians. He started off with a dream debut taking five wickets in his first Test and scoring a few runs along with it as well. Among his five wickets, there were a few which were not against good deliveries. But he got those wickets and that is what matters.

Botham has come a long way since and has to his credit over 200 wickets and 3,000 runs as well, plus over 50 catches, which truly speaks of his ability. At the end of the day, it is sheer statistics that go to prove a person's ability and not the words which are written about him. When a person plays Test cricket over a period of time, it is really the figures that speak. For too long people have gone on saying that so-and-so is a great player because he has done very well in county matches or other first class games. But these matches do not really matter. It is only Test matches which really matter and when the form seen in Test matches is seen over a period of years, the ability of a person is proved. Botham has proved that he is the topmost all-rounder in the world today. His ability to change the fortunes of a match with his batting, with his catching and with his bowling is now legendary and while he is on the field no team can take things easy.

I first met Ian in the Brylcream Double-Wicket Indoor Championship played early in April in the 1978 season. And at first appearance, he looked to me like one of those French detectives of whom one reads about in novels. I do not know why that impression stuck in my mind, but that is the impression I carry of him ever since. He was obviously restricted because of the rules which specified that one could be caught off the net on the side of the wicket and one could not bowl from a long run-up because the lighting was not so good. Yet you could see the enormous talent in that man. He hit some huge sixes during that event and his strokes flew like lightning on that surface which was an artificial one. The way he fielded those scorching hits by the West Indians and the other players was amazing. This man showed absolutely no regard for the hardness of the hits and feared no injuries while stopping some of those hits. Fear of injury never entered his mind and he stopped everything that came at him. Derek Randall and he won the tournament that year and also the following year, when the double-wicket tournament was organised at the same venue at Wembley, London.

That year, in 1978, he routed the New Zealanders and the Pakistanis with his bowling and batting and was really the star of the season. There was nobody to touch him but, at the same time, there were also unkind remarks that he had scored his runs and taken his wickets against second-rate opposition. He was to prove later of course, that he could score runs and take wickets against all kinds of opposition. But the successes of those years were clearly written-off because some of the best cricketers were playing for Kerry Packer. What people forgot was that Ian Botham had not picked the opposition sides and he was only playing against those available and to decry those performances is very unfair. Not that it mattered to Botham because he is the type of person who enjoys the game immensely and if he is successful, all the better. He is not the kind of person who would brood over his lack of success and let failures overtake him and subdue his bubbly spirit.

When it was our turn to play in England in 1979, Ian Botham was the one man we were worried about because he was the one person who was capable of turning the fate of a match. In the first Test, he was not required to do much because David Gower scored a double hundred and Boycott ground out a hundred and fifty runs. There were useful scores from almost everybody in the England batting line-up. But in bowling, it was Botham who struck at vital times and as a fielder at silly point, he put a lot of pressure while the spinners were on. He played his part in that victory with crucial wickets.

When the second Test came along, it was hotly debated whether Botham would be able to get his hundredth wicket in that match and thus become the player to get the fastest double. Well, he did that having got my wicket to a brilliant diving catch by Brearley off his bowling, and that was something which annoyed me tremendously. I was determined not to get out to Botham, particularly in view of the fact that he was in line for his hundredth wicket. That over during which he captured his hundredth wicket still gives me the shivers. I missed a hundred which was there for the asking, if I could have kept just a little control over my eagerness to attack. The first ball, which he bowled, was shortish, more of an attempted bouncer which did not come up and I gloved it off and it went of the second bounce to Mike Brearley in the slips. The next ball was a slower one. I smacked it hard but as the ball came rather slower than intended it went uppishly to Randall's left and he stuck out a hand, not expecting to catch it, but to stop it. The ball fell to the ground with Randall wringing his hands and me cursing myself for having missed four runs.

Botham seemed to be charged with that particular delivery and the next one was a beautifully pitched outswinger which I played and missed. At the next ball, which was again a shortish ball outside the off-stump, I thought to myself that here comes four runs again. The ball was a little closer to my body and as I was a little cramped in playing that shot, a back-foot forcing shot, the ball hit the bottom of my bat, just kissed the bottom edge, and went low to Mike Brearley who dived to his left and held on to it - a marvellous effort. To my mind it was a waste of a wicket as far as the Indian team was concerned. I was fuming to myself, though I offered a congratulatory hand to Ian, who, in his eagerness to go over to Brearley, completely overlooked that. I was furious with myself for having missed out on a big score as well as letting the team down.

Another over which comes to my mind was when I was batting with 99 in the Bangalore Test and he bowled to me four genuine outswingers when the ball was not even new. The first such ball just pitched on good length on the off-stump, forcing me to play at it and then luckily missing an edge. This happened for about four times in that over and the fifth and sixth balls he brought in and hit me on the thigh pad. That was one over which I was glad was finished as I could have been out four times, though that was not to be. That is what the luck of the game is all about, and one can hardly complain about one dismissal and be complacent about dismissals at other times.

Bottam played, an incredible innings of 138 in the Test at Leeds when he smashed all our bowlers all over the park. It was hitting which was controlled and, at the same time, savage. Every time Kapil or Ghavri bowled a little short of length, it was hooked into the car park of the Leeds cricket ground. It looked at one stage as if he was more keen on smashing Geoff Boycott's car parked there but, fortunately, that kind of thing did not happen and he managed only to smash the confidence of our bowlers. Till he came on the scene in that Test our bowling was looking really good. Kapil struck early blows and Mohinder had managed to get an important wicket. Ghavri had also bowled very well. So it looked as if we would have England on the run but then this man came in and changed the entire complexion of the game. He had managed to hit 99 runs in the session before lunch and he did not know that he had scored that many because in the last over before lunch from Kapil he played out a maiden over, which was unthinkable, considering the mayhem that had preceded in the 118 minutes before lunch. That also goes to prove that Ian Botham is not a man who looks at figures but just plays his game. Any other man would have tried to get that extra run but that was not the case with Botham. When he got out he was four runs short of scoring 1,000 runs in Test cricket, and missed that coveted double. He eventually did that in the next Test - the fastest double in Test - but it could have been one Test earlier. This reiterates the fact that Botham does not care for records.

In the next Test he was run out owing to a misunderstanding with Boycott which was something of a sight and shall remain in my memory for ever - the way Botham walked off, swearing away at Boycott. Boycott, for once, did not look too repentant and almost seemed to have a gleam in his eye! It seems, the story goes, that in New Zealand while the Englishmen were going for quick runs and for a declaration, Botham had gone in and got Boycott run out deliberately so that the scoring rate could be accelerated with Boycott's departure. Well, the tables seemed to have been turned at the Oval and it was a fuming Botham who went off the field.

When we were batting and I had got my hundred, he turned around to me and said that he had dreamt the previous night that I would score a double century. He also said that he would see to it that the dream is proved wrong. Well, I did get the double hundred and it was very, very thoughtful of him that at the end of the day after I was out and the Indian batting was going on trying to overhaul the target of 438 set by England, he picked up the stumps and kept them as souvenirs for me. That was the gesture of a person who has always treated the game as a sport. It was a gesture which goes to show how warm-hearted he is and appreciative of others' performances.

He then moved on to Australia to prove to the doubting Thomases that his successes earlier were not just against second-rate opposition as they seem to have been thinking. He proved to them that he had the ability to get wickets and score runs against the best that Australia had to offer.

Then came his greatest performance when in the Jubilee Test at Bombay he single-handedly won the match for England. He started off by taking eight wickets and the nonstop bowling spell in Bombay's sultry heat was a sheer test of stamina. He put everything into his bowling. The wicket this time was as green as one can ever hope for a fast bowler. It was hard underneath and, therefore, there was a fair amount of bounce in the track. Botham utilised it in a magnificent way, not giving batsmen a chance at all and running through our side. When it was our turn to field, Kapil Dev and Ghavri bowled excellently and restricted England to 57 for five when Botham, along with Bob Taylor, staged a grand recovery. Botham scored 114, a superb innings, because he did not play a single rash shot. He put his head down and was prepared to wait for a loose delivery. It was an extremely responsible innings. It was an innings which showed that he could play with his head down if he wanted to and if it was required by his side. In fact, it was one of the best I have seen because Kapil and Ghavri were really moving the ball and making it talk.

Ian was not finished with the game and in the second innings, he took another five wickets to see that we were skittled out, leaving England only 90-odd runs to win which they did without losing a wicket. Ian must have gone back a very happy man because England had not had a very successful tour of Australia, having lost the series 3-0, and therefore did not have a victory under their belt till the one in Bombay.

It was during the Jubilee Test at Bombay that the offer of playing for Somerset was made to me. Not by Ian as many people believe. I was, however, not very keen at that stage to get involved in a seven-day-a-week programme of English county cricket and, therefore, had to decline the invitation. But I took it up later when I realised that I was required to play only for a short while and not for the full season. That gave me an opportunity of studying Ian Botham more closely and I have been friends with him ever since. When one plays in opposition, one can never really be friends because there is still a certain reserve which is difficult to break. There are very few friendships between cricketers of opposite teams. But then having played together for Somerset, Ian has since been a good friend of mine.

410

You come to know a person a little better when you spend time in the same dressing room with him. That was the time I came to know Ian Botham as a person. He has remained untouched by all the successes he has had, all the glamour he has been surrounded with and the adulation received from the crowd. I also found out that he did not particularly like the criticism that came his way sometimes and especially from some of the spectators when he had to give them the old Harvey Smith salute which, as captain of the England team, was perhaps not the right thing to do.

The captaincy of England really did not change him and he went on in the same way as he had gone about before. This was quite the right thing to do. Captaincy is something which succeeds by what one has been doing before and one need not change after being appointed captain. Perhaps the Harvey Smith signal could have been replaced by a clenched fist which would perhaps convey the same meaning to the offender and you can get the thing off your chest as well.

In the dressing room he was an absolute terror because he never could sit still and had to keep doing something. If he did not find anything to do, he would punch you viciously on the arms, dip his teaspoon in a pot of boiling water and while you were sitting unawares, he would try to cause burns on your hand with the spoon or just a lighted match stick. Many other variations of his technique would startle and stun you. I believe if the British Secret Service or the police wanted somebody to do a bit of torture, and get information out of people who have not been talking, Ian Botham is the right man to contact.

Knowing my fear of dogs, he never missed an opportunity to lead a stray dog in Taunton into or near the dressing room which meant I would be stuck in the room for hours on end.

411

Once I remember going just outside the dressing room, as there were no telephone facilities inside, into a public call booth which was ten yards away. The moment he saw me inside the booth, he got hold of a big dog and both the dog and Ian were parked outside the booth. In spite of the fact that there was a big queue outside, there was no way I could come out. I stuck there in the booth for about twenty minutes and the people outside were getting very annoyed. I had to signal to tell them to take the dog away and only then could I step out. Ian eventually took pity on me, and may God bless him for that! He took the dog away and I came out and heaved a sigh of relief.

At other times he would just lounge about in the dressing room. He could really eat, because any sandwich, any piece of cake or any eatable left over would be devoured by him hungrily. Not only that, between the lunch and tea intervals, he would send for his famous steak and kidney pies and keep on eating them. No wonder, his girth increased during that early summer season, as not much cricket was played which meant that with inactivity, Botham kept putting on weight. That perhaps hampered his bowling, because one could see that he was not able to bend his back as he would have liked and as much as he was doing earlier. So his outswinger was not as dangerous any more and a batsman could play him with comparative ease.

He did not have a particularly good season against the West Indians and his figures, both batting and bowling, did not do him justice at all; but that did not seem to affect him at all. He was horsing around as usual. On the last day of the season there was no play owing to rain and both the teams, Somerset and Warwickshire, decided to play a game of football. Botham was at his best during the game and he really enjoyed it. When everybody was in the team bath at the end of the game, Ian suddenly got out and dumped the pad and boot whitener into the bath while the others were still there and, amidst angry howls of protest, sped away. Then he sneaked into the Warwickshire dressing room where most of the players were dozing off after a hectic night in Taunton. They were woken with a bucketful of water being splashed all over them. Dilip Doshi was lucky because he was in a three-piece suit and Ian threatened to douse him with water too. I do not know what happened, but in spite of an urging from me he did not do so. He was quite fond of Doshi and obviously did not want to spoil the expensive suit he was wearing. On that day he would not have bothered about anybody and so Doshi must count himself lucky on that score.

His car driving, is as dangerous as his bowling. Just as his deliveries seem to dip in and out between a batsman's bat and pads, he weaves in and out of lanes, and speeds along at breakneck pace which is not permissible under law. He has been lucky that he has not been caught for speeding but I believe that he has recently been booked. The police obviously have newer faster cars now to be able to catch up with him.

I was not very sure about my way around Somerset and when we were away playing matches I would follow one of the other players' cars. As it happened, once we were playing at Bath, and I had to follow Botham's car. I told him frankly that since I was going to stay within the speed limits he should also strictly follow the same. Botham was really agitated when we finally reached Bath. He said that he would have driven faster in reverse gear but for the restrictions imposed by me.

Well, that's Ian Botham the man who has been living his life fully. There are no short cuts for him, no brakes for him. It is just one beautiful innings he is playing. I hope with advancing age and diminishing reflexes, which is the case with every individual, the fun that he is getting out of the game and giving to the people, who come to watch, is not in any way reduced and the spirit in which he is playing the game remains as buoyant as ever.

15

Ian Chappell

IN THE YEAR 1969-70, MOST OF THE COLLEGE CRICKETERS IN
INDIA, particularly in Bombay, started wearing their hair over the
collar. Long hair was in fashion and it was also due to the fact
that one of the most charismatic cricketers of our generation,
Ian Chappell, also did so just an inch or so above his shoulder.
Unfortunately, with my wavy hair, I could not wear hair above
my collar but the rest of the fellows with their straight hair could
do that, being true fans of Ian Chappell.

And then as luck would have it, the Australian team came
down to India in the latter half of our winter in 1969-70 and
all eyes really were on Ian Chappell. Just a season before in
Australia he had punished the West Indies attack for over 500
runs, including three hundreds. And with his flamboyant manner,
he was the main attraction. There was, of course, Doug Walters,

415

who had also scored an equal number of runs the previous season. He was the first player in the world to score a century and a double century in a Test match. But then Walters has been a very quiet individual, not the same kind of outgoing personality that Ian Chappell was. Walters was a more humorous person than Ian ever was. But most people were eager to see only Ian Chappell when the tour team was announced.

Bill Lawry had come to India in 1965 and so also Graham McKenzie, but then they were two players who attracted attention because of their stature. Johnny Gleeson was another player who invited attention with his ability to turn the ball both ways without any noticeable change in his bowling action.

Before that series, however, India played a three-Test series against New Zealand and just managed to draw it. So when the Australians came with all their might, it was generally believed that India would be lucky to draw the series. As it turned out, India put up a good performance and it was only because of the lack of solidity in the middle-order batting that we lost a couple of Tests.

The first Test was in Bombay at the Brabourne Stadium and as soon as the first wicket fell, it was a sight for anxious eyes as Ian Chappell came out with his collar rolled up. This, to the Indians, is a sign that the man is swollen headed. The reason for turning the collar up is simple, and that is to protect the neck from the fierce heat of the sun or to protect it from a stiff wind.

His manners were a bit cocky, a little arrogant, and he only gave a glimpse of his ability then. However, he came back in the Delhi Test with a brilliant hundred on a wicket which was turning and which afforded all kinds of help to our famed spinners. He then followed it up with a superb 99 in Calcutta. Over there, I am given to understand that it was the excitement of the large crowd that got him dismissed one short of his century, though I can't believe that a player as experienced, crafty and professional as Ian Chappell could be dismissed for that reason. In fact, the crowd wanted him to get his hundred and were disappointed when he was out. In that series the ease with which he took some brilliant slip catches was remarkable. His style was a little peculiar in that he did not really bend down from the shoulders as most slip fielders do. Most slip fielders are used to almost squatting down on the field, but Ian Chappell had a different way of standing - a habit which was picked up in Australia where the ball comes up, the wickets being bouncier. The ball comes over the waist or near the shoulders rather than near the boots as it happens in England and India.

When the Australian team went to South Africa after the Indian tour, their captain, Bill Lawry, made a statement that Ian Chappell was the best batsman in the world. Of course, Lawry made that statement in all honesty. Ian had scored runs on the England tour of 1968, then in Australia against the West Indies. On the spinning tracks in India too he was successful, where the ball turned from the word go. He had scored about 400 runs on the Indian tour and naturally Bill Lawry felt so about Ian. A host of other followers of the game all over the world also held the same view that Ian was the best batsman in the world at that time. But this riled the South Africans. They put in more efforts to get Ian Chappell out. Though a lot of people tried to explain away the Australian failure by saying that the South African leg of the tour came after the tiring Indian tour, they, however, forgot that the Australians are a tough and resilient lot. The Australians could not cope with the South Africans in 1969-70, as the latter must have been a really good side.

Australia were really whitewashed in that series in South Africa and Lawry's captaincy was in jeopardy. But the Australian selectors gave him another chance when the England team, captained by Ray Illingworth, came Down Under for the Ashes series. Lawry's performance as captain in this series did not meet the approval of the selectors who thought that he was not able to get as much from his team-mates as they would have liked him to do. So for the seventh Test – this was added later as one of the Tests was completely washed out by rain – Ian Chappell was appointed captain. Chappell lost that Test but under his captaincy, the side somehow seemed to be a revitalised side with new determination and purpose. Poor Bill Lawry was not even picked for that Test, although he gave good performances as a batsman at that stage.

It was then the turn of the South African team to come down to Australia in 1971-72, but the Australian government did not give them permission to come over. The Rest of the World XI team was assembled to replace the South Africans. The idea of having a Rest of the World side was the brainchild of Sir Donald Bradman. Gary Sobers at that time was living in South Australia and these two got around in Adelaide for the formation of the Rest of the World XI. Sobers was the captain of the World XI and Ian Chappell that of Australia. The void thus created by the cancellation of the South African tour was filled for the Australian season.

It was not a truly representative World XI because some big names were missing from it. Boycott and Barry Richards, who were considered to be the two best opening batsmen in the world were not there and so also was Alan Knott; but they had previous commitments and could not join the party. Still, it was a good side, although it lacked a genuinely quick bowler which would have been an advantage on the hard, bouncy Australian wickets.

In the first Test itself Ian Chappell gave Australia a tremendous start on a slightly rain-affected wicket by scoring a hundred. His hundred was adorned with brilliant drives, cuts and pulls. He was particularly superb in playing the spins of Bedi and Intikhab Alam. Whenever Bedi flighted the ball, Ian was down the track, reaching the pitch of it for driving and every time Bishen pitched it short, he was very savage with his pull. He, therefore, neutralised any advantage the spinners got from the rain-affected wicket. The Australians, helped by another decent score from Keith Stackpole, piled up a good score. The Rest of the World also did not do badly with Hulton Ackerman and Rohan Kanhai adding over 150 runs for the second wicket and both scoring hundreds.

Ian Chappell believed that the Australians were a better side and so in the second innings he decided to take the attack by the scruff of the neck and carved out another hundred, even more brilliantly than the first innings. With a century in each innings, he set the tone of the series. Unfortunately, the rains came and the match was abandoned as a dull draw, contrary to Ian's expectations. In the second Test Lillee tore our hearts out by taking eight wickets for 29 runs, and, although Rohan Kanhai scored another brilliant century in the second innings, it did not stop the Australians from running away with victory.

The third Test in Melbourne, of course, was well fought where Gary Sobers scored that unforgettable 254 not out. It completely dwarfed the efforts of Greg Chappell, who was playing in his first Test of that series, and a century by Doug Walters before lunch. The World XI won that Test to tie the score at one-all. With the Sydney match washed out, the last one was a crucial match for both the sides.

The World XI was a better balanced side and their batting was strengthened at that stage by the arrival of the Pollock brothers. We won the last Test in Adelaide to take the series. But one could see that Ian Chappell had inculcated a fierce determination to win and the Australians, as always, were a difficult side to beat. They never seemed to give up and every time Ian called out in the field for greater efforts, his team-mates responded. His leadership was flamboyant. Every time a wicket fell or a catch was taken, he would rush to the bowler or the fielder, embrace him, congratulate him, which meant plenty of encouragement to them. The rest of the team members also rushed in to congratulate the bowler or the fielder which amounted to a kind of assault on the bowler or the fielder. But this kind of feeling brought along with it a sense of participation and team effort and a feeling of one-for-all and all-for-one. Ian was the vital cog around which the Australian team was revolving. The players used to look to him for inspiration in the field and instruction and he became gradually a revered figure as a batsman and also a tremendously respected captain.

So competitive did the Australian team become that they also practised the art of "sledging" to perfection. Sledging is a short-term for sledge-hammering. It was a term which was invented because the Australians were very vocal and never felt shy to tell the opposition what they thought of them; whether it was the opposition batsman or the fielder. The Australians have this habit of giving nicknames to persons or things meaning exactly the opposite of what the nicknames are, for example, somebody who is a very quiet person will be called Rowdy. Similarly, sledging meant that the views the Australians had of the opposition on the field would be conveyed to the opposition in as subtle a manner as a sledge-hammer if ever a sledge-hammer can be subtle.

That's how the word sledging came into being and the credit for it should go to Ian Chappell for giving shape to it. Former players touring Australia have admitted that the practice was there. However, those days, it was followed by only a few team members and not all. This is not cast any aspersions on

Ian Chappell but just to show how competitive the Aussies were in gamesmanship which in their view lay in unsettling the opposition and scoring over them.

Thus, the team under Ian Chappell came to be known as the "Ugly Australians" because if an opposition player got into arguments with them, almost the entire team told him what they thought of him. This was unprecedented in a way and, therefore, the Australians did not make too many friends wherever they went. They thought that winning was everything and didn't really care for the norms and traditions of this gentlemen's game.

Along with Ian Chappell there was Dennis Lillee, another fiercely competitive cricketer; and Rodney Marsh, Ashley Mallet and Greg Chappell lent him able support in his campaign. These were the players who formed the nucleus of the Australian teams of those years.

When the Australian side went to New Zealand in 1973-74, Ian Chappell had a public altercation with Glenn Turner after which Turner declared that he would never share the same dressing room with Ian Chappell. Of course, professional cricketers should never make statements like this because somewhere along the line there comes a time when you have to share a room with the same player. Glenn may not agree but then he went to South Africa with the International Cavaliers, a team assembled by former Australian captain Richie Benaud, and Ian Chappell was also included in the side. Eventually he had to share the dressing room with Ian Chappell.

Anyway Ian Chappell did not come out of the incident creditably. He was very unpopular with the Australian administrators and his relationship with them was quite stormy, to say the least. There was a public uproar also when he dropped his trousers to tie a loose thigh pad, though for the life of me, I cannot understand how a player could ever tie a thigh pad without dropping his trousers. What is normally done when a thigh pad comes undone is to request the wicketkeeper and close-in fielders to form a kind of shield around the batsman while he adjusts the thigh pad. Probably, Ian would not dream of asking that favour from the opposition and, therefore, he thought it was all right and just changed the thigh pad on the ground. The media in Australia, which is always looking for something sensational, projected him as someone who did not care for traditions.

Then, of course, there was the incident where Ian Chappell had to appear before Sir Donald Bradman for having incited South Australian players not to play in a Sheffield Shield match. He went to the meeting smoking a cigar and with a pint of beer in his hand, which certainly did not seem to be the most respectable thing to do.

But then he did what he really thought was right and damned everybody else. This did not make him very popular with the officials and they were always waiting for a chance to get back at him. Chappell also made it clear that he would not give the Australian officials a chance to sack him as captain and, therefore, after a very successful tour of England in 1975, he stepped down from the captaincy, though he was available to play for Australia in Australia.

The following year, in 1977, a great coup was staged and Kerry Packer signed up all the leading players from Australia and the rest of the world. Ian was the main brain behind this movement and did everything possible to make the World Series Cricket very popular. He went to the extent of ridiculing the India vs. Australia series in 1977-78 and thought that these were not real Test matches.

That was Ian Chappell and, once he stuck by a person, you could be assured that Ian would give his life for him. He came to Delhi for the Abbas Ali Baig Benefit match and took this opportunity to try and sound me about joining the Packer series. His approach to me was typically direct and forthright. He came to me near the dressing room and said, "Sunny, I want to have a yarn with you." We then sat around and discussed the pros and cons of joining the WSC. He was quite impressive because he placed before me only the best aspects ahead of me. He did not quite mention the disadvantages, though he made it very clear that it was I who had to make the final decision and that I should make proper inquiries from different people as to the kind of cricket and the kind of security that was involved in the World Series Cricket.

Talking to him then, I realised how much of a morale booster he must have been to the players. Every time the team was down in the dumps, he had the knack of talking to the players which would boost their morale and make them rally round him. He pointed out that if I did not join the WSC there would be something missing in my life. It was such talk during their team meetings at the intervals that must have made the Australian cricketers do their best for the team. That is what made him one of the great captains of Australia.

He retired as captain and then came again as a player to play against the English in 1979-80. In that series, the Australians simply overwhelmed the English 3-0. He would have loved to score runs, particularly against Ian Botham whom he did not rate very highly when he burst on the international cricket scene. The story of his clash with Ian Botham in a Melbourne pub is well-known. It is one of the few occasions when Ian Chappell came second best in an argument or brawl.

He then became a commentator on TV Channel Nine after his cricket was finished and his comments were, very knowledgeable. In fact, his comments were precise, to the point

423

and he gave superb insight into the cricketing psychology that prevails when a Test match is on. Later on, so impressed was Channel Nine that they gave him a sports programme to compere. It became very popular and here again he did a marvellous job.

One day, not realising that the mike was live, he uttered an abuse which was heard by millions of viewers. He had to apologise and was suspended for some time. He came back again and he hasn't so far made a mistake, using a wrong word here or there. One can be assured that the defiant spirit of Ian Chappell is still alive and it won't be too far in the future when Ian Chappell is in the news again.

There is an interesting story about how Ian Chappell became a fiercely competitive cricketer. On his first tour with the Australian team to South Africa in 1967, he was playing in a Test match when a ball came up, off a length, and as he hurriedly fended it off, he lost sight of it as it went off his bat. The next thing he knew was the chorus of appeal and so he turned round to the fielder who had the ball in his hand and asked him: "Did you catch it?" The fielder said: "Yes, I did." Ian walked back to the pavilion. In the dressing room, the rest of the team members were furious with him and told him what a sucker he had been made. They told him that the ball had lobbed before the fielder had taken it. Ian Chappell was furious about it and at the end of the day cornered the fielder and checked with him why he said he had caught the ball when he hadn't. The fielder replied: "You asked me whether I caught it but you did not ask me whether it bounced first. Did you?" And it was from then on that Ian Chappell stopped walking away from the wicket and became an aggressive cricketer. He would do everything within his powers and within the rules for his team and he came out of it successfully.

Most Australian cricketers of that era believed that Ian Chappell was a better player than his brother Greg. But this is difficult to accept because Greg is so much more correct a player than Ian was. They believed that on difficult wickets and under difficult conditions, Ian, with his fighting attitude and never-say-die spirit, would come out on top and play a much better innings than Greg, who according to them was not as good a player as Ian was. The Australians believe that if there was one player whom they would choose if it came to saving their lives, they would unhesitatingly vote for Ian Michael Chappell.

His attitude on the cricket field for not caring for reputations, not giving a damn to the authorities, is reflected in his life. He dressed very casually, hated suits, and only now that he has become a compere for TV programmes has he taken to wearing ties. But he preferred to be in jeans or shorts and open-neck shirts.

He offended people by running on the field to dispute an umpire's decision in shorts in one of the World Series Cricket matches. And during his time, the Australian cricketers also dressed casually and were often called the most sloppily-dressed cricketers in the world. For them they were just being themselves, dressing in whatever was comfortable.

Ian's attitude towards the discipline of the team was also similar. He believed that each player selected to play for Australia was capable of understanding his responsibilities and, therefore, did not believe in curfews or things of that sort. He is reported to have said that a little beer did not give anybody a hangover and, in any case, it passed off in a few moments in the morning. With such a person at the helm, it was but natural that the Australian cricketers responded warmly and gave everything that was possible. To ask an Australian not to drink beer is nothing short of cruelty and so it was absurd to ask Ian not to have a beer can in his hand.

Perhaps the officials didn't like him; perhaps the media, which castigated him at every possible opportunity, didn't like him either for his abrasiveness or his give-a-damn attitude. But it was he who brought in the crowds more than anybody else, maybe with the exception of Lillee and Thomson. It was Ian Chappell, the cricketer, that every cricket-lover admired for his style, for his attitude towards the game. It was Chappell who took Australian cricket by the scruff of the neck, brought it right on top of the world and made it the pride of all the Australian sporting public.

16

Imran Khan

WHEN WE PLAYED WORCESTERSHIRE IN 1971, A SKINNY BOY WITH an unruly mop of hair came up to bowl. He kept on pitching short his medium-paced stuff. Ajit Wadekar and myself who were involved in a big partnership kept on helping ourselves to some useful runs, mainly through cuts. Three years later, when we saw this fellow again, he was a little bit quicker but just didn't seem to have filled in physically at all. He still had a small freckled face and the unruly mop of hair was still there. Years later when we saw this young man he had grown into a wide-shouldered, narrow-hipped man and had all the requisites of a bowler of genuine speed. This man was Imran Khan.

When one saw him first in 1971, one could not have believed that this man, in a matter of three or four years, would be troubling the best of the batsmen in the world, and make them dance to his tune with his ferocious bowling. In 1974 he dismissed one of our batsmen in the very first over with a bouncer. The batsman tried to duck and held the bat hanging up like a periscope lobbing an easy catch. But then Imran had worked very hard at building up his physique and the result is one of the most magnificent bodies one can hope to see. In 1971 he was still growing. My impression of Imran of 1971 is that the man was a little shorter than what he is today.

One then heard of him when he skittled out Australia at Sydney in 1976-77 and caused their downfall, thus leaving Pakistan with a small target to clinch victory, their first on Australian soil. At the end of the match, Greg Chappell wrote in his column that Imran, at times, bowled as fast as Dennis Lillee did. And that we thought was a wee bit ex-aggerated. But then Greg Chappell knew what he was talking about and Imran himself has said in many of his interviews since then that he himself did not believe till then that he could bowl quick. He went to the West Indies from there and though he did not have the kind of success as he gave promise of in Australia, he was still fiery and the West Indians could not afford to treat him lightly. As Sarfraz was also in the team, there was obviously no bumper war, because the Pakistani bowlers could have easily retaliated, if not in the same measure as the menacing West Indian fast bowlers. Pakistan had enough guns to cause a little bit of discomfort.

After that brilliant beginning, Imran joined the World Series Cricket which saw him away from Test cricket for some time. The seventeen-year-old lad, who had come down to England in 1971, had now come to stay as Pakistan's main bowler. His success in the World Series Cricket on the harder, faster and bouncier wickets of Australia saw him establish himself as a bowler of world class. People now started talking about Imran in the same breath as some of the West Indian quick bowlers. In 1978, the World Series Cricket episode was forgotten by the Pakistan Cricket Board and all the players were recalled to play in the India vs. Pakistan series which was resumed after a long lapse of twenty years. Imran was one man on whom the Pakistanis pinned their hopes for the attack. But at Faisalabad, he bowled far too short. That gave our batsmen enough time to either avoid the delivery or play it down safely. It was at Lahore on a greenish wicket that Imran came into his own and really ran down our batting along with Sarfraz and Salim Altaf for less than 200 runs.

Imran bowled really fast and some of his deliveries were being taken by Wasim Bari in front of his face as they were still climbing. Bari was standing quite a few paces behind the wicket. Till then we would not believe that Imran had genuine speed. That performance proved that he had become one of the great quick bowlers in the game. He did not move the ball much because he pitched it too short. His main target seemed to be between the ribcage hoping that the batsman would fend off the ball but that kind of approach does not always pay in Test cricket. He got most of his wickets by bringing the ball up and letting it do the rest. Even in Karachi, he bowled fast but he was not so successful, as much as one would have hoped, but his furious hitting when Pakistan were chasing a target won the game. And it was those 19 runs that changed the complexion of the game. It was altogether an unexpected victory.

He then went to Australia and New Zealand where he bowled superbly and had all the batsmen in trouble. When the Pakistan team came to India, he was suffering from fitness problems, having first suffered a side injury at first, then a back injury because of which he was not able to take part in the full tour. He made a mistake by playing the Bombay Test as he missed out a real green-top in Kanpur which was the Test site following Bombay. I think it was Imran's dream to play in the Bombay Test as he had a large following there and he did not want to disappoint his fans there. This was a mistake as far as Pakistan were concerned, because that aggravated his injury which had occurred in the previous Test in Delhi. In Delhi, he bowled three overs of real scorching pace before he broke down. If he had bowled another over to me, perhaps I would have batted with no feeling in my knuckles, so badly were they smashed in those fiery three overs. He broke down then and did not bowl again in that Test in which Sikander Bakht went on to take eight wickets and then the marathon knock by Dilip Vengsarkar almost clinched a victory for us when we missed the target by just 26 runs.

Came the Madras Test and Imran was fit. The Madras wicket is known to be a hard one which gives enough bounce to a fast bowler. Imran was a dangerous proposition on that track. But fortunately everybody in the Indian team seems to have applied himself to the task and the Imran threat was nullified to a great extent. In the Calcutta Test, Imran exploited a patch which was on the centre of the track and as the ball reared up it made life miserable for the Indian batsmen. The ball really flew to unexpected heights and caught the batsmen unawares.

On this tour Imran seems to have concentrated more on his bowling, and his batting is something which did not get the recognition it so deserved. If you see his county record, it is excellent. He is a useful batsman, but somehow he has not scored for Pakistan consistently as he should have. Perhaps, when he found a place in the Pakistan team, it already had a very good batting line-up. The only time when his turn came to bat, he was required to do some slogging to get some quick runs. This obviously is not the best way to build up one's batting. Imran suffered because of that. But now that Pakistan needs his batting he should bat higher up in the order.

It was on the last tour of Australia that his batting in the one-day internationals as well as in Tests was something extraordinary. He now realises that Pakistan needs his batting and also that he himself is capable of batting well at the Test level and the results are there to see. He is still young and that means that there are many years ahead of him as a quick bowler and a brilliant all-rounder.

Off the field, Imran is a lady's man. He can sweep women off their feet. During the Abbas Ali Baig Benefit match which was played in Delhi, the players were not put up in hotels but billeted with families. Imran and I were with one family and one should have seen the rush of girls at this family's house. How they came to know about it and how they contacted him was beyond comprehension. Hordes of girls visited him. He always welcomed them and had time for most of them – something he is free to do being one of the most eligible bachelors in the cricketing world. I believe in Pakistan his telephone number has to be constantly changed so that girls do not disturb him and his family members.

The Abbas Ali Baig match was played in April 1978 and when I went to Pakistan in September 1978, I was a little disappointed to see a change in Imran. He had certainly become less communicative. This was perhaps because I was the opening batsman and perhaps he being the opposition opening bowler thought that he should not be over friendly with me. But thankfully, when he came down to India in 1979, his attitude had changed. He was his normal friendly self and someone who would talk about cricket for hours on end.

Girls continued to surround him on the 1979-80 tour also

and the cry "Hi Imran" was heard throughout the length and breadth of the country wherever the Pakistanis went. He is still a popular figure in India, still the heart-throb of thousands of girls, not only in India but all over the world. And I am sure these girls await with bated breath till "Prince Charming" makes his final choice. He still has a long way to go as far as setting up some more bowling records is concerned. The recently concluded series against India was a phenomenal personal success for him. He is now not only the leading all-rounder in the world but also a popular and successful captain. It would be a pity if his shin stress fracture were to stop him from bowling, because Imran running in to bowl is a sight for Gods.

17

Javed Miandad

TWO CRICKETERS IN 1977-78 CAPTURED THE IMAGINATION OF THE cricket-loving public in the Indian subcontinent. One was Javed Miandad of Pakistan and the other was Kapil Dev of India. These two cricketers have taken the cricket world by storm and, within a short span, have won over countless admirers from both the countries.

Javed Miandad made his debut much before Kapil Dev did. He is one who has been more in the forefront because of his glorious performances in his country and also in county cricket which Kapil Dev has only recently started playing.

I remember Javed Miandad as a little kid, just barely out of his teens. He hadn'teven began to shave then. He had come to play in the Prudential World Cup in 1975. Mushtaq Mohammed was the captain of Pakistan though not for the World Cup. He

433

had said that Javed Miandad was the most promising youngster he had seen. "This boy should go places", Mushtaq had added in 1974, a year before Javed was picked to play for Pakistan in the World Cup.

Javed was a very shy and a diffident character then and not the brash, self-confident and cocky person he is today. I remember sitting down in the lobby of a London hotel when Javed shyly asked for directions to go to a Chinese restaurant round the corner. He did not speak much English then and I was not very fluent in Hindi and so there was a bit of a problem making him understand where the restaurant was. But later, one found him in the same restaurant, sitting by himself and eating shyly. The other thing I remember about him is how he was trying to warn a team-mate of his against trying to flirt with a cricketer's wife. Javed knew the lady in question, a fact which his colleague in the team did not know and thought she was just one of the fans who had come to meet the players. That expression on his face trying to warn his colleague, who was still seen flirting, is still vivid in my mind. Of course, Javed would not be averse to flirting a bit on his own as now he has come a long way since he was a little kid in 1975.

In the World Cup in 1975, he did show glimpses of his ability to play the quick West Indian bowlers and score some runs and then chip in with the valuable wicket of Clive Lloyd. Pakistan had as good as won the game when they had nine wickets of the West Indians down, still needing 62 runs to win. But then Deryck Murray and Andy Roberts played some sensible cricket and took the West Indies to a sensational victory, thus preventing Pakistan from qualifying for the knockout stage of the tournament.

Javed stayed back after the World Cup and played with a club. He came back again the following year to play league cricket. Then he was asked to register with Sussex in order to qualify to play county cricket. In 1976 he took the cricket world by storm by scoring a hundred on his Test debut against New Zealand and with a double hundred in the last Test. He narrowly missed the distinction of scoring a double hundred and a hundred in the last Test when he was stumped out at 85. Thus a brilliant Test career was launched. He has not looked back since and has been a most consistent scorer in the subcontinent. In fact, if there is one person who is likely to score the maximum number of runs in the subcontinent, it is going to be Javed Miandad, because he has youth on his side and the confidence and ability to score all those runs.

The tour of Australia following that was a bit of a disaster for him because he did not get many runs there as also on the tour of the West Indies that followed. When he came back in 1977 to play against the visiting England team, he looked in good shape though he did not make as many runs as was expected of him. It was obvious that his performance was improving and the trips to Australia and the West Indies had done him a world of good.

The following year it was India's turn to return the visit to Pakistan after almost twenty years. It was a resumption of Test cricket between the two countries after a very long time. The last series played between India and Pakistan was in India in 1960 which was followed by a period of political uncertainties between the two countries. The atmosphere was neither healthy for any tour nor for any sporting contacts and it was only towards the early part of 1978 when the Pakistani hockey team came to India that the conditions became normal for a cricket tour. Before that, however, the Pakistan team had gone through a drastic change due to the Packer saga, which put a lot of pressure on Javed Miandad at the tender age of twenty-one. To be the team's main batsman as well was no easy thing and, obviously, it told on his form and he had a miserable tour of England. Against India, all the Packer players were recalled; Asif Iqbal came back from retirement to play in the series and all the leading players were back in the fold. Thus a load was off Javed's shoulders and as he was just one of the players in a team which boasted of a tremendous batting talent, Javed could play his natural attacking game.

In the first Test he scored 153, reaching his 50, 100 and 150 with enormous sixes which showed that he still had that cheeky spirit and that he was not afraid of lofting the ball whenever the occasion demanded it. But for the greater part of that innings, he was watchful, waiting for the right delivery to come and very seldom did he jump out to drive. He batted as if he had made up his mind to score a hundred runs, only in singles, and he took a long time over his innings. But in that match, it was Zaheer Abbas's 176 that overshadowed Javed's innings. Zaheer stroked the ball beautifully from the word go and so Javed was content to play second fiddle to him.

I do not think Javed got too many runs in the second Test, again dominated by Zaheer Abbas with a career-best of (for the India-Pakistan series) 235 not out and there was really no need for Javed to exert himself. In the third Test he scored a very good hundred runs on a wicket on which Kapil had found his rhythm and was beginning to pose a threat to most Pakistani batsmen. It was Miandad's running between the wickets in the second innings and his daredevil batting that won for Pakistan the Test when it looked, at one stage, as heading for a draw.

Credit should also be given to Asif Iqbal and Miandad for the way they ran their singles, for the way they hit good balls for runs and the way they kept on moving up the score. I do not think they even thought for a moment that they would not be able to score

436

the runs. The manner in which they played they even won the match with three overs to spare, was a considerable achievement considering the target they had been set.

Then, of course, came one of the many incidents in which Javed was involved. There was the running out of Rodney Hogg in the Perth Test in Australia when "Hoggy" went gardening. Miandad picked up the ball, threw down the wicket and appealed for run out which was upheld. Mushtaq asked the umpire to reverse the decision, but the umpire refused and "Hoggy" knocked down the bails and created an ugly scene. So that was one of the first incidents in which Javed was involved. It seems he had picked up a lot of these tricks while playing professional cricket with Sussex under the captaincy of Tony Greig. There is nothing wrong with these things because they form a part of the game in cricket and Javed, standing in the same position as Greig used to, was not afraid to give a bit of talk to the batsman who would lose his concentration. Javed, who till then had scored runs only in Pakistan, showed that he could score runs outside Pakistan as well, cracking a brilliant 130 on the Perth track against Rodney Hogg bowling at his fastest. Earlier, Hogg had unsettled the English who toured Australia but Pakistan was a different story, although Australia won that Test with a brilliant effort of 300 runs scored in the last innings. Meanwhile, because of the registration rules in county cricket he had to change counties and opted to play for Glamorgan because Imran Khan and Kepler Wessels were playing for Sussex.

The 1979-80 tour of India by the Pakistan team was one of the important events of the year as far as Indian cricket is concerned. Nowhere was a side looked forward to as much as the Pakistan side was. Even the West Indians when they arrived in India in 1966 and again in 1974 with the best of the

437

cricketing talents paled in comparison. Only the previous year they had thrashed us soundly by 2-0. So the cricketing public of India expected that they would thrash us again. Even I had serious misgivings and months before, in fact in May, when we were due to proceed to England I had written, when we saw the itinerary, that the Pakistanis would smash us to pulp. That statement was made considering the fact that we had just finished a season in which we had played three Tests against Pakistan, six Tests at home against the West Indies and with just a six-week rest, we were leaving for England to play in the World Cup, after which we were due to play four Test matches in England. A week after returning from England we were due to play a six-Test series against the Australians and then the Pakistanis, which meant that we were playing 25 Tests in a matter of sixteen to seventeen months. On the contrary, the Pakistan team had a long lay-off after that 1978-79 tour of Australia and New Zealand. And even those who played county cricket in England had a sufficient break before they came to India. The Indian players would be tired with the continuous playing and perhaps would not be in a proper physical and mental condition before taking on the might of the Pakistanis.

As it turned out, my fears were unfounded. What really happened was that the six-Test series against Australia, which we won convincingly 2-0, gave us new hopes. We were charged with more enthusiasm to tackle the Pakistanis. Before the Pakistanis started their first Test, a number of team meetings were held where the strategies were evolved. Among these was the strategy whereby we tried to limit the scoring abilities of Zaheer Abbas. We succeeded with Zaheer, but in the case of Javed Miandad, it was difficult to devise any strategy. He was so versatile in his range of shots. It was Javed who we were really afraid of because of his totally unorthodox batting and his

438

daredevil stroke play. He was capable of changing the fortunes of the match with his quick running between the wickets and thus unsettling the bowlers. This is what he did, although he failed to score a hundred in the series. He played extremely well at all times. Perhaps his best innings was the 60 he scored on a vicious turning track when Dilip Doshi and Shivlal Yadav were really making the ball hop. He batted extremely well, was sweeping Doshi on that turning track with all the control in the world and he was generally making batting look really simple. Even in the Madras Test which the Pakistan team lost to eventually lose the series, it was Javed Miandad who delayed our victory with a defiant knock of 50.

He was always dangerous and in the field he was always brilliant. I once jokingly told him that electrified heels should not be allowed on the field because he moved so quickly to chase the ball stopping it yards within the boundary.

His batting was not exactly, from the purist's point of view, a delight but from his side's point of view his improvisation was an abject lesson to viewers. Javed on the field was a tough customer. He had an answer to everything. He was not averse to exchanging words with you. But this man Javed is one of the friendliest of fellows and I particularly think leaving all his animosity on the field behind him.

There was no doubt on that Test that he had a sharp cricketing brain. He was always on Asif's side explaining to him and cajoling him to bring a particular bowler on or to shift a particular fielder this way or that way. Javed for all his inadequacies, as far as education, etc. go, is a great cricketing brain which exposes weaknesses in the opponents and plans ahead.

It is a pity that because of internal problems, Javed Miandad has lost the captaincy. But one thing is certain: whether he is captain or not, his brain will keep on ticking, providing the captain with ideas so that the team can do well. I personally feel that he is the one man who is likely to break most of the batting records in this subcontinent. He has time on his side, he has talent in plenty and, more importantly, the determination to do it.

Different strokes.

(facing page, top)
Sunil Gavaskar with the
Benson & Hedges trophy.

(below) ... declaring his
retirement from captaincy.

Any records to be broken here? I'm game!

Sunil Gavaskar with

... fellow commentator Tony Greig.

... Kapil Dev

... living legends *(top)* Sir Gary Sobers ard *(below)* Lala Amarnath.

... Ian Chappell.

(facing page) ... Ian Chappell, Mohinder Amarnath and

(below) ... Mark Mascarenhas

... Krishnamachari Srikkanth, his favourite opening partner.

... Ravi Shastri.

... *(top)* Imran Khan and *(below)* wife Marshneil.

18

Jeff Thomson

WHEN THE ENGLAND TEAM LED BY MIKE DENNESS ARRIVED IN Australia in 1974, they were greeted with Lillee's comback stories in the newspapers. Lillee had been out of action for more than a year owing to back trouble which, at one stage, had looked like finishing his career. But Lillee came back strongly, thanks to his hard work and the fitness programme charted out by·his doctor to get him back into top physical condition.

Along with the report about Lillee's comeback, there was this news about Australia having discovered another demon bowler in Jeff Thomson. The English dismissed this story as just another created by the Australian press to cause worry to them. The English were not worried in the least about tackling Thomson because in his only Test, two years ago, against Pakistan, he was hit all over for 100 runs and could claim only one wicket. They forgot, for a moment, that Thomson had bowled in that Test with a fractured toe and so they concentrated on how to tackle the fury and pace of Lillee. They went to see Lillee bowling in a Sheffield Shield match and were relieved when they saw him bowling only medium pace in his comeback match.

Then came the first Test at Brisbane in Queensland and the Englishmen were shaken out of their complacency by Lillee and Thomson. Lillee, of course, had very intelligently conserved his energies and saved himself for the big occasion, building his speed, confidence and accuracy for the Test matches. He did it very gradually and the climax was reached when he went flat out in the Test. So did Thomson. His run-up was not very long, but he had powerful shoulders. He was an immensely strong man and had a whipping action. He concealed the ball behind his right thigh and at the point of delivery, he was just about impossible to be picked. He was so quick that he did not have to move the ball at all.

On a wicket full of grass these two simply ran through the English batting order and put back the careers of a lot of established English batsmen. Thomson bowled into the wind because Lillee, being the senior partner, more experienced and craftier, was given the choice of ends to bowl, with the breeze behind him to get that additional pace. Yet, Rodney Marsh thought that Thomson, bowling into the steep breeze, was even quicker than Dennis Lillee, which is saying something.

At the end of the first session, Rodney Marsh turned to the slip fielders, Ian and Greg Chappell, and told them that his fingers were hurting from the battering they were taking from Lillee and Thomson's thunderbolts. But he added that despite the hurt, "I still love it."

Australia thus found a combination which could match the legendary combinations of Hall and Griffith, Lindwall and

Miller, Statham and Trueman of the bygone days. And between them these two put a scare into the England batsmen and gave Australia such a psychological advantage that England never recovered from it at all.

Thomson, prior to the series, had got himself into trouble. He had said in a magazine interview that he liked to see the batsmen on the field with blood flowing because that's the way he could get them out. If he could not get them out bowled, he would like to see them knocked out and sent back to the pavilion. Either way was fine by him. This interview, of course, was great stuff, first class sensationalism to attract attention and invite people through the turnstiles, but not exactly the cup of tea for Cricket Boards all over the world. Though the Boards would like people to come for matches in large numbers, this statement of Thomson was not in keeping with the traditions of the gentleman's game. But the Australians always like to speak their minds without worrying about the consequences. Thomson later denied having given that interview, but for a moment it made enough impact and created a reputation for Jeff Thomson.

When the Englishmen met Thomson, though they were confident of tackling him on account of his poor performance in the only Test played against Pakistan, they were shaken out of their smugness by the scorching, electrifying pace that Thomson achieved. His most dangerous deliveries were those which rose from fractionally short of a length and which gave the batsmen no time to play any kind of strokes. Batsmen had bruised knuckles and blows all over the chest to show for their efforts to get behind the line of the ball. In this Test, every time Jeff tried to bowl a bouncer, the ball went sailing above Rodney Marsh's head and struck the boundary fence for four byes. And one ball went so high above Marsh's head that it struck the boundary fence on the first bounce, which tells how quick Thomson was and how hard, green and bouncy the track was. On such a track, Lillee's craftiness and Thomson's pace was enough to destroy the confidence of the best of batsmen, not just Englishmen, who always shout about other batsmen's weaknesses against pace, without showing any kind of technique or attitude towards pace themselves, considering that in English county cricket, there is at least one, if not two, quick bowler in every county side.

From that Test, Lillee and Thomson became household names in Australia, but the connoisseurs of fast bowling loved Lillee for his rhythmic approach, delivery action, his strides, his follow-through and also his craft with the ball. The Australian kids went wild for Thomson, his unruly mop of hair bouncing as he ran in to bowl with his unusual action and his hatred towards the batsmen seemed to drive the children crazy. Suddenly, Thomson found himself the idol of millions of Australian kids and he did not quite know how to react to that. His attitude was to be his normal self and as he is a calm, composed man off the field he took it all, after initial amazement, in his stride. He was always obliging towards giving autographs. He used to say, "Never refuse an autograph to any kid, he might have an elder sister."

In those days Thommo became the darling of the press. Whatener he did was reported with gusto and with a lot of spice added to it as well. But his image of a man, who would like to see the batsmen in pain, suffering under his onslaughts, was one thing and the other was his image of a man who liked to see the sun come up in the morning and spend his time with beautiful girls. Basically he was a law unto himself. This image is, however, highly exaggerated, but at that time it suited Thommo, and it suited the Australian press and the Australian team led by that mercurial but outstanding captain, Ian Chappell. It gave them a certain feeling of toughness and also brought the crowds flocking to the Tests.

By the end of the fifth Test, Thomson had picked up thirty-three wickets and looked as though he was going to overtake the series record set by Clarie V. Grimmett way back in 1935-36 when he had taken forty-four South African wickets. This, however, did not come off because on the rest day of this Test, Thommo had an injury. On the rest day, both the teams traditionally go to Borossa Valley which is a vineyard with facilities for playing tennis and swimming. They relax and enjoy Australian hospitality and, of course, the wine. Here, while playing tennis, Thommo damaged his shoulder ligaments and was unfit to play not only in this Test but also in the next. That ruled him out from setting the series bowling record for most wickets taken. Lillee too damaged his foot and went off the field under this handicap. Without the Australian fast bowling twins, the English had a hayday and amassed a big total with Fletcher scoring 100 and Mike Denness 188. The mastery that Lillee and Thomson had established over the English had gone. The English side went on to win this Test to overcome a little bit of the ignominy that they had suffered at the hands of the Australians right through. This victory also helped in regaining their confidence and they left for New Zealand in a much better frame of mind.

At the end of that series, the English press, which always has excuses, sometimes ridiculous, for the performances of their side, accused the Australians of having resorted to a bouncer war. However, they forgot that the bouncers were, in fact, started by Peter Lever and Bob Willis who bowled short at the Australian batsmen in the first Test. It was the English themselves who started it since they had not reckoned with

Lillee's comeback to peak physical fitness and Thomson's arrival, which they thought was figment of the imagination of the Australian press. So to a certain extent the tables were turned on the Englishmen and they lost very badly. That series had caught the attention of the people back in England. When the inaugural World Cup was due to be played that summer in England, Lillee and Thomson were the ones who were the star attractions, even more than the West Indians who were the favourites to win the World Cup. During the series in Australia, reports mentioning "Lillee and Thomson" made headlines in the English press and that led old ladies in England to wonder why and how a woman called Lillian Thomson could rip through the England team.

When the team assembled for the World Cup, all attention once again was focused on Lillee and Thomson. After the World Cup, there was a series between England and Australia in England and that meant that the two bowlers were again to meet the Englishmen, this time on their soil. The English press had faithfully picked up from the Australian press what they had been writing about the exploits of Jeff Thomson off the field and painted him with garish colours making him some sort of a villain.

In the first World Cup match played against Pakistan, they all went to see Jeff Thomson bowl and some other action. Thomson did not disappoint them. Having some trouble with his run-up and having been called for no balls often, he found to his dismay the crowd cheering his discomfiture and cheering every no ball he bowled. Not used to being booed and this kind of reception, his immediate reaction was to show two fingers to the crowd. And this gesture, though more out of frustration than anything else, made the headlines the next day. The more perceptive writers knew of Thomson's predicament, but the

446

others cashed in in the hope of producing good copy, hinting that the Australian umpires were reluctant to find this fault in Thomson's delivery. But the height of Thomson's unpopularity came when he was playing against Sri Lanka. Earlier, the Sri Lankan batsmen had batted very confidently on a flat Oval track. Then Thomson decided to go flat out and knocked Duleep Mendis on the head. Duleep was lying flat on the ground and Thomson, instead of going up to him and inquiring about his injury, just turned his back. This reaction was condemned by everybody.

Hardly had this incident been forgotten, when Thomson was involved in another. He bowled a yorker to Sunil Wettimuny which hit him on his foot. Thomson refers to his yorkers as "sandshoe crushers". As the batsman was out of the crease, writhing in pain, Thomson ran down the pitch and broke the wicket, appealing for a run out. This again did not meet with anybody's approval and though he was technically right, the ball seemed to be dead and that was what the umpires ruled. Thomson again made the headlines the next day. This was all very frustrating for Jeff and it was certainly not helping him in any way. However, he showed great imagination and determination when in the final of the World Cup, Lillee and he batted sensibly and took the Australians within 17 runs of victory against the West Indies. That was a great final, thrilling all the way. There was some great fielding, particularly by Vivian Richards, great batting by Clive Lloyd and Rohan Kanhai and this last partnership between Lillee and Thomson which almost snatched victory away from the West Indians' hands.

At the end of the World Cup the Australians applied themselves to the task of facing England in the four-Test series to follow. The biggest problem was to with Jeff Thomson overstepping the crease which had by now reached alarming proportions. And this was causing his team management a lot of worries. However, during the Test matches, Thomson came good and although he had the occasional trouble of overstepping, he took care not to annoy the umpires as well as his captain. The wickets in England that season were more like what you see in Pakistan or India, devoid of any grass and more whitish in appearance than green. Obviously, the English were not prepared to take risks with Lillee and Thomson in the attack, supported by Max Walker and Gary Gilmour, who had done very well in the World Cup and were also a force to reckon with.

The Australians won the first Test very comfortably after Mike Denness had opted to field and then suddenly found that the weather had upset his calculations. Thomson, though not bowling at his fastest, got vital wickets and proved that his performance in Australia was not a mere flash in the pan. Lillee, of course, was there taking his usual quota of wickets and on his way to becoming the greatest fast bowler of the decade. The two completely mesmerised the English batsmen in that Test and this forced Mike Denness to step down from captaincy making way for Tony Greig to take over. He did a thorough job of revitalising the English team and he brought in players who were not outstanding or crowd-pulling but thorough professionals who would do their best for England. One of them was David Steele and he fitted firmly in Tony Greig's plans, batting with care and caution against the twin menace of Lillee and Thomson. Thomson, after his first Test success, was not quite the bowler he was and the wickets hardly afforded him any help. Also, he was not particularly happy with the cold, damp conditions in England, though it was an extraordinarily good summer. The wickets were drier and there was hardly any scope for seam bowlers to do anything extraordinary once the ball had lost its initial shine.

Thomson returned from that tour without damaging his reputation but also without enhancing it any further. He waited for the West Indians to come "Down Under" later that season for what was labelled as the "World Championship Series". The Australians completely annihilated the West Indians and it was the pace bowling of Thomson and Lillee that did the damage. We were touring the West Indies in 1976 and it was interesting to hear stories about how quick Jeff Thomson was from some of the demoralised West Indians. They admitted they had never played pace bowling of the type Lillee and Thomson hurled at them on that tour.

Throughout that series, Lillee and Thomson bowled shortpitched deliveries at them and completely mastered them, the only exception being when Roy Fredericks scored 169, racing to his century in 71 deliveries. This was one of the most memorable Test hundreds in cricket history.

Apart from that battering, Thomson was his usual devastating self. He was back in familiar surroundings, on harder, bouncier tracks from which he could extract life and bounce. This, together with the West Indians' natural fondness for the hook, was the downfall of the batsmen. The Australian grounds being larger than most West Indian grounds, their hooked shots turned into catches. They were not hooking badly, but the shots which would have been certain sixes on other grounds fell short and were caught. That was a bit of a disappointing series for either side with such an array of fast bowlers on both. It was predicted that it would be an evenly-contested series, and the West Indians at that stage were a talented lot but still were not in that professional, ruthless streak of winning which they were to fall into the following year.

For Jeff Thomson that was a satisfying way of making a comeback into big wicket-taking league and he now waited patiently for the new Australian season to start when the Pakistanis were going to visit Australia. He had memories of his first Test against Pakistan when he had broken his toe but had not informed the selection committee. Because of that broken toe, he had not been able to get more than one wicket and was hit for over 100 runs by Pakistani batsmen. He, thus, had a score to settle with them and was eagerly looking forward to that series.

Unfortunately, everything went wrong for him in the first Test itself. Having captured two quick wickets, Thomson bowled a steep rising bouncer to Zaheer Abbas, one of the best batsmen in the team. Zaheer went for the hook and hit it high with the splice of the bat and Thomson, following through, collided with Alan Turner, who was running in from mid-wicket to take the catch and both fell in a heap on the ground. Thomson was then seen getting up holding his shoulder. The collision made a terrific sound like the crack of a pistol and that meant that there was something seriously wrong with Thomson's shoulder. It was later discovered that the shoulder had not only dislocated and fractured but that the injury would heal only after inserting a metal pin in his shoulder. At that stage it looked as if Thomson's career was at a very sad end. However, he made very good recovery and after having satisfied the Australian selectors he went on the England tour in 1977. That was the year when Kerry Packer had signed up cricketers all over the world. Some of the Australian players were not invited to sign and the result was that there was a clear division in the Australian team's ranks. Thomson had Pascoe as his partner to share the new ball as Lillee had opted out of the team because of his old back trouble. The Australians could never get going. Then good leadership by Mike Brearley and the emergence of Ian Botham as a world-class player and all-rounder combined to cause their defeat by a 1-3 margin.

By the middle of this series, Thomson was involved in a controversy. The WSC people claimed that he had signed up with Kerry Packer, while his agent David Lord claimed that no way could Thomson have signed and, even if he had it would not be valid for the simple reason that Thomson had a previous contract with a radio station in Queensland.

As a result Thomson had to withdraw from the WSC Australian side and was brought back in the official Australian side. He was the only leading player of the side. Bobby Simpson was appointed captain of the Australian team after a lapse of ten years, because there was no one experienced enough to lead the side which was totally depleted. Simpson insisted on discipline at all cost, not only on but even off the field. He wanted the players to stop coming to the ground in T-shirts and jeans and insisted on them wearing the Australian tie and blazer. He insisted that the Australian players must feel proud of wearing their colours as representatives of the country. This policy brought in a new look to the Australian team. They were a determined lot and with Thomson in their ranks they were raring to go against India.

It was a well-contested series because both the sides were equally balanced. They won the first two Tests mainly because of Thomson's bowling and the second Test additionally because of his batting at the crucial stage. The Indians won the next two Tests and the fifth Test was the deciding one. Australia coasted to a 500-plus total and Thomson captured the first two wickets. He then strained a ligament in his leg and did not participate further part in the match. That was a severe blow to the Australians. The Indians almost won that Test, falling short by just 45 runs.

Thomson had a very good series and was rewarded with the vice-captaincy of the Australian team that toured the West Indies immediately thereafter. Here, somehow, the old views of Simpson and the modern views of Thomson did not agree and created quite a few problems. The relationship between the two was apparently not what should have been between a captain and a vice-captain. The result was that Thomson could produce only one electrifying spell in Barbados when he had the West Indian batsmen on the hop. People in the know said that it was the fastest spell of bowling they had ever seen in the West Indies.

After that it has been a series of ups and downs for Thomson. He has been in and out of the Australian team, sometimes owing to injuries and sometimes owing to the fact that the Australians produced some fine fast bowlers to partner Lillee, and that Thomson was not always able to keep his place in the team.

He was dropped from the side that went to England in 1981 and he instead signed for Middlesex in the county championship, something he was not in favour of earlier because it involved playing cricket seven days a week. Over there, he had to return midway through the season as he was required to undergo an operation and Middlesex could utilise his services for only part of the season.

Thomson is not cut out for the seven days a week hard grind. He would love to play for shorter durations and go fishing between matches, which he admits is his favourite pastime.

He did not have a very successful season in 1982-83 when New Zealand and England toured Australia, nor could he do anything extraordinary in the World Cup in England earlier in 1983. In fact, he was dropped from some matches because of his indifferent form.

Married to a beautiful one-time model, Thomson still has a lot of fire in him, though it seems to surface only occasionally. Still he is an attractive fast bowler who even today draws the crowds. Thomson will go down in the cricketing history as one of the most fearsome fast bowlers of the 1970s.

19

John Snow

WHEN THE INDIAN TEAM WAS PLAYING IN THE WEST INDIES IN 1971, we got regular reports about the series in Australia where John Snow was running through the Australian batsmen and making them hop. Geoff Boycott was scoring all the runs and John Snow was getting all the wickets. As luck would have it, both of them were not there for the vital sixth Test which was being played. Boycott had broken his arm and Snow his finger in this Test itself and was unable to play in the second innings.

When we came to England, the talk was mainly about these two English players. Both had been picked because of their performances earlier in the winter, both were also in for some criticism for their behaviour on the tour. Boycott had thrown down his bat when he was given run out and Snow had altercations with the umpires about the bouncers. Both were controversial characters, Snow to a lesser degree than Boycott. But that summer Snow was much more in the news. He had not played against the Pakistanis earlier in the summer owing to some injury and he was due to make his comeback against us in the Lord's Test. Till he actually played, one had no idea as to his bowling action or the kind of deliveries that he specialised in. Of course, it was believed that the bouncer was his lethal ball. But nobody could give us any indication whether he moved the ball off the wicket or either way. That was something which we had to find out ourselves when the Test started.

The Nursery end at Lord's is a place where teams practise before and during the match as nets are out of the ground behind the stands at the northern end from the pavilion. So on the morning of the match, most of the Indian players were trying to get an idea of how John Snow bowled. He bowled off a short run-up to the English batsmen. The balls used at the English nets are seldom new ones and we could not get an idea about his bowling ability but got to see his bowling action.

It wasn't long before that opportunity came and we could see why Snow had been rated as the top fast bowler in the world. But before that, Snow contributed with the bat and led an England recovery with Raymond Illingworth. England were not in a happy position when Snow walked in to bat and he just stuck around there by sheer dint of application and plenty of determination. He wasn't able to read Chandra, wasn't comfortable against Bishen, but carried on gamely for 71, before Chandra had him caught. These runs were indeed invaluable and helped England put up a reasonable total. That batting effort seemed to have warmed him up for the bowling that was to follow. He bowled fast and furiously and soon a short one had Ashok Mankad lobbing a catch to Norman Gifford at forward short-leg. He didn't have too much success after that because he bowled too short and perhaps his line and length were still adjusted to Australian wickets and not the English ones.

Therefore he did not get too many wickets in that game and frustration was telling on him. The Indian batsmen have gained a reputation for not liking real fast bowling, though I don't think this is correct when it is hinted that others in the world are more adept at playing fast bowling. No team in the world is good at playing fast bowling and at various times one has seen how the best of the teams have fallen. To India's defence, it must be said that they rarely get anything above medium-pace in domestic cricket and, therefore, have failed to have enough practice against the bouncing ball. And so their vulnerability to fast bowling is understandable because they just do not have the opportunity to play the kind of fast bowling the rest of the world has. Look at the present performance of India in international cricket and it can be seen that they are sometimes better than those countries which regularly get practice against fast bowling and yet do not give good performances!

Well, with this kind of a reputation, Snow thought that he would be able to run through the side. When he faced resistance, at times defiance in the wake of Ajit Wadekar's brilliant innings, another good knock from Vishy and the stubborn defence of Eknath Solkar, the frustration was quite evident. When we began the second innings, he tried bouncers, and when he found that they did not have the desired effect, he was getting a little difficult.

Then came the famous incident which almost everybody knows but I want to record it for the benefit of those who missed it. Snow was bowling and a delivery hit Engineer on the thigh pad and went down to where short square-leg would have been, in front of the wicket. We were chasing runs at that stage and taking quick singles to keep the scoreboard moving. As I dashed off to take that single as the non-striker, I suddenly found Snow coming in my path. As I swerved away, I found Snow following me. The next thing I knew was that a hefty shoulder had dug into me and I went sprawling. I reached the crease on my hands and knees as the bat was knocked out of my hands. I was furious at this incident. I turned round to see Snow standing there with my bat in his hands which he tossed to me and was off and away. The umpires had a word with him but it was a very annoying thing which upset me a great deal. It took me a long while to recover.

Snow was asked to apologise for that incident by the chairman of the England selection committee, when play started after lunch. He was also disciplined and not picked for the team for the second Test. Peter Level took his place, scored 81, and that meant that Snow was not in the team for the third Test. But an injury to Lever ruled him out and Snow was recalled for the third Test at the Oval.

When our turn came to bat, Snow's first ball, as expected, was a bouncer to me and he gave me a stare as if to say that because of me he had been suspended for one Test. In any case, that ball was a waste but later he produced a beauty that went through my defence, through my bat and pad to knock off my middle stump. I still remember how quickly it nipped back and ripped through the gate. Snow really bowled well but was not very successful on that Test. It is now history how India went on to register their first Test victory in England at the Oval.

Snow got me out in the second innings when I offered no stroke, the ball coming outside the leg-stump. I was surprised that I was given out leg before. Be that as it may, the experience of watching John Snow was tremendous, because here was a great fast bowler. His run-up was short, not long as you see today with most fast bowlers. It was rhythmic, smooth and his final delivery stride, though not really sideways on, ended with a lovely action. He had the whipping method of delivering the ball. He predominantly bowled inswingers or made the ball cut in off the wicket. His outswingers but were not as lethal as his inswingers.

For a fast bowler, he had the usual good bouncer, but he did not have an effective yorker to follow it. He made you play the bouncer all the time and did not waste it at all. The ball seemed to be coming at your throat, which meant that you had to throw the bat up to protect yourself and then if you were unlucky you would lob up a catch.

It was this bouncer that got him into trouble in Australia because he bowled one to Terry Jenner which did not come up and Jenner turned his back and received a sickening blow on the back of his head. Jenner had to retire hurt. At this stage, the umpires cautioned him for bowling too many bouncers. Snow and an agitated Illingworth argued with the umpires about the ball being called a bouncer. In their opinion the ball wasn't a bouncer. As if to prove his point, Snow bowled a bouncer the next ball and turned round to the umpire and said, "that was a bouncer and not the previous one." The umpires warned him promptly and told him that if he did that again, he would be taken off the attack. Fortunately, Snow kept his cool thereafter because of his importance to the England attack and went on with his judicious mixture of bouncers to win the match for England.

In the last Test, just before he broke his finger, he was fielding at the fence and a drunken spectator came up to him and caught hold of his shirt. Snow did not do anything to retaliate. But that was enough for Ray Illingworth to take his side off the field because he thought the his team was in danger.

It was then at this very spot when play resumed later that Snow broke his finger while going for a catch off Stackpole and crashing into the wooden fence, dislocating his little finger of the right hand, his bowling hand. He was out of action in that vital innings when the Aussies required 180-odd runs to win and Ray Illingworth and Basil D'Oliviera spun England to a victory.

Snow played in 1972 when the Australians were around and again in 1973, though he was surprisingly not picked to tour with the team to the West Indies in 1973-74. I am sure the England team must have missed him because on the previous tour there in 1968, Snow was very successful as he got quite a few wickets in that series. In fact, in that series, he became the only bowler in the world to get Gary Sobers out twice off the first ball he had bowled to him. He got him out again in the 1970 series when he bowled him with a shooter.

We met again in 1975 when the World Cup was staged in England for the first time. Snow was brought back to the England team though he was not included when we were there in 1974. He was going back to his bowling mark when we played England in the World Cup and he turned around and told me, "Don't try those singles," remembering the 1971 incident that had taken place at the same venue, four years earlier.

Snow has always been, apart from that incident, a good friend off the field. Like all fast bowlers he has got that aggressive streak in him when he is bowling to opening batsmen. Even after that 1971 incident, we sat together and had long discussions on South Africa. I remember Solkar, Illingworth and I sitting together and it was only when Col. Adhikari, our manager, insisted that we go to bed that we decided to part. Not very often does one come across people with Illingworth's experience as a cricketer. At that stage of our career, Solkar and I were newcomers to cricket and whatever Illingworth was discussing we were taking in. Snow also joined in the discussion and one could see that there was a great deal of affinity between the two.

Cricket-lovers in India wanted to see Snow in the England team that toured India in 1976 when Tony Greig captained the side. But Snow was not picked. He had gone more or less off the Test scene, though he did make sporadic Test appearances for England.

Later, we kept meeting often. In 1979 when the Indian team was in England, I bumped into Snow. He talked a great deal about Sandeep Patil who had played for his club, Edmonton, and he thought Sandeep had good prospects. His words did indeed come true. Patil has established himself. At that stage Patil had not played in Tests and John Snow helped him a great deal in playing the moving ball.

Snow has now set up a travel agency and he hopes that when the new business is settled and is on sound footing, he will avail himself of a free ticket and come to India, the country he had not visited as a player. Maybe, as a former player he can come on a holiday and play a couple of matches and show the cricket-lovers of India what John Snow the cricketer is all about.

20

Kapil Dev

IN 1978 RAJ SINGH DUNGARPUR CALLED ME OVER TO DISCUSS THE team for East Africa. While discussing that team, I remembered an over bowled to me earlier in the season in the Wills Trophy. A young lad called Kapil Dev had not only shown enormous potential but also a willingness to learn. I remember telling him in that match that he should come closer to the stumps because his outswinger then would be more effective. Mind you, all that happened when we were playing against each other in the same match.

A couple of players from his team rushed to him thinking that I was trying to make him bowl the wrong line. But that was farthest from my mind because after a long, long time, there was a bowler in Indian cricket who was promising and fast in the competition. It is always good fun to play against good bowlers,

461

rather than try your ability against less fast bowlers. Kapil was a quick learner and in the next over, one could see him making an effort to come closer to the stumps and bowl. As soon as he got that right, it was apparent that he was going to be a force to reckon with.

He bowled extremely well in that match in Madras and his bowling set us back a great deal and helped his side to win. His side was strong anyway and could have won under normal circumstances. Kapil's spell, however, was a particularly memorable one. It gave him a lot of prominence and brought him into national focus. This match was at the back of my mind when we sat to pick the team to go to East Africa. This was going to be a friendly tour and the team comprised experienced Test players and those who were highly promising. We had included Pataudi, Vishwanath, Yajurvinder Singh and Eknath Solkar among Test stalwarts and among the youngsters were Kapil Dev and Suru Nayak. The two were picked to get some experience of foreign conditions which could have helped them considerably. Playing abroad against an opposition which is different, under different conditions with different bowlers and players comes in handy at all times and goes a long way towards making one a better cricketer.

Kapil did well on this trip. He was not only the bowler who got us vital breakthroughs, but he also batted magnificently, hitting many a towering six, and winning the hearts of East African cricket-lovers. One noticed on this trip how Kapil improved match by match and towards the end of the tour in a three-day game against the strongest East African side, he was well nigh unplayable. After the team returned to India, Kapil was selected to play for the Rest of India in the Irani Trophy match at Bangalore. It was a trial game before the team for Pakistan was selected. Kapil scored a hurricane 61 and bowled most impressively. He thus found a berth for himself in the side to go to Pakistan, although even at that stage, it was doubtful if he would really find a place for himself in the Test team. It was thought that the tour would give him a lot of experience and so when the West Indies team came to India later that season, Kapil could be very useful.

However, his performance in Pakistan in the beginning was such that he could not be ignored and he was picked for the first Test at Faisalabad. It was a good strip which afforded a fair amount of bounce to the new-ball bowlers. In the first few overs Kapil forced Sadiq to discard his green Pakistani cap for a helmet. As it turned out, it was a wise move as in the very next over, a bouncer from Kapil hit Sadiq flush on the helmet and went away for four byes. With that one delivery Kapil had proved that he could not be taken lightly in Test cricket and India, after a long, long time, had not only a bowler who could use the new ball, but also bowl with fire.

Thereafter, there was no stopping Kapil. He scored 59 as a night-watchman and thus earned the tag of an all-rounder. He confirmed this later in the season when he scored a century against the West Indians. The only time the tag of an all-rounder did not fit him was on the 1979 tour of England when this dynamic cricketer failed with the bat. He bowled with his customary fire and efficiency in the Test matches and also in other matches but somehow failed to get the runs. He used to get out in his eagerness to hit the ball in the air, rather than take his time and play his shots. This, of course, was solely due to inexperience, which was amply proved on the 1982 tour of England, when he almost scored 300 runs in three Test matches.

After that 1978 tour, his career graph has been on the rise. He is now reckoned to be one of the top all-rounders in the world, if not the topmost. People talk about Imran Khan, Ian Botham, Kapil Dev and Richard Hadlee as the leading all-rounders in the world. It is indeed difficult to pick the best among them all. But one thing is sure: any captain would love to have all four of them on his team and win a match, because all of them are attacking cricketers; all of them have put in sterling performances; all of them have performed under pressure and proved that they have the flamboyance and ability to take on any opponents at any given time. Picking the best player out of them is basically a subject of extensive exercise. There would always be conflicting opinions on the merits and demerits of each player.

In Kapil's case he has the disadvantage of not having a strike bowler along with him which means that the entire pressure of taking wickets is entirely on him. The opponents also know that since he is the only player capable of running through the side, they are extra careful while playing him. Thus he does not always capture the kind of wickets which are expected of him. Also during Kapil's time, the Indian batting has not been consistent, with the result that he has hardly time to take off his bowling boots and put on his batting shoes before he is called upon to go in for the rescue act. This has undoubtedly put a lot of pressure on Kapil and it has, at times, made him play some loose shots which has brought about his early dismissal.

But with greater experience and added responsibility after becoming the captain, such shots have become rarer and will definitely contribute to a consistent performance in future. And I am convinced that if Kapil had more experience, the 1979 Oval Test which we drew and did not win, falling short by nine runs, could easily have been won. Kapil went there, promoted in the batting order, and the first delivery itself he tried to whack out of the ground and ended up being caught at long on.

Kapil's greatest triumph, however, has been leading India to win the Prudential World Cup in June 1983. Nobody could have dreamt that India, so often the underdog in one-day cricket, could have ended up as winners. But Kapil led by example in the game against Zimbabwe when five Indian wickets had gone for 17 runs to a mixture of good bowling and poor strokes. Kapil went out and played an innings that is truly unforgettable. His first 70 to 80 runs were really calculated in the sense that he pushed and nudged the ball and only hit those which he was convinced should be hit. After that, he had enough confidence and when he saw that he had partners who would stay with him, he launched a counter-attack the likes of which one had never seen before. It was absolutely unbelievable stuff. He was hitting the bowlers as if at will and we were applauding each and every shot. Our hands became weary but each shot was absolutely thrilling. When he was around 160, we all had our hearts in our mouths. We knew that the record score of 171 was so near. Perhaps Kapil was not aware of it, and in his anxiety to get as many runs as possible, he would perhaps play an ambitious shot and get out.

It was obvious at this stage that he was a tired man and might hit a tired looking shot and get out. But fortunately, he didn't do that and went on to make 175 not out, which is a record in the Prudential World Cup. Then he came on to bowl four overs of tight medium-pace bowling and did not give Zimbabwe players any respite at all.

That was the turning point of the tournament and thereafter, the Indian team really went from strength to strength taking Australia, England and the West Indies in their stride. With this win, Kapil has become a household name not only in India, but all over the cricketing world. His grinning face holding the Prudential Trophy with sheer joy stamped on it has become as memorable as the win itself.

His brothers have started a hotel and named it after Kapil. "Hotel Kapil" is a tribute to him from his brothers for all the glory he has brought to India and to the family. His success has given encouragement and impetus to thousands of youngsters all over the country and not only in metropolitan cities. This will act as a spur to many youngsters to give their best in international cricket.

Kapil's advent in international cricket is the best thing that could have happened to Indian cricket. We've always had spinners who earned a name for themselves and the country but there never was a fast bowler to uplift India's prestige so high in the past. With Kapil's example before them, boys in the street are walking to their marks purposefully, coming in from a distance and hurling the ball quickly at the opposing batsman. Today's cricket is jet-age cricket where speed is more important than subtleties of spin. Speed follows the batsman wherever he goes and with the likes of Kapil Dev to inspire the youngsters, more and more of the younger lot will take to fast bowling which will be good for Indian cricket. And even if all of them cannot make the Test grade, at least they will be able to provide adequate practice to our batsmen so that they are not found wanting when facing the fast bowlers from other countries.

Kapil's brand of cricket is also the attacking brand which makes him a crowd pleaser everywhere he goes. It will certainly go a long way towards ensuring that the cricket India plays is the kind which will bring in the crowds. No longer will Indian cricket and cricketers be called "dull dogs" as was the case in the early fifties and people will come to believe that the team can play attractive cricket.

It has been a rapid rise for a lad who batted at No. 11 in East Africa to come to the fore as one of the leading all-rounders in the world. Kapil, to this date, remains the same simple fellow that he was in 1978, with, of course, a lot more confidence in dealing with people than he had in 1978. This confidence came as he gained more successes in international cricket. But with this confidence, and with these successes, his attitude towards people has not changed. He is still polite and courteous to the senior cricketers and lends an ear to everyone. These characteristics have been difficult to find in recent years and Kapil is richly endowed with these along with his many splendoured cricketing talents that God Almighty has showered on him. He is still twenty-four and has years and years of Test cricket ahead of him. I am confident that these will be the years when the standard of Indian cricket will keep rising and reach the greatest of heights.

21

Mohinder Amarnath

WHEN I STARTED WRITING THIS BOOK, SOMETIME LAST YEAR, Mohinder Amarnath did not figure in the list of my idols. Until then he had always been a very fine player who had not somehow produced a performance befitting his potential at the Test level. The transition from a very fine player to a great player came only last season when, with the consistency which is the hallmark of great players, he started producing centuries and big scores in all the matches that he played.

The dividing line between a great player and a good player is that the former scores runs when the team really needs them, while the good player scores runs when everybody else is on a scoring spree. Mohinder Amarnath's performance in the last season was outstanding. His batting displays in the West Indies ought to have been preserved on films because he showed that the West Indies bowling could not only be attacked but also attacked successfully and consistently. Apart from that, his ability to judge which deliveries to leave alone, clearly separated him from other players in the team. No wonder, therefore, that he got 300 runs more than the next best batsman in that series for India.

One first heard of Mohinder Amarnath in 1965 when the Cooch-Behar Trophy matches were in progress in Bombay. The newspapers in those days used to cover the University and Cooch-Behar Schools Tournament in greater detail and gave them plenty of prominence. Amarnath bowling with a short run-up attracted attention because of his similarity in bowling action, though not the delivery stride, with his illustrious father, Lala Amarnath. Scribes, who had also seen his father in action, went on to describe how Mohinder resembled his father in his run-up and also in his ability to make the ball swing late both ways. It was thus as a bowler that Mohinder first came to be noticed in the cricketing world.

His elder brother Surinder was a batsman and though Mohinder was also a useful batsman at that stage, nobody paid much attention to his batting ability. During the visit of the London schoolboys later that year, both Mohinder and Surinder were in the Indian schoolboys team. Although they didn't have outstanding successes their ability was never in doubt and it was only a matter of time before they would follow in their father's footsteps and become Test players. Both are quiet and it was very difficult to get anything out from either of them. However, if a leg-pulling session is on, both join in. But as it happens, at school level, when sons of former Test players are involved, no one fools around with them too much for the simple reason that schoolboys being what they are and anxious about their future, do not wish to jeopardise their chances.

Both of them immediately after played for Punjab in the Ranji Trophy in 1966. I had played with them in the school tournaments, and for one who was not even in the reckoning for the Ranji Trophy cap, I used to follow their progress in the tournament with great interest. The All India Schools side that year was a very strong one with Eknath Solkar as captain, Ashok Gandotra - another talented player who went out of first class cricket too soon to concentrate on his career, Ramesh Nagdev - who but for his migration to the USA, would have made the higher grade - and Sunil Gavaskar, of whom the world probably had not heard, the Amarnaths, Milind Rege, Arun Kumar, Asif, Ajit Naik and Dhiraj Prasanna. All these cricketers were a lot of fun. This side was full of cricketers of promise and most of them went on to play for India or their state with distinction.

Mohinder was soon making progress, mainly as a bowler, and though his pace was of a friendly variety he was a shrewd mover of the ball, keeping it just outside the off-stump and getting wickets as the batsmen played rash strokes, underestimating his ability. It was, therefore, not much of a surprise to find his name in the Test 12 at Madras when the Australians came to India in 1969. He stood up courageously to the Australian fast bowlers and made his name by clean bowling Stackpole and Ian Chappell. That, however, was the last Test of the series. There was no way Mohinder could find a place in the team next year when the Indian team went to the West Indies because Tiger Pataudi was no longer the captain and he had been instrumental in picking Mohinder for the Madras Test.

After that successful tour of the West Indies, the Indian team was to go to England. For the last place in the team, Mohinder and Kirmani were selected, but only one was to go

470

depending upon whether Engineer was available for the tour matches other than Tests. Subsequently, Engineer's county, Lancashire C.C., decided that he could not be released for other matches and so Kirmani had to go as second wicketkeeper and Mohinder was out of the team. There was this unusual inclusion of three wicketkeepers in the team. At this stage, Mohinder developed the phlegmatic attitude that has remained with him all these years. Disappointed to miss the tour, he kept quiet and never tried to make an issue of it. He went on training and practising in his own way trying to prove the selectors wrong.

It was not until 1976 that Mohinder came back into the Indian team for the tour of New Zealand and Australia. On that tour he impressed everyone with his ability to take a few knocks on the body. He was not at all worried by the pace or spin. In fact, in the first Test against New Zealand, which India won, we were indebted to Madan Lal and Mohinder for their invaluable partnership which gave us a big lead and thus enabled Pras to strike his form and bowl us to victory. In the second Test at Christchurch in the cold and windy conditions, he and Madan Lal kept on bowling for hours and captured five wickets each. In the last Test at Wellington when New Zealand routed India, Mohinder stood bravely against the battery of their fast bowlers with a courageous batting display.

With his elder brother Surinder showing indifferent form, Mohinder was promoted to No. 3 in the series against the West Indies and he rose to the occasion magnificently. In one of the Tests when I was at the non-striker's end, I remember a ball from Holding, who was twice as quick in 1976 as he is today, rising awkwardly. Mohinder was caught unawares but he was unperturbed, and took the missile on his chest. He did not even try to rub the area where the ball had hit him. When I walked down the track to ask him if he was all right, he said with a

471

shy smile on his face that it was okay. He must have been in pain. That must have been his way of saying that it was indeed a painful blow. Then in the last Test he was the only player to offer some resistance, scoring a fine 58, with three sixes when Holding was at his ferocious best.

At the end of the series I was convinced that Mohinder, if he showed the same kind of application and a little more discretion in the choice of deliveries he picked up to hook and score runs off, would not only be more consistent but would also become a great player. But unfortunately, that wasn't to be, because immediately thereafter, that winter, New Zealand and England toured India. He did not score as many runs as were expected of him. That was the series when Tony Greig used his intimidating tactics and to handle that a lot of established players had to be dropped from the Indian side. Mohinder was no exception. He found himself out of the team to accommodate Madan Lal who then was the only genuine new-ball bowler in the side. With Chandra, Prasanna and Bedi in the team, the Indians could not afford the luxury of another seam bowler. The spinners used to come on the scene within a couple of overs as the ball started turning almost from the word go. The exercise of opening the bowling from the other end used to be entrusted to a batsman who had to turn his arm over for an over or two at the most.

However, Mohinder was the first to be selected when the side to tour Australia was announced in 1977-78. Here too, his liking for pace bowling was evident, for he handled Jeff Thomson at his best and fastest. His hooking was thrilling to watch and his running between wickets was a greater joy to see. We batted together on many occasions and he responded to my calls for singles. I am a great believer in taking singles because not only does it keep the score-board moving but it also keeps the strike rotating. As a result no bowler gets to bowl too many balls continuously at you.

Mohinder's courage again come to the fore in the second Test. He was batting with 80-odd runs when a ball from Sam Gannon smashed into his right temple as he went to hook it just before lunch. Mohinder was carried off the field and a big lump formed just above the eyebrow. It was hideous, black and blue, and really looked nasty but Mohinder just got it attended to during the forty minute lunch interval. And contrary to all advice, he went on to bat again, scored 90, before falling to another short ball. However, the century he missed came in the next innings when he played all bowlers with ease. At the end of the series he had established himself as No. 3 batsman for India. Cricket can be a very funny and at the same time a cruel game.

When the Indian team toured Pakistan in 1978, Mohinder, in spite of these excellent performances, found himself down the batting order with brother Surinder taking his No. 3 position. Mohinder batted lower down in the first two Tests. It was in the Lahore Test that Mohinder took another painful blow when he turned his eyes away from a short ball from Imran and was hit a sickening blow on the back of his head and fell down unconscious. We all feared for his life. His wife – they had got married only six months ago – was most upset at that. However, Jimmy came out of that crisis without any scars and was subjected to a bumper barrage as soon as he came on to bat. He fell to one such bumper while trying to hook and fell on his wicket. Soon a whispering campaign was started that he would always get out to short-pitched deliveries.

Surinder Amarnath was indisposed during the second innings of the last Test and Mohinder was promoted to No. 3. With Chetan Chauhan falling early and the new ball still fresh, it was expected that the Pakistani bowlers would see that no ball was pitched in his half of the wicket in view of what had happened previously in the series. Sarfraz and Imran threw more deliveries at him which were short-pitched and thought that Mohinder would back away and get out. But instead, Sarfraz and Imran saw Mohinder's courageous side who hooked and timed his strokes perfectly. However, his innings of 58 was the only knock of note in that series and there was intense pressure on him to be able to keep his place in the team. Therefore when he failed in the first innings of the Bombay Test against the West Indies, which followed on the heels of the Karachi Test, Mohinder had to go. Anshuman Gaekwad was picked to bat instead. Chetan Chauhan and I opened the innings. But when Chetan was injured, Gaekwad opened and Dilip Vengsarkar was promoted from No. 5 to No. 3 position. There was a thrilling partnership between Gaekwad and Vengsarkar and the latter thus clinched the No. 3 position for some time to come.

But players of Mohinder's class cannot be kept away for long and he came back in the last Test at Kanpur where everyone scored, as India amassed 644. Mohinder scored his second Test hundred and ensured his place in the team to England in 1979. It was here in England that he again got hit on the head and sustained a hairline crack which meant that now there was a big question mark against his ability to play the short ball. People forgot that he would hit most of them and it would only be the odd ball which caused injuries. But since injuries had come fairly frequently, it was, therefore, a tough decision for the selection committee to make. Mohinder produced a fitness certificate and because of his known ability, the selection committee was forced to include him for the last Test at Bombay against the Australians in 1979. It was anticipated then that he would be bounced at and that's what happened. Rodney Hogg bounced one and Mohinder in an attempt to play that ball slipped and fell on the wicket. He was batting in the old sola hat which the players used to wear in the 1930s and 1940s and this came in for much ridicule.

The sola hat is tough but not quite a helmet. Mohinder, who is such a professional cricketer in his attitude, did not wear a helmet for so long apparently because his father would not allow his sons to wear them. With this dismissal, which was unfortunate, Mohinder missed out and was not selected against the Pakistan team which came to India. It was in this series that Sandeep Patil made his mark and with Yashpal Sharma showing dogged qualities, the Indian middle-order looked settled with Vengsarkar at No. 3, Vishwanath at No. 4, Patil at No. 5 and Yashpal at No. 6 and with Kapil and Kirmani to follow. It was, therefore, a tough job for Jimmy to break into the side unless any of these players failed consistently.

Mohinder seemed resigned to his fate and knowing fully well that he had no chance of staging a comeback, accepted a contract to play in western Australia for the 1980-81 season. He went to Australia even before the Irani Trophy match, which is considered to be a selection trial. In fact, the team to tour Australia was to be selected on the basis of performances in this match. He did not take his chance and play in this match, otherwise he would have been considered for selection.

In the 1981-82 season, Indian cricket saw another young player come up in Ashok Malhotra. He was an added asset to the players mentioned earlier who have been consistent in our middle-order batting. It was when Sandeep Patil failed in four consecutive Tests that Malhotra took his place and did a good job in the first Test innings he played. He was considered to be a promising cricketer. Consequently, it was difficult for

Mohinder to stage a comeback for two consecutive seasons. However, his name did come up for selection when the team was being picked to go to England in 1982, mainly because of his phenomenal innings of 170-plus in that incredible final of the Ranji Trophy when Delhi scored over 700 runs to beat Karnataka which had already totalled 700.

The selection committee, however, decided to bring back Patil. Mohinder was considered mainly as a batsman and with Patil, Malhotra, Vishwanath, Yashpal and Vengsarkar in the team, forming a solid middle-order batting, Mohinder lost out to these players. It was a pity that people made a big noise about his omission. They forgot that Mohinder was now coming into consideration only as a batsman and he had to miss out because of the superior performances of the others.

Undaunted, Mohinder came back at the beginning of the 1982-83, season, scoring a hundred and a double hundred. He was selected to go to Pakistan and the axe now fell on Malhotra. What happened later is now history and we all know what a magnificent comeback he has made in Test cricket. People say that the use of helmet has changed his fortunes and helped him. They also believe that his two-eyed stance has also helped him. I would not like to argue with them. All I would like to say is that Mohinder had the courage, ability and the vital element in cricket that every successful cricketer needs, i.e. luck which was with him. He grabbed this opportunity with both hands and not only has he consolidated his position in the Indian side but has become, in my opinion, for whatever it's worth, the best batsman in the world. Nobody plays fast bowling better than him. Nobody plays fast bowling with such an assurance and this is all the more praiseworthy because Indians do not get to play fast bowling in their own country.

Off the field, Mohinder, called Jimmy, is always smiling and likes to joke about others and himself too. He is basically a quiet type and does not venture to express his opinion, unless he is asked. He is non-interfering and in recent instances has shown that if there is a controversy, he can take care of it by dismissing it very maturely. He has done himself ample justice even though he is only thirty-three. He is a fitness fanatic and a very dedicated cricketer. There are yet plenty of years ahead of Mohinder and with two series in India this winter, Mohinder, I am sure, will utilise these Tests to consolidate his position.

His best years which are ahead of him, will be savoured by Indian cricket followers, because India is playing mainly at home and thus it will be the Indian cricket crowd which will have the opportunity of seeing Mohinder at his very best.

22

Padmakar Shivalkar

ONE OF MY FAVOURITE CRICKETERS HAS BEEN PADMAKAR SHIVALKAR. Paddy, as he is affectionately called by fellow cricketers and cricket-lovers, has played cricket with nothing but complete enjoyment. And perhaps the only sad thing is that he has not been picked to play for India in an official Test. I always admire this man's uncomplicated approach to life, just as his approach to the wicket was simple and rhythmic.

It is an irony of fate that players like Shivalkar and Goel were born at the same time as Bishen Bedi, and so were deprived of playing for India in Tests. Any other country would have gladly picked them and included them in teams.

Paddy's misfortune was that when he came on the scene, Bapu Nadkarni was already an established left-arm spinner for Bombay. Nadkarni used to get plenty of wickets in addition to

478

a number of centuries which he got with monotonous regularity in local as well as Ranji Trophy cricket. And when Bapu Nadkarni was about to bow out, in came Eknath Solkar and with his extraordinary fielding and ability to bowl seamers as well, blocked Shivalkar's entry to big cricket for some more time. Shivalkar hence, had to wait very long before he got picked for Bombay.

He had gone to Australia with the Cricket Club of India team in 1962 and impressed everybody not only with his batting figures but also with a bagful of wickets. On those hard Australian wickets, he bowled brilliantly, teasing the batsmen with his flight and forcing them to play shots which normally they would not have played.

It was finally in the 1967-68 season that Shivalkar was selected to play for Bombay in the Ranji Trophy Championship matches. I was then in the reserves for the Bombay team. I recall the excitement with which he came on the eve of the match to our room and talked about how he just needed a little luck now that he had his break so that he could become a permanent fixture in the Bombay team. It took him a couple of seasons to do this but since then he has hardly looked back. Only in the last couple of seasons has the selection committee decided to do away with his services and bring in some young aspirants.

Padmakar Shivalkar's has been a truly, tremendous success story. He started off like everybody else in those days at Shivaji Park Gymkhana. In the early sixties this gymkhana produced cricketers of the highest quality, much the same way as Dadar Union used to do in the late sixties and seventies.

Shivalkar started his career there and attracted the attention of the cricket-lovers in the city. Followers of cricket in Bombay are most discerning and because a lot of cricket is played there, it becomes easy for them to spot talent. Shivalkar's name started buzzing around the Bombay club circuit, and he soon became the highest wicket-taker in a Ranji Trophy season. Like all bowlers, he was very proud of his batting ability and he saved Bombay on a couple of occasions by staying there stubbornly till the regular batsman had got the winning run. In those days only one team used to qualify for the knock-out rounds from West Zone. The matches used to be very close in the league stage and on a number of occasions, Shivalkar came to Bombay's rescue with his batting ability. There used to be, invariably, a mix-up when he and Abdul Ismail were batting. There were occasions when both batsmen were at the same end and one was run out. These mix-ups were a great source of all-round hilarity in the dressing rooms and we all used to enjoy them greatly.

In the dressing room, Paddy was, to begin with, very quiet. But then, as he became an established member of the Bombay team, he opened up, and showed that he too had a dry, naughty sense of humour. In fact, he was the player who was very helpful in the thick of tension. His remarks would help ease tension all around. One does need players of this character in moments like this.

Paddy was very good as a thinker on the field. He would spot the batsman's weaknesses right away and start attacking him accordingly. On a turner, he was absolutely unplayable and even now, when he is in his forties, it is impossible to score runs off him on a turning track. Today, the old nip, of course, is not there as before but it is very difficult to take any liberties with him. This goes on to show how bowling has become such a practised exercise for him. This perhaps gives one the impression that his heart is not in his bowling, but so much has his body been used to running up and bowling that dainty three-step run-up that you cannot score too many runs off him even if you want to.

Today he is a very accomplished singer. A few years ago, he approached me to cut a disc with him. I was very happy to do so. He sang his version of the disc in a very professional and lilting manner and a particular song composed by Shantaram Nandgaonkar is about how one misses an opportunity if luck is not on one's side. Paddy put his heart and soul in rendering that song. It was almost the story of his cricket career: how he came so close to getting an India cap but did not. It was indeed a very touching song. Now he sings in a lot of programmes and shows. He is very popular because he sings without any fuss and has good control over his voice.

Shivalkar's behaviour on stage has been impeccable, just like his behaviour on and off the cricket field. He has carved out a niche for himself as a popular singer. He is totally engrossed in his singing and spends a lot of time practising. When he is running in to bowl, one gets the impression that he is humming a tune under his breath. Most certainly he does that while fielding on the boundary fence and one knows that he is practising for the evening's show.

A simple and a modest man, he likes to wear sports clothes, particularly when he is not playing cricket. He has always given his best for his team, and this too knowing fully well that he is not going to get an India cap. It speaks volumes for the man's contribution to the game. He was one man who always wore a smile. Keep on smiling, Paddy. There are very few cricketers like you in the world. Your contribution to the game has been just as immense as all the top Test players.

23

Rajinder Goel

THERE ARE TWO CRICKETERS WHO WERE DESPERATELY unlucky not to have played for India. They are Rajinder Goel and Padmakar Shivalkar, both left-arm spinners of the highest order. But because of the presence of Bishen Singh Bedi, these two have not been able to play in Tests. Before Bishen came on the scene, they had to contend with Bapu Nadkarni and Rusi Surti who were more all-rounders than specialists and, of course, that genius of all-rounders, Salim Durrani. So Goel and Shivalkar could not make the Indian Test team.

Once Bishen came on the scene, he was certainly miles ahead of them as far as bowling was concerned because of his variation and he could not be displaced at all. But given the choice of facing Bedi and Goel at their peak, I would prefer to play Bishen because with his flight, Bishen gave you a bit of a chance of coming down the track and converting those deliveries into drivable balls, while Goel, with a flatter trajectory, was almost impossible to hit. Not that he could not flight the ball, but the flighting was minimal and because he could obtain turn on any track, the flighting was just not necessary.

Rajinder Goel has got over five hundred wickets in the Ranji Trophy, not to mention the wickets he has captured in the Duleep and Irani Trophy matches. This is a record in the Ranji Trophy and looks as if it will remain so for quite some time. There are not too many people with 400-plus wickets in the Ranji Trophy playing today. The only person in this category is Venkataraghavan and he will also take some time before he can catch up with Rajinder Goel. Meanwhile, Goel plans to play for another year and thereby complete over twenty-five years of playing in the Ranji Trophy, which will be another record for him.

I do not know if any other player has had such a record in the Ranji Trophy though there are some careers which have been flourishing for quite some time. Notable among them being Ashok Mankad's which started in 1962 and is still there on the scene after twenty years, although he missed out one season because of differences with the Bombay Cricket Association selection committee. Rajinder's stamina is unbelievable for a man who is over forty and once given the ball he can bowl right till the end of the day's play without seeming to lose any of the nip that he possesses. It is true that his turn today is not as sharp as it used to be a few years ago, nor is the nip off which he claimed many of his victims, bowled or leg before as quick. The accuracy is still there as is the willingness to bowl long spells.

Kapil Dev's advent on the Haryana scene has certainly taken the load off Goel's shoulders and now he does not have to work as hard as he had to before. He is a simple man and a totally unassuming character; a person who is an ideal to follow on account of his behaviour on and off the field.

He is an absolute professional who takes pride in his craft and is forever trying to think the batsman out. His batting is strictly No. 11 stuff though he has got a few runs by throwing his bat about, his best shot being the sweep shot which he plays even against the quicker bowlers. But it is really a pity that somebody like him never got a chance to represent the country and one fails to understand why, when we picked two right hand off-spinners in the side, he was not picked. In partnership with Bedi he could have worked wonders where victories were missed by just a few wickets, or by a few runs.

When he was unexpectedly picked for the Test team in 1974, because Bishen was disciplined, he was a surprised man and he had to buy a new pair of boots, a new bat and the entire kit to make it to the Test. It is a pity that he was dropped then and two off-spinners were picked, but against the mighty West Indians, there was no place for anybody to make a Test debut. I have a feeling that the selection committee was not prepared to play him because if he had taken a few wickets, Bishen's return to the team would have been delayed for some more time and it would have been quite embarrassing for the selectors.

He had been on the fringe of Test cricket for a long time and played in the unofficial Test against Sri Lanka. He did very well but he was considered not good enough to be picked on a tour with the Indian team, which would have meant that he would have at least worn Indian colours, although he would not have technically won the Indian cap as he had not played in a Test match. But the man still went on playing Ranji Trophy cricket, and did it with pride, knowing fully well that he had no hopes of playing for India. He did his job faithfully as only he knows how to. I wish there were more cricketers like Rajinder Goel in this country. I also wish there were younger cricketers who followed his example and kept on serving their state associations for a longer time even if somehow owing to bad luck, they could not play for their country.

When we played North Zone in the Duleep Trophy, it was him we were more afraid of than Bishen Bedi because he was the one who pegged us down. It was Goel who would take the wickets on a turning track and it was him who was the most likely to run through the side. He has done that on a few occasions and caused enough problems, chipping in to take a lot of wickets, just the vital ones, and then waiting, withdrawn from the attack, till called again and again delivered the goods.

He is the one bowler whom I have really dreaded facing in my life, because I have never been able to feel comfortable against his left-hand spinners. Goel has been the one who, because of his flatter trajectory, has not given me the opportunity to step down the track and drive. Our bowlers, who bowl with a flatter trajectory, often commit the mistake of either bowling short or overpitched and so can be driven, cut and pulled, but Goel has done that very seldom in his career and that too perhaps when he had started bowling his twenty-fifth or twenty-sixth over. All the overs before that were deadly accurate. We were lucky to scratch a single or two off those and lucky if we survived.

He was quite a good fidder too. He took most of the catches that came his way and even now he throws without any trouble. His throw is perhaps not as powerful as it used to be, but it is as accurate as his bowling has been and that is very important.

He is a simple and modest man, almost self-effacing about his tremendous achievements in the Ranji Trophy. He is a person who is a pleasure to talk to and, as I said before, an ideal for the younger cricketers to follow. Although he is not a Test cricketer, to me he is one of the greatest I have played against and it has indeed been a privilege.

24

Richard Hadlee

NO OTHER CRICKETER HAS STIRRED THE IMAGINATION OF THE
SPORTS-loving public of New Zealand in recent years more than
Richard Hadlee. New Zealand has produced its great players
over the years and Bert Sutcliffe, John Reid, Glenn Turner are
names that come easily to one's mind. But Richard Hadlee
towers above them all.

In sheer performance, charisma and crowd-pulling ability
there is no one who has done as much for New Zealand as
Richard Hadlee. I remember my former office colleague and
friend, Tony Fernandes, who had gone to Tasmania to play a
season of club cricket, coming back and raving about Richard
Hadlee. At that stage the New Zealand team had gone to
Australia to play a three-Test series. The year was 1973 and
Richard Hadlee, though not very successful, impressed Tony

Fernandes who came back and said: "Here is a bowler whom much will be heard of."

Tony hasn't been proved wrong and Richard Hadlee has simply improved with time. Now after almost ten years in Test cricket, Richard can claim to be one of the finest new-ball bowlers that have played a Test match.

Unfortunately, Richard's batting ability has not been given the kind of importance that one would have liked and because, perhaps, of his inconsistency with the bat he's not being talked about as an all-rounder in the same breath as Ian Botham, Kapil Dev and Imran Khan.

He's got a beautiful run-up; he generates genuine pace and has one of the best outswingers in the business. Having played county cricket he has added the inswinger to his repertoire and he is certainly a most difficult and awkward customer on a green and lively wicket.

His run-up starts off in a somewhat odd fashion because his body seems to move forward and he leans out and then instead of taking off his right foot comes back as though he's going into reverse. Then suddenly he starts off again with that run-up of his accelerating into a beautiful action and a fine side on delivery, as classical as one would hope to see.

He is an intensely competitive player as the Australians have found out and it is no wonder, as they are very competitive players themselves and would like to battle with someone like Richard Hadlee. The Australian crowds also find him a customer that they cannot ignore.

Richard Hadlee was almost a one-man unit for the New Zealand team for the last few years, until Geoff Howarth came on to the scene and established himself with his quiet firmness and dignity and took over the New Zealand captaincy. With Geoff doing such a good job of leading New Zealand,

Richard found the pressure taken off him to a great extent and one found Richard's performances improving by leaps and bounds. Till then, because Richard was the only world-class player in the New Zealand side, the pressure was so much on him that one got the impression that he tried too hard. Because he is such an outstanding fast bowler, although he got wickets, when it came to batting he wasn't able to contribute as much as New Zealand would have liked him to or he himself would have liked to, as the bowling had taken a heavy toll on his energies.

But with Geoff Howarth coming on to the scene and scoring runs fluently for New Zealand, this pressure seemed to have gone and New Zealand became a better side. With Geoff there to score his runs, Richard bowling his heart out and New Zealand fielding being top class as always, it became a side which, though without too many outstanding or world class players, always fought for every run in the field. So even if the New Zealand team did not score too many runs, its fielding gave the impression that there were many more runs at hand than the ones on the board. You really had to get through the cordon - people used to dive about, throw themselves at the ball and generally be very stingy about giving away runs.

When the Indian side arrived in New Zealand in 1976, Richard Collinger and D.R. Hadlee were the main bowlers for them. Richard Hadlee was in the New Zealand fourteen but not in the playing eleven. In the second Test at Christchurch he was picked to play for the side and though he did not get too many wickets he bowled at a good speed and gave enough trouble to the Indian batsmen.

At this stage India was one up in the series and the last Test was to be played at Wellington, normally a very windy place - probably the most windy place in my cricket-playing memory

489

- where, with a green wicket, the ball would certainly help the seamers. What was predicted before the match was that Richard Hadlee would be made the twelfth man. But the New Zealand selectors decided to pick him in the eleven. He became an instant hero by capturing four wickets in the first innings and followed it up with seven in the second to destroy India and level the series for New Zealand.

That was the beginning of Richard's exploits and thereafter, barring injury, he has been a permanent fixture in the New Zealand team.

The following year when the Australians were in New Zealand, Richard Hadlee captured the imagination of the crowd. First, he smote the great Dennis Lillee back over his head for a six. He played a very defiant innings that had the crowd on their feet. When he went in to bowl, the crowd started chanting "Hadlee, Hadlee" as they used to shout "Lillee, Lillee" when Lillee used to bowl in Melbourne. That was the first time that the New Zealand crowd got so involved in a cricket match and in backing their own particular player. The Australians and the New Zealanders, being neighbours, have always had an extra bit of competitiveness in their matches. The New Zealanders feel that they have not been treated in quite the manner that they deserve by the Australians, and the Australians have always treated the New Zealanders as kid brothers and beginners in Test cricket. And, therefore, they have not always sent the best possible team to New Zealand.

All that, of course, has changed now and the full Australian side goes to New Zealand to play in its games. Richard Hadlee was perhaps one of the persons responsible for bringing about this change. He proved with his performance that there was a backbone to the New Zealand side and the Australians could ill afford to send a second team to new Zealand.

Since the time the Auckland crowd got up and gave him the kind of support he wanted, Richard Hadlee has become the darling of the New Zealand cricket-loving public. Ever since then, Richard, whenever he comes on to bowl, at all the possible New Zealand centres, evokes this chant of "Hadlee, Hadlee" and it is quite unnerving for the batsman who is facing the ball. But perhaps not as upsetting as the Calcutta crowds' chant of "B-o-w-l-e-d" everytime Chandra used to come in to bowl. That was something else altogether and that perhaps will never be matched because of the sheer numbers of the Calcutta crowd.

Richard, after that performance, was one who was eagerly watched. In the series when the New Zealand team came down to India after the Indian team had been there earlier in the year, he and Glenn Turner, who was captaining the side, were the two persons who were most eagerly awaited. Neither of them did disappoint, because Glenn with his impeccable technique and Richard with his aggressive attitude captured the attention of all the people who had come to watch the New Zealand series.

India won the series 2-0 rather easily and it was mainly due to first class bowling by our spinners – Bishen, Chandra, Venkat and Prasanna. Our batting also stood up to the test quite impressively which made the task of the New Zealand cricketers a little more difficult.

Richard bowled excellently in the first Test as well as in the second, though not with much luck. He had quite a few chances "grassed" and he beat the bat very often without getting the edge. At this stage of his career the inswinger was not a very important part of his bowling armoury and in fact he rarely bowled the inswinger; he just concentrated on the outswinger and the ball that went straight through.

He also had surprisingly, a good bouncer which came up of a short length and one had to play it. Either you played it in front of your face or you tried to hook it. Mohinder Amarnath got a fair share of Richard's bouncers and although he scored quite a few runs off them he was never able to hook them as well as he hooked other bowlers.

In the third Test there was a bit of an ugly incident. Richard got upset with the umpire's decision not to give Anshuman Gaekwad out hit-wicket, when all the New Zealand fielders thought that Anshuman had hit the wicket. Anshuman himself believed that he did not touch the wicket at all. However, with the bails having fallen, the New Zealanders were a very upset lot and there were ugly scenes around. Richard, for once, could not control himself and he flung the bail at the umpire, hitting him in the stomach. He also said a few things which made the air around a little tense.

But then that is competition and at that stage the frustration of the New Zealand players was reaching its saturation point, having gone through a tough tour. This is one of the reasons why they could not stomach a decision which did not go in their favour.

However, Richard was not to be on the field for a long time after that because the heat got to him and he suddenly collapsed while he was fielding on the deep fine leg fence. Madras, at most times, can be pretty hot and stuffy, and Richard had just bowled a spell of two or three overs. He suddenly found the heat too much and had to be carried off the field not playing any further on that day.

The New Zealanders lost that series fairly easily by a margin of 2-0. But the performances of Glenn Turner and Richard Hadlee were memorable ones in that series. By the time the Indian side played Richard Hadlee again in 1979 in the World Cup he had already become a famous name. He had played for Nottingham in the county championships with distinction and along with Clive Rice he had formed one of the most dangerous new ball attacks in county cricket.

The experience of having played county cricket added a lot more guile to his bowling. He now just did not come in and bowl as fast as possible but kept himself in reserve and only rarely did you see him bowl a genuinely quick delivery. He concentrated more on using the new ball well, swinging it both ways, testing the batsman outside the off-stump and also coming in with a surprise bouncer. These are the varieties he added to his bowling after he had played county cricket.

In 1979 he bowled very well in the World Cup match at Headingley. The wicket was ideal for him, just slightly green, and with enough bounce in it for him to exploit. He never gave us much of a chance and although we mustered up a fair total he saw to it that we did not put up an imposing total.

Later, just before we played the last match at the Oval, the penultimate match of the tour was against Nottinghamshire and Richard, along with Clive Rice, bowled on a real green top and defeated our team. It was only the second defeat for our team in the county games. The first was the unexpected one at Gloucester where Mike Procter had run through us.

The Holts Trophy and the prize money would have run into quite a few thousand pounds for Gloucestershire but Nottingham prepared a real green wicket and saw to it that they too got a part of the share by defeating our team.

It was in this game that Hadlee hit Mohinder Amarnath on the head with a bouncer and caused a crack in the skull which, though not very serious physically, was not very good for Mohinder as far as his confidence was concerned. Hadlee's bowling in that game was an abject lesson on how to keep the ball up and never give the batsman any rest. At the other end Clive Rice was faster but certainly did not look as dangerous, because Richard was the one who was making the ball move around and do all kinds of things off the wicket.

The 1980-81 season in Australia, in which India shared a tour with New Zealand, found Richard Hadlee one of the main attractions of the tour. He did not belie that expectation, by constantly playing aggressively with the bat and bowling with real speed at the Australians. His clashes with the crowds became fairly notorious, and the crowds used to love to bait him when he came on to field at the fence between his overs. The Australian crowd being what it is and their attitude towards New Zealanders being well known, it was but natural that one day Richard would lose his cool and do something drastic. That's what he did in one of the finals of the Benson and Hedges matches when he picked up a spectator and threw him over the fence as the spectator had come across and stopped him from fielding a ball which was just going to the boundary. That was Richard Hadlee's competitiveness. He apologised the next day, although he made it very clear that he wasn't too happy with the the Australian crowd.

We went to New Zealand immediately after that tour of Australia. In the three Test matches, we lost 1-0. In the first Test, Richard bowled New Zealand to victory when we had to chase a total of 250 runs on a wicket which wasn't looking as lively as it did on the first day. I had put New Zealand in after winning the toss because the wicket looked very green and lively and I thought that with Binny, Yograj and Kapil Dev on our side it was better to put the other side in and see what Kapil could do.

Kapil and Yograj got quite a genuine amount of pace out of the wicket but unfortunately for us they seldom found the target and that allowed New Zealand to settle down and post quite a good score. Surprisingly, when the Indians batted, it was not Richard who got most of the wickets but Lance Cairns, who destroyed our batting with his medium paced swing. Richard, perhaps like Kapil Dev, had tried a bit too hard on that wicket and although he beat the batsmen, he wasn't able to get the wickets.

In the second innings our bowlers found the ideal length and we dismissed New Zealand for just over a hundred which left us with 250 runs to win. We thought our chances were fairly good if we got off to a good start but that wasn't to be, because Richard got Chetan Chauhan, who had been batting consistently well, cheaply and then ran through the side with four important wickets that really set us back in that game.

After that in the Christchurch Test, as well as in the Test at Auckland, Richard did not have much to do because the wickets did not enable him to do much. The Christchurch Test was, unfortunately, ruined by rain for the major part and in the Auckland Test the ball was turning a fair bit.

Yet, simply by that second innings in the first Test when he got four wickets he had seen to it that New Zealand had ended up on the winning side again, just as his own performance had seen New Zealand beat the West Indies for the first time in New Zealand the previous year.

He cracked a hundred and also got wickets in every Test though it was a tour that was marred by the West Indians' displeasure at the umpiring decisions of New Zealand's umpires. However, one cannot take away the credit from the admirable qualities shown by the New Zealand team in playing together so much as a team that even the mighty West Indians could not get away from the pressure tactics and competitiveness shown by them.

This facet of intense competitiveness shown by the New Zealand team is owing solely to Richard Hadlee. Geoff Howarth, although competitive, is a fairly mild person, compared to

Richard who, being a quick bowler and having the temperament of a quick bowler, brings out the competitive element in the rest of the team. And that makes it an altogether formidable combination.

However, off the field Richard is a very warm and friendly person who is always willing to have a chat and a drink. He has come to India and played a couple of benefit matches as well. He has always been popular with the Indians because of his warm, outgoing nature off the field.

There's one story of how a collector of photographs and albums from newspaper clippings over many years - a person called Shashikant Zarapkar - went across to Richard during the benefit match played for G.S. Ramchand and inquired timidly whether he was Fred Titmus. That was the only time when Richard was found stumped for an answer and also his sense of humour at that stage failed him because he turned around and asked if he was looking as old as Fred Titmus. However, that was only a passing reaction and Richard quickly saw the funny side of it. He was very happy to go through the album and sign some of the pictures which Shashikant Zarapkar so religiously collects.

Hadlee's wife also plays cricket. She represents New Zealand in women's cricket. Richard's father also played for New Zealand and was chairman of the New Zealand Cricket Council after he retired from competitive cricket. His brother Dayle played for New Zealand and his other brother, Barry, was in the 1979 World Cup side, though he did not play an official Test for New Zealand. So it must be quite a family, as it has produced so many sportsmen of international calibre.

Richard always travels with a medicare bag which takes care of his minor injuries. There was a season, 1980, when he was plagued by far too many injuries and hardly played in the county championship. That almost made him want to give it up. He added that he wouldn't be coming back to play for Nottinghamshire. But the supporters of the Nottinghamshire County Cricket Club prevailed upon him to change his mind. They went back to tell him that even if he was absent for the major part of the matches it did not really matter. That was a tremendous compliment, because for an overseas player to prove as prized as Richard is, I think, a tremendous tribute.

Richard did not disappoint Nottinghamshire because when he came back in 1981, he was bowling over a slightly shorter run-up and along with Clive Rice destroyed most of the county attacks. Nottinghamshire won the county championship for the first time in many, many years. Richard's contribution to that was immense with the ball and the bat as his competitiveness must have rubbed off on his colleagues at Nottingham as well.

Richard and Glenn Turner are the only two professionals in the true sense of the term that New Zealand has produced. Glenn has had many a row with the New Zealand Cricket Council and therefore has not been playing Test cricket, but Richard has somehow managed to get everything together and is still available for New Zealand.

I sincerely hope for New Zealand cricket and for the cricket-loving public in the world that Richard Hadlee continues to play for many, many years, although I hope that every time I play against him he gives me a half-volley first ball so that I can get off the mark!

25

Rodney Marsh

RODNEY MARSH TODAY HAS THE HIGHEST NUMBER OF VICTIMS behind the stumps, and he is considered to be the best wicketkeer in the world. And to think that when he started playing for Australia, he was nicknamed "Iron Gloves" by the critics in Australia and England! I am not too sure if the same critics have retracted their words, which is seldom done. They jumped to the conclusion after seeing him in action in just one Test. The first Test for any cricketer is bound to make him nervous and tense and that's what happened to Marsh. He might have dropped a couple of catches, his gathering might not have been the cleanest, his collection of throws might not have pleased the purists, but there was no denying the fact that he had the determination and competitiveness to do well and in this respect he was a typical Australian.

His critics thought otherwise. Perhaps this opinion was based on a comparison with his predecessor, Brian Taber, and it was thought that he was not good enough to replace Taber. But Brian Taber has recently said that Marsh is one of the best wicketkeepers that he has ever seen which should silence any critic.

If that is not enough, his record speaks for itself and though there are people who would always run down statistics and statisticians, it has to be admitted that over a period of time, it's only statistics that gives one an indication of a player's class. Over a short period, it might not be possible to judge a player's class but over a long period, it is statistics that tell you how good or bad the player was, as despite the "class" tag, players are unable to produce it in the Tests. Rodney Marsh does not fall in this category and his performance has been superbly consistent right through.

When he first played for Australia in 1970, he was a roly-poly cricketer, overweight, and came in for criticism for that as well. In the following year, having played in six Test matches against England, he made up his mind to lose weight and this he did by hard training and sensible intake of food.

Rodney has not been lucky to keep wickets to top-class spin bowling. It would have been a great sight to see him keep to the bowlers of the calibre of Bedi, Pras and Chandra. mainly, to the unpredictable Chandra, because he himself at times did not know what he was going to bowl.

People in India have been rather unfortunate to miss Rodney Marsh in action just as they have missed Greg Chappell, Dennis Lillee and Jeff Thomson. With the sort of programme chalked out between the two Boards, it is extremely unlikely that these players would be seen in action in a Test match in India. All of them are well past their prime, they are now above thirty, and the Australians are known for their reluctance to continue in the game beyond that limit. Indian spectators should keep their fingers crossed. If these players are not able to play in India in a Test match, they should hopefully be able to come down for an odd benefit match and share their talents with the Indian cricket fans.

Rodney Marsh has a batting ability to add to his excellent wicket-keeping. And that must have tilted the scales in his favour when he first came on the Test scene. He did not let the Australian selection committee down on either count. In the second Test match on his home ground, which was the first ever Test in Perth, Marsh scored 92 not out and Bill Lawry came in for heavy criticism for having declared the Australian innings when Marsh was only 8 runs short of his Test century. Lawry has always been an uncompromising skipper. He always put his team's interest first before individual glory and therefore, when the team needed a declaration, he applied the closure. It was the same Test in which Greg Chappell made his memorable debut with a Test century.

Marsh has not looked back since and has been a regular member of the Australian team. In fact, his has been the first name to be ticked when the Australian team is selected in recent years. The only time he missed playing in the Tests was when he opted to play for the WSC. His tally of catching victims would have been even greater because he missed out on a number of matches during that three-year period. Certainly the Australians missed him more than anybody else. It is an acknowledged fact, and Dennis Lillee agrees, that many of his victims were claimed only because of Marsh's tips to him as to how to bowl to a particular batsman. Lillee had publicly acknowledged this fact by rushing down the wicket, after taking a wicket, to congratulate Marsh.

Besides Ian Chappell, Rodney Marsh has been one of the shrewdest cricketing brains in Australian cricket. Standing next to Ian Chappell who was in first slip, Marsh learnt many a trick from him, not only of cricketing but of sportsmanship too. However, this aspect of Marsh was evident when Ian Chappell was around. Now, after Ian's retirement, it has disappeared completely. Captains do influence their colleagues as far as behaviour on the field is concerned. With Ian Chappell it was always a no-holds-barred contest between his team and the other teams and he would go to any length to ensure a victory. The Australian team in those days was, therefore, labelled "Ugly Australians". But Rodney Marsh is far, far removed from this tag and his image has been of the friendliest kind.

When we first saw him in 1971 during the Rest of the World series in Australia, Marsh was still a corpulent cricketer. He has since lost a lot of weight. Already in 1971 he was at least thirty pounds lighter than what he was in 1970. He continued with his weight loss and is now one of the fittest players.

It is quite a sight to see him in the dressing room in shorts or with a towel around his waist. He has got thick muscular legs, almost like tree trunks. An Australian colleague of his said that his legs should have been on his arms and his arms on his legs as he would then have been a better and prettier sight. But the fact remains that Marsh has very strong legs and it is only in recent years that his knee has started giving him problems. If he had been the same weight as in 1970, you can imagine how he would have carried himself for all these thirteen years.

I will not forget the way he bumped into me one night during that Rest of the World series. A fire had started in a building near where we had gone partying. Tony Greig and I went down the street to see the fire. The heat generated by the fire was

501

intense and we were continuously pushed away by the firemen and police personnel. Suddenly, we saw Rodney Marsh walking in and staring at the fire with a lost expression on his face. We wondered whether he was staying in that building. Thankfully it was not so and the three of us went down to a cafe for a bite. That's where he told us that he was walking down the streets a bit nervously because he was expecting to be a father and his wife was in the advance stages of pregnancy. It was truly an unforgettable sight. In the restaurant, one could hardly believe the way Marsh and Greig talked. Both were at loggerheads on the field in the previous two games. Such is the spirit of cricketers that all the harsh words are exchanged on the field are easily forgotten and many friendships are made which last lifelong.

After that World Series, we again met after nearly ten years in 1980. We played Australia in 1977-78 and again in 1979 but then Marsh was with the WSC. He could not come to India with Kim Hughes' team in 1979 because of the Packer connection. I found him to be a very amiable person, and not the hard competitive cricketer that he had been made out to be by the press.

Sure enough, he was tough on the field and no one expected him to be otherwise. What was refreshing was the way he would come down at the end of the day's play and have a word with us, not necessarily on cricket, but on any topic. He had a keen interest in India. He added he regretted not being able to play in India and also hoping that he would be able to do so. This desire of his does not seem likely to be fulfilled now.

The wicketkeepers of all teams make a beeline for him to know about his experiences and take valuable tips on improving their own technique. They are also prepared to take a tip from him to improve their batting. Marsh has always obliged. He has the ability to spot the weaknesses of others and pass on this information to their captains. He advises the captains as to what type of field should be set for a particular batsman. From behind the wickets, he constantly encourages the bowlers when they are getting a thrashing. This way he ensures that the bowlers' spirits do not drop. Marsh has hence, contributed a great deal to Australian cricket.

It is a pity that he was never given a chance to lead Australia. I am sure that he would have done a marvellous job if he was given that opportunity. Perhaps, it is Australia's loss and the opponents' gain. But Rodney Marsh would not let such things affect him, although there was a period in late 1979-80 when there was a bit of resentment when Kim Hughes was asked to lead the side in preference to Marsh. There was also a bit of ill feeling in Western Australia when Hughes was appointed skipper after Marsh had successfully led western Australia in the Sheffield Shield competition in the previous year. However, the true sportsman that he is, he did not show any resentment, but carried on, as best as he could, doing his job, which was wicketkeeping. Not for a moment did he show any resentment that he was deprived of the captaincy. Whenever Hughes asked for his guidance on the field, he gave him all he could in the interest of his side. He is a perfect team man and therefore he is held in high esteem throughout Australia.

With Ian and Greg Chappell and Dennis Lillee, Marsh has dominated Australian and world cricket over the last decade. Along with the three, he has been talked about as the most controversial cricketer in Australia though he has not involved himself in as many controversies as the others. He has had his fair share of them but now he seems to have mellowed with age. Therefore he is less troublesome to the administrators and officials.

He is very good at golf as well. His brother, Graham Marsh, has earned quite a reputation for himself as a professional golfer.

Idols

At one time it was debatable whether Rodney Marsh would take up golf or cricket. There was apparently some sort of understanding between the brothers and one of them opted for golf and is doing fairly well at it. Similarly, Marsh has done remarkably well in his chosen profession. Rodney Marsh is an epitome of a hard-working cricketer who has risen above criticism and his own performances. He is a fine example for budding cricketers, and particularly budding wicketkeepers, to follow.

26

Rohan Kanhai

ROHAN KANHAI IS QUITE SIMPLY THE GREATEST BATSMAN I HAVE EVER seen. What does one write about one's hero, one's idol, one for whom there is so much admiration?

To say that he is the greatest batsman I have ever seen so far is to put it mildly. A controversial statement perhaps, considering that there have been so many outstanding batsmen, and some great batsmen that I have played with and against. But, having seen them all, there is no doubt in my mind that Rohan Kanhai was quite simply the best of them all.

Sir Gary Sobers came quite close to being the best batsman, but he was the greatest cricketer ever, and he could do just about anything. But as a batsman I thought Rohan Kanhai was just a little bit better.

My first impression of Rohan Kanhai, my first view, was in

505

the game in 1958 when the CCI played against the touring West Indians. I don't really remember much about that game but in the Test that followed I remember quite clearly how brilliantly Rohan Kanhai batted and made our bowling look very easy. He drove, he pulled and he cut with time to spare and he looked a shade above everybody else. Between periods of studious defence he would come out with an explosive shot which went like a rocket to the boundary. When Manohar Hardikar bowling his first over in Test cricket got him out leg before most of the stadium erupted in joy. But I was disappointed because Rohan had missed his hundred. Perhaps it was at that time but unpatriotic, my idol had failed to score a hundred which indeed was very disappointing.

He made up for it in the latter part of the series with 256 at Calcutta which is still talked about and a series of other knocks which proved what a great player he was.

The other memorable part about that 1958 Test, which incidentally was the first Test match I ever saw, was Rohan's fielding. His anticipation, his sprinting to the boundary to chase the ball, stopping it a few yards inside and then hurling it back parallel to the ground and into the wicketkeeper's gloves were thrilling. I stood up in my seat every time he did that to get a better view from the North Stand.

The next time that Rohan Kanhai came to India was in 1966 with the West Indian side which was then captained by Gary Sobers. Bombay didn't see him at his best. That was the first match which I saw from the pavilion, though, according to the Cricket Club of India rules, I was not really entitled to sit there because I was under eighteen. I thus got a closer look at my hero. There was also M.L. Jaisimha who was my other hero. Here I was seeing both of them in the flesh, so to speak, from such close quarters and went home feeling thrilled.

Jaisimha, though he appeared nervous - and who wouldn't having to face Wesley Hall and Charlie Griffith - still managed to smile a lot and convey the impression that he was thoroughly enjoying himself.

Rohan Kanhai, on the other hand, seemed very temperamental. He would sit in his corner of the players' enclosure and would not look too happy with the world. Maybe, he had problems at that stage and I know each Test cricketer goes through such a period. There are many Test cricketers who get very worked up during Test matches and are hardly ever their normal self. They're grumpy, they're grouchy and very irritable. Away from it all - away from the Test match scene - a lot of them would be jovial and absolutely top-class company, but when the Test match fever gets them they are not good company at all.

Maybe that was what was happening to Rohan Kanhai that day. In fact, I was surprised later when the Test started and the shot he got out to. It was the first time the West Indians were playing Chandra who really had all of them foxed. Chandra bowled a short one and Rohan tried to hit it out of the ground but only managed to hit it high in the air. Abbas Ali Baig from mid-wicket ran back about twenty-five yards and took a beautiful catch.

That was the end of Rohan in the first innings. In the second innings too he didn't score much At least I don't remember anything about the second innings. What is memorable about that match is Clive Lloyd's batting when he clubbed Bapu Nadkarni savagely. I don't think Bapuji was ever treated as roughly as in that particular Test.

The next occasion to see Rohan was when we played against his team in the West Indies in 1971. Rohan was reticent at first; he wouldn't make much conversation excepting a very formal and polite hello and for me, a newcomer, it was impossible to get close to him and have a couple of words.

I had heard so much about his falling sweep shot and I was looking forward to it. He didn't disappoint me when in the second innings during his marathon 158 not out he played a few of those shots off Prasanna. That made my day, and also the fact that he had scored a hundred which meant that one could have a longer, closer look at his batting technique.

Our new-ball bowlers did not trouble him too much and he seemed to go on the front foot almost immediately, even before the ball was delivered. But one could see when he was facing the spinners, particularly when Bishen was bowling with Prasanna, that he would wait till the ball was in the air before committing himself either forward or back. In this way he found enough time to play his shots. The only time he had a bit of trouble in that innings was when Eknath Solkar came in to bowl and he did not know whether to go forward or back because Eknath was bowling at a much quicker pace than Bishen Bedi or Salim Durrani.

At the end of that innings when I went to him and said "well played" he smiled, said "thank you" and asked me my name. After I replied he just nodded and raised his eyebrows when I mentioned the words "opening batsman". He turned round and said, "Well, I wouldn't want to be an opening batsman ever. Thank God I'm not an opening batsman. All these crazy fellows trying to knock your head off."

I instantly warmed to him. All my apprehension after I watched his temperamental behaviour in 1966 vanished with that one remark. From then onwards it became easier to get to know him and slowly our friendship developed.

What won me over completely thereafter was the interest he took in my batting even though I was in the opposite side.

If I played an shot and if I turned back to see the slips I would see him shaking his head to show his disapproval. If I played some good shots, at the end of the over while passing from slip to slip he would mutter under his breath "good shot" or "well played" or something like that. That was his way of giving encouragement to an opponent. I really appreciated that because it was my first series and Test cricket being what it is today none of the players went out of their way to be helpful to oppouents. In this way Rohan Kanhai showed himself to be different from most Test cricketers, while I must also add that Gary Sobers was also very generous with his appreciation every time our boys did well. These two great cricketers proved that you did not have to be nasty to your opponents to win matches.

The other thing that got us closer was the fact that he was very much interested in seeing Alvin Kalicharan don the West Indian colours. Kali and I and, of course, Vishy, the three shorties, hit it off almost instantly from the first time we met. In fact, I remember a very funny incident when Kalicharan thought that during the West Indies-Board President's XI match when he had got out cheaply in the first innings he had lost his chance of ever playing for the West Indies. We were at a barbecue dinner and Kali was crying about the fact that he had muffed up his chances. There was Vishwanath, probably an inch shorter than Kali; and I, maybe a quarter of an inch shorter than Kali; Vishwanath with four Test match experiences behind him; I with no Test experience. We were consoling and advising Kali like veterans not to give up and that he should fight it out. That was also the beginning of our friendship. When Rohan came to know that the three of us were good friends he was amused about it because he said to Kali later, "It's quite natural that the three of you with just an inch separating you all should get together and become friends." People were talking about Kalicharan as the left-handed Rohan Kanhai. Now Kali is a very fine player indeed but he could never be a Kanhai. For that matter, nobody could be a Kanhai.

After that first hundred he got a few good scores of 30s but never went on to score a hundred in that series. We met again in England playing against the counties. He was, as usual, pretty good, though he seemed at that stage a little less warmer than he had been in the West Indies. I don't blame him. Probably it was the weather, the English weather, that made him seem a little less friendly than before. During my trip to Bermuda where I was part of a double-wicket tourney, I spent some time with Kanhai. We were together during that period and I spent a lot of time in Bermuda talking to him, trying to get the finer points of batting out from him. It was very difficult to get him to talk cricket at the end of the day, particularly because Bermuda wasn't as serious as other cricket centres were. But one got the impression that he wasn't very happy talking cricket. In fact, there were traces of annoyance when I pestered him about batting techniques. At that stage I thought that it was better to leave him alone rather than annoy him and perhaps lose his friendship in the bargain.

There was a surprise waiting for me. When I returned from Bermuda I was informed that I was selected to play for the Rest of the World party which was going to replace the South African team. The invitation to the South African team was withdrawn by the Australian government and therefore they had hurriedly formed a Rest of the World side and Rohan was going to be playing with them.

Well, that was tremendous, because I thought this was just the right opportunity for me to be with two of the greatest players I have ever seen - Rohan Kanhai and Gary Sobers -

and learn from them. It is a fact that when one is touring, the players in the team come to know each other much better, because they spend most of their time together. You share moments of joy, tension and sadness on a tour.

So I was very keen for this trip and fortunately for me it was good to have not only Rohan and Gary, but also the very competitive Tony Greig, the perfect gentleman Intikhab Alam, and Graeme Pollock who came down just before the third Test. There was also Bob Taylor, apart from our very own Bishen Bedi and Farokh Engineer.

Farokh and I had gone earlier to Bangkok. The team came from London and we joined the onward flight to Australia. It was good to be with the fellows and one could instantly feel that each one was trying to size up the other. It is a very difficult task to get people from different countries to form into a team and play another country. In that sort of a tour the first few days are very crucial. So one can imagine how wary each one must have been when people from different countries came together to play for the Rest of the World.

However, Gary Sobers, with his magnificent approach and total lack of any (to use the Indian word) "nakhras" (pretensions), instantly put everybody at ease. He is, and has always been, such an unassuming man that it was very easy for the ice to be broken amongst the team-mates. This was helped to a great extent by Norman Gilford and Tony Greig and also the dry humour of Richard Hutton.

The first few days, however, Rohan seemed to be in a shell of his own. He didn't want to mix around too much. He'd been to Australia a few times before. In fact the previous year he'd come down to Tasmania to coach, so he knew a lot of people and had a lot of friends in Australia . He obviously wanted to spend some time with them before the major part of the tour began. It was therefore difficult to reach Rohan Kanhai and speak to him about batting because he was preoccupied.

He did take me to a couple of parties and it was good fun meeting his friends in Australia. But soon we were back to the serious business of playing cricket and one could see how much dedication Rohan showed to batting. He trained a lot, practised a lot and was very keen to see that he was successful. However, injuries came his way quite often and deprived him of playing many matches.

He missed the first match because he was struck in the indoor nets in Melbourne by a ball from Asif Masood which just shot off a good length and dealt a very painful blow on the left forearm. Our fear at that stage was that it was broken. It was, however, badly bruised, and swollen. But he missed that game and the next one.

Came the first Test against Australia at Brisbane and Rohan was raring to go. Brisbane at that time was very hot and Rohan was wearing his white floppy cap while batting. He batted at No. 3 and along with Ackerman got a hundred in that game.

At that stage in the tour we didn't think that Lillee would be a great danger because Ackerman and Rohan had played him very well while scoring their individual hundreds. McKenzie looked just a shadow of his great self. However, the Test at Perth was a different story altogether. Lillee knocked the Rest of the World side out for 59 runs in their first innings. This was a pathetic performance in spite of the fact that the wicket was by far the fastest one had encountered. With the kind of batting line-up that we had there was no excuse for us to get out for 59 and that too within two hours before lunch. We had time also to come down for ten minutes' batting in the second innings, during which time we lost Farokh Engineer, which meant that we lost eleven wickets in that session.

It was during this Test that the greatness of Rohan Kanhai's batting became evident to me. I had the rare opportunity to stay along with him in a partnership and it was simply amazing the way he played that day.

Earlier in his innings, a short ball from Lillee hit him on the chest. It was painful but he shrugged off all help and stood his ground. The next ball expectedly was another short one and Rohan imperiously hooked it wide off mid-wicket for a four. That was a great shot. An absolutely unbelievable shot, because Lillee was bowling genuinely fast and to have the time to get up on one's toes and smash the ball down like a forehand overhead shot in tennis requires some talent.

That's precisely what he did. He just smashed the ball to all corners of the field and scored 117. I've seen quite a few century innings, but that, to my mind, ranks as the best century I've ever seen. For sheer guts, for sheer technique, for the sheer audacity of his shots, that century was worth preserving on film.

However, another hundred – a double hundred – in the same series and in the next Test by Sir Gary Sobers completely erased Kanhai's hundred. But I feel Rohan's was the greater hundred as it was one played under more tension – it was a hundred played when the bowling was really fierce. Mind you, I'm not dismissing Sir Gary's 254. It was a great innings, all right, but Rohan's 117 in Perth was just that one shade better.

After that innings Rohan seemed to have gone into a bit of decline. He didn't play the Melbourne Test nor did he play the Adelaide Test – being laid down with injuries – and that was a blow to our side. He'd been hit so often on his arms or on his chest and had gone for so many x-rays that after one trip from the radiologist, Richard Hutton refused to sit next to him saying that he would be "radioactive".

During that tour Rohan and I became good friends. He took

a genuine interest in my batting. He was very disappointed that I wasn't scoring many runs. He tried to explain to me how important it was as an opening batsman to try and see the new ball off. His favourite words used to be: "Give the first hour to the bowler and the rest can be yours."

And this was precisely what I was not able to do because on that tour in my very first match I scored a hurricane 30 and a very impressionable twenty-two-year-old got carried away with all that publicity about fast scoring and tried to repeat it in the rest of the game – at least until the second Test ended – with disastrous results. It was during the Perth innings that Rohan told me the importance of building an innings, of staying there when the other batsman was scoring a lot of runs, so that the other batsman keeps on playing his shots and does not come under any pressure.

These are little things, but one has to learn them and it was great education to be at the other end while Rohan Kanhai batted.

We met quite often after that. He used to come over for the benefit matches in India or stop over on his way back from some trip. He had a lot of contracts to play cricket in Australia. Invariably on his return journey he would stop over in Bombay, stay with his friends and we would spend an evening or two together.

Rohan has plenty of friends in Bombay and I'm sure all over the world as well. With women he's utterly charming and wins them over by his impeccable manners.

He teased me a lot in Australia in 1971 when he used to say that in 1961 when the West Indies team was first in Australia, there used to be a line of girls outside his room. He seems to like Australia as a place and he's tried to settle down there but not with success. He has since returned to Blackpool in England.

Even now in league cricket he's scoring runs and passing on tips to younger players. We meet on trips to England and he always calls up to wish the team luck. He is now very much involved in organising tours to different parts of the world. Only a couple of years ago he took a Rest of the World team to Pakistan to give their players practice before they went to Australia.

He'd love to bring a team to India and perhaps he might do so very soon. I know that people in India have a soft corner for Rohan and would welcome him with open arms. I am also one of the many Indians who are genuinely fond of the man not just as a cricketer but as a person. I have had the honour of naming my son Rohan after the great man and if only Rohan Gavaskar becomes half as good a player as Rohan Kanhai (if he becomes a cricketer at all) I shall be a very happy man indeed.

27

S. Venkataraghavan

RAMAKANT DESAI RAN UP TO BOWL WITH THAT SMOOTH RUN-up of his, pitched the ball just short outside the off-stump. Barry Sinclair, the New Zealand vice-captain, square-cut powerfully but uppishly and when most heads were turned towards the boundary, a tall and slim figure stood up with a half jump and snatched the ball with complete ease. The entire Brabourne Stadium rose to a man to applaud this magnificent catch by a youngster who was playing his first Test series. That youngster was Srinivas Venkataraghavan, India's veteran cricketer today.

He has since then become almost a specialist in taking overhead catches, particularly off slashes off spin bowlers which come at blinding speed. That catch was of a kind that the Indian cricketing public and the Bombay crowd took notice of and took this pencil-thin youngster to their hearts. Bombay crowds love a brilliant fielder and Venkat had won their hearts even before he had started to weave his magic web over the batsmen of the Test-playing countries.

The next Test was in New Delhi. It was here that Venkat gave notice to the cricketing world that another first class spinner had arrived on the scene. He captured eight wickets in the first innings and five in the second. Apart from that he was brilliant in the field. With a performance like this behind him, he should have been the automatic choice in the Indian teams thereafter but strangely, with the advent of Prasanna and his subsequent comeback, Venkat found it hard to hold a place in the side.

I remember watching Venkat bowl in the Test against the West Indies the following year when he trapped Gary Sobers plumb in front with a quicker delivery. However, the umpire thought otherwise and did not give Sobers out. Sobers then went on to score a brilliant 50, but as soon as the appeal had been negatived, he turned round to Budhi Kunderan who was keeping wickets, and with a grin said: "Hard luck, old chap". That was one chance the Indian team had in trying to contain the West Indies team to a reasonable total. Venkat bowled well but without success, and shall I say without much success in that series. Towards the end of the series he was replaced by Prasanna. Before that, the Indian selectors in a bold move had picked Bishen Bedi to play in the second Test, after having watched the Sikh in the Board President's XI match at Delhi. So with Chandra in the side, Prasanna making a comeback and Bishen beginning to establish himself, Venkat found himself out of the Indian side.

That season was memorable because the spin trio, and later the spin quartet, came into being that year. They mesmerised the batsmen throughout the seventies. Venkat made the trip to

England in 1967 but Tiger Pataudi did not seem to have much confidence in Venkat. He plumped for Prasanna who had more variation and more spin than Venkat and was the better bowler of the two. It was this tour that saw Prasanna come into his own. He was an automatic choice in the side that went to Australia and New Zealand within two months of the England trip.

Venkat was inexplicably dropped from the team and Prasanna consolidated his position capturing forty-nine wickets in eight Test matches in Australia and New Zealand. It was a superlative performance but it also meant that Venkat had by now realised that he had a competitor and would have to fight hard to get his place back in the Indian team. Venkat has always been a fighter and the word defeat does not seem to exist in his dictionary. He never gives up. This never-say-die spirit strengthened during this period of absence from Test cricket and later been developed to perfection in the season that followed.

When the New Zealand and Australian teams returned the visit in 1969-70, Venkat was back in the Indian team but merely as a third or fourth spinner and would come on to bowl only when Pras and Bishen were tiring. He never let go the opportunity, though, and saw to it that after the two bowlers had finished their stints, runs were not easy to come by off his bowling. His job then was to see that he bowled tight so that both the spinners would come back and strike the vital blows. To my mind, this is where Venkat lost out to Pras and that too in the larger interests of the team. Venkat realised that he would have to be more economical than Pras. Hence, he sacrificed his natural loop and beautiful flight which he had when he first came on to the Test scene, so that Pras could get the wickets at the other end.

Not many people, except those who had seen Venkat in action in the 1965 series, would realise that this change had taken place. I don't think Venkat is the type who would talk about it as well. It is only now in recent years that, with Pras off the scene, Venkat has come back to his original style, giving the ball plenty of air, inviting the batsman to play his shots and thus getting wickets. That, plus his physical fitness, as well as his indomitable spirit have kept him in remarkable shape and kept him going as a Test bowler even now.

In 1970, to everybody's surprise, Venkat was appointed captain of the South Zone team. This was a clever move engineered mainly to see that he became the vice-captain of the Indian team to tour the West Indies in 1971. To many, this move also seemed deliberate and done with a view to see that Venkat did not get a raw deal when bowling for the South Zone. The South Zone team also included Pras and the previous captain tended to rely more on him rather then Venkat. With Pras tending to tire quickly, it was Venkat with his stamina who bowled long spells while Pras came in short, quick bursts, to take quick wickets. Venkat was duly appointed vice-captain of the Indian team. With Pras also in the side, it was going to be difficult for both bowlers to play in the same Test team. Chandrasekhar was not in the team and thus our spin combination included Salim Durrani, an all-rounder, Eknath Solkar, also capable of left-arm spin, Bishen, of course, and Pras and Venkat.

To Venkat's credit it must be said that he never dominated and made use of his position. He was extremely fair in his treatment of Pras. Pras, however, was injured and did not play in some Tests, so Venkat grabbed the opportunity with both hands and ended up as the highest wicket-taker on this trip. With India winning this series against the West Indies for the first time ever, Venkat had no problems in being appointed vice-captain again. However, this time instead of Chandra being dropped, it was Salim Durrani's turn to be axed and Chandra went to England. On this tour too India made history by winning the series for the first time ever. The chief architect of our success at the Oval was Chandra, when he destroyed England for a mere 101, taking six wickets for 38 runs. But what people tend to forget is that Venkat kept a very tight leash on the batsmen and did not allow them to take any liberties with his bowling. He also dismissed the troublesome Alan Knott to a brilliant catch by Eknath Solkar and thus he also had his share in this success.

When the English team returned the visit in 1972-73, Venkat found himself in the background with Bishen and Chandra among the wickets. Chandra took a record 35 wickets in the series, closely followed by Bishen. With Pras coming on with his flighted guile, Venkat found himself relegated to the rear. This must have been a severe blow to one who was the vice-captain of the country the previous year. This, however, went on to strengthen Venkat's resolve not to give up.

In 1974 India visited England with Ajit Wadekar as captain and Venkat as vice-captain. This tour produced different results altogether, India being beaten completely 3-0. It was a trip beset by weather and other problems and it never appeared that the Indian team would do anything of significance on this trip and that is how it was.

The West Indies team, which was in the process of building itself as the champions of the world, came to India in the winter of 1974-75. That was a winter of turmoil which marked Ajit Wadekar's exit and Tiger Pataudi taking over as captain. This was a severe blow for Venkat who was vice-captain till just a few months earlier, on the trip to England, when Pataudi had refused to join the team for reasons best known to him. In those days, people did not bother to know if a player withdrew for personal or business reasons.

To my surprise, I was told on the eve of the first Test that I was appointed vice-captain but was asked not to make it public. That led to an embarrassing situation when Tiger Pataudi was injured during the first Test while taking a catch and had to go off the field. I knew that I was the vice-captain but as I was fielding on the deep-mid-wicket fence, it took me some time to reach the centre of the field and realise that Pataudi had gone off without informing the senior players who was to take charge. Venkat felt that he being the vice-captain on the previous tour, would automatically be the captain. Traditionally and normally, the seniormost player takes over if the captain goes off. Farokh Engineer thought that he would be in charge. It came as a surprise to all of them when I rushed and told them that I had been appointed vice-captain and was in charge. It really was very embarrassing when senior players like Chandra, Engineer and Venkat were in the side and someone like me who had just started his career was asked to captain them. However, I didn't have any problems but I really did feel sorry, at that stage, for Venkat.

When Tiger Pataudi got injured, I was appointed captain for the second Test in Delhi, but hardly a week before this match, I injured my index finger playing for Bombay against Maharashtra on a matting wicket at Nasik. With the chairman of the selection committee turning up only on the morning of the Test match, India woke up that morning of the second Test without a captain. It wasn't a situation for anybody to make his captaincy debut. Venkat, who had been asked to lead the side, could be hardly prepared to do the job. How can one discuss any tactics or strategy when one does not know who is going to be the captain? Thus it was that Venkat's debut as captain was a disaster. Added to that was the decision of the umpires to start play in spite of a rain-affected wicket, just half an hour before lunch. For the life of me, I could not understand how the umpires could not wait the extra half an hour before lunch, have lunch and start afterwards. After all it was a five-day game and there was enough time to be made up.

With the umpires insisting on play starting early, India lost quick wickets, never recovered from that situation and lost the Test. But worse was to follow. Having captained the side in this Test, Venkat found himself relegated to the position of twelfth man in the next Test. What a demoralising blow it must have been for him, but never did Venkat show that he was hurt by the treatment meted out to him by the selectors and nor did he ever say anything to anybody. He just carried on gamely bowling to the Test players in the nets, giving fielding practice, taking his share of catches and making himself useful in the dressing room. However, he was back in the side, soon and at the end of the series Pataudi announced his retirement from Test cricket. That meant that India had to find another captain.

The selection committee once again showed its whims and fancies by disregarding the claims of the appointed vice-captain for that series and appointing Venkat as captain for the Prudential World Cup. This was probably owing to the fact that Venkat at that time was playing county cricket for Derbyshire and was thus experienced enough in the finer points of one-day cricket to be able to lead the side. However, England proved too strong in this game and they rattled up a record score of 334 which only recently has been bettered by Pakistan in the last World Cup. With my inexplicable innings of 36, India had no chance whatsoever in that tournament.

Back home, Bishen was appointed captain for the tour of New Zealand and West Indies. The reasoning of the selection committee was now beyond anybody's understanding. They had started off by making Venkat the vice-captain in 1974, then recalled Pataudi as captain, making me vice-captain in 1974-75. After Pataudi's retirement, recalling Venkat as captain, me as vice-captain and finally making Bishen captain in 1976. However, this was an enjoyable trip but with Chandra, Pras and Bishen being among the wickets, Venkat found it difficult to get into the team except when Pras was injured. Here again he didn't let the side down and bowled particularly well in the West Indies. It was only due to Kirmani's lack of experience of the West Indies wickets and his poor keeping in that series that Venkat didn't get the rewards that he deserved. There were many moments when the great Viv Richards was stranded out of the crease, but with Kirmani found wanting, he could get back and make most of his "lives" to start a tremendous sequence of runs.

When New Zealand and England came to India in 1976, Venkat again found himself in and out of the side. It surely does not do anybody's confidence much good to have such treatment. However, Venkat had a big heart and, as a result, he kept on doing his own thing and went about his own ways.

The Australian tour in 1977-78 wasn't a very successful one for him. When the Indian team went to Pakistan in 1978, Venkat didn't play even a single Test. Zaheer and company had literally hounded Chandra, Bishen and Pras. Venkat, not having played in a Test, escaped their wrath. So, he was picked to play against the West Indies team. He bowled very well in that series. The only disappointment was that he was not able to run through the side on the rain-affected track in Delhi. The Indian team had put up a massive total and the West Indies team collapsed against Ghavri and Kapil Dev. They had to follow-on on a rain-affected pitch but Venkat could not do anything extraordinary with three left-handers in their side.

At the end of the season, I was deposed as captain, allegedly because of some statements my wife had made to the media.

Venkat was once again appointed captain of the Indian team to tour England. That tour started disastrously with England scoring 600 runs in the first Test and beating us comfortably by an innings. Thereafter, rain came to our rescue more often than not and we went into the last Test again facing a defeat. Fortunately, that was not to be and we just missed winning the Test by 9 runs, with two wickets in hand. A victory would have been possible but for some fairly tough decisions by the English umpires which left us struggling when we should have been in a position of dominance.

On the flight back home it was announced that Venkat was deposed as captain. He took that very well. However, midway through the Australian series that followed, Venkat found himself out of the side. Shivlal Yadav, the young Hyderabad off-spinner, had come to the fore and was bowling very well and was getting wickets while Venkat was finding it difficult to get them.

Thus Venkat, after three Test matches, was dropped again. He was out of the side for almost three years when he was picked to go to the West Indies in 1983. On this trip he bowled well without getting any rewards and was very useful to some of the youngsters who would go to him for advice. His comeback after a gap of three years is proof enough of the man's fighting spirit and it is something worth emulating by young players.

As a captain, Venkat was difficult to understand mainly because he set very, very high standards. If he found anybody falling short, he was not averse to giving the player a firing. In fact, his temper has become something of a joke in the Indian team. Venkat now is more sporting. He also understands that his temper is the cause of a bit of leg-pulling, but he is very nonchalant about it and often laughs at himself. His temper was perhaps the reason why he was not able to get the best out of the players that he had.

I have found him to be good company because right from the beginning, from my first tour, way back in 1971, we got along well. In 1971 in Jamaica, when I was nursing an injured finger, Venkat, who is a bit of a palmist, read my palm and predicted big things for me. I was very interested in finding out from him whether I could make the trip to England, because no cricketer's education is complete if he hasn't played in England. He said that not only would I make the trip, but I would also be successful on this current trip. I was amazed when his predictions came true. I did not know whether his predictions were merely a way of giving encouragement to a young player on his first trip or whether he could really read one's palm. I have not asked him about to that the day and I would rather believe that whatever he said, had come true.

On the 1976 trip to the West Indies, where Dilip Vengsarkar was making his first tour, one could see the personal interest that Venkat took in Dilip and impressed upon him that with his height, he could make an excellent close-in fielder. Dilip has a very safe pair of hands but his reluctance to stand in the close-in positions is, to me and the Indian team, very surprising.

Venkat was good company also because he could talk on a variety of subjects and it is particularly refreshing not to talk cricket at the end of a day's play. If we went out for a meal together, Venkat would talk on any subject but cricket and that was a great relief. He was dropped from the side that won the World Cup in England in 1983. But knowing the man and his determination, one could be certain that he would be raring to go when the Indian season began as he was back in the side. He had not played a Test against Pakistan but he achieved that ambition when he played at Bangalore in the first Test. Here is wishing him luck and may he achieve the success that is his just reward, but which has been denied to him for a long time.

28

Sir Gary Sobers

THE GREATEST CRICKETER I HAVE EVER SEEN IS SIR GARFIELD Sobers. He was the complete cricketer. He could bowl medium pace and could be quick when he wanted to; he could bowl spinners, the orthodox as well as the chinaman variety. He could bat at any number and he opened the innings once in a Test. I am sure, he could also keep wickets. As far as fielding is concerned, he was one of the safest catchers in the close-in positions and till the later years, when his bowling used to tire him out, a swift-moving fielder in the outfield.

My first trip to the West Indies in 1971 saw the West Indies captained by Gary Sobers. Gary had run into a bit of controversy, having just toured Rhodesia to play in a double-wicket tournament. The governments of Jamaica and Guyana were not very happy about it. I also think, though I could be wrong, that the West

526

Indian public wasn't happy about the fact that he had married a white Australian girl, because, after all, Sobers was a national hero in the West Indies, much like what Vivian Richards and Andy Roberts are in Antigua today.

In the first Test match of the series in Jamaica, Sir Gary scored 40 runs but, even before that, when we batted, he took a blinder of a slip catch off Jayantilal when he dived sideways and picked that ball up inches from the turf. As he tumbled and came up with the catch, I turned round and said to Eknath Solkar, who was sitting next to me, "Wow! All I want to do now is to see Rohan Kanhai play his falling sweep-shot and it doesn't matter if I play on this trip or not."

I was on the injured list at that time with a whitlow on my middle finger and so was just a spectator as far as that match was concerned. That match also showed how Gary Sobers could tear an attack apart, while Rohan Kanhai, in the second innings, resorted to playing a waiting game. Gary went out with the intention of showing the Indian bowlers where they really belonged. He just smashed everything. Neither Bishen nor Pras could make any difference to him. He had stormed into the 90s, when Ajit gave the ball to Eknath Solkar and, wonder of wonders, Solkar got him caught behind when he was trying to assay a back-foot drive through the covers. But then that was typical Sobers, no caution for him. He just went out and played as he could naturally. Thanks to that effort, as well as Rohan Kanhai's marathon one, the West Indies saved the game.

That game also showed that even a great cricketer like Gary Sobers can make a mistake unaware of some of the laws of the game. With the first day's play having been washed out completely, the match became a four-day contest and, therefore, the follow-on margin became 150 runs. Since we had a lead of more than 150 and less than 200 runs, Ajit very rightly enforced the follow-on. This completely stunned Gary Sobers and he had to be told by the umpires that Ajit was right. But I also believe that this stung Gary Sobers because this was the first time in so many matches that an Indian team had enforced a follow-on on the West Indies team. When he went out to bat the second time, the determination could be seen in the way he handled the bowlers. That was one of his missed centuries and there were not many more occasions when he got out in the 90s.

When the second Test started, I was making my debut and got to see the great man at very close quarters. He was bowled trying to sweep Venkataraghavan and I was in leg-slip. I thought that it was a very unbecoming stroke, particularly from such a master batsman as he was, but obviously, we could not complain because once we get somebody like Gary Sobers for less than 50, it is a bonus.

That evening we started our innings and aware that I was making my debut, and with a not very impressive score by his team, Gary crowded me with fielders. I managed to survive that evening. The next morning, Vanburn Holder, who was very much quicker than what we saw of him in 1974 or 1978 - in fact, he was genuinely quick in 1971 - bowled me a shortish ball outside the off-stump. I went for a back-foot drive and the ball just moved, took a thick outside edge and went low to Sobers at second slip. Gary missed that catch and, though he tumbled in trying to take it on the rebound, the chance was grassed. That was the first time, to my mind, when Sobers seemed human. There was nothing one could do after that excepting try and capitalise on this lapse - a very unusual lapse - by such a great fielder.

When he was bowling he tried everything. He tried bouncing; he tried bowling across; he bowled around the wicket; he bowled seamers and he bowled spinners; he bowled back-of-the-hand stuff and one could not but help admire the versatility of this man. It just seemed that there was nothing in the world which was impossible for him. But then, that was not his day and we managed to get a fairly useful lead.

In the second innings, Salim Durrani bowled him a beautiful delivery, pitching just outside his off-stump, and as Gary went out to push, the ball sneaked in between the gap and bowled him. Here I must say that Gary was never one of those who pushed the pad forward. He always played positively and never used his pads, unless he was beaten; but the first idea, the first aim, was always to meet the ball with the bat unlike what we see today where players push the pad forward hoping that the ball would hit the pad and not the bat. With Gary's wicket, we knew that unless the tail wagged or unless there was an astonishing recovery by the West Indies, we were in with a chance of winning that Test. And so it happened. We won that Test. That was also the time when I had myself photographed with Sir Gary Sobers just outside the dressing rooms, my first photograph with the great man, and it is something I treasure.

Came the Guyana Test and once again Gary didn't do too well, and neither did the West Indies. When our innings began, Grayson Shillingford bowled me a similar kind of delivery like the one Holder had bowled in the second Test. Only this one was shorter, and I thought I would square-cut it. The ball bounced a little more than I expected and, off a thick outside edge, went to Sobers at second slip. Wonder of wonders, Gary grassed it again. That was the fifth ball of the over and as he passed by, I could hear him explaining to Rohan Kanhai, who was in first slip, that he did not see the ball at all. That could be quite true because Guyana is one place where the background makes it very difficult to see and sight the edge. Most people believe that slip catches are easy. They look easy when you are 75-80 or maybe even a 100 yards away because you have that much more distance in which to see the ball travelling from the bat's edge to the fielder. But when you are out there in the middle and it is like a rocket coming at you from barely ten yards, it is very, very difficult.

I wasn't unhappy because it was the second time in the series that Sobers had given me a "life" followed by another one a little later. It was when Noreiga was bowling and I was on 94, on my way to the first Test century of my career. Noreiga bowled and as I moved to play forward, Sobers, who was at short square-leg, trying to anticipate, rushed to his left and tried to pick the ball up almost off the bat but. Unfortunately for him, the ball jumped up a bit, took my glove and went to where Sobers was originally in position before he left for the ball. Sobers's flailing right hand was useless and instead I got myself one more run. Therefore, when the next day's play started, Sobers said to me jokingly, "Man, let me touch you because I need some of the luck which you seem to have."

Remember, he was having a fairly lean time by his standards. After his score of 93 in the first Test at Jamaica he had not scored very many runs in his last three innings and people were saying that he should be dropped. But then this is what happens when you are such a great player as Gary Sobers and nothing short of the best at all times is expected of you. Well, Gary went out in the second innings and hit us for a 100, though many from our side believed that he had been caught for a zero by Dilip Sardesai off Salim Durrani at silly mid-on. The very fact that we could have two short legs, Dilip Sardesai and Eknath Solkar, just goes to show how uncertain Gary was till that innings. After he got his bearings and the pitch started easing, Gary hit Bishen and Salim Durrani for enormous sixes; the one off Salim Durrani, which was a gift-wrapped full toss, was hit out of the ground, clean over the pavilion, into the car park. This Test was drawn and that meant that we were still one up, but what was more ominous was the fact that Gary Sobers had scored a 100.

In the next match against Barbados, Sobers scored another 100 and one could see that the great man was just coming into form. There was no letting up after that and, true enough, in the first innings of the fourth Test at Barbados, he smashed us for 178 glorious runs and the "Bajans", as the Barbadians are called, went wild. Here was their home-grown product, their national hero, doing everything that they wanted and wished him to do. The strokes were all there, the delicate late-cuts off, the off-spinners, the flicks through mid-wicket off the front-foot, back-foot and off the left-hand spinners. Sobers was virtually standing, without moving his feet, and crushing Abid Ali on either side of the wicket as if to say, "I don't need foot-work against your pace."

For a twenty-one-year-old like me it was a great education and Gary didn't let up even after his 100. In fact, he just accelerated to put his batting in one more gear and was blazing away. What the West Indies lacked in that Test was a good off-spinner, because the foot-marks made by Eknath Solkar's bowling follow-through were just right for an off-spinner to exploit. I think, at that stage, Gary did not bowl his chinamen because he was having some trouble with his shoulders – his chinamen would have been perhaps equally dangerous to the right-handers.

With only one Test left and India still one-up, the West Indians were obviously looking for the kill. No one was more determined than Sir Gary Sobers. The Test started with a bit of a controversy about the toss. Both Sobers and Ajit thought that he had won the toss. The great sportsman that he is, Gary did not make a scene and gallantly allowed Ajit to have the right of winning the toss. This kind of thing can happen quite often if different coins are used. It happened to Venkat and Mike Brearley in 1979 and once to me and Kalicharan.

When they batted, the West Indians were obviously in a big rush because they had to force the pace and dismiss us quickly in the second innings to get in with a chance. Sobers scored another 100. That made it four tons in a row for him, before a ball from Prasanna, that kept low, bowled him as he went in for a cut. Before that, when our innings started, Gary was in the second slip, as usual, and there he dived to his left to catch Ajit, off John Shepherd. As he fell clutching the ball to his chest, the impact drove it into his chest and left him dazed. He went off the field at lunch, didn't take the field again and Joey Carew led the side for two days. The second day we did not hear a word from Sobers though he was in the pavilion. Otherwise, as the dressing rooms were adjoining, one could always hear his hearty laughter coming through.

On the third day, as soon as he arrived at the ground, we heard that unmistakable laughter. We groaned because we knew that Sobers was fit and he showed how fit he was by knocking off another century. He still continued to come up to me every morning saying, "Let me touch you for luck." I do not know whether he really believed in that or he was just pulling my leg. But if a great man like Sobers pulls my leg, it really does not matter. Remember the first time he came and touched me and said, "I want to touch you for luck" he got his first 100? Maybe like most cricketers who are a bit superstitious, Sobers thought that this was bringing him luck. Whether it did or not, he did not have to rely on luck at all. All the natural talent was there and it was just a question of his getting into his batting rhythm. At the end of the series, he paid me a great compliment privately, when he said that I should get a lot of runs in England and his words of advice were: "Try and avoid cutting in June but do that in July and August." He also said that I should go on with my hook shots, though there were times when I hooked in the air and he said, "Such a shot you play well and you have not got out so far in a Test match. It has got you many runs, just keep playing it." The very words that he used, "Your team should do well in England", were a great source of encouragement to me because coming from a man of great skill they were highly cherished.

We met him again in England when we were playing the Nottingham county game and Sir Gary didn't play in that game. County cricket being such a tough game, he had to take a break from cricket. He could only do so in a non-championship game against the tourists. He was there with his son Matthew, watching us very keenly and had a word for almost every member of our team.

When the proposed South African tour of Australia later that year was called off, Gary Sobers persuaded the Australian Cricket Board to include me in the Rest of the World's side to play Australia that season. My opening partner was to be Hylton Ackerman and Farokh Engineer was going to be the third opening bat. Geoff Boycott and Barry Richards were at that stage the acknowledged best opening batsmen in the world. Richards was, however, contracted to play for a club in South Australia and so was not picked. I am unaware as to why Boycott was not picked.

When we landed in Melbourne, Sir Gary was there to welcome us and told us about the incident involving Tony Greig, Hylton Ackerman and Sir Don Bradman. Ackerman and Tony Greig had arrived earlier from South Africa and at the Adelaide airport Gary Sobers had gone to receive them along with an elderly looking gentleman. When the introductions were being done, Greig and Ackerman, who were feeling sleepy from their long journey, did not quite catch the name of the person Gary introduced them to. When Ackerman had to leave to go to the toilet, he handed over his overnight bag to the elderly gentleman and left. After he returned from the toilet he tried to make polite conversation and asked the elderly gentleman, if he had anything to do with Australian cricket, to which the elderly person smiled and nodded and said, "Yes, a little bit". Ackerman then posed the question which has become a well-known story now. He asked the elderly man, "I'm sorry, I didn't get the name; what did you say your name was?" and the person replied "Don Bradman". Ackerman at that stage looked as if he could have been swallowed by the earth.

I don't know who actually made the booboo. Ackerman said it was Tony Greig and Tony said it was Ackerman who asked that question. Well, whoever it was, both Gary and Don Bradman had a hearty laugh.

During that tour of Australia, Gary was criticised for not being with the team, particularly for net practices, and playing golf instead. In fact, Gary was there for most of the net practices that the team had. But it was only after we played a three-day game that he opted out of the next day's practice, particularly because one travelled long distances in Australia to get to the next centre. That accusation was very unfair because Gary was really concerned about the team's performance as this was one which he and Sir Donald had selected and therefore was very keen to see that it gave a very good account of itself.

The first Test was drawn and that was our first sight of a bowler called Dennis Lillee. In this Test Ackerman and Rohan Kanhai got centuries and Sir Gary was hardly under any pressure. It was the second Test which turned the tables on us and after Australia were all out at the end of the first day we started our innings next morning. The wicket which seemed to have sweated under the covers assumed dangerous proportions. Dennis Lillee made the ball fly from just short of a good length and he had both Clive Lloyd and Gary Sobers off successive deliveries trying to fend off the balls from their chins, caught in the slips or caught behind by the keeper. That was great bowling and even in the second innings Lillee bowled extremely well in spite of one of the greatest, if not the greatest, Test centuries I have seen by Rohan Kanhai.

It was at this stage that the Australian press really started to give Sir Gary a hard time with regard to his absence from net practices and his fondness for golf. And so he was really a charged man when the third Test began at Melbourne. Ackerman opened the innings and he obviously still hadn't recovered from the previous evening's revelry, the Test having started on New Year's day. One could make out as we walked out to bat with him that he wasn't going to be in any good shape to do any good. He was bowled third ball by Lillee for a duck. Lillee also got Graeme Pollock, who had flown in on the previous day from South Africa, edging a catch to Marsh. Sir Gary was out to the first ball he played when a short rising delivery from Lillee was nudged straight to second slip Keith Stackpole. The look Gary gave Lillee was one which was full of meaning. It was for the second time in succession that Dennis Lillee had got Sir Gary out playing a shot like that and Gary certainly wasn't pleased about it.

Another remarkable thing is that Sir Gary never wore a thigh guard in his life and the bat which he used was always a light-weight one unlike the heavy ones which are in use now. The speed with which the ball went to the boundary showed what superb timing he had and that one does not always need a bat with a lot of meat in it to hit the ball as powerfully as one wants to. One six off O'Keefe was lifted effortlessly into the stands and that too without advancing down the track. People who have been fortunate to see the film of that stroke have raved about it. But remember that those were just the highlights which were shown and what can really be seen or how much can be seen in half-an-hour of highlights? Till Sobers reached his 50, the ball met the middle of the bat consistently but with the minimum of footwork. After 50 the foot started going to the ball and it started going more speedily to the boundary. This was really vintage batting and one which completely turned the match upside down as far as the Australians were concerned.

When we fielded, Sir Gary contributed with two sharp catches at leg slip to get rid of the Australians enabling us to level the series. That was a great way to start the new year, and we were all buoyant with hope that with our skipper in such great form and Ackerman and Kanhai who had already hit big hundreds, we would be able to beat the Australians.

The fourth Test was at Sydney. That's where Bob Massie who had already played in Melbourne, but not with much success, came into prominence. He took seven wickets, including that of Sobers, and the moment he did that he obviously was noticed, and not only that, he also had Graeme Pollock's wicket. Bob Massie hence immediately attracted the attention of the cricket-loving public of Australia. Rain spoilt that game but we were not in a great position at that stage. Sir Gary was bowled in the second innings by Inverarity when he tried to turn a full toss to mid-wicket, missed and the ball went off his pads on to the stumps.

Came the last Test and the series was still one-all. Both the teams were looking for a win, but with the Adelaide wicket noted for its spin, the Australians brought Mallet. It was expected that Intikhab and Bishen would do wonders for us. That is what happened. Both Intikhab and Bishen bowled extremely well,

536

although there was a very good partnership between the Chappell brothers. At one stage, Intikhab took two wickets in an over and we had a very close field when Inverarity came in to bat. I was at silly mid-on where very few cricketers are comfortable and as Intikhab bowled that ball and Inverarity played it, I was taking a step back as the ball shot off a thick inside edge and I caught it. Sobers, who was at backward square-leg, came to me laughing and said, "You were retreating when the ball came to you. Anyway, well caught", and I said to him, "Well, I am not used to standing in that position!" He said, "Don't worry, you are too small a person to make a target. If I was standing there, I would be a bigger man and a bigger target because of my size." There was some sense in that kind of talk.

We duly won that Test to win the series 2-1. The Australian side was just shaping up at that stage with the up and coming Greg Chappell and Dennis Lillee, with Ian Chappell making his impact as a captain. The only problem they were facing was a sound opening partner for Keith Stackpole at that stage. There was Massie as well. Rodney Marsh had proved to his critics that he was a world-class wicketkeeper in the making and so the Australian side was really looking good.

It was during this last Test in Adelaide that a farewell dinner was organised and Sir Don Bradman came and spoke at length on how the tour came about, how important it was and how the tour had gone. This dinner was only for the members of our team and the manager and Sir Don Bradman were special invitees. Bradman then spoke about each member of the team, what his impressions about that member were and how he had contributed to that tour. Before that, welcoming Sir Don to the dinner, Sir Gary also spoke of the role that Sir Don had played in getting the tour going and giving it every encouragement. While this was going on a very senior cricketer sitting next to me said, "Well, these two chaps keep on praising each other, don't they?" That may have been so, but there is no denying the fact that these two cricketers were the greatest ever the world has ever seen. One, Sir Don, the greatest batsman the world has seen, and the other, Sir Gary, the greatest cricketer the world has seen till now.

Thus ended for me the first tour with so many top-class players from the world and my only regret, apart from not getting a century in the unofficial Tests as well as in the first-class matches on the tour, was that I could not get a big partnership with Sir Gary Sobers. There could have been so much to learn from him had I batted along with him, just like batting along with Rohan Kanhai in Perth had helped me in so many ways. One thing I noticed about Sir Gary when he was at the other end was that he never gave any kind of advice to his partner. If the partner played a bad shot there was no shaking of the head or no glare. Sir Gary would simply get back to his crease and stand and look stoically elsewhere. Similarly, if the partner played a good shot there would just be the hint of a smile and a nod so that he would know that while the shot was appreciated, there was no need to be carried away by that. This is what I noticed when India played the West Indies and also in our brief companionship. Still, partnering Sir Gary was an experience I was not fortunate to have. This is one story I regret I will not be able to tell my grandchildren.

On that tour Sir Gary had grown a beard because his razor was stolen during the first match of the trip. He bought another one which too was stolen. The third one which he bought was also stolen, obviously by people not wanting to steal but to keep something as a memento of the great man. But Gary resolved at that point not to shave again on the tour. His remark was simple, "I cannot afford to buy razors all the time."

So he just grew a beard, but he was lucky because he did not have much of a growth on his cheeks with just a bit on and beneath the chin.

Gary Sobers was fond of night life. We once went to a night club together and I was astonished at the way he could knock back a drink. He kept on having a dig at me for drinking cocacola and said that it was more harmful to the intestines than liquor. I told him that I wasn't worried about my intestines but I was worried about my brain, to which he gave a hearty laugh and said, "That's a good one." But to his credit, he never forced me to drink with him unlike some of our senior cricketers who force the young players in the team to take a drink. Fortunately, this trend in Indian cricket is now on the wane but, certainly, it was there when I was a beginner and an attempt was made to see that all the young players also joined in the drinks. This trend has virtually disappeared since 1977 and I think it is better today that in the Indian team, we find very few players who take alcoholic drinks or smoke. In fact, the one addiction of the current Indian team is music and that is what they get their kick from.

I kept on meeting Sir Gary off and on after that and always the greeting was, "How are you then, my little fellow?", and the greeting was always very warm and affectionate. On the 1976 trip some of the Indian cricketers were fortunate to be invited to his house in Barbados for a party which the boys thoroughly enjoyed, but what one did not enjoy afterwards was Sir Gary's driving in his Jaguar, through the narrow streets of Barbados when he was dropping us back at our hotel. The streets of Barbados are very narrow with sharp curves and the way the great Gary was driving we thought we would be lucky if the four of us in his car reached the hotel alive. It was Prasanna who asked him why he drove so fast and how did he know that there was no other car coming from the opposite side when he was taking a sharp curve. Gary replied, "It's my nose, man, I can smell a car if it's coming the other way."

His nose must have sure been sharper than ours! All we knew was that we were happy that we reached back safely, although those fifteen minutes from the time we left his house till the time he dropped us back at our hotel were filled with great discomfort and worry. But that is Sir Gary Sobers. He lived his life like that, fast. He played his cricket fast and not only did he enjoy life but he also gave enjoyment to those who came to watch him play cricket.

29

Syed Kirmani

IN 1967, AJIT NAIK, WHO WAS THE CAPTAIN OF THE INDIAN
Schools team to England, invited me to meet the vice-captain
of the team, but he warned me before that, "Don't be surprised;
although we have a schoolboys' team, the vice-captain smokes,
so don't get upset by it at all." Actually, I did not understand
the reason why that should have been surprising, because lots
of schoolboys get up to more mischief than smoking.

I was eventually introduced to Syed Mujtaba Hussein
Kirmani. What struck me was the warmth of that person, his
charm, the way he talked in typical Hyderabadi manner, very
polite, bending down almost to the ground while being introduced
and generally being very respectful. That impression of Kirmani
has not changed over the years, even after he became a Test
player and became, what must be universally accepted, even

by the Australians, recognised as the best wicketkeeper in the world.

In the recently-concluded Prudential World Cup, he won the best wicketkeeper of the tournament award if proof be needed. I firmly believe in that for the simple reason that he has been keeping wickets to the spinners and keeping them extremely well, throughout the seven or eight years he has been playing Test cricket. Of course, like any other wicketkeeper, he has had a bad patch. In fact, he had a terrible series in 1976 in the West Indies. But the standard of wicketkeeping that he has displayed has been of the very highest order. The consistency he has shown over that period is enough proof that he is amongst the top wicketkeepers of all times.

Rodney Marsh has an edge on him because Marsh stands up to the faster bowlers and thus he is able to see the ball a little more when he brings out those incredible catches. But then, Syed Kirmani has also brought off so many incredible catches off the medium-pacers when he is standing back. Where he scores over Rodney Marsh, is in keeping to the spinners.

To get back to Syed Kirmani's rise to Test cricket. That schoolboy tour of England in 1967 was highly successful for him and opened up the doors of the Ranji Trophy cricket for Mysore as soon as he returned. Mysore had been struggling to find a good wicketkeeper, although Budhi Kunderan was keeping wickets for them. But Budhi perhaps found the duties of both wicketkeeper and captain rather strenuous and so he must have been very relieved when Kirmani came on the scene.

Incredible though it may sound now, when Kirmani went to England with the Indian Schools team in 1967, he went in as a batsman and not as a wicketkeeper. They had two regular wicketkeepers on the team and it was known that Kirmani could keep wickets. He was, however, not picked up. But in the Mysore team they picked him as a wicketkeeper. He has not looked back since.

Kiri himself recalls how he started keeping wickets in the matches that the boys played in streets using a brick as a glove and that "keeping glove" was harder than what he does now. His beginning, therefore, has been right from the bottom rung and that's how it should really be, since there are no short cuts, no half-measures to the top.

Kirmani first came into prominence when he played in the Ranji Trophy match against Bombay in Bombay. He scored runs and kept wickets very competently and showed that his temperament was suited for the big time. That match against Bombay brought a lot of young players in the national reckoning, particularly Brijesh Patel and Kirmani, to name only two. While Vishwanath, who was already a Test star, once again proved his progress towards greatness in that particular match by scoring an incredible 95. Thus, with the all-India schools tour behind him and his performance at the Ranji Trophy level brought Kirmani into the limelight to attract the attention of the Test selectors.

When the Indian team was going to tour England in 1971, there was some doubt about Farokh Engineer's participation in all the matches of the tour and there was a tussle for the last place in the team between Mohinder Amarnath and Syed Kirmani. Krishnamurthy had already been chosen as Engineer's deputy and another wicketkeeper was required only if Engineer was not available for the county games. Engineer was at that time only available for Test matches. Eventually, this was resolved when Lancashire C.C., for whom Engineer was playing, intimated that he would not be released for all the matches, but only for Tests and an odd game before the first Test. Thus, Mohinder Amarnath was dropped and Syed Kirmani came on the trip to England.

He didn't have much scope on that tour because Krishnamurthy kept wickets in most of the county matches and Kirmani was there just to get some experience.

I remember a very funny incident. Syed is very fond of taking his afternoon nap and this he does religiously if the team is not on the field. And if the side is batting, you can safely assume that between lunch and tea, provided that the situation is all right, and he is not required to bat, or be padded up, Kirmani would be in some corner of the dressing room fast asleep. On this tour, he was just doing that, sleeping in a corner when the late Ram Prakash Mehra, the second official on this tour, woke him up pretty roughly and asked him to watch Alan Knott. We were playing Kent then and he wanted Kirmani to watch Knott and improve. Mehra believed that Kirmani, who was then a youngster, could learn much by watching Knott. Kiri complied and got up, watched the proceedings with an air of boredom written all over his face. As soon as Ram Prakash Mehra got up to get a fresh packet of cigarettes, he slipped away into the physio room, stretched himself once again and was fast asleep, When Mehra got back, he could not find Kirmani and he inquired where he was. Someone said that Kiri was watching Alan Knott from near the sightscreen. Mehra was impressed by this and remarked that one had to push the youngsters a bit otherwise they would never try to learn.

We did not want to disillusion Mehra at all, but not watching Alan Knott or any of the other top cricketers at that stage hasn't in any way affected Syed Kirmani. Because one can learn only a bit by watching the great players, but to assimilate that knowledge into your own game is extremely difficult. One has one's own style, a set pattern of play and to change it after watching someone else is very difficult. To learn good points from great players to improve your own game is to gain in confidence, but one should just keep them in mind while having one's own style. Kirmani had to wait in the wings for a fairly long time, although he made another trip to England in 1974 as Engineer's deputy. The 1976 tour of New Zealand and West Indies found him as the first choice wicketkeeper in preference to Krishnamurthy, though the latter was on that tour and had been consistently the second wicketkeeper to Engineer. Engineer had not been picked as he could not come to India and play in domestic cricket as stipulated by the Board then.

Kirmani was capped as a wicketkeeper in a Test match for the first time in Auckland. He kept wickets confidently. His batting was also spectacular and he proved on many occasions that as a batsman he was difficult to dislodge. It was, however, in the second Test of that series that he gave a superb display behind the wickets when the conditions were blistering cold. Our spinners could not do well on that grassy wicket. They could not turn the ball an inch as they could not even grip the ball. Thus, we had to rely on our medium pacers who made life difficult for the New Zealanders. Kirmani took some excellent catches and one catch in particular, off Glenn Turner, was outstanding when he dived full length to his left to pick up a leg glance. This has now become Kirmani's hallmark and his catching off the fine leg glances, with which a batsman normally expects to get himself four runs, has now become legendary.

However, after this magnificent debut in the three-Test series in New Zealand, Kirmani's form somehow fell when the team went to the West Indies. Viv Richards, who was to embark on his run-getting spree in that series, benefited by Kirmani's lapses and the main bowler to suffer was Venkataraghavan. In fact, the situation was such that in the last Test after Rafique Jumadeen skied the ball up in the air, between the wicketkeeper and me, at leg slip, and when I made the catch, Venkat rushed and thanked me for taking the catch because he had lost confidence in Kirmani's keeping in that particular series.

Perhaps the memory of that series was in Venkat's mind, when as a captain, he was a party with the selection committee to the dropping of Kirmani for the 1979 tour of England.

However, when Kirmani returned to India in 1976, his wicketkeeping was once again at its best and the West Indies tour aberrations were soon forgotten. Cricket-lovers at home then got to see with their own eyes that the country had found an adequate, if not better, replacement for Engineer. Kirmani, of course, was not the same kind of batsman as Engineer. Engineer was flamboyant, dashing in his approach and his shots were sometimes outrageous, very bold, very daring and he was a crowd pleaser. Kirmani's batting was more careful. His approach was merely push and prod, not that of hit-for-four-runs. That meant that it was more difficult to get Kirmani out than Engineer because the latter's enthusiasm meant that he was prone to the odd mistake here and there. Kirmani's mistakes were induced by a bowler.

In 1977-78, when the Indian team went to Australia, his inclusion as a wicketkeeper/batsman was certain. He was more than a useful batsman and many times down the order, he contributed handsomely and saw to it that the Indian team would reach a respectable total. His wicketkeeping on that tour was of the highest class and it was no wonder that when the World Series Cricket were looking for Indians to take part in its cricketing activities, Kirmani's name figured very prominently in the list. Kirmani thinks very carefully and after having weighed the pros and cons, he was prepared to join the WSC. The fact that it did not materialise and everything was sorted out between the WSC and the world cricket officials is another story.

That was used as an excuse, or so it appeared, when Kirmani was dropped from the team which went to England in 1979.

If Sunil Gavaskar was captain of that Indian team, he would have been accused of regional considerations in dropping Kirmani. But in this particular instance, the captain and the manager came from the same state and the wicketkeeper to be the beneficiary from the dropping of Kirmani was also from the same state. At that stage, these facts didn't enter anyone's mind. And why should they? For Sunil Gavaskar is the only captain who is thought capable of such regional considerations and none else in Indian cricket is when he is picking a side! I am making these comments because the dropping of Kirmani in 1979 agitated my mind considerably and I felt the same way when Chetan Chauhan was dropped in 1981-82, sharing the sentiments of cricket followers all over the country.

There have been other selection omissions which have caused plenty of anguish, notably those of Karsan Ghavri and Dilip Vengsarkar, but these stories will have to wait for another book.

When Kirmani came to know that he had been axed from the England tour, he was in a daze. He jumped into a taxi and asked the driver to drive anywhere and as long as he pleased. I do not know how much the taxi fare came to, but the damage to Kirmani's purse would not have been a fraction of the damage caused to him psychologically.

The Indian team to tour England in 1979 had to undergo a physical conditioning camp at Bangalore and Kirmani had arranged his wedding date during the camp so that he would be able to take his wife to England with him for a sort of cricket honeymoon. These plans did not materialise and it was a tremendous blow to him mentally. But typically of the man, he came out bravely, fought back and worked hard to regain his place when the Australians came in 1979. Sent as a night-watchman, he contributed an invaluable 65 and proved his usefulness as a batsman as well.

He has not looked back since then and in the last Test of that series he even scored his maiden Test century. This was when he was sent as a night-watchman again and he responded to the humid heat of Bombay by scoring a brilliant hundred. That effort sapped his energies to such an extent that one found Kirmani on his knees between deliveries when Kapil Dev walked back to his bowling mark to send the next delivery. It appeared at that time that Kirmani was saying his prayers, but in effect, he was so tired and the heat had so drained him of his energies that he was in no frame of mind to stand up. But he kept well and proved what a good keeper he has been over the years.

Since then he has been on top and every time there is talk of replacing him with another wicketkeeper, he comes back with a superlative performance to silence his critics.

The latest example is the World Cup which India won and his wicketkeeping was of the highest order. He won the best wicketkeeper award in the World Cup tournament and the presentation was made by no less a person than Godfrey Evans, one of the greatest wicketkeepers of the past.

Success in international cricket hasn't touched Kirmani. He is the same affable person that he was in 1967, showing the same courtesy, the same charm and the ability to win friends. He has plenty of friends spread all over the world and so too are his fans who have become his friends now. He has also made it a point to go wherever his fans are and meet them.

He is a very religious person and never forgets to say his prayers during the day. He has also made a couple of trips to Mecca in recent years. After his first trip to Mecca, he shaved his head. He thus solved a problem. His receding hairline required him to comb his hair across the rest of the head when he disembarked from a plane or when he was waiting to be introduced to a guest or a VIP. It has now become easy for him as he need not worry about his hair flying and exposing his balding pate. One thought that this would enable him to be punctual at ceremonies or be ready to leave with the team, but Kirmani just loves his sleep and it is not always that he is on time. The team members always laugh when he gives his excuses for being late as the bus or coach starts.

Kirmani has many, many years of international cricket ahead of him. He is very conscious of physical fitness and keeps himself trim. He is not much of an eater and doesn't drink at all. His only vice, if it may be called so, is smoking, but in recent years he has been able to cut it down considerably.

It will be very difficult for any wicketkeeper in India to replace him in view of his recent form. I cannot visualise it, barring an injury to him. Of course, little injuries do not bother him; such is his commitment to the Indian team.

When he was vice-captain in the West Indies, he confessed that his ambition was to reach the top, be at the helm and get out by 1989. That is six years away and I sincerely hope that his ambition of becoming India's captain is fulfilled. His dedication is well-known, his ability is legendary and I am certain that his experience which has been gained over the years will certainly help him in achieving his ambition. I wish him well. I also wish to express how great an admirer I have been of his cricketing abilities and I pray that he goes on as long as he wishes to.

30

Vivian Richards

WHEN THE INDIAN TEAM ARRIVED IN ENGLAND IN 1974, ONE OF the first games they played was at Eastbourne against Robbin's XI. During this game which was captained by Brian Close who was also captaining Somerset, he was asked what kind of a team he had. Brian Close, normally not a man to waste his breath praising cricketers, went on raving about a young West Indian lad who was making his debut for Somerset and who he thought would be one of the best batsman the world would ever see.

There were knowing glances exchanged by the other county cricketers who were present, as if to convey the impression that, well, this is what Brian thinks, it doesn't have to be necessarily true. But I knew that this was something that had to be taken very seriously, because in 1971 Brian Close had given us a tip about a horse which then came through at the unbelievable odds of 14 to 1.

I remember that incident very vividly simply because I had my wallet picked just the day before, which left me penniless. It was only because of the tip Brian Close gave that I requested another team-mate to put in a pound for me and ended up getting fourteen.

That was a bet which came in very handy and I knew then that Brian Close does not waste his words. So when he talked about Viv Richards in such glowing terms even before Viv had played first class cricket for the county, we knew that we would get to see a star when we played in Taunton later in the summer.

It was bitterly cold in Taunton when we did land up there. Viv was seen loitering about in the covers, very quick on his feet and very eager to get on with the game. When his turn came in to bat, he smashed Abid Ali imperiously through mid-on for four and the crowd sat back expecting some more fireworks. However, Abid had the last laugh when he forced Viv to play another attacking shot off the back foot to a ball which was pitched up for that kind of a shot and the resulting inside edge knocked off his stumps.

So we saw Viv Richards for a very short period and one could not form any impressions about his batting, though his fielding was outstanding. Later in the summer one came to know that he had been picked for the West Indies team touring India later and one looked forward to seeing how this man had progressed.

He became the first West Indian to get a 100 on that tour in the first match itself and although the West Zone attack wasn't exactly menacing, one could see that the young man had adapted himself very well to the wickets and the shift in the bowling from pace to spin. He looked a predominantly on-side player but he also cut the ball well.

In spite of his scoring a 100 one did not expect him to be picked in the team ahead of people like Lawrence Rowe, Alvin Kalicharan, Clive Lloyd, to name a few. But it was during the same game in Poona that an ailment in Lawrence Rowe's eye was detected and he had to fly back to London to get it treated, which left a batting place vacant for the West Indies. Viv Richards, with his hundred as well as his brilliant fielding, was a certainty to play.

His Test debut was not auspicious as a batsman – Chandra got him out quickly in both the innings. But his debut was memorable for his fielding. In the Indian first innings he caught both the openers, Farokh and me, brilliantly, and treated the Bangaloreans to as fine a spectacle in fielding as one could see when he was in the outfield. His running, picking up and throwing on the turn and throwing on the run were unbelievable. The power of his throws was to be seen in the way Deryck Murray wrung his gloves every time he received a ball from him from the outfield.

The West Indies won that Test largely due to a superlative innings of 163 by Clive Lloyd, which turned the scales completely in the West Indies' favour. When the second Test came along, Viv Richards decided to announce himself to the cricketing world and to the bowlers of the Test nations that a new star had arrived.

He scored 192. But more than that it was the manner in which he scored those runs that was memorable. I was injured after having been appointed to lead the team in place of Tiger Pataudi who was also injured but I decided to make the trip in any case – and what a wonderful sight it was to see Viv Richards play!

Bishen Bedi had been recalled to the Indian side after having been dropped for disciplinary reasons in the first Test at Bangalore Bedi, Venkat and Chandrasekhar were a formidable attack. Yet, Viv treated them in a cavalier fashion, particularly after he had got his hundred. He was watchful, but never dull till he reached his 100. Once he reached that magic figure he just seemed to go berserk and was smashing everything out of sight. To Venkat, he just stepped out on the track and lofted the ball into the adjoining football ground - a hit which must have been a 100 yards, if not more.

He also lifted Bishen and Chandrasekhar into the crowds for huge sixes. There were four sixes in his 192 and many other attractive shots. The West Indies won that Test also with ease.

The Indian team came back in the third Test, thanks to a great century by Vishwanath and his fighting partnership with Karsan Ghavri. The West Indies started very confidently and it was Viv Richards' dismissal - two short of his fifty - that turned the tide in India's favour, a position from which India did not look back for the next couple of Tests.

The third and fourth Tests were also won by India to level the series with one Test to be played. This was the fifth Test at Wankhede Stadium in Bombay, a new venue. All kinds of doubts were expressed about the quality of the wicket and about the stadium. All these doubts were proved wrong and the West Indies won this rather highscoring - highscoring in the first innings - game rather comfortably midway through the last day.

Clive Lloyd scored a mammoth 242 not out and with that effort a brilliant 100 by Roy Fredericks was overshadowed as also Viv Richards' two little gems in both the innings. His effort in the second innings when he scored 30-odd runs in half an hour, playing shots which have now become his hallmark - moving away to the leg-side and hitting the ball through the off-side - was marvellous in the sense that he played with such ease and with such a carefree attitude that even in the opposition one could not but admire the man who played them.

The West Indies duly won that Test and with that the series. And at the end of the series Viv Richards had justified his inclusion in the West Indian team. He had just one big hundred to his name but plenty of 30s and 40s. Somehow he seemed to be getting a rush of blood in his head when he was in his 30s and 40s to try for an ambitious shot and got out when a little more care would have assured another 100 for him.

His impetuosity got the better of him on those occasions and fortunately for India, these periods seemed to come more often when he was in his 30s or 40s.

When we next played against him in 1976 the earlier impetuosity was gone. The aggressiveness was still there but it was tempered to the extent that one thought that Viv was a little cautious in the choice of ball to defend.

During his Test century in Barbados, his first of the series, he seemed to be able to despatch the good balls into the crowd, yet when the half volley was bowled he would block it very meticulously, almost copybook fashion. This was perhaps his way of tempering himself and telling himself to play a long innings and not get carried away.

He was the scourge of our attack and he scored runs in every Test match that we played. He had a 100 in the first Test, a 100 in the second Test, and again a 100 in the third Test. And he looked like getting a 100 in the fourth Test as well when he was 60-odd runs before he got out. And thank God for that!

But it was amazing to see this man play such long innings. Just a year and a half ago it looked very unlikely that this man would like to be kept quiet but here in this series there were periods when he went scoreless for fifteen to twenty minutes, but it didn't seem to bother him. In the series in India in 1974, if more than a couple of overs were bowled without him having scored, you could bet he would try and play a funny shot and get some runs. But all that had vanished and he was looking more solid than ever before. We came to know that he had taken some hypnotherapy in Australia which enabled him to gain confidence and crack almost 250 runs in the last two Test matches that he played, including one hundred and another near hundred. He had caught on the century habit. This was evident because immediately after our series he went to England and plundered over 800 runs in just four Test matches. While in England, he became ill and was not able to play the Lord's Test in 1976. To score 800 runs in England is certainly a tremendous achievement, because the English do not make things easy at all for you. They pride themselves on their professionalism. When they know that they can't get you out they try to see that you don't score too many runs off them. They keep you tied so that you lose your patience and get out playing a foolish shot. The fact that Viv was not only able to keep scoring runs, and score them in such a big way, indicates his complete mastery over their attack.

The summer was one of the best summers they have ever had. There was hardly a day in the entire summer when it rained. When a match was interrupted because of rain, and for the West Indians, who like the Indians are used to having the sun on their backs, this was, indeed, a Godsend. How they managed to make use of this freak weather in England is well chronicled. The outstanding performances of the tour were by Viv Richards in the batting department and by Michael Holding and Andy Roberts in bowling.

The side was superbly led by Clive Lloyd and they just did not give England a chance. They completely cleaned up the series and seemed to have been spurred on by the comments of Tony Greig who, before the West Indian team arrived in England, said that the the former were susceptible to pressure and that he would make them grovel. Now grovel is a word which we all know is derogatory, particularly to the West Indian race, and this seemed to make them try all that harder. It is no wonder then that Viv Richards was not happy with just 230 in the first Test but went on to score 291. I think getting out at 291 must not have been as painful to him as the fact that he got out bowled to Tony Greig.

Whenever Tony Greig came out to bat, Michael Holding, Andy Roberts and all the big bowlers would find extra strength and bowl yards faster at this man who had uttered those words. Many times in that series one found Greig's stumps sent flying before his bat came down, so quick were the balls delivered by the West Indian fast bowlers. Yet, for the West Indian fast bowler, to be able to bowl consistently, with attacking fields, they needed big totals and this was where the genius of Viv Richards came into play. He missed out on the Lord's Test but scored runs in just about every other Test match with two double centuries, and a century and an innings of 60 in the Headingley Test where on a whole day's play the West Indians plundered almost 400 runs, something unique as far as today's Test match scoring rates are concerned.

Viv Richards was the one man the English team had to get rid of, and Viv never really gave them the pleasure unless he was well past his hundred. The West Indies were well established on their way to a big score. Although he missed out on the Lord's Test because of a virus infection, he made up for this absence by scoring a hundred the next time he played at Lord's in a Test match. This was in 1980 when he scored 145 and one of the best that England has seen in recent years. But Viv Richards, like all great players, had to go through a fairly lean patch by his own standards, and that came about in 1977 when the Pakistan team was touring the West Indies. Now after all his big scores the previous season, everybody expected him to plunder the Pakistan bowling on the West Indian wickets, but in fact Viv's highest score in the series was a 90-odd and he failed to touch a hundred, which was remarkable because at no stage did he look as if he was batting badly. But the old impatience seems to have crept in and with it the desire to try and dominate the bowler from the first ball.

The newspapers also said that he had become a little overconfident, but who wouldn't become overconfident after having scored almost 1,800 runs in the previous year? This was just one of those phases which every batsman goes through. Viv too went through that, although he had a harrowing time at the hands of the West Indian spectators who expected their champion to blast the Pakistan attack. The crowds were disappointed, and some were pretty vocal in expressing their sentiments. The pressure on Viv was therefore increased and he wasn't happy with the way the West Indian public had treated his efforts against Pakistan.

It was during this time that the famous Packer episode took place and the entire West Indian team signed up to play for Packer. This in effect meant that Viv missed out on a few Test matches, for example, the West Indian team that toured India in 1978-79. I'm sure, had he played he would have scored a packet of runs. India at that stage were going through a phase when their spinners were on their way out and Kapil Dev was just making his mark. It was just the kind of attack that Viv would have loved and unfortunately for the Indian spectators but fortunately for the Indian team, Viv was not there. He was playing in Australia and was scoring a lot of runs against the Australian teams on wickets which were hard, lively and bouncy, just the kind he liked.

When the Australian team came to the West Indies in 1978, the West Indian Board had decided to accept the World Series Cricket players and Viv, along with his West Indian colleagues, was back in the West Indian side. His duel with Thomson in the first Test was memorable. It was mainly because Thomson was inspired with a batsman of Viv Richards's class at the other end, that he bowled some of the fastest overs he has bowled ever since his unfortunate accident when he had damaged his shoulder.

Viv did not come out of the battle unscarred, though one shot of his, a parallel hook into the stands, proved how he was unafraid of the fastest deliveries. When a bowler like Thomson is firing on all cylinders even great batsmen like Viv Richards find him difficult to handle. This was one of the Tests where Thomson got the better of Viv Richards. However, after a couple of Tests, the old problem of the World Series Cricket surfaced when the players refused to give it in writing that they would be available for the Indian tour later in the year, which meant that the West Indian Selection Committee had no option but to try other players who would be available for the tour of India, later in the winter. So Viv and company were out after playing the first two Test matches and this was quite a blow to the West Indian spectators who showed what they thought of the series by attending in very few numbers the remaining three Test matches. The series was won by the West Indies by a margin of 3-1 and the last three Test matches were much closer because the West Indians did not have their full side.

In the winter Viv went away again to Australia and played another season of World Series Cricket, another exciting season in which the West Indians dominated the Australian team, but the matches were much closer than in the previous season.

In 1979 after the West Indies had a fairly ineffective tour of India it was decided that all the WSC players would be called back into the fold for the World Cup. The inaugural World Cup in 1975 having been won by the West Indies, the West Indian Board and the public wanted the best side sent across so that the World Cup could be retained.

In the 1975 final Viv Richards had not contributed a great deal with the bat but his brilliant fielding had accounted for the Chappell brothers being run out when both were looking dangerous for the West Indies team. In 1979 Viv Richards was already the best batsman in the world and what a place to prove that once more and with emphasis! He scored a brilliant 138 and those who have seen that innings will never forget the last two shots which he played. He flicked a six off the last ball of the sixty overs. He moved away to the off-stump and as Mike Hendrick banged down the inevitable yorker, Viv was quickly into position. He converted it into a full toss and flicked it over the square leg boundary for a six.

That was one incredible shot, but even more incredible shots had been seen during Viv's earlier part of the innings and in his partnership with Collis King. The ball was regularly beaten against the boundary boards of the Lord's cricket ground. It was West Indian batting at its exciting best. Collis King and Viv Richards, in spite of the fact that the West Indians were under pressure at that stage, proved that strokes could be played and played without any nervousness. Both of them played the kind of innings the West Indian public have been privileged to see and what the rest of the world hears about. This was the kind of approach that has made the West Indians so popular all over the world and that's how they won the World Cup.

It is true that in 1979 the West Indians had the formidable fast bowling quartet of Roberts, Holding, Croft and Garner and they weren't let down at all by these four who saw to it that not many runs were scored against them by any team.

And that is precisely what happened; they virtually ran away with the World Cup in 1979, finding very little opposition from anybody. In 1975 they had a little problem with Pakistan and they scraped through the series, thanks to Deryck Murray and Andy Roberts for keeping their heads level. But in 1979 they had very little opposition and they just ran through the World Cup opposition.

That winter Viv was again in Australia. It almost seemed that he was destined to go to Australia every winter. That winter he played official Tests because the previous two winters he'd been playing WSC, which was not recognised by the international cricket boards. But here in this season, after a settlement had been reached between the WSC authorities and the Australian Cricket Board, a series was organised with the West Indian and England teams called to participate in a triangular tournament where the Australians would play three Tests against the West Indies and three against England along with a number of one-day matches which would be triangular matches played between the three teams.

The West Indies not only won the Benson and Hedges Championship for one-day cricket but they also won the three Test matches that they played against the Australians and they never looked in any danger at all. Viv was unfit, having a problem with his back and his thigh. He still managed to score a brilliant 140 virtually on one foot. He also contributed his bit in the field by diving to his left and snapping up Allan Border. These were truly the efforts of a man who has always played for his side when they needed him most.

His innings of 140 included memorable shots again - a flat-bat hook off Jeff Thomson at his fastest, which went between mid-on and mid-wicket. This was the shot of the match, and so also a flick off Lillee when he pitched the ball a shade up which was bisected through mid-on and mid-wicket. The Australian bowlers thought that Viv was not so hot on the off-side and fed him on the off-stump. Viv was there with his cover drives and thumping straight drives. The innings was a lesson in batting for all the young players who were privileged to watch it.

Also memorable among Viv's efforts in Australia that year was a 153 he took off the Australian attack in a one-day game. To score a hundred in a limited overs game is a very rare thing. Not, of course, for Viv, but for most batsmen. Viv not only reached a hundred but went on to score 50 more runs! Greenidge and Viv just demolished the Australian attack and made victory for the West Indians a mere formality.

By this time Viv had been appointed vice-captain of the West Indian team, in recognition of the authority that he wielded with the bat and the respect and command he got from the West Indian players.

In 1980 when Clive Lloyd brought the West Indians over for a full Test series in England, Viv got a chance to lead in the last Test after Lloyd had pulled a muscle in his leg. Lloyd was not always at his best in this series, suffering from muscular injuries, though he scored a brilliant hundred in the Old Trafford Test, his second home, in Lancashire. Viv was the man who set the stands alight with his knock of 145 in the Lord's Test. It was a joy to watch the way he smashed Bob Willis. He continued it in the next Test, though he got out bowled to Ian Botham in his 60s. This was one of his inexplicable dismissals when he looked so much in command and so completely in control. It was therefore a surprise to see him get out in that series for anything less than a hundred.

By this time he was universally acknowledged as the best batsman in the world. He proved it again when the England team went down to the West Indies in the winter by thrashing

200 off their attack, the second hundred being one made specially for the occasion of Antigua's first ever Test match. Viv hails from Antigua and the people of Antigua had only read about and maybe seen a little bit of Viv on film and television and were getting the opportunity to see their hero bat in a Test with their own eyes. He did not let them down. Viv scored a hundred, and it looked at one stage that the hundred would come in less than a hundred minutes. That was the way he started. He had seven fours in his first 28 runs and he looked in superb control. However, he suddenly seemed to realise that too much of a good thing would not be the right way to try and get a hundred, maybe overconfidence would bring about a fall, and so he played a game which was different from his usual game. He waited and waited for a loose ball. It almost looked as if he was determined to see that he got out for nothing less than a hundred, which he eventually did. He scored the hundred and the whole of Antigua went wild.

Before that, Antigua had another reason to celebrate when Viv married his childhood sweetheart Miriam. According to reports it seemed as if the entire population of Antigua had turned up for the wedding, though obviously not everyone could have been invited for the wedding! But nobody would have wanted to miss the wedding of their prince. That's how dear Viv is to the population of Antigua.

My only season in county cricket came about because Viv was going to be with the West Indies team in 1980 for the major part of the season and I was required to play only for the time Viv would be absent from the Somerset side. I enjoyed that period and even after Viv returned I was with Somerset. One of my lasting memories is of sharing a flat with Joel Garner and the West Indian contingent in the Somerset side turning up religiously every evening for a meal cooked by Joel.

I have never been much embarrassed about my being a very poor eater but the only time I really felt embarrassed was when Viv, Joel, Hugh Gore and Hallam Moseley came over to the flat and had their meals. The way they tucked into their food was a sight to be seen and in spite of the huge quantities they consumed they never seemed to put on weight. Their waists seemed to be as narrow as ever and the quantity consumed did not seem to have any effect at all.

They would be joking and laughing all the time while eating. Typical of West Indian style the whole body would take part in the laughter. While laughing one of them would crumple under the table in fact, and while the person was cracking up with laughter somebody would pick up the food from his plate and eat it up. It was truly an incredible sight and something which I'll never forget.

I confined myself to toast and tea that time mainly to avoid being dubbed a poor eater by them, because I would have been really embarrassed to eat or pick at my food which I normally do. Yet, I just couldn't help but admire the way they ate If I eat a little more than usual the effect is instantaneous and I always feel overweight But nothing seems to happen to Viv whose waist seems to be the same as when one saw him in 1974. He is deceptively strong. From a distance he doesn't look very big because when fellows like Clive Lloyd, Colin Croft and Holding are around he looks smaller than them but as you come closer to Viv you realise what a barrel chest he's got and those muscular arms stare at you straightaway.

Viv is also very fond of dressing well. He's got an incredible wardrobe and, if I'm told correctly, he never wears the same shirt twice in a county season. That must mean that he possesses an unbelievable variety. It is easy to believe that, because one sees him always immaculately dressed. A briefcase is his constant companion as he gets involved in the business aspect of being a cricketer and Viv today must have a bit saved up in the bank.

I know that the Indian public is waiting anxiously to see this great player again. The opportunity will arise in 1983-84 when the West Indian team is due to tour India. I feel that at that time Clive Lloyd will have called it a day and it will be Viv Richards who will be leading the side to India.

As we go to press we learn that Lloyd has been reappointed captain and Viv is vice-captain which perhaps is good because then Viv can concentrate on making runs and show to the Indian crowds why he is the best in the world.

31

Zaheer Abbas

PROBABLY THE ONLY TEST WICKET THAT WILL EVER BE CREDITED to me is Zaheer Abbas'. The great man was on 96 in the second innings, and he was set for the second century of the match, having scored 176 in the first innings in the first Test at Faisalabad between India and Pakistan on the 1978 tour. That wicket is still etched in my memory. It was more a moment of sorrow than of joy for me.

Zaheer has been a personal friend since we toured together with the Rest of the World team in Australia. For me to get his wicket when he was just four short of a landmark was most painful. I still remember the ball. It was an innocuous delivery. I am still surprised that Zaheer mishit that delivery. Earlier, with the match petering out into a draw, I had been fooling around a bit with different versions of a run-up. There was a bowler who used to bowl at the Hindu Gymkhana and I was trying to imitate his leg-breaks. Suddenly, in this over, I decided to bowl with my normal run-up and bowled one, to which Zaheer came down the track to loft straight over the bowler's head, for the boundary which would have given him his hundred, but instead he managed to get an edge and the ball went to Chetan Chauhan at mid-on for a catch. Normally that ball could have been or should have been hit anywhere. Zaheer could have driven it along the ground or he could have flicked it past the mid-wicket or he could have still cover-driven it. But why he tried to lift it over my head is still a mystery to me. There was still time left for a few more overs during which he could have definitely got his hundred. Though he has not yet scored a century in each innings of a Test, he has the enviable record of scoring a double century and century in a match on four occasions. This is a world record which nobody has come close to. His consistency is amazing. Today, he has over 100 hundreds in first class cricket to his credit. He was the first Asian to join the ranks of those who have scored a hundred hundreds. It was an achievement treated with pride in India and Pakistan. At last an Asian had joined the select band of those who have scored a 100 hundreds.

Zaheer Abbas came into prominence on the 1971 tour of England by Pakistan. In his first Test against England he hammered 274 runs and I have always asked him how he got out at 274. Was it out of fatigue or was it due to overconfidence? He told me that he had tried to sweep Illingworth and somehow the ball came a little slower than he had expected. It took an edge and he was caught at square-leg. Zaheer is very fond of setting up records and he had the record of 365 before his eyes when he got out. Because he is so energetic and his concentration is so amazing, that it was not a surprise when in 1974 he went on to crack 240 against England. This time he again disappointed by not going on to a triple hundred by chopping a ball from Underwood on to his stumps. The next double hundred came against India when he scored 235 not out at Lahore. This was another brilliant, stroke-full innings. The declaration came as Pakistan were going for victory, the first Test having ended in a draw. Pakistan had to declare and give us some time before knocking us out. That they did it is now history and that is how the stalemate of draws was broken in this match at Lahore in the 1978 series.

I first met Zaheer when he was brought to our dressing room at the Oval in the 1971 Test by Abid Ali. Zaheer at that stage was much thinner than what he is now. And everyone just wondered how this frail-looking man could have scored 274 runs. When you shook hands with him you could feel the strength in his wrists. When we saw clips of his 274 and saw those wristy shots we knew how those runs had come.

We got along fairly well at that stage. We both found ourselves in the Rest of the World team that toured Australia in 1971 when the Australian Board withdrew the invitation to South Africa and the Rest of the World team was hurriedly got through after the English season to substitute for the South Africans. Right from those days we got along well and even today we are very close friends.

Over in Australia, Zaheer dominated the initial matches with plenty of runs and the fastish Australian wickets seemed to suit his style of play. As the ball came up, he was able to deflect it over his hips or drive it on the up. He had a most peculiar-looking flick shot to anything pitched on the legs at that stage, because he was committed on the front foot. If he wanted to flick he was sort of hopping and jumping at the same time hitting the ball with enough punch past the square-leg umpire for a boundary. As far as his off-side strokes were concerned, they were mainly in the cover region and very seldom did he straight-drive or off-drive a ball. All the runs were scored from the extra-cover region onwards and he got most of his runs with that shot and the flick shots. He was not afraid to hook, though he employed that shot on rare occasions if the ball was really a short one and he was confident of hooking it.

In the first Test he did not get too many runs and in the second he was going on well when he was run out. In the early days his calling was not in the top drawer and not as precise as his batting was. In the third Test he was dismissed cheaply in the first innings as at that stage of his career he was found vulnerable to an outswinger pitched well up. He tried to drive without getting into the proper position and edged the ball quite often to the slips or the wicketkeeper. But in the second innings of the Melbourne Test he was the one who took the sting out of Dennis Lillee's bowling, making 86 before he was out to a wild-looking shot and was caught in the slips thus missing a hundred. That was most unlike a Zaheer shot because when he gets near the magic figure, he seems to concentrate more and has no nerves in the nervous nineties. He used to get through that with just a few attacking shots to his hundred. In this case, he was out for 86, abd in the fourth Test he did not get many runs getting a fifty in the fifth Test. He showed another facet, his weakness, when he was talked out by the Australians. Keith Stackpole was giving him a bit of lip for the way Zaheer had played a few shots earlier and the latter was trying to hit Stackpole out of the ground when he was bowled. Stackpole had won a tactical victory. Thereafter Zaheer and I kept in touch whenever we were in England. But the most unfortunate thing was that when the 1971 tour was on, the war between India and Pakistan broke out. A new nation, Bangladesh, was born and that was the time our friendship was put to test because we used to get conflicting reports from people as to the way the war was going. That was the time when we were tense and as the eyes of the media were on us, our friendship was seen in its true colours. All of us, Asif, Masood, Intikhab Alam, Bishen Bedi, Zaheer and I used to go out together to a Pakistani restaurant for snacks and dinner and not once did we talk about the war though Bishen seemed to be understandably worried because Amritsar, where he lived, is very close to the border. Never was the war discussed amongst us. At the end of the tour, in a general discussion on politics, Zaheer had something to say about our leaders and I had to express my opinion about Pakistan. Of course, these were not opinions of any earth-shattering nature but opinions of individuals who were following the fortunes of both the countries and we were just expressing it in a manner of discussion.

Zaheer signed up for Gloucestershire for whom he has been playing for the last ten years with great success. On the 1974 tour of England the Pakistanis had a very strong side led by Mushtaq Mohammed. In addition to a strong batting line-up, they had a very good bowling side and though they did not have anybody of genuine speed – Imran had still to find his confidence of bowling genuinely fast – they had bowlers good enough for the English conditions. They did not win the series, despite scoring well in two of the Test matches. After not scoring well in the first two matches, Zaheer came with a bang in the last Test, thereby erasing all his previous failures. Thereafter, Zaheer seemed to have got into a bit of decline as far as his batting form was concerned because he did not hit a century for a long, long time, though he got very near that figure against the Australians in 1976. Against the West Indians too, when the Pakistan team went there in 1976-77, he was not able to score too many runs. In fact, he had a broken toe. He was also lucky that he was not drowned, because he and Wasim Bari, while surfing, had met with an accident. They were carried away by waves, but fortunately rescued by lifeguards. When he came back to Pakistan, he had to play against the Indians. Scores of 176 and 96 in the first Test, 235 not out in the second, were ample proof of the man's awesome ability. He scored over 500 runs in the three Test mini-series and he was the man responsible for destroying our fearful spinners.

In 1977, there was a bit of controversy when the Pakistanis were released by Kerry Packer from their contracts so as to enable them to assist Pakistan against England who were touring Pakistan. But the English did not want to play against the "deserters" of Test cricket, so the Pakistani professionals were not included. In any case, Zaheer's arrival in Pakistan created a storm of protests, though the Test eventually went on peacefully. The point was not lost on the Pakistan Board that they would have to invite their WSC players to play against India. Unfortunately for India they all came and reinforced the team and saw that the Indian team had no real chance.

When the Pakistan team was due to play in India in 1979-80, the two players we were really worried about were Javed Miandad and Zaheer Abbas. While we could plan a bit of strategy for Zaheer, to try and curb his run-making, it was almost impossible to think of such a plan for Javed Miandad. The plan for Zaheer's strokes succeeded in a large measure due to the excellent bowling by Kapil Dev and Karsan Ghavri, supported by Dilip Doshi. The bowlers bowled to a plan and, fortunately for us, Zaheer fell into the trap so much so that the Zaheer Abbas we knew in Pakistan in 1978 was nowhere in evidence. We are told that in the last Test he did not want to play and made way for another player. It was typical of Zaheer, who had always kept the interest of the team before his personal interest. All cricketers who score profusely give an impression that they are worried only about their individual scores. That is not always the case and Zaheer Abbas is a prime example that comes to my mind of a player who plays for his side rather than for himself.

Thereafter, Zaheer had a wonderful season with Gloucestershire scoring ten hundreds. There was a period when he scored 1,500 runs in a month. This was an amazing sequence of run-making even by Zaheer's standards and his greed for runs does not seem to have diminished at all. The Indian public were disappointed that they could not see this great player in action as much as they wanted to but the Indian players and the bowlers were very happy that Zaheer Abbas kept on getting out match after match.

The Indians returned the visit in 1982-83 and once again found "Zed", as he is known in the cricketing world, in great form. With a double hundred in the first Test he became the first Asian to hit a century of centuries. If we thought that he would stop there we were mistaken, because with another two centuries Zed amassed over 600 runs and also became the first Pakistani to score 4,000 runs in Test cricket.

He has one ambition and that is to score a Test century in India. So come September, Kapil will have to watch out for this gentle, smiling murderer of bowlers.

ONE-DAY WONDERS

1

Captaincy

RAVI SHANKAR SHASTRI USED HIS FINGERS TO PICK UP SOME
ICE from the icepail, dropped a couple in his drink and asked
me if I wanted some in mine. I proffered my glass and he put
a few cubes in it. To readers it might seem unhygienic that Ravi
(since he seems to have dropped the Shankar from his name)
should use his fingers instead of ice tongs. As a cricketer one
is diving about, throwing oneself on the ground and often
coming up spitting grass and dust; so using fingers to put ice
in a drink was no big deal.

Ravi stretched his long legs across the table, almost touching
my knees, and then looked at his wristwatch. I looked at mine
and said, 'It's twenty minutes to nine, Bach. So neither you nor
I am the Captain. Try and relax, okay?'

We were sitting in his room on the first floor of Hotel

Mountview, Chandigarh. I had come up to his room after having spent some time with the irrepressible Lt. Col. Surendranath, who was our team manager, in his suite which was next to mine on the ground floor. Suri, as Surendranath is affectionately called, has the envious knack of looking at the brighter side of life and one can come away from his room in nothing but a cheerful frame of mind. It was in this frame of mind that I had reached Ravi's room, having found out previously that he was not busy. Ravi appeared anxious, not tense, to know what was happening, particularly since a member of the Selection Committee had informally asked him in the morning if he would be willing to captain the Indian team to Australia.

Having lost the Madras Test and thus being one down, with one Test to go, meant that at best we would draw the series, which we should have won easily. Having been beaten in the one-day series by a 3-1 margin before we came to Chandigarh, almost everybody was looking for and wanting a change in the captaincy. Funny, how the blame for losing is heaped only on the captain. While his team-mates may just get a negligent curse, the Selection Committee, which may in fact have been responsible for selecting the losing team, is hardly affected by the mud that gets flung about and invariably ends steering clear. Everybody was convinced that the captain was going to be changed. Mohinder Amarnath and Ravi Shastri were the names bandied about. Ravi had been talked to by a Committee member and he had suddenly started being very careful how he spoke that day. The team members were quite convinced that it was going to be Ravi, unless, of course, Mohinder were to suddenly turn up in Chandigarh. Ravi also had to put up with a lot of banter from us because we had plenty of time, since overnight rain had left the ground and the wicket in a sorry state, delaying the start of the last one-day international against England.

Thus I could sense and understand Ravi's anxiety as we sat sipping our Thums Up in his room. I knew that the Selection Committee were divided over my appointment and hence the selection was postponed from the first day of the fourth Test to that moment. Normally the appointment of a captain does not take very long, though the Committee might deliberate for a while longer on the composition of the team. The announcement thus is sometimes delayed, giving rise to much speculation in the press. The board also does not help by trying to withhold facts More harm is done by this speculation than if the media were to be taken into confidence. While it is difficult to divulge reasons for an omission or selection, a brief statement by the Secretary and the Chairman of the Selection Committee would go a long way towards meeting the demands of the media.

Since the match had finished at five-thirty it was presumed that the announcement would be made after two hours, at the very latest. But there we were, almost three and a half hours after the committee had started its deliberations, with no announcement made yet. By this time I was convinced that somebody else had been made the captain and since Ravi had not been informed, it was obvious he also had missed out.

The telephone rang and as Ravi picked it up I could faintly hear a female voice at the other end. I presumed it to be one of Ravi's millions of admirers and smiled as Ravi began to talk. Within seconds, however, he turned to me and said, 'It's Pammi'. I was wondering what the matter could be, since I had been with her in Suri's room and had just left her to come up to Ravi's room. I picked up the phone and said, 'Yes, Mrs G, what can I do for you?' The reply was, 'You ordered some peanuts and crisps and they have just arrived.' That stumped me, because I had done nothing of the sort, but I felt excitement building up in me because her voice too had an undercurrent. I made some excuse to Ravi, which I am sure did not fool him, because we were going to order dinner in a short while and Ravi is too sharp anyway.

I went down to the room to find Pammi, hand extended, saying, 'Hi, Captain'. I was surprised, because while I was hoping to be appointed skipper I did not think that after such a long time had passed I would be given the job. Pammi then told me that I had to go to a car parked across the road from the hotel where the Board Joint Secretary, Ranbir Singh Mahendra, was waiting to drive me to where the Selection Committee was meeting. She said that I should not go by the main entrance, as the press was waiting there, but scale the wall that ran alongside the lawn.

This did not make any sense to me, because if I was the captain, why play hide and seek with the press, I argued, but she said, 'Just go and don't waste time discussing this with me because I am only conveying what Ranbir said to me when he came here with the news.'

It was in the act of scaling the wall and dropping to the road on the other side that my mind was made up that I would quit the job after the Australian tour. To me it made no sense that the captain of India should stealthily sneak out to join the Selection Committee. I did it only because I had no time to think and had to rush because the members of the Committee were waiting for me.

When I arrived there I could easily make out who were the ones who had opposed me, because they refused to look me in the eye as they shook hands with me. It didn't matter to me, because now we had to do the important job of selecting a good side to take to Australia.

As far as I was concerned there were no surprises, excepting the omission of Sandeep Patil, whose brand of batting is ideally suited for one-day cricket and who has the performance to show for it. Later, people were surprised that L. Sivaramakrishnan was picked, but to my mind he was going to be a vital cog in our bowling machine.

The team looked well-balanced, with the batting strength more visible than the bowling strength. It was, I thought, a blend of experience and youth and a team capable of lifting a season of total despair to one of hope.

The Press Pass

IT WAS THE EVENING THAT THE KANPUR TEST FINISHED THAT I SAT down with Chandu Borde, the Chairman of the Selection Committee, and told him of my decision to step down from the captaincy of the Indian team after the Australian tour. Chandu Borde is a very likeable man. As Chairman he conducted the selection meetings with great dignity and carried himself extremely well. I got along with him very nicely and respected his judgement. It is easy to respect someone like Borde, because he has gone through the ups and downs of a cricket career and yet come out on top. His record speaks for itself and I had witnessed his glorious stroke-filled century against Hall, Griffith, Sobers and Gibbs in 1966 at the Brabourne Stadium. I admire him as a cricketer.

He speaks slowly, as if choosing his words with care, and

has a habit of saying 'Acchha!' more like an exclamation than like a question.

We sat and had coffee and discussed why we had lost the series to this English side. At the end I told him of my decision. He sat back and asked if the result of the series had anything to do with it. I replied, 'Partly; though my mind was being made up during the first Test itself.' He then asked me if I could announce the decision in Australia, since I had told him I would hand in my letter to the Board before our departure to Australia. I didn't see any reason for doing so and thus when Qantas had a cocktail party on the eve of our departure I cornered the Cricket Control Board Secretary and gave him the letter. He did not even ask me what it was and just shoved it into his coat pocket.

Next morning we (the Bombay players) were summoned urgently to the President Hotel where the team was staying, as Mr Salve had wanted to talk to the team over breakfast. So I had to drop whatever plans I had and rush to the hotel. Unlike during Tests when even the local players have to stay at the hotel, we were not required to do so before our departure.

We could go home at nights and spend that time with our families. This is ideal, because it gives the player time to go about his own business before embarking on a tour. During Tests it is better for the players to stay together, as one can have urgent meetings and discussions on the Test in progress and also be able to go together as a team to the ground and to social functions.

When I landed at the hotel I found Vengsarkar and Shastri missing. They were probably not informed, since this was a last-minute meeting summoned by the Board President. However, their absence the previous day at the cocktails was disappointing. Bombay players should consider themselves lucky that most flights out of the country take off from Bombay; so that gives them more time to be with their families than the players from other cities who have to leave their homes a few days earlier to reach the city. Thus to plead that one wants to spend time with the family and not attend a team function is not right, in my opinion.

Mr Salve gave us a pep talk at which, apart from the team, Mr Kanmadikar, the Board Secretary, Ranbir Singh, Joint Secretary, and P.M. Rungta were present. I informed Mr Salve about my decision and he was very upset that I had not taken him into confidence before deciding anything like this. He then asked me if I had informed the press. I told him that officially the announcement should come from the Board and so I had not told the press anything, though a couple of my friends in the press knew about it. Yes, I do have friends in the press; though reading the reports of the series against England one could have been excused for thinking otherwise. I have no complaints against the press for their criticism of my cricket and captaincy. That is the way they see it and even if I do not agree with them I will certainly not hold it against them. My disappointment lies in the fact that they make up certain stories which have no basis in truth.

I will give only three examples of their disregard for truth. The first one was after we had lost the Delhi Test and Kapil was dropped from the squad. The papers reported that after Kapil got out in the second innings there was an altercation when ·he returned to the dressing room. The truth is that not a word was said by either of us. While I was certainly disappointed and upset by his mode of dismissal I knew there was no point in saying anything, because it would not have made Kapil go back to bat. Yet, the papers made a big issue of a nonevent and had recourse to evasions like 'alleged altercation' and 'according to dressing room sources'.

By the way, the discussion to drop Kapil had started before I joined the selection meeting. I was late in joining the selectors because I was urging the players to forget the Delhi disaster and look forward to the remainder of the series as a three-Test series. My opinion was certainly sought when I did join the meeting later, and it was given in no uncertain terms, but again, it was I who got the sole blame for Kapil's omission.

In fact, one Delhi reporter even went to the extent of quoting me at the meeting. That, of course, was total fabrication, but in his case I'll be surprised if he ever gives me a pat on the back. Actually, I know the reason for his antagonism towards me. While I have not spoken about this before, I do feel the time has come to reveal what I feel are the reasons behind his constant animosity.

When I was playing in the Vizzy Trophy in Delhi in 1968-69 this person offered to take me to the rehearsal for the Republic Day parade. I went straight from the ground in a car with him and saw the very impressive Beating the Retreat. It had become quite dark as we were returning to the hostel we were staying at and on the way to the hostel this person made an indecent advance which I promptly repulsed, even telling him that he was like an uncle to me. He said, 'Do not tell anybody; or else I will ruin your career.' Since nothing really had happened, I did not bother, but confided that evening over dinner in Ajit Naik who asked me to forget it and just concentrate on my game. It is obvious that while I didn't even think much about it, this person has not forgotten the rebuff and has been critical of everything that I have done, ever since. Ajit Naik jocularly remarked the other day, 'What he could not do to you physically, he is doing in print.' All I can say is good luck to him. I actually feel sorry for him now. Coming back to the second example of press misreporting, it was after I declared the innings in the Calcutta Test, some, not all, reported that this was done only because the police in Calcutta had told me that the crowd would riot if I did not declare. The police never entered the dressing room. I have a lot of regard for the Calcutta police, because they have a most difficult job during Tests and they do it splendidly. So that was another imaginary story.

The third, of course, was during the Kanpur Test when Azharuddin set up a world record by scoring a century in each of his first three Tests. This time even a paper like the *Hindu* printed as a box item the news that I did not come out to applaud Azhar's feat and stayed put in the dressing room. This hurt me considerably, because I believe the *Hindu* to be absolutely top-drawer, which would not malign somebody without checking the facts.

I was in the dressing room and watching the game on the TV there when Ajju turned the ball off his hips to take the single for his century. The moment I saw that he was going to complete the single I ran outside and stood applauding the achievement. Obviously I could not be seen in the front because everybody was standing up and clapping and it's not my style to push and come to the front to get attention from TV cameras or photographers. Yet the press, sitting on the opposite end of the ground, made it an item of sidelights of the game that I did not applaud Azhar's feat. Nobody bothered to check with me but went ahead and wrote, as Gavaskar was everybody's favourite whipping boy by then. Not that I shall cease to be so after this book appears, but I write this only because the public which laps up everything that's written about cricket tends to believe what it reads without pausing to think whether it might be true.

While the players' conduct on and off the field gets written about, I feel there should also be a code of conduct for the press so that they do not depart from facts, nor misrepresent them.

The other day I was watching a video cassette of my twenty-ninth test century. It might be interesting for my friends in the press to see who among the Indian team were present and applauding when I got my ton and who were absent. I believe if one has made up one's mind to criticise a player, no matter what then, nothing will do. After all, the written word is digested immediately and no clarification made later is going to make any big difference.

If I seem unduly sensitive, then I must confess that I am so. Nobody likes to be criticised. While I accept that as a Test captain I will be under greater scrutiny and that more criticism will be levelled against me than against the other players, I feel that the criticism should concern the game and not other aspects like the Azhar episode, about which I was most hurt. I am writing about it openly, because I believe that my opinion should be expressed. I do not wish to behave like some other players who resent the press, but nevertheless will be 'correct' with them just to get a good report. Once again, let me emphasise that my grouse is not against the press in general but only against those particular members who indulge in fanciful reporting.

There were many other cases of misreporting, but these three were the most glaring and the most galling. It is a pity really, because the other honest reporters who straight forwardly report the match in a straight forward manner and do not take sides get a cold treatment from the players when, in fact, both should come together to contribute to the progress of Indian cricket.

3

Peach Melba

THE DIFFERENCE BETWEEN FLYING AIR INDIA AND ANOTHER AIRLINE was at once apparent when Qantas gave us scattered seats. Although we travel economy class, Air India almost always upgrades the team and makes sure that the players sit together. The friendliness of the Air India crew also means that the flight, especially if it is a long one, is always jovial and time passes fairly quickly. In his few appearances in the one-day matches in India, Sadanand Vishwanath had shown himself to be quite a character and on this flight it was he who regaled us with his stories. During one of the meals a player noticed Vishy eating cheese with the cellophane wrapper on, but when it was pointed out to Vishy he nonchalantly replied, 'That's the way I like it.'

When we landed in Melbourne, another aspect became clear; that we would be treated like other passengers. Now, really, there is nothing wrong at all in that but when teams visit India some official comes forward and collects all the passports and completes the immigration formalities. Here we were, after a gruelling flight, standing in a queue and moving slowly up the line. Not quite a friendly welcome, we all felt.

We fixed up a team meeting for the evening and decided to rest. Most players turned up for the meeting looking bleary-eyed. Only Sadanand looked alert and it was obvious that in the few hours between our landing and the team meeting he had done some shopping. He had taken a tram to the city centre and walked to the shopping area, found out the various prices, found where the restaurants were, especially the Indian and Chinese food joints, the grocery store and the laundromat. Even those who were on their third tour of Australia would not have been able to do so. As Vishy continued to tell us his afternoon experiences in his wide-eyed manner it became apparent to the rest of us that here was an enterprising person who would pep up the side when morale was low. He had become an instant hit with the team.

Pras spoke to the players about his hopes and aspirations for the team and I told the players about the need to discipline themselves, because Australia offers various delights and the greatest danger is of putting on weight. We decided to lay emphasis on fielding practice and physical fitness. When the meeting broke up it did so with the sound of laughter. Everybody looked relaxed and happy with each other. Pras, Kapil and I sat down later to chalk out a probable eleven and decide how best to get them more practice than the others who were unlikely to play in the first few games. Some local Australian fast bowlers were also recruited to bowl at us, not only to give us some much-needed practice against quicker bowling on the bouncier Australian wickets but also to see that our own bowlers did not get overworked at the nets.

The nets were arranged at the Richmond Football Club, which was adjoining the Melbourne Cricket Ground. Since our hotel was bang opposite the M.C.G., we walked across to the ground, from where we were directed to the Richmond nets. The cynosure of all eyes, naturally, was Azharuddin, with Siva being followed by an equal number of cameramen, all trying to catch the moment when Siva would bowl his googly. The mischievous fellow that he is, Siva did not bowl a single 'wrong one' in the session but just concentrated on line and length. There was turn and some bounce in the wicket and after every delivery Siva's smile became wider and wider. Ravi Shastri also expressed his happiness at the turn and bounce he got and after a knock in the nets looked pleased as punch with Australia.

The next morning was spent trying out our coloured clothing. Only after we had landed in Australia did we find out that every game was to be played in coloured clothes and with a white ball. We were under the impression that the day games were to be in whites, so all of us had brought our regular kit along. I promptly cornered Judge Kanmadikar who sheepishly confessed that he had presumed we would be aware that all through only coloured clothing and gear would be used. He, however, agreed to carry back to India my white leg-guards and clothing, since he was leaving earlier.

After a session with the outfitters for coloured clothing it was now the turn for signing as many as five hundred bats. When we last visited Australia in 1980-81 we had a similar session. That time there were sixteen chairs put up in a big room with about thirty bats in front of each. The players were made to sit on the chairs and sign the bats in front of them. After finishing the lot a player got up and went to the next chair and signed the bats there. By this rotation no player felt fatigued and it was over very quickly. On this occasion the bats were laid up on a table and the players just moved from bat to bat. This was more tiring, as the players had to bend down to sign with a huge pile in front. It looked like a daunting prospect. As we moved away after signing the bats we were each given a Benson & Hedges carrier bag. We were also told that each player and manager would get a bat each. That meant that everybody signed carefully and not just scribbled, because there was the danger that they themselves might land up with a bat on which they had scribbled their autograph.

We had a light lunch organised by Benson & Hedges, for whom Alan Turner, the former Australian opening batsman, is now working as an executive. He was somehow quite certain that we would do well and expressed the hope that Australia and India would meet in the finals. One can understand his feelings, because the Aussies had beaten us convincingly on their short tour of India and as an Aussie what better way to end the season than with an Australian victory in the Benson & Hedges Cup.

We also had to attend a press conference organised for all the captains and managers. When we arrived at the venue, Pras and I were in cricket clothing since we had to rush off for net practice immediately after the conference. Allan Border was the only other captain present with the team manager Bob Merriman, while the West Indians had sent only their manager Wes Hall. The English team was playing a friendly fixture which was to prove quite expensive, as they ended that day with two of their players breaking their wrist bones. The Sri Lankans also were playing a friendly match where the Pakistanis and the New Zealanders were engaged in a test series in New Zealand.

The day the tournament began there was a parade where all the teams went round the ground to a thunderous ovation from the crowd. The West Indians and, naturally, the Australians got the biggest applause but it was heartening to see the Indian tricolour being waved from the crowd. The authorities had never expected a turnout like this. When I had woken up that morning and had a peek outside I was surprised to see people queueing up to enter the ground. This was around 8.30 in the morning for a match starting at 2.30 in the afternoon.

The Australian prime minister, Bob Hawke, was present and after the speeches he tossed the coin for the match between England and Australia. We watched a bit of the game and then went away for a net session. It was another hard session and the team was led through the training by Jimmy Amarnath. Held day after day these sessions can be boring, but Jimmy wisely invited some individual players to stand next to him while the rest of us formed the usual circle and performed the exercises. When Jimmy invited a player to stand next to him his intentions became clear, because then that player would try and match Jimmy, as all our eyes would be on him and he would not shirk the exercises or do them casually. Every player obviously has his limitations, but often one tends to go through the motions of the exercises, smilingly.

That evening the Indian Association organised a dinner for us. Dr J. Rao, who is the honorary Consul General for India in Melbourne, was the inspiration behind these dinners, which the team has been attending since 1977. It is good to meet Indians who have settled and made a life for themselves in Australia. They are keen to hear at first-hand about the situation in India. The only problem at these parties seems to be the endless flash of cameras. We rushed back from there to the M.C.G. to get an idea about the lights and the atmosphere.

Australia did not seem to be doing well, but picked up through Kerr and Jones and overhauled the modest English score, much to the delight of the big crowd which had come to see their team do the Pommies in. They went away happy amid a splendid show of fireworks which was launched as soon as the game finished. It was truly a magnificent spectacle and went on for quite some time. When we reached the hotel we could still see the fireworks from our rooms.

Our practice session the next day was scheduled for the morning at the M.C.G. The vast ground was empty, though there were still signs that there had been a big crowd present the previous evening with the odd beer can lying about. What was most obvious was the gleaming gold-coloured Audi which had been put on display. This car was to be presented to the Champion of Champions of the tournament, selected by the commentators of Channel 9 network.

As we did our training exercises in front of the stand where the Audi was displayed there were at least five members of the side who pointed to the car and said that on 10 March the car would be theirs. Thereafter, every time we had a practice session at the M.C.G. the players would look at the car and smile, each living his own private dream. The Pakistani team had arrived from New Zealand where they were denied a win by some stubborn batting by Jeremy Coney and the last batsman, Chatfield. Their confidence was boosted by the arrival of Imran Khan who was to play for his country after a lapse of two years. His shin fracture had healed and he was back in the business of bowling fast. His very presence in the side must be a great morale booster for the players because like all top all-rounders he has the ability to change the course of the match single-handedly. In Imran's case it is more so with his bowling, but others like Kapil, Botham and Hadlee can do so with either their bowling or batting or both.

591

On the eve of the match we practised under the light for the first time and found that though the lights were very good those in Delhi were much better. Most eyes, however, were focused on Imran who was limbering up at the other net. He came in with his full run-up and bowled and though the speed looked marginally less than before, any doubts regarding his fitness were dispensed with.

Imran is a splendid example to budding young fast bowlers. He really works hard doing several laps of the ground and then his own special brand of exercises. However, the most notable part of his bowling, as also Kapil's, in the nets is that they never bowl no-balls. Thus a no-ball from Imran or Kapil in the match is a rare event. Many young and even established bowlers do not bother about no-balls in the nets and overstep blithely, believing that everything will come right in the match. What they are tampering with is their rhythm and once this is upset, it becomes a real uphill task.

There are certain bowlers who like to take their time and think before they deliver the ball, while some like Lance Gibbs want to fire in ball after ball quickly. I recollect how upset Gibbs was when I took my time after each delivery he bowled, looking around the field or simply adjusting my leg-guards or gloves. He not only gave me a verbal rocket but also bowled a bouncer out of anger because I was making him wait at the top of his run-up. At first I was only trying to get the extra seconds to get my breath back after a hard run of a two or three but as I realised that I was upsetting his rhythm, I kept doing a bit more of the delay. Yes, I indeed was a naughty 21-year-old!

Since it was pretty late when we finished practice and the match next day was in the afternoon, the team strategy meeting was postponed to 11.45 in the morning. Apart from the strategy to be adopted if we won the toss, we discussed each Pakistani player in detail, his strengths and weaknesses and discussed how to curb his effectiveness. What was good about this meeting was that a newcomer like Sadanand Viswanath showed much spirit and his points, made animatedly, were important. There seemed to be a new determination, a new inner strength may be because the meeting was held minutes before we left for the ground. Often when meetings are held on the eve of the match a lot of fellows are distracted. Held on the mornings, of the match the meeting would mean that with the match a couple of hours away, the strategy and discussions are fresh in the player's mind and he is really charged up for the game.

Pakistan were put in to bat after I won the toss. The opening pair surprised us, because we thought the tried and trusted Mohsin and Mudassar would open. Instead it was Qasim with Mohsin, possibly because of the fine form shown by Omar in New Zealand. It was Mohsin who left early when a ball from Binny rose awkwardly and brushed his glove on the way to Vishwanath. Sadanand's joy and relief could be seen on his face; relief, because earlier he had dived to his right when Omar edged Binny and the catch which was coming to me directly was dropped and deflected for a single. I've always believed wicketkeepers must go for a catch they think they can reach. With their gauntlets they stand a better chance of the ball sticking on than the slip fielder who, unless he gets the ball smack in the right place, is likely to have it bounce out.

Vish suddenly was a different player after taking Mohsin's catch. I had to have a quiet word with him after his lapse earlier, because he was swearing at himself very loudly and I reminded him of the sensitive microphones which were probably picking his every word. He suddenly stopped and flashed that grin of his and I knew that he had forgotten about the microphones. Too often even established and seasoned players keep thinking of a mistake they may have made on the field, which means that with their concentration impaired they are likely to make another one soon.

Qasim and Zaheer were kept quiet by some excellent bowling by Kapil and Roger and after each had bowled five overs Pakistan were barely averaging over two runs per over. Madan then came in and bowled a good tight spell and as soon as the limitation on the fielders for the first fifteen overs within the 30-yard circle was removed I brought on Sivaramakrishnan. We had planned in the team meeting to have Siva bowl round the wicket if he found bowling over difficult. Qasim swept him for two boundaries and he and Zaheer also got their singles by driving on either side of the wicket. Then Siva went round the wicket and immediately struck when Zaheer hit back a catch which Siva grabbed and held on to at the second attempt as he fell. Qasim completed a well-compiled fifty and was out soon after when he mistimed a drive and Siva took another return catch.

Rameez Raja did not stay long too. When Binny was brought back he induced Javed into playing early and the resultant catch was taken at mid-wicket by Siva. Our fielding practice was showing results and the crowning piece was Mudassar's run-out. He swung at a ball, got the outside edge and the ball went to third man to Kapil's left.

Kapil charged, collected and threw the wickets down in one single motion as Mudassar vainly stretched to reach the crease. The ball had to hit the stumps or else Mudassar would have completed the second run. It was brilliant cricket and the crowd loved it. Having got a piece of the action Kapil was not likely to let go and he had Imran attempting a slog only to be caught at extra cover off a skier. Madan then got into the act by having Tahir Naqqash caught by Amarnath at deep mid-wicket. With hardly any resistance from the tail Pakistan were all out for 183.

This was not a big score, but somehow 183 brings back memories of Lords 1983 and I kept my fingers crossed that we should not become overconfident like the West Indians in the Prudential Cup final. Besides, there was a man called Imran Khan who was making a comeback in the international scene, no doubt anxious to prove to all that he was now fully fit and back at the top.

The tour selection committee had decided earlier that Ravi Shastri should open with Srikkanth. Not only had Ravi been successful as an opener in the limited-overs matches but he also would act as the ideal person to balance Srikkanth's ebullience. I had also noticed a tendency on Srikkanth's part to go into his shell whenever he opened with me and so it was decided that Ravi should open. He went in the first over to Imran and just when we were breathing a little easier Imran struck with the fifth and sixth ball of his fifth over, having Srikkanth and Vengsarkar caught, to leave us reeling at 27 for three.

I joined Azharuddin at this stage and was immediately put at ease by Azhar's calm composure. My first task, however, was to make sure that I got a run to my name. Before we left for Australia my son Rohan said to me that since the first match was on his birthday I had better not give him a zero as a birthday present. I nodded then, thinking to myself how time quickly changes attitudes. Only a couple of months before Rohan was asking me to score centuries and here he was now, seeing my bad form, asking me not to score a zero!

I scored my first run off Rashid Khan who had replaced Imran after the latter had bowled his sixth over, Azhar having safely played out the hat-trick delivery and playing the entire over. It is at this stage that a captain has to take a gamble. Imran had fired three batsmen and was possibly a little tired, having bowled six overs, and with four overs of his quota left the captain had to decide whether to remove him and use him in two spells of two overs each or take a gamble and give him the seventh over. I had not faced a single ball from Imran since Azhar had played out his sixth over. Since he had played confidently and as there was no certainty that I would be there to face Imran if he was given the seventh over, Javed decided to rest him and bring Rashid Khan on. Wasim Akram also was removed from the attack and Naqqash brought on. The pressure eased considerably and Azhar and I began to build the innings up slowly by looking for singles and trying to convert ones into twos and twos into threes. Azhar is a superb runner between wickets, responding eagerly to a call; and not only that, he is a good judge of a run. One can be a quick runner between wickets but one must also be able to judge the risk in taking a run. This Azhar did to perfection and with him being in top form soon he was flicking the ball away off his legs and driving beautifully through the off side.

Early on in our partnership I went to drive a ball from Rashid and snicked it very faintly but the umpire negatived the confident appeal much to the chagrin of the Pakistani bowler and fielders. I stood my ground, because though my first inclination is to walk, there are two teams against whom I will never do so. One is Pakistan and the other is Mafatlals in the inter-office tournaments. TV slow motion replays did not show any deflection and those in the dressing room thought I was nowhere near the ball.

After that there was hardly an anxious moment, even after Imran came in for his second spell. Though I was out leg-before to Mudassar we needed only a few runs to win, with lots of overs to go. Azhar remained not out on a dazzling 93, unlucky not to reach his century, and Mohinder kept him company when the winning hit was made with almost five overs to spare.

Though one hates to be out, in this case I was secretly happy to be so, only because if I had been unbeaten and Azhar had remained on 93 my friends in the press would surely have blamed me for not letting Azhar get his century. Sometimes things do work out for the better.

In Australia the practice is for the captains to meet the press after they have finished the TV presentation, which is live, and here in Melbourne, luckily, the press was gathered in the room next to our dressing room. When I entered the room Javed was answering questions. He had almost finished when I pulled up a chair next to him. I heard him say that but for an appeal for a catch behind the wicket, which was disallowed, Pakistan would have won. When pressed by the journalists he said that the appeal he was referring to was the one against me. Till now it was Javed's show and so I kept quiet but seeing me sit next to him the journalists couldn't but help ask my opinion and I replied that it did not matter what I thought or what Javed thought. The only important thing was what the umpire thought. However, the umpire being an Australian in an India-Pakistan game, there was no bitterness in Javed's complaints. If the umpire had been an Indian, then allegations of bias would have been levelled, but an umpire from a third country only provokes a complaint and a shrug of the shoulders.

The victory was a turning point, because the team's morale suddenly shot up sky high. We were now looking forward to the clash against England in Sydney. Although England beat us 4-

1 in the five one-day games in India they were close-fought, with one or two wayward overs costing us the matches. Also we had some new faces in the squad and this meant that they were not suffering from the trauma of that defeat.

4

Settling Scores with England

SYDNEY HAS PROBABLY THE BEST PRACTICE WICKET IN AUSTRALIA;
neither too bouncy nor too slow, just an even bounce and pace
for bowlers and batsmen alike. Before we arrived in Sydney we
had a day in Melbourne and we spent that day practising, even
though the match had finished only at ten the previous night.
By the time sleep overtook most of us it must have been close
to dawn. The problem with a night game is that it takes a good
three or four hours for the body and mind to unwind from the
excitement, pressure and tension of the game. It is invariably
around two or three in the morning when one drops off to sleep
unlike in a day game when one can unwind early

After the game against Pakistan most of us went for dinner to a restaurant because none of us had eaten much during the interval between the innings and then spent some time in the hotel disco. All the teams were in the same hotel and so there was a fair sprinkling of players from all sides.

Thus to get up early in the morning and practise was a bit tough, because the one-day game is more exhausting than the regular Test match and the body seems to get more stiff. All of us were there for practice. Most people were surprised because the day after the game almost everybody relaxes and stays put in the hotel. But this team was a motivated team and though the practice session was not as hard as the previous ones it was good to give the reserves a chance to limber up and get some useful knocks. It was good to see the players use the nets with a purpose. Often nets are used to bat wildly, with the result that faults, previously unknown, start appearing, which become difficult to first detect and then correct.

There was not much practice we could get in Sydney as the rains came down with a vengeance and even the match looked doubtful. Fortunately it stopped, and though the outfield looked a bit soggy, the match was to start on time.

I lost the toss and David Gower turned round and said to me 'same format'. He was referring to our one-day practice of putting the other in after winning the toss, in the series played at home. I replied, 'Of course, different result though.'

I signalled inside that we were batting and ran to the other end of the ground where I was to be interviewed by Channel 9 on the advisability of the use of the helmet. Somehow owing to some disturbance or the other the interview could not be recorded properly and so by the time I reached the dressing room, the players were entering the ground and I could only whisper 'best of luck' under my breath as Ravi and Srikkanth passed me on their way to the wicket. That was terribly wrong of me. I should have been in the dressing room, available for any questions, though we had had the team meeting earlier in the morning where we discussed everything.

Srikkanth got off to a blazing start and the Channel 9 commentators, especially Bill Lawry, were captivated by his batting. He was not afraid to loft the ball over the fielders. He does this regularly, but today he was timing the ball well. Foster bowled a good tight spell while Cowans did not know what hit him. Ravi was taking his singles, intelligently leaving the strike to Srikkanth. Ravi got out flicking uppishly and Srikkanth, after an electrifying 58, was run out to a brilliant throw from deep square leg by Norman Cowans.

Azhar got into his stride immediately. The English bowlers must dread the sight of this slim batsman from Hyderabad. Every time he had gone to bat against them he had made a substantial score. Here he began to stroke the ball with the silken grace that only Zaheer in present day international cricket seems capable of. Allan Lamb summed up Azhar's batting in a very succinct manner saying, 'Batting is like f-- to him. Just go out and do it.'

Azhar is also a superb runner between the wickets and the dressing room was in splits when he started calling Vengsarkar for singles and threes. The outfield being slow, as a result of the rain, even the hardest hits were slowing down enough for the English fielders to get to before the ball crossed the line and this in turn meant that the batsmen had to keep running. Dilip was just about reaching his end and then resting with one hand on his hips, with the other leaning on to his bat when he would be called for another run. This often happens and one feels little out of breath at first. Then as one gets used to the running one seems to get a second wind, so to speak.

In Dilip's case after the earlier hustle he settled down and was driving crisply, as is his wont. When he gets on to that front foot and drives, Dilip is a majestic sight. One cover drive off Foster was a beauty, while another flick off his hips left Cowans and Lamb, the two men on the fine leg fence, converging upon each other, with the ball neatly passing for a four. It was superb batting. However, both Azhar and he fell in quick succession. Kapil had been promoted to lay about the bowling and when I joined him he was just looking like tearing the attack apart. Cowans was brought on and I drove him high and straight first bounce into the fence. I enjoyed that shot. Cowans had given me some bother in the Calcutta Test, mainly because I was determined not to hook and the ball kept coming slower than I imagined. Just as a bowler loves tormenting a batsman who may have heaped runs against him, a batsman also likes to get his own back against a tormentor.

Kapil and Mohinder fell quickly and when Binny and Madan did not contribute much, it looked like we would not even total 225, but Sadanand Vishwanath played well and we took the score to 236 when he was run out, trying to go for a third run. The score, though not enough by limited-over standards, was a fighting total and if we got a few quick wickets then we could be in with our second win.

Fowler started the England innings with his usual play, miss and whoosh. There are batsmen who make the bowlers go down on their knees in different ways: the likes of Gooch, Richards, Kapil, Botham, Srikkanth who smash their way around leaving the bowlers demoralized, the likes of Zaheer, Vishwanath, Roy Dias, Azhar, Gower who hit the good ball for runs and make the bowlers wonder what to do next; the likes of Boycott,

Amarnath, Greenidge and, by recent accounts, Ravi Shastri who, with their seemingly impregnable defence, look as solid as steel and often make the bowlers feel they are bowling to a brick wall. Then there is somebody like Fowler who will play and miss, edge the ball exactly between third slip and gully and play a superb shot, all in one over. His kind makes the bowler want to tear his hair out in frustration; the fielders begin by looking heavenwards as if begging for divine intervention and as Fowler prospers their language becomes unprintable. He simply demoralises the opposition by his playing and missing. Having said that, one has nothing but admiration for the way he carries on with his job. The fact that he is a very pleasant man, not averse to a joke or two on the field, makes all his runs appreciated, however sketchily, by his team-mates and grudgingly so by the opposition.

In this match he fell to Binny when, in trying to lift a ball over square leg, he succeeded only in getting a top edge and the ball went high in the air. Vishy, running to his right, judged it perfectly and held on to it much to our delight. Moxon took his time to settle down and he and Gower were looking like taking the game away from us when Siva did the trick. At 99, with half the overs gone, England looked poised. Within a few overs, however, the game slipped completely from their grasp. Siva started the slide by having Gower caught in the deep by Vengsarkar off a full toss. He then had Moxon caught and bowled and then cunningly bowled Allan Lamb a googly which the batsman played all over and was bowled. Ravi Shastri then had Gatting, going for a cut, caught behind by Vishwanath and England's innings was in shambles. However, Marks and Downton had rescued England from a similar situation in the past and so the match was far from over. Shastri had other ideas. He got Marks stretching forward and brilliantly stumped. Edmonds also fell quickly and then Vishy took a real beauty of a catch standing up to Madan Lal when Ellison tried to cut.

5

Aussies Crestfallen

OUR VICTORY HAD MORE OR LESS ASSURED US OF A place in the semifinals but it was important that we maintained a good run rate in our final group match against Australia who had been beaten convincingly by Pakistan a couple of days earlier. Whether the run rate would matter depended on the Pakistan-England game on the day before we played Australia. If England won then we would be through to the semifinals anyway, with the match against Australia only deciding who would top our group in case Australia won against us.

The Pakistan-England match was thus followed with much interest by all in Australia. They were of course hoping that England beat Pakistan so that Australia could qualify by beating India. There were some in the Indian camp who also felt that an England victory would be ideal, as then the game next day against Australia would not be critical because we would have qualified anyway.

Exactly the opposite happened. Pakistan beat England, though if England had not had to achieve their target of 213 in 32.4 overs the result could have been close. Allan Lamb in a breathtaking display almost made it possible, but after his dismissal England collapsed, to be all out for 146 in 24.2 overs. It was a spiritless effort.

Now the pressure was on both Australia and India. Pakistan had a run rate of 4.39 and to get past that Australia had to score 225 and India 221 or something like that, according to the papers. Frankly speaking, I was not bothered, because the pressure was more on the Aussies. They had to win the match to qualify. I was confident that in spite of having lost to them earlier in India, the way our team was playing meant that we were just beginning to peak.

We were to play on the same wicket that had been used the previous day and having seen Lamb's innings we knew it was a lovely wicket to play on.

Allan Border could not accompany me to the toss because of an upset stomach and so Rodney Hogg came along to toss with me. The walk from the M.C.G. dressing room to the wicket is one of the longest and as we walked, Hoggy said, 'You guys have been playing incredibly. You really seem to do well outside India, don't you?' I just nodded back but I was happy to note from his remark that the Australians were worried. I won the toss and asked Australia to bat. This was the only day game we played. The others were all day-night events. So if there was any moisture it would help our seamers. And that's exactly what happened.

Kapil was now running in sharply and Roger with that languid walk back to the mark is deceptive when he turns around and bowls. Kapil struck first, getting Kerr bowled as he shouldered the bat and found the ball deflecting off his leg-guards onto the stumps. Wood was bowled by Binny in the next over with a beautifully pitched delivery that darted into the gap between bat and pad to knock his off stump out. In Binny's next over he had the Australian captain bowled in a similar manner to have Australia reeling at three for 17.

Then came the kind of intelligent thinking that makes Kapil such a great bowler. Knowing Wessels' fondness for the front foot, Kapil dug one in short and Wessels, suddenly finding himself cramped, played an involuntary hook shot in the air and the ball went to the safest catcher in the world, Madan Lal. In the same over Phillips cut hard and uppishly and Azhar diving to his left got his hands to the ball but was unable to hold on to it. The Australians would have been 18 for five wickets if Azhar's great effort had resulted in a catch.

We had to wait a little longer for the next wicket. It seemed long, because with the earlier four wickets we had got them in four overs from either end. Amarnath had replaced Binny while Madan Lal had come in for Kapil. Amarnath succeeded when he had Dean Jones chasing a widish delivery to be caught behind. Things looking were good for India at -- 37 for five. The Pakistanis must have been sporting broad grins at this stage, knowing that it would take a superhuman effort by the Australians to reach the 225 runs that were needed for qualifying for the knockout stage of the tournament.

Simon O'Donnell and Wayne Phillips began the rebuilding operation, but the overs were finishing quickly and they had to chance their arm. O'Donnell went first, going for a big hit but only managing to hit the ball in the air where Mohinder held on to the catch. In the next over Siva foxed Lawson into giving a return catch and it was 85 for seven wickets. Both Siva and Ravi were bowling beautifully, giving the ball just the right amount of air and thus managing to get enough turn to beat the attacking stroke.

I crowded Rodney Hogg hoping that he would go for the big hit and misstime. He did but he also hit it cleanly to get a four, over mid-wicket. I had removed the deep mid-wicket to tempt him into the shot. Ravi was not happy, so I put the man back on the job of patrolling that area. Hogg played sensibly, nudging the odd one here and there. Phillips, in the meanwhile, had reached a well-compiled 50. He is a dangerous player, because he can be very unorthodox and has the uncanny ability to find the gaps. With his individual score at 60 he went to sweep Siva, got a top edge and Amarnath took his second catch.

Hogg, McCurdy and Alderman each contributed a bit before the Australian innings ended at 163. For the Australians to qualify, they had not only to bowl us out but do so for less than 161.

The score did not look imposing, but there lies the real danger, because the earlier batsmen sometimes tend to take things easy, thinking that the batsmen down the order can do the repairs. This often means that wickets are down quickly and there is a collapse, putting enormous pressure on the all-rounders. Luckily for us, we had the levelheaded, conscientious Ravi Shastri to see that there was no collapse and Srikkanth too, after seeing off a hostile spell from Lawson and Hogg, during which the two bowlers overstepped often, opened out in his typical fashion to see that we were through without any anxiety.

The pair added 124 runs before Shastri departed, caught behind, for 51. Srikkanth continued to plunder runs, hitting unconventional shots and then shrugging his shoulders and smiling at the non-striker, which must have made the bowler even angrier. Simon O'Donnell certainly did not find anything funny as he repeatedly got hit over the top or glided through the vacant slips for boundaries. He had earlier dropped Srikkanth off McCurdy; one of the easiest catches that one could hope for, but O'Donnell had muffed it. He swears a lot on the field, so perhaps he should have tried the catch with his mouth instead of his hands!

Azhar got his first, and hopefully last, duck for India playing back to Alderman and being adjudged leg-before. However, there were no further alarms as Srikkanth, joined by the experienced Vengsarkar, saw us overtake the score of 163 with plenty of overs to spare.

Thus we had topped our group, winning three matches. Pakistan also qualified by having won two matches, followed by Australia with one win and England with nil. During the course of our innings Javed Miandad had dropped into our dressing room and was looking very happy, as with our dismissal of Australia for 163, Pakistan had qualified irrespective of who won our game. As always, he had words of advice as to how we could have dismissed Australia for less than 163 if only we had done this and that. Dilip Vengsarkar, who revels in egging Javed on, just about said that we should have dismissed Australia for less than 75. I joked that then the match would have been a non-contest and it certainly would not have looked very nice that the hosts should be humbled so. Javed left, saying that at least they had qualified and if they lost it would be to the eventual champions, West Indies.

6

Kapil Snatches a Victory

WE TRAVELLED TO SYDNEY THE NEXT MORNING AND WERE TO
PLAY New Zealand on Tuesday. This, I thought, was a bit hard
because having played a game on Sunday we were getting only
a day's rest while New Zealand had qualified eight days earlier
and in fact gone back home to play a domestic tournament.
They had had a longer break. Also, Pakistan had played on
Saturday, while West Indies had played a week earlier. So three
teams in the semifinals were lucky to get a long break to be
fresher for the fray. Our team would get hardly any rest, but then
such was the luck with the draw.

We practised, stiff limbs or not, and once again the
enthusiasm of the players was most remarkable. With the

manager Prasanna himself bowling in the nets, challenging the batsmen to hit with an imaginary field placing, batting in the nets was not simply a chore but an enjoyable and stimulating experience. Pras is still a very crafty bowler and one has to watch him in the nets. He bowled Azhar with a beauty that went straight through, after having sent down three previous deliveries with sufficient turn to beat the bat. Genius is genius, whether you are twenty-four or forty-four.

There was a huge contingent from New Zealand to support their team. With plenty of New Zealanders working in Sydney there was no dearth of encouragement for Howarth and his team.

Geoff Howarth is one of the most likeable cricketers in the world and so are the members of the New Zealand team. They are very friendly and, though they play hard, are good losers, which I am afraid cannot be said of many others.

I won the toss and asked them to bat first. Kapil struck immediately, getting John Wright caught behind off the third ball that left him after the earlier two had come into the left-handed opener. Good start. Binny bowled well, though he looked to be having trouble with his run-up. Roger is hardly the one to complain. He takes everything in his stride with a shrug of his shoulders and that shy smile of his. Having been driven gloriously through the cover for a boundary by McEwan he produced an unplayable delivery that lifted from a length. McEwan could only snick it to Vish behind the wicket. After the boundary shot, the N.Z. supporters had begun to sing one of their popular cheering songs, but Roger put the dampner on their joy. Strangely, the next time also the same thing happened, as Crowe got out after a boundary and the exultant singing by the supporters. Thereafter they stopped singing, perhaps thinking that it was unlucky for their batsmen.

Howarth, who has taken to batting in spectacles, was run out when a ball flipped his pad, broke the top buckle and definitely hampered him as he went for a second and was run out by a direct throw from Kapil. Another brilliant piece of fielding from this great trier.

Coney and Reid were men in form. Both play very sensibly, avoiding flashy shots and concentrating on taking every possible opportunity to score. Reid reached a well-made 50 but left soon after when he tried to hit Shastri for a six and found instead the ball landing in Kapil's hands at long-on. Smith was promoted ahead of Hadlee, which looked a bit strange to us, because with the spinners operating one would have thought the big-hitting Cairns or the experienced Hadlee would come in.

Amarnath had, in the meanwhile, bowled a most crucial spell of seven overs in which he gave away only 24 runs. I had been bringing Jimmy on, to try and have a little flexibility, in case the major bowlers got carved around a bit. However, the two or three overs that I planned extended to seven overs because Jimmy was bowling so well and was difficult to get away with.

Coney and Smith ran their singles well and just as they were lookng dangerous, Shastri tempted Coney into cutting his armer and knocked back his stumps. Hadlee then holed out to Madan Lal for three but his exit meant that the big-hitting Cairns now came in. Somehow he just seemed to be interested in nudging singles and twos and both he and Smith ran like mad men. Smith was lucky to survive a leg-before appeal off Madan, but going for a big hit in the following over he lifted a catch to Mohinder.

It was now that Cairns decided to take charge. He smote Madan high over mid-on for a four, then over square-leg for another one. He hit another almighty up in the air and Srikkanth, normally a safe catcher, floored it. Off the very next ball he went for another hit and hit it wider Srikkanth's left but the Tamil Nadu opener not only did not try for the catch, which was admittedly a bit far away, but did not even try to stop the ball. This was what upset me, because runs are important and though Sri must have been dejected after his miss he should have made the effort to stop the ball going for a boundary. I immediately shuffled the fielders, because this was the last over of the innings and time did not matter. So Kapil came to deep mid-wicket from deep square-leg and Srikkanth went to Kapil's place. In cricket there is a saying that the ball follows a fielder whether he is catching or dropping everything. As if to prove that, Cairns flicked the next ball over to square-leg and this time Srikkanth made no mistake. His sigh of relief was almost audible round the ground and the entire Indian team was grinning from ear to ear at the turn of events. Snedden then was caught at deep midwicket next ball as New Zealand were all out for 206 runs.

A score of 206 is not much by international standards. Once again the simple principle of one-day cricket, which says, 'Keep wickets intact and score at a fair average so that when the slog overs are on one can take risks without the pressure of being all out before fifty overs are complete', was applied.

The New Zealanders were not going to give up without a fight and their bowlers, backed up by splendid fielding, kept the batsmen quiet. Srikkanth left early and then came the man the New Zealanders wanted to see, Azharuddin. Earlier in the week, Imran Khan, writing in a newspaper, had said that Crowe would be the batsman of the 1980s. With the 1980s almost half way over and the likes of Miandad, Border, and Gower still around and young talent like Azharuddin, Saleem Malik to challenge, Martin Crowe is going to have a tough time justifying Imran's confidence.

The New Zealanders had obviously studied Azhar well and planned their strategy to tie him up on his legs with four fielders from backward square leg to mid-on and a fifth at deep fine-leg. Azhar was thus kept in check. The overs began to run away and the score moved in a trickle. A message was sent at the drinks interval and Azhar started to take risks. He clouted Coney over his head for a boundary and the score now began to move, but still there was plenty to make up. Azhar's innings was terminated by a fine running catch by Coney. More than half the fifty overs had been bowled and we were nowhere near the 100 mark.

Kapil had been sitting and watching the match along with our Consul General in Sydney. If there was a batsman who could change the complexion of the game it was Kapil. There are only two other batsmen capable of doing so. One, Srikkanth, was already out and the other, Sandeep Patil, was playing the Times Shield and Ranji Trophy in Bombay. I asked Kapil to pad up. He sprang up as if he was expecting this all along. When Azhar fell he looked at me and I motioned him with my hand to wait. I wanted him to go after thirty overs had been bowled and certainly not while Cairns was bowling. Cairns is a much underrated bowler. He swings the ball into the batsman most of the time and has a beautiful leg cutter and a slower ball, well-disguised. It was this slower ball which I was afraid of for Kapil and so wanted him to go after Cairns was taken off.

Our 100 came up in the thirty-first over, as also Shastri's half century. Hadlee, brought on for a new spell, got Ravi slicing a drive to backward point and at this stage Kapil strode in to bat. It was a make or break situation. Hadlee's following over was unforgettable. Off the first ball Kapil square cut off the full face of the bat to the point boundary. The next one went a little finer for another boundary.

In the Indian dressing room the atmosphere was now charged. The weather outside had turned chilly and we had been distributing sweaters and blazers and track-suit tops to relations and friends who were sitting in the stands and were exposed to the winds. This chill had somehow entered the dressing room. But after those two cracking shots from Kapil the dressing room certainly was a warmer place. As Hadlee walked back to his mark, Ashok Malhotra turned around and said, 'I hope he doesn't do anything silly now. He has already got runs and should nudge away for singles and twos.' Hadlee came charging in and bowled a well-concealed slower ball. Kapil launched into a drive and as the ball went up in the air a groan escaped our lips, only to be replaced by a deep sigh of relief as Reid dropped the catch at mid-off. There was everybody talking at the same time saying, 'I told you so. He just gets carried away,' etc. Fortunately the next ball was to be bowled and we all waited with bated breath to see what would happen. Hadlee came and bowled and five seconds later the ball was ricocheting off the extra cover fence from as glorious a cover drive as one could ever hope to see. When Kapil took a single in the next ball we were relieved, because in this vein he is apt to get out trying only for boundaries. Vengsarkar, who was now taking strike off Hadlee's last delivery, slashed a square cut away for another boundary; this time Chatfield, the fielder at deep third man, was running vainly to his left to try and stop the ball, after having been made to run to his right earlier in the over by Kapil's square cuts. Seventeen runs in the over and we had now broken the shackles that the New Zealand bowlers had put around us. Hadlee had been punished for 26 runs in two overs and now the target did not look too distant.

Dilip seemed to be invigorated by Kapil's batting and they literally carved the bowling to all parts of the ground now. Suddenly the Indian tricolour was fluttering more frequently than earlier from the stands. There was a huge crowd of Indians who had come down to support the team and were being treated to an exhibition of batting they will always remember. Vengsarkar, tall, correct and orthodox in his stroke making, seemingly caressing the ball, while Kapil at the other end, also tall, but certainly not always orthodox either in his shots or the choice of deliveries to hit. It was heady, brilliant stuff and the silent Indian dressing room was now agog with chatter. Typically, as we were moving closer and closer towards a victory, Indian supporters started invading the dressing room. This is a conduct common to Pakistan and India, where the privacy of the dressing room is often shattered. None of the supporters seem to have the patience to wait outside. If there is a place the cricketers are sensitive about, it is the dressing room. It is one place where they are away from the eyes of the world. This is the place where they can get rid of their tensions in different ways: shed a tear, scream and swear, perhaps throw a bat. This is also often a place where cricketers are not always properly dressed, to put it mildly, and so when an outsider barges in he is certainly not welcome. Even when a player's friend comes in, there is silence, because players are not certain of him and hold their tongues. Only if somebody is known to the team, does everybody carry on as usual.

During these invasions by supporters, lots of players have lost their equipment and that is more than enough reason not to allow strangers in the dressing room. Of course, not all behave in that manner. They are often well-meaning, but in countries outside India they are mainly under the influence of liquor and can be quite irritating.

Kapil and Dilip took us to victory with thirty-nine deliveries to spare, which did not look possible earlier. It was an outstanding performance.

The press conference after that was an enjoyable experience. At every conference I was giving new and different reasons for our team's performance. What else can one do when people refuse to accept that this game is full of uncertainties and thus the performance is likely to change from one day to the other. I was particularly looking forward to meeting a TV commentator from New Zealand who had asked me after our win over Australia in the previous game if India's wins were not flukes and reminded me that our record against New Zealand was not so good. The only answer I gave him that day was that our one-day record against Australia was not good either, and here we were through to the knock-out, having beaten Australia.

Now after this win over New Zealand, I was waiting for him to ask him if he thought this win was a fluke too. I also wanted to ask him how many major wins New Zealand had out of their country. Unfortunately, he turned up far too late, when most of the press had dispersed. Since he had questioned me in public after the Australian game, I was not going to ask him an inconvenient question when no one was around. I thus accepted his congratulations and went back to our dressing room. Most of the players had left and I only hoped they had done so in more peaceful circumstances than the previous game at Sydney against England.

Later, a few inebriated Indian supporters had offered Kapil, Madan and Chetan Sharma a lift but were politely refused because not only had taxis been ordered, but their car was parked a fair distance away in the car park and no one wants to lug a heavy cricket bag a distance. The Indian supporters took offence at this rejection of their request and the next thing one saw was bats being swung. Fortunately it was all brought under control very quickly or else there was every likelihood of a few broken bones.

7

Pakistan Comes Through

THE NEXT DAY WAS THE OTHER SEMIFINAL BETWEEN PAKISTAN
AND West Indies. We had a free day. Typically, and indicative of
the fierce desire to win which had now enveloped the team, most
members stayed put in their rooms to watch the telecast of the
match from Melbourne. We saw the West Indies batsmen throw
the match away, playing a sequence of astonishingly poor shots
and then their tail-enders showed little appreciation of the value
of sticking out till fifty overs were completed. While Lloyd was
batting, there was still a chance, but the way Marshall and the
others got out was not befitting the champion West Indian side.

Still West Indies had scored 159 and Pakistan were yet to
get them. Incredible things have been known to happen in
cricket and with the dreaded West Indies fast bowling machine
in operation anything could.

619

Marshall and Garner bowled a tremendously fast opening spell in which they got Mudassar. The manner in which the catch was taken showed how nervous the West Indians were. Mohsin wisely eschewed shots and concentrated on pushing the ball for singles while Rameez Raja plundered runs with audacious shots. Winston Davis came in for some punishment when he kept banging the ball in short without any attacking fielders and thus got pasted all over the ground. The second wicket fell at 97 and the third at 116 before Javed and Omar guided Pakistan into the final. This was a real upset win and Clive Lloyd said that one of the reasons was that his team had not played cricket for almost a week.

This reason was exactly opposite to that given by Allan Border when he complained that Australia had lost because they had had too much cricket. I thought Border's excuse a bit flimsy because apart from Wessels, Lawson and Border himself, the other members of the Aussie team were new and thus could not complain of overexposure. We had played the same kind of cricket and we also should have been tired. However, it is in such circumstances that one's determination and temperament scores. I am not for one moment suggesting that the Australians do not have determination, because if there is one team that fights till the very end they is the Australians.

Border, after their loss against Pakistan, rebuked former captain Kim Hughes in a press conference. Predictably the next day's headlines were only about Hughes having departed immediately after the match because he had a flight to catch, without even the courtesy of informing Allan Border. The fine performance of the Pakistan team was thus relegated to the background. If this was a ploy to avoid criticism of the Australian team it was magnificent stuff thought up by the Australian skipper. Poor Kim Hughes really had it. My sympathies were entirely with him because when we were rival captains in 1979-80 he was outstanding not only as a player but for the manner in which he carried himself. Also I had experienced very recently the kind of all-round criticism that he was being subjected to and so naturally I was with him.

When Allan Border had failed to come forward and congratulate the Indian team after we beat them, I saw my opportunity and inquired why Border did not have the simple courtesy of popping into our dressing room and offering his congratulations. 'He did not have a flight to catch, did he?' I asked the Australian press. Not that it made any difference, because if the media like you they will make any excuse for you, even avoid printing news but if you are their favourite whipping-boy, then like Hughes you will get blamed for every little thing.

8

Javed's Premature Jubilance

THE DAY BEFORE THE FINAL, JAVED AND I WERE ASKED TO COME
down to the M.C.G. to pose for pictures with the glittering
Benson & Hedges Cup. The chirpy Javed said to me while I
held the cup that I could keep it for the day but the next day
he would be the one holding it high. His words sent my mind
back a month. On 10 February, I had just finished my bath and
was wrapped in a towel when a vision of me holding the cup
aloft came before my eyes. So I said to my sisters-in-law who
were in the house at that moment, 'Next month on 10 March
I will be holding the B&H Cup'. They just looked at me and
smiled more in amazement than politeness. I rarely talk cricket
at home and very seldom with them. As Javed said those words,
the vision of that day came back to me and I was quietly
determined to have it come true.

Javed went back to the hotel, while we went and practised

under the lights. Surprisingly, the Pakistan team did not turn up as they had practised in the morning. It was thus fairly obvious that they were going to bat if they won the toss next day. However, what is most important is fielding practice under the lights, as unlike during daytime the velocity and trajectory of the ball falling from the dark skies is difficult to gauge. Perhaps they were overconfident, having beaten the West Indies in the semifinals. Perhaps they simply wanted more than twenty-four hours rest before the finals.

Our fielding practice as usual was intensive. Most of the players had earlier done catching and throwing in ones and twos while the nets were on. After everybody had finished batting and bowling we got down to fielding practice together. Roger was asked to hit the catches. He really gave us some steeplers, hitting the ball with one hand. Every time he sent a ball a mile high, one of us would shout 'beef and pork' meaning that diet was the secret of Roger's incredible strength in hitting the ball so high, one handed. For most of us it is difficult to hit the ball half that height with two hands and here he was doing it effortlessly with one hand. The swirling wind, the dark skies and the falling temperatures made everybody's hands sting as they went for the catches. Every time Kapil and Siva ran for catches my heart would stop beating. In their case a slight miscalculation would mean an injured finger and their inability to bowl their best the next day. I even asked them to leave but they would not listen. Mohinder and Madan were the other two who worked hard. Even after we all had finished our catches Madan and then Mohinder took over from Roger and gave each other some really hard catches.

As we walked back to our hotel I thought that we had truly practised hard, right through this tournament and we deserved success, if only for the efforts that the players had put in.

We went for dinner to Dr Sada Anvekar's where we saw part of a Hindi film on the video before realizing that it was almost midnight and time to catch up on sleep.

I had a 'do not disturb' on the phone and the door, so when I woke up next morning and read a message that had been shoved under the door saying that Mohinder wanted a doctor urgently, I was worried and called up to be told by Jimmy that he was all right but Roger was not. Apparently he had come down with flu and was in bed. The doctor had come and given him a shot and since the match was still five hours away there was still some hope that he would be fit to play.

We kept on inquiring and were told that he was asleep and that it would be better if he came down only before the game was to start. We had our team meeting in the Manager's room just before we left for the ground. Since we had already played Pakistan once there was less discussion on the individuals, though we talked about Rameez Raja who had played so well against the West Indie in the semifinals. We also speculated about the probable composition of their eleven. Most of the team felt that Zaheer, with his excellent record against us, would play. There were some who thought that Javed would not pick Zed, while some others thought Zaheer, though fit, would declare himself not so and thus be out of the game. I told Chetan that he could be playing in case Roger declared himself unfit. Roger had not attended the team meeting.

We came down to the lobby to be met by some Indians who had flown in from various parts of the world to watch the game. I am sure so had the Pakistanis come to see their team win. People had come from Fiji and Singapore, and from Muscat, Kanaksi Khimji had come who loves cricket and had organized the benefit match for the late Vijay Manjrekar. One expected Abdul Rehman Bukhatir, the inspiration behind cricket in the Gulf, especially since it was an Indo-Pak final. He did not turn up but I am certain his mind must have been in Melbourne though physically he may have been thousands of miles away.

Just as we had done through the earlier rounds we went straight to the lunch room for a light lunch and then went for practice. The Pakistan team had now finished practice and were now trooping in for lunch which left the ground free for us. We went through our usual training schedule, batting and bowling. The wicket looked good which was important. Far too many one-day matches have been spoilt by having wickets which aid the bowlers too much, resulting in low-scoring matches and hardly any strokeplay. We had earlier decided upon the usual one-day ploy of ours of putting the opposition in, in case we won the toss.

The toss was to be done in the presence of a Channel 9 commentator, usually Ian Chappell. Ian would then ask the captain who won the toss why he opted for the decision to bat or field and his general strategy and hopes for the game. He would also ask the opposition captain about his strategies etc. I had been warned by a couple of journalist friends that Ian would be asking me about my decision to quit captaincy. Ian and I had got along well in discussions behind and in front of the camera

Now I waited for him to appear at the wicket so that Javed and I could go out to toss. It was almost two in the afternoon, just a half-hour before the finals were to begin. Both of us walked down the long passage, stopping to sign autographs for spectators. When we entered the ground it was about twenty minutes before the start of the game and yet there was no sign of Ian Chappell. As we walked to the wicket both of us decided to play a prank. We went and inspected the wicket, I tossed in the air, Javed bent as if to pick up the coin, shook hands with me and then both of us raised our hand and waved to our dressing room as if we had won the toss and started walking back towards the rooms. The Channel 9 cameraman was in a panic, because we had to toss with a special coin and also talk to Ian.

When we started to laugh he realised that we had not tossed at all. He breathed a sigh of relief, gave us the special coin which fell the way Javed had wanted. Javed told me about his decision to bat first, which surprised me because I thought that having lost to us earlier by batting first they would try and put us in and chase the runs. I don't know what the Pakistan team planning was but at least now one could understand why they had not bothered practising under the lights the previous evening. Since we had decided to field first it was as good as having won the toss and the players were cheerful when I broke the news to them in the dressing room. Only Roger, understandably, was feeling dejected. He had been there right through the tournament and given us vital breakthroughs in all the games. Now he was out of the finals with the flu. It was unbelievable really that a strong man like Roger should go down with something relatively mild like flu, and instead of being part of the action in the 'big one' Roger was lying on the massage table and resting. Most of the team went up to him and sympathised with him, adding that they'd try extra hard for his sake, which really goes to show how popular and well-liked Roger was.

Kapil began the finals by bowling to Mohsin and Pakistan were off to a quiet start. Chetan Sharma, who had come to the squad for Roger, also warmed up nicely and bowled well. Just as it looked that the Pakistan openers were going to survive the opening spell, Mohsin turned a ball from Kapil off his hips and Azhar at square-leg took the catch to give us our breakthrough. In the next over Kapil struck again when he induced Mudassar to chase a wide outswinger for Vishwanath to come up with a fine tumbling catch. Mud looked disgusted with himself as he rightly should have left the ball alone and the umpire would have called it a wide. The next ball to my mind was the best ball of the entire tournament. It was a fast straight yorker and it went through Qasim Umar's defence and bowled him. This brought in Javed and we crowded him, as he was facing the hat-trick ball. He negotiated that and fluently drove the next past mid-off for a boundary.

Now came the difficult decision. Should I give Kapil another over or keep him for a final burst? My strategy in previous games was to have Kapil bowl five overs and then bring him in two more spells of two and three overs. Here he had bowled six overs already and had captured two wickets in his sixth over. I decided to take the risk and ask him to bowl a seventh over, because Javed was the only recognized batsman, though Rameez was at the other end and Imran, Malik and Wasim Raja were to follow. If Kapil could get rid of Javed, Pakistan's back would be broken and we could dismiss them for a modest score. I also had, at the back of my mind, our encounter against Pakistan in the first match of the tournament, when Imran had taken a wicket with the last two balls of his fifth over. I was in next but I did not face Imran because his entire next over was played by Azhar. Javed took Imran off to keep him for the 'charge' overs. I thought he should have taken a risk and given Immy another delivery so he could have had a crack at the new batsmen, me. By the time Imran was brought again I was set and Azhar was batting like a champion. In fact we took more runs off him in those two overs than in his entire first spell of six overs.

Kapil bowled a good over but went wicketless. Chetan Sharma, however, made up for Kapil by getting Rameez out, caught low down at square-leg by Srikkanth. The batsman was not sure that the catch was taken cleanly, but we had no doubts as also the umpire and so Rameez had to take the long walk back to the pavilion. Imran then came in ahead of Salim Malim, which was a bit surprising because I think Salim Malik is destined for great things. He had taken a century off us in the Faisalabad Test earlier in the year, which was so thrilling that even being in the opposition one had but to applaud. Perhaps Imran's greater experience tilted the scales in favour of his coming in to bat before Malik. One ball and one raised finger was all that it would have taken to prove that Javed had made a mistake. Chetan Sharma intelligently produced a bouncer and Imran went to hook and quite palpably gloved it to be caught by Viswanath but the umpire thought otherwise and Imran continued with a sheepish grin. Thankfully he did not try to indicate that he had not touched it, but just put his head down to face the next ball. Many batsmen have this habit of rubbing some other part of the body or spreading their arms wide to show that they did not touch the ball which is abetting a wrong decision, because everyone around, with the exception of the umpire, knows that they have got a snick.

Chetan Sharma was shattered by the decision and I had quite a job pacifying, first Sadanand Vishwanath, the other fielders and then running across to Chetan. I tried to explain to him that since he had already induced Imran to make a mistake surely he could deceive him into making another. I urged him not to spoil the good work he was doing by getting upset and bowling stupidly. He is a good listener and a quick learner and he went on bowling well, which was so essential at this stage to keep the pressure on.

The ball was still hard and had been finely maintained by Kapil and Chetan; so when Madan and Mohinder were brought on they could move it. Madan is a great trier and Mohinder who 'hits the deck' is apt to make the ball deviate disconcertingly and get surprising bounce, especially on Australian wickets. Imran and Javed, realising that they had to bind the pieces together, did not try any flashy shots but as the overs went by one could sense a feeling of restlessness in them. It was time to bring the spinners on, because they would invite some risky shots. Ravi had to be brought to bowl with the wind behind him. Not only does he like to bowl that way but he is also likely to be hit because he is more predictable than Siva. But hitting him against the wind would be a tough task. Siva was brought on after a truly superb spell by Mohinder in which he was decidedly unlucky not to have Javed given out, caught behind, by the same umpire. It was interesting to watch Javed's face as he looked on with apprehension and then relief as he realised that the umpire was not going to uphold our appeal. Even more interesting was when he came to me at the drinks interval and said in Hindi to tell Sadanand not to shout so much behind the wicket. 'Insaan khel rahe hain, jaanwar nahin' (Human beings are playing, not animals). I laughed in his face and asked him sarcastically to repeat what he had said. He didn't obviously catch the sarcasm because he repeated his complaint. Coming from Javed Miandad, this was quite hilarious.

By no means can Javed be called shy. He certainly has not been so on the cricket field where his opinions, wisecracks abound and come thick and fast, especially when he is fielding. He then believes it is his right to try and get the batsman out in any way possible. He does not like being talked to when he is batting. This we realised when Pakistan had come over to India in 1983 and for a few overs we gave him everything we could and he was as visibly upset as he was now.

I reminded him that Sadanand was only encouraging our bowlers and not saying anything to the batsmen which was perfectly acceptable. He should complain to me if Sadanand said something nasty to him. Today most wicketkeepers try to keep the morale high by shouting encouragement to the bowlers and fielders. Ashraf Ali, the Pakistan keeper, once called out 'well bowled' to a ball declared wide in a Test match when Javed was fielding in the slips.

Sadanand's influence on our team was remarkable. He consistently boosted our spirits with his peppy style of keeping and speaking to bowlers and fielders. Off the field his dress sense always brought a smile on the faces of his colleagues. Another aspect of his character needs mentioning. He found that in Sydney a friend of his was in hospital suffering from bone marrow cancer. Every time we were in Sydney, Sadanand would go off directly from practice to the hospital to visit his friend and sit with him for hours. People will talk about the many reasons why we won the Benson & Hedges Cup but one of the main reasons was the presence of Sadanand Viswanath.

After the drinks interval I went up to Sadanand and told him to keep up the good work. He understood and smiled. Javed was getting pretty angry now and was trying some unorthodox shots but Ravi and Siva were bowling extremely well. The fielding was giving nothing away, with Kapil and Madan being outstanding. Our two fleetfooted outfielders Azharuddin and Srikkanth were never seriously tested, which meant they were reasonably fresh for their batting stint to follow.

The Imran-Javed partnership had prospered and was beginning to look dangerous. We had begun to give the umpire, who had negatived our appeal, long looks. Disaster, however, was round the corner when Imran played Siva to my left at point and started off for a single. Now our strategy was that the short third man, point and cover point would rush to prevent the single because we had a man on the fence behind us if we were beaten, while the extra cover would be a little deeper to give him room to move on either side. As soon as I saw Imran stretching forward defensively I was on the move. Luckily the hours of fielding practice paid off because the ball was picked and the single visible stump was hit, with Imran way out of his ground. That was the breakthrough we wanted. Imran walked away giving dirty glances to Javed but it was he who was clearly at fault. There was no single there even if the ball had gone to a portly 35-year-old.

Salim Malik was lucky that Shastri's valiant attempt to catch him was in vain. However, Chetan Sharma made up for it with a beautifully judged catch at long-off to see that Siva was not deprived of Salim's wicket.

Next delivery Siva worked his magic, flighting the ball, inviting Javed to step out and pitching it perfectly so that it spun away and beat Javed's bat. In a flash Vish had the bails off, running towards the square-leg umpire to confirm the dismissal, then running towards the bowler and still finding time in between to mouth two words that told Javed what to do.

Tahir Naqqash was on a hat-trick and he played an extraordinary shot first ball. He just swung the 'wrong one' over the long-on's head. He was lucky that with the Melbourne boundaries being longer the fielder was a good fifteen yards inside the fence but credit must be given to him for hitting the ball so well. He did not last long and was out when he attempted an ambitious shot off Shastri and got a snick, which was gobbled up nicely by Viswanath behind the wicket.

Anil Dalpat hit a wide half-volley from Siva to Shastri at extra-cover and Pakistan were nine down. Again a lot of calculations had to be made after Azeem Hafiz survived that over. The time was two minutes to five-thirty and if Pakistan were to get all out before 5.30 then we would have had to play a few overs before the 6 o'clock time for the break. No opening batsman likes to bat at such a time. He has not only to survive what is an unusually attacking field but also to begin getting set and concentrate all over again. And in a limited-overs game valuable overs are thus lost.

With all this at the back of my mind I signalled to Chetan Sharma who was the fielder at the deepest end to come and have a go. I was not perturbed when I found his attention elsewhere. It enabled me to lose some precious seconds. Typically, when he saw me signalling him, he ran like any 17-year-old, full-of-energy youngster. I had to motion him to take it easy and with one eye on the clock I began to arrange the field as if Chetan was going to bowl. As he took the ball from a startled Shastri and began to mark his run in, I saw that it was almost five-thirty. I then made if I had changed my mind and sent him back to the fence and recalled Ravi, who was trudging away to field, totally perplexed as to why he was being removed when he had taken a wicket in his previous over. When I called him and explained to him why, he threw back his head and laughed. When he finished his over and Kapil was brought on from his end the umpire Tony Crafter came up and said, "Aha! Now I know why you played that charade!"

Azeem and Wasim played sensibly and they added valuable runs; so when fifty overs were completed Pakistan had scored 176 with some wickets in hand. This was the first time in all the matches that we had failed to bowl a side out within the fifty overs. Yet we had contained the total to a reasonable limit. Now all that mattered was some sensible batting after surviving Imran's first spell.

As we walked into the pavilion most Indian supporters thought that we had as good as won the match I tried to remind them that in cricket anything could happen and we had to get 176 runs before we could grab the cup. The one man who could take it away from us was Imran Khan.

He was sitting in the lunch room along with Mudassar and Mohsin who seemed to be good friends of his. Mud as usual was in lively spirits and he said something to me with a wink which I did not catch on. Mud is sometimes too fast with his words but he is one of the most likeable fellows in the team. The previous evening we had sat together in the hotel lounge sipping a drink. As we watched the Indian and Pakistani supporters walk in and out of the hotel he turned and remarked, 'The actual match will be between them and not us, because we will play and go away but these fellows will talk about the rights and wrongs of the final forever.' We had been involved in a few verbal skirmishes in our first encounters in 1978 and 1979-80 series and he said 'we were told by our senior players that we had to be competitive and that meant talking tough; so we swore away at you in particular and they hid behind their faces like gentlemen and we got the bad name.'

Now at lunch (or should we call it supper?) Mud got up from his table, threw a grape at Madan and went back to his dressing room leaving Imran and Mohsin alone. Mud's leaving the table gave me an uninterrupted sight of Imran and I was simply staggered to see the man eat. He polished off some salad, then

633

the big steak (and Australian steaks are big), then some fruit salad with ice cream, popped in a few grapes, peeled off a banana and ate it with great relish. A he got up he picked up another banana (Australian bananas are big too). I couldn't help exclaiming, 'Immy, what's going on?'

He completely misunderstood my question because he said, 'Sorry about that. I was about to walk, when through the corner of my eye I saw no reaction from the umpire and so I stayed put.' He was of course referring to our first ball appeal against him. I was only flabbergasted that this man was now going to go out and bust his guts trying to bowl us out and that too on a full stomach. Most of us tend to eat sparingly at lunch so that it does not make one lethargic and here Imran had eaten almost twice as most of us do.

It was therefore interesting to watch his first over. In our previous game he had struck in his first over, getting rid of Shastri as we watched him with bated breath. He took his time to reach peak pace though he had loosened up considerably, prior to taking the field, by bowling to the wicketkeeper near the boundary of the dressing room. Only the fifth and sixth balls of his first over were quick and they were safely negotiated.

Azeem Hafiz also kept a tidy length and in the first few overs the runs came only in trickles of ones and twos. This is not something that Krishnamachari Srikkanth prefers and in Hafiz's fourth over he flexed himself and launched into a mighty off drive which landed a few rows behind the boundary. Hafiz could not believe his eyes and the Pakistani fielders who were agile till then suddenly let their heads droop. In the Indian dressing room there was nervous laughter and a shaking of heads that meant only Srikkanth could play an incredible shot like that. He has the quickest eye in our team and he picks the line, angle and speed of the ball that fraction earlier than most and therefore is in a position to play a shot before most players.

During the 1983 World Cup we were practising at the Indoor School at Lord's and after his batting stint at one net Sri went into another where Sandeep Patil was fiddling with a bowling machine. The machine luckily only only tennis balls and Sandeep was fooling with the dials that regulated the speed with which the machine would release the ball. At first Sandeep kept it at a moderate speed with the snout of the machine pointing at a good-length spot where the ball would pitch. Suddenly and without warning Sri, Sandy increased the speed to 70 mph and pointed the snout at the batsman's head. The ball went like a bullet, yet Sri was able to jerk his head away quickly, which not many of us would have been able to do. By the way, even at 70 mph the ball was going much faster than is bowled by Test bowlers. I wonder how therefore one arrives at a speed of 90 mph when one talks of Marshall & Co.

Technique has never been Srikkanth's strongest point and up until the time he got 80 - plus in the Kanpur Test there was a question mark against his temperament too. Happily he has overcome that aspect of his cricket. The problem with him is not so much his aggressive outlook but his tendency to be premeditative which gets him into a mess. Study his dismissals and you will find that the bowler has seldom got him out. Its Srikkanth with a predetermined shot that has got himself out.

After that magnificent six off Azeem Hafiz we kept our fingers crossed that he would keep cool and play each ball on its merit. That was what he fortunately did and after Imran was taken off for a spell, he really settled down and began to play some glorious shots. Ravi at the other end was his usual self, flicking anything pitched on the middle and leg stump past square-leg for ones and twos. Both of them ran well and with the long boundaries they had to run quite a few threes. Mudassar, like Imran, gives everything he has and has to be watched carefully. He started off way back in 1978-79 being a change bowler but has developed so well that he can truly claim to be an all-rounder. He induced one or two doubts in the batsmen's minds but luckily no damage was done. Just a bit of playing and missing and the odd ball hitting the pads.

There was one moment of tension when Srikkanth hit Wasim Raja high and Rameez running with his eyes on the ball, collided on the iron fence as the ball bounced into the crowd for another six. The collision was sickening and as Rameez staggered and fell it was even more sickening to find a lot of Pakistani players trying to pump him on the chest as if his heart had stopped. If Rameez was not seriously injured his team-mates' honest but misguided efforts almost made him so. Luckily, he only had a bad bruise and came off the field. When I went into the Pakistani dressing room, he was on a massage table in pain, but it was not very serious.

Srikkanth had gone way past his 50 and was looking good for another when Imran, returning for his second spell, had him cutting uppishly for Wasim Raja to take the stinging catch. The openers had put on 103.

Azhar walked in to a tremendous ovation as Srikkanth walked back, admonishing himself and shaking his head sadly. He knew he had missed a century but importantly, he had given us the start we needed. We needed now not to lose our heads but carry on from Sri's drive. We had just the right men in the middle: two of the coolest customers one can find on the cricket field, both far more mature than their years suggest. The only time Ravi Shastri gets excited on the field is when he is swept for a four. Perhaps he should stop and think about the excitement when he sweeps so many girls off their feet. Off the field Ravi gets upset only if he does not get the food he wants. When he came into the Bombay team we were amazed at his capacity to eat. It seemed as if his stomach was a bottomless pit. Then he suddenly shot up in height and perhaps that made him stop and think, for he eats much less than he used to, almost normal now. Fortunately that does not show on him. His utter dedication will not allow it. The most encouraging aspect of today's young players is their awareness of and keenness about physical fitness. Ravi leads the pack. He exercises fanatically to maintain the standards that are expected of him now.

Azhar is also extremely fit and many seem to have overlooked in the brilliant light of his batting performances his ability as a fielder. A quick, graceful mover with a powerful throw, Azhar again belongs to that new breed of Indian cricketers, who are brilliant fielders. He had won the admiration of the Australian crowds and was a popular figure with the kids there too. Thus the ovation he got as he walked in to bat was no surprise. He was quickly off the mark and settled in, seeing off dangerous Imran's second spell. Azhar also likes to play on the leg-side and is particularly good at the ball coming into him which he whips off his hips either to the right or left of the square-leg umpire and often through his legs.

Imran wisely did not give him anything pitched on his legs but concentrated on his off stump and Azhar was content to play it quietly. He knew we had overs in hand and it was important not to cause any panic by losing quick wickets. He was lucky to have Anil Dalpat drop him behind the wickets, admittedly a difficult chance, but one nevertheless. These things do not disconcert him. He has a superb temperament and this enables him to keep cool even in the most trying circumstances. He had scored 24 when he got out, but by then the match was very much in our bag and only the formalities remained to be completed.

Ravi, however, was taking no chances and he preferred to push away for singles while the large contingent of Indian supporters wanted the tension to be over and preferred some boundaries to finish the match. In the dressing room the atmosphere was lighter and well-wishers were streaming in pumping our hands. The Indian High Commissioner in Australia, Mr Ansari, the Consul-General, Mr Banerjee, and the Honorary Consul-General in Melbourne, Dr T.J. Rao, brought in champagne. The High Commissioner came all the way from Canberra to witness the matches and the Consul-General, Mr Banerjee, is a cricket fan, so he did not miss a match either. The Honorary Consul-General, Dr Janardhan Rao, has been a friend of the Indian cricketers since our tour of 1977-78. This soft-spoken ever-smiling gentleman was at hand at any given time for the team. He even provided Srikkanth with a cooker so that Sri, a strict vegetarian, could cook his rice and some curry from the curry powder. I wonder if Sri ever managed to cook in his room!

The Channel 9 TV crew was now at the dressing-room windows poking their camera to record the reactions of our team members as the moment of victory drew closer. Sadanand Vishwanath was shaking the champagne bottle and spraying it around in the dressing room. It was a bit premature and old-timers would have frowned but there was simply no way we could have lost now.

There were to be no glorious uncertainties of the game, only the certainty of our winning. Since the coverage was being aired home live all the players came up to the viewing room and got into the frame so that their friends and relatives at home could see them. The dressing rooms in Melbourne are on the lower ground floor and one climbs up a few steps to reach the viewing room from where one can watch the play in the middle. From there one goes to the field of play through a passage on either side of which crowds sit. Mostly it is relatives and friends who sit there. They are also the most expensive tickets at the ground. While the players in the viewing room can look and identify their friends, people in the stands cannot see anything in the viewing room as the glass has a special tint. When the sun is out shining brightly Aussie girls strip to get a tan and so the attention is often diverted from the field of play. The binoculars then shift to watch the swing of things, in more ways than one. However, when we were batting the lights had come on, the girls were covered and the match was far more important anyway. As Dilip turned Wasim Raja for the single that got us the victory, the dressing room, already noisy, got even noisier. The V.C.A. officials were now in the room with their congratulations and a request to get the team ready for the presentation ceremony. The players were going crazy, embracing each other, and shaking each other's hands, shouting, singing, throwing their clothes and gloves at each other. The scene was indescribable and unforgettable. It was really difficult to get the players out on to the ground for the presentation ceremony.

We were told by Alan Turner, the former Australian opener, that Ravi Shastri was the Champion of Champions and had won the Audi 100, while Srikkanth was the man of the finals. This was like the proverbial icing on the cake. To have two of your colleagues win awards along with the championship was fantastic. These announcements were greeted with shouts of delight and as the Indian High Commissioner to Australia, Mr Ansari, handed me a message from the Prime Minister, which I in turn read out to the team, there was bedlam. Perhaps for the Prime Minister it was just sending another message during his busy schedule, but to us players a simple message like that meant a lot and we were absolutely delighted to receive it. When I inquired of the High Commissioner how he got hold of the message at the M.C.G., he whispered in my ears that the message had come in a couple of hours earlier. That means the P.M. must have watched or kept in touch with the game and our innings to see that there were no causes for alarm before confidently sending out his message.

We then trooped out to receive the Cup. Some of the Pakistani players were squatting on the ground in disappointment. We shook hands all round and then the presentation was made. It was an emotional moment for me and I thanked the team for their wonderful present to me. Hardly had I got off the rostrum when the players surrounded me and so did the photographers. One of the players, probably Jimmy Amarnath, poured champagne over my head and then the others followed. Some poured champagne into the Cup and we all had a sip from there. It was Ravi's turn to be presented with the keys of the Audi and Ian Chappell, whom Ravi admires, handed him the keys. Unknown to Ravi we all had sneaked into the car and when Ravi turned after expressing his feelings about being the Champion of Champions he found he only had one unoccupied seat in the car. Unfortunately for us the keys were in his possession; otherwise our plan was to let Ravi hold the microphone while we ran away with the car. The ride in the car round the stadium was fun and soon we had players on the bonnet, on top and behind the car. It was my job by virtue of being in the front seat to navigate Ravi because the players on the bonnet were blocking his view. He almost knocked down Adrian Murrell and Patrick Eagar, the photographers. Fortunately, the ride ended without any damage except to the seats in the car, where some champagne had spilt. The Australian crowds loved it, because although a car had been presented every year for the last few years, none of the winners had done anything more than pose with the keys in front of the car. Here the whole team had spontaneously enjoyed the ride. The Audi people were overjoyed, because as the TV cameras followed us it was good publicity for them.

I was looking forward to the press conference. I enjoy the bantering I can have with the foreign pressmen because they understand when I say something tongue-in-cheek, while in India even if I say something in a lighter vein, the humour is almost always lost. One of the Indian sports magazines had their reporter saying before we left for the championship that at the end of the tournament the Indians would be sitting under the gargantuan stands wondering what went wrong. I cast my eyes towards him now and found him avoiding eye contact, looking sheepish and wondering himself what went wrong with his prediction. He did not have any questions to ask. The others, particularly the English scribes, were only keen to find why there was such an amazing transformation in our team's performance. At the end of the conference I asked them if Javed had had any complaints against umpiring this time. He, of course dared not have any, because not only had he benefited from an error, so had Imran. Because the umpire was Australian no fuss had been made. This strengthens the lobby which wants neutral umpires, because when the umpire is from a country other than the participating ones it is easier to accept his mistakes.

When I went back to the dressing room most of the players had left and I gathered my gear and left the ground. In our previous encounter against Pakistan I had lost the bat with which I had scored 50 runs. This time I made sure everything was neatly packed and left only with my clothing. By the time I reached the hotel most of the clothing was gone. People who were waiting had come up to ask for souvenirs and I had only my clothing to give. Lest readers misunderstand, let me clarify that the clothing I gave away was the spare clothing one carries.

At the hotel lobby there were some people around. The Somaiya family who had been so good to us and had recorded the TV highlights for me were there in strength and so was the Honorary Consul, Dr Rao. He and our Consul-General in Sydney, Mr Banerjee, could not stop grinning. Mr Banerjee, an avid cricket follower, had been giving me valuable information, having watched the earlier season and had also provided us with some video cassettes to study. All these had come in handy, because some of the Australian players were new to us and we could thus get at least an idea of what to expect after viewing the video cassettes.

After going up to my room and taking a shower I rushed down, because when we had reached the hotel it was almost midnight. The bars in the hotel were about to shut down and so there was little time to celebrate. I rushed down to join the Somaiyas and Wulf, a friend from Amsterdam, who had come all the way to watch the games. The Somaiyas had, with foresight, ordered some champagne; so even if there was no one to attend to as at the bar we could help ourselves. When we went back to the room I went on a phone ringing spree calling all my friends all over the world.

When I woke up the next morning and looked out of the window across towards the ground there was nothing but an almost eerie silence. When I looked down, the signboard which had put up signs for all the B & H matches at the M.C.G., now read, 17 March – Melbourne Tattoo.

9

Homecoming

THE MORNING AFTER OUR WIN THERE WAS A CALL FROM BISHEN
Bedi from New Delhi congratulating the team for the win and
me personally for the wonderful job I had done. As I thanked
him I could not withhold a grin, as it was no secret that Bishen
did not want me as the skipper for the tour. He then asked me
what the conditions in Sharjah would be like and what the
changes should be. I said that he should discuss this with
Kapil who had been appointed skipper. I had had enough of
being blamed for various selection committee decisions as if
I was a one-man selection committee. In fact the captain has
no vote in the selection committee. He is just invited for his
views. Whatever views I may have expressed, the final decision
was that of the selection committee. Yet it had become a
fashion to pin the blame on me. So I did not have anything

to say to Bishen about the composition of the team for Sharjah.

Later in the day I found that Manoj Prabhakar had been left out of the squad. Nobody told him about it. Eventually in Singapore I had to break the news to him. He wanted to buy something and he came to me asking whether it was advisable to buy the item in Singapore or in Dubai where he was told it was slightly cheaper. It was then that I had to tell him that he had better buy it in Singapore as he was not in the team going to the U.A.E. At first he did not believe me but seeing the expresion on my face, was convinced. It certainly spoilt his day and mine too for having been the one to give the news to him.

Before we left for Singapore we had a benefit dinner for Erapally Prasanna, our Manager, hosted by the Indian Association in Australia. It was a magnificent gesture by the Association and it was well attended. Most of the players who had played with Pras spoke on the occasion. Pras too spoke movingly about his experiences. The best speech of all was by Sadanand Vishwanath. He had us all listening to him with rapt attention as he spoke about his admiration for Prasanna. The only disappointment was Dilip Vengsarkar, who refused to speak. Dilip's reluctance to express himself has come in the way of his progress to cricketing hierarchy. Otherwise, a man with his experience and cricketing intelligence should have been seriously in the running for the captaincy. Now Ravi Shastri, very much junior to him, had stolen a march over him by being appointed vice-captain to Kapil for the U.A.E. tournament.

Our game in Singapore was a friendly one and we won that without much problem. The trip was organised by the Indian cultural office in Sydney, Air India and Hotel Oberoi Imperial Palace kindly provided the hospitality. It was a much-needed break after the hard work the players had put in. There had been hardly any time for shopping in Australia and in any case Australia is a very expensive country to shop in. So Singapore it was. The Air India manager there, Kishore Sabnis, was extremely helpful but his efforts to get us on an Air India flight back to Bombay failed as Quantas refused to entertain his offer that he would give them an equal number of passengers so that there would be no loss of revenue to them.

Most members of the Indian team prefer travelling Air India, maybe because the Indian team is spoilt by the airline and we expect the same standards from other airlines, which perhaps is expecting too much.

When we landed we found that there was a media boycott because the press and TV were not allowed in the customs enclosure. Not that it made any difference. I've never understood why TV cameras should pan into a player's suitcase as it is opened for customs examination. Surely that is a gross invasion of privacy and is hardly of any interest to viewers. Also with the current security problem it is absolutely essential that all cameras, etc., be away from sensitive areas and the customs enclosure is a sensitive area. After all, a camera can identify customs men in plainclothes, which is not going to help them perform their duties unobtrusively in the future.

There was thus no press conference at the airport though I did give a TV interview at the airport. I enjoyed that, though I felt sorry for Milind Wagle, who is a friend, for getting my back up by asking whether we expected to win. No team goes into a tournament wanting to lose and although our form prior to the tournament was not encouraging, we all know that cricket is a game which can confound the greatest experts. Haresh Munwani then asked if I thought our victory was a fluke. I answered firmly, tongue in cheek, that since this was the age of sequels to hit-movies like *Jaws I, Jaws II, Rocky II.* etc., this win could be termed *Fluke II*. I had a heavily bandaged middle finger as well as a tape on my forehead where extra skin growth had been removed and inevitably there was a question as to what happened. That was the question I was waiting for. My answer: 'I had a fight with Kapil Dev.' Of course everybody laughed. We had won, so there could not have been a fight, but since we had lost earlier it was believable that there could have been one. The practice is to look for excuses other than cricketing ones to explain away India's defeats.

The crowd outside was nothing compared to the crowds that welcomed the team on its arrival after winning the 1983 World Cup. It was just as well, because we have always had excessive praise or excessive abuse. Somewhere in between might be ideal, but having been in both the boats during my career I know it is difficult for the cricket-loving public to exercise moderation. All I can say is that it feels good to be welcomed warmly with cheers.

There were no felicitation functions either, nor did the Cricket Control Board jump on to announce any cash bonuses to the team, which was really not surprising. Ever since the Treasurer of the Board scrapped any incentive bonuses, any that the team may have dreamt of has remained just that -- a dream! What we hoped was that at least the prize money, which was substantial, would be distributed quickly to the team, since this does not depend on the manager's report. Normally for an overseas tour a player is given fifty per cent of the tour fees before departure and the balance is given only after the manager gives a clean chit to the player for his performance and behaviour on the tour. Very seldom has a manager given an adverse report against a player and that's mainly because Indian teams that I have been part of have been invariably well-behaved, though there has been the odd rowdy occasion as well.

After a couple of days we went to Delhi to show the Prime Minister the Benson & Hedges Cup. He was very charming and said that since we were shortly going to Sharjah we should not rest on our laurels but do well there too.

10

Mopping it Up

THE TEAM WAS TO LEAVE SHORTLY FOR THE ROTHMANS CUP IN Sharjah and so most players probably had only a couple of days to spend with their families before leaving for the Gulf. The teams participating in the Cup were Australia, England, Pakistan and India. A lot of withdrawals left the England team looking like a completely different outfit from the one we had played against in India and Australia. Some of the Australians also had withdrawn and though that really did not affect their team it does have an effect of giving the opponents a psychological advantage. The Pakistan team was minus the great Zaheer Abbas who had still not recovered from his ailments. The Indian team had only one change from the fourteen that won the world championship in Australia. A selector did propose that all those over thirty should be dropped. It was a fine way of getting rid of two cricketers. He did not like Mohinder Amarnath and me. And for that he was prepared to sacrifice his favourite, Madan Lal, who was the third player over thirty years old.

So when the team landed in Sharjah we were referring to Mohinder, Madan and myself as O.T., acronym for 'over thirty'. Our first game, the semifinals, was against Pakistan and Australia and England were to contest the other. In the Melbourne championship Pakistan had batted first on both the occasions we had played, and lost. So as soon as Javed won the toss he asked us to bat.

The match started off on a sensational note, with Ravi Shastri being leg-before off the first delivery from Imran. What a great leveller this game is! Here was the Champion of Champions gone with the first ball. That was not all as Srikkanth mishooked and was caught at square leg. Vengsarkar went, caught behind on the leg-side and I went caught behind on the off-side. Amarnath was bowled by an inswinger and our back was broken. It was a devastating spell of fast, swing bowling and if there were any doubters in the world about Imran Khan's ability to bowl fast after his long lay-off they must have been clearly convinced that he was literally bouncing and fit.

Azhar and Kapil did a salvage operation of sorts but that was not enough, for when our last wicket fell a good half-hour before lunch we had totalled only 125 with Azhar top-scoring with 47 runs. There was silence in the dressing room while next door the Pakistan room was full of excitement. Since it was a Friday the regulations said that the lunch hour would be one hour to enable the faithful to say their afternoon prayers. That, plus our dismissal a half-hour before lunch, meant that it was almost ninety minutes. We barely had a bite and filed back into the dressing room. Surprising as it may sound, within minutes everybody was fast asleep. When we were finally woken up, only twenty minutes were left for play to start. Kapil said to the players 'C'mon, lets make them fight for each run'. I firmly believe that our snooze helped us considerably. Not only did we wake up feeling refreshed and thinking our dismissal was a bad dream but we were saved of the brooding and worrying had we been awake.

The first couple of overs were incident-free. Mohsin then drove Kapil hard and straight to Mohinder and took off for a run, which at the best of times was risky. He was barely past the half-way stage when Mohinder's pick-up and throw, hit the stumps directly. We all converged round Jimmy as he shyly accepted the hands proferred. It was Madan who put extra energy into us by coming up and saying, 'Well done, O.T.' The whole team now was bustling with this breakthrough and just when the bubble of enthusiasm was about to burst with a wayward over from Binny, he induced Mudassar to nibble at a ball outside the off-stump and I caught the resultant edge. Once again everybody crowded around and this time Mohinder and Madan said, 'Shabash, O.T.'

Kapil took himself off and brought Ravi Shastri on. He got one to turn and bounce at Javed, and once again the edge came to me at slip. With Javed gone and without Zaheer in the team we knew we could put presure on the inexperienced Pakistani batsmen. At the other end, surprisingly, Ashraf Ali was sent in ahead of Imran or the talented Saleem Malik. When Siva was brought in he played a very awkward looking defensive jab off the backfoot and Vengsarkar at silly point dived to his left to come up with the catch. Two balls later Imran was making his way back to the pavilion, stumped, when he missed a big hit off Siva. Now Pakistan was in real trouble and not only did they and we knew it, the whole crowd knew it too. The Indian supporters who were quiet at lunch were now jubilant and

650

shouting away while the Pakistani supporters sat with worry creasing their brows.

The match, however, was far from over. Pakistan's two most talented batsmen were on view: Rameez Raja and Saleem Malik. Between them they began to build up the total, lofting the odd ball to the boundary and taking their singles smartly. They took the score past 70 but the overs were also running out for them. Ravi's last over of his quota had Saleem cutting a sharp catch to me in the slip. That was the wicket we wanted and though the match was not won we were now convinced that it was ours. As if to make doubly sure, Kapil, who replaced Shastri, had Rameez edging a drive to me at slip, my fourth catch of the game, and after that it was just a matter of minutes before the Pakistan tail-enders catapulted. Madan had given excellent support by bowling to a line and length like a true professional. This was the most vital phase, because if the Pakistanis had managed to get him away then the pressure would have eased but he did not even give them a sniff of a loose ball. With their top batsmen out they could not even take the risk of charging down the track to attack him.

As we ran back to the dressing room we were engulfed by our supporters and it was back slapping all the way till it hurt. But one forgets the pain at such moments. Inside the dressing room everybody was embracing each other, while our manager, Ramakant Desai, just could not stop laughing and shaking his head. Now it was our dressing room which was agog with excitement while the Pakistani room was quiet. Amid our mini-celebrations, Javed came in with some of their players to offer his congratulations. Imran came in when there was more silence in the room to return a couple of magazines which I had given him to read. He is featured very often in magazines in India and I have this habit of carrying plenty of reading material with me on tours. Seeing our celebrations he wished us and quietly went back. He must have been particularly horrified at the way the Pakistani batsmen threw the match away by some shoddy batting, after he had set us back by his superb bowling. The prize of the Man of the Match was hardly any consolation.

I had not been able to get hold of a black arm-band earlier but I was wearing one when we fielded to mourn the passing away of Dattu Phadkar, earlier in the week. Apart from being one of India's finest cricketers, Dattubhai, as some of us called him, was my father's colleague in their college days. My father always spoke warmly about him and even Dattubhai inquired of him whenever he met me. We had also spent some time together in the selection committee meetings when he would defuse a tense discussion with a witty remark. He was also the manager of our teams when I scored my highest in test cricket. He was very popular and also respected by the players.

Since nobody thought of respecting his memory in any manner I thought that on my own I would do so by wearing a black arm-band. At the end of the game a reporter from one of the Gulf newspapers asked me why I was wearing one and I told him the reason. He turned around and said, 'Oh! One of your newspaper guys said that you must be protesting against the lunch, breakfast or something or the other because you were the only one wearing it.' In recent times very seldom have I been rendered speechless, but this was one occasion when I stared at him and would not say anything. I just shook my head and walked away. One has heard the term jumping to conclusions but this surely was a jump longer than Bob Beamon's.

We now had a week for the finals and had to wait for the result of the Australia-England match to know who our opponents would be. Australia it was, with their thrilling last ball victory over England.

England and Pakistan played to fight for the third and fourth places and that match was eagerly watched because the same wicket was to be used for the finals. In this match the ball turned from the word 'play' and Shoaib Mohammed, known more as an opening batsman, got wickets with his brand of off-spinners. This naturally set up talk that we would drop Binny and bring in Ashok Patel.

The selectors, however, decided to stick to the same eleven as in the game against Pakistan. The Australians got off to a good start and after Wessels went, Amarnath turned the game in our favour by getting Border and Hughes in quick succession. Our fielding again was top class, with Srikkanth, Azhar, Siva and Binny outstanding and Ravi bringing up some superlative diving saves on the boundary. We had to score 137 to win.

Our innings again got off on the wrong foot as Srikkanth went leg-before to McDermott. Ravi and Azhar steadied the boat somewhat, before Ravi fell, caught down the leg-side and when McDermott had Azhar caught behind square-leg we were three down for 37 runs. This was a crucial phase. In the Gulf one would have thought that there would be little support to the Aussies from the crowd but surprising as it may sound, there were many Pakistanis in the crowd vociferously cheering Australia on. The Aussies don't get this kind of support even in Australia and they must have been really cheered to find Asians supporting them rather than another Asian team.

Coming back to the match, Dilip and I had a good partnership. He played a crackling innings. In one over from

Murray Bennett he hammered four boundaries: two sweeps, during which he pulled a groin muscle, two drives, one off the front foot and the other off the back foot through the covers. In that one over he got rid of our greatest danger and though we both fell within a few runs of each other there really was no danger to us with the kind of batting depth we had in chasing a modest total.

Kapil and Binny got out, bowled by Greg Mathews who was turning his off-breaks a long way, but in Madan Lal and Mohinder we had cool, experienced heads and they got us victory in a splendid fashion. If ever a selector received a resounding slap it was now, because it was the over-thirty duo who had got the win.

Champagne corks popped in our dressing room again and the discussion centred round who would be the man of the series. I half-jokingly ventured that it should be me and was most pleasantly surprised when it was announced that it indeed was me. The Australian team was not amused by the choice, though they were somewhat pacified by the presentation of a special prize for Greg Matthews.

The prize distribution dinner was, as usual, a magnificent affair, at the end of which there was a belly-dance thrown in. Most of us were too tired at this stage and only wanted to return to our rooms. Four of us were to play an exhibition game in Bahrain the next day.

The international commitments for the season were over. What was left was to make sure that the Ranji Trophy stayed in the offices of Bombay Cricket Association. Ravi Shastri's performances ensured that and thus ended what I had termed the season of hope. Our performances against England made it look more like a season of mope than one of hope, but the two one-day trophies were a good way to balance the scales.

From under the debris after the England series, to be on top down under, and finish the season catching up with the desert mirage was fantastic.

What's the new season going to be like?

Index

Index

Index

Index

Index

Index

Index

Index

Index

Index